Department of Economic
and Social Affairs
Statistics Division

World
Statistics
Pocketbook
2015 edition

United Nations, New York, 2015

The Depa............ .. .. and Social Affairs of the United Nations Secretariat is a vital interface between global policies in the economic, social and environmental spheres and national action. The Department works in three main interlinked areas: (i) it compiles, generates and analyses a wide range of economic, social and environmental data and information on which States Members of the United Nations draw to review common problems and to take stock of policy options; (ii) it facilitates the negotiations of Member States in many intergovernmental bodies on joint courses of action to address ongoing or emerging global challenges; and (iii) it advises interested Governments on the ways and means of translating policy frameworks developed in United Nations conferences and summits into programmes at the country level and, through technical assistance, helps build national capacities.

Note

The designations employed and the presentation of material in this publication do not imply the expression of any opinion whatsoever on the part of the Secretariat of the United Nations concerning the legal status of any country, territory, city or area or of its authorities, or concerning the delimitation of its frontiers or boundaries.

The term "country" as used in this publication also refers, as appropriate, to territories or areas.

Visit the United Nations World Wide Web site on the Internet:
For the Department of Economic and Social Affairs,
    http://www.un.org/esa/desa/
For statistics and statistical publications,
    http://unstats.un.org/unsd/
For UN publications, https://unp.un.org/

ST/ESA/STAT/SER.V/39
United Nations Publication
Sales No. E.15.XVII.9
ISBN-13: 978-92-1-161596-8
eISBN: 978-92-1-057393-1

All queries on rights and licenses, including subsidiary rights, should be addressed to United Nations Publications, 300 East 42nd Street, New York, NY 10017, USA, e-mail: publications@un.org, web: http://un.org/publications

World Statistics Pocketbook, 2015 edition
© 2015 United Nations
New York, NY 10017, United States of America

Contents

Country profiles

Contents (*continued*)

Contents (*continued*)

Introduction

The *World Statistics Pocketbook* is an annual compilation of key economic, social and environmental indicators, presented in one-page profiles. This edition includes country profiles for 224 countries or areas of the world. Prepared by the United Nations Statistics Division of the Department of Economic and Social Affairs, it responds to General Assembly resolution 2626 (XXV), in which the Secretary-General is requested to supply basic national data that will increase international public awareness of countries' development efforts.

The indicators shown are selected from the wealth of international statistical information compiled regularly by the Statistics Division and the Population Division of the United Nations, the statistical services of the United Nations specialized agencies and other international organizations and institutions. Special recognition is gratefully given for their assistance in continually providing data.

Time period

This issue of the *World Statistics Pocketbook* covers various years from 2005 to 2015. For the economic indicators, in general, three years - 2005, 2010 and 2013 - are shown, unless otherwise indicated. Due to space limitations, data for one year only are shown for the indicators in the social and environmental categories. For the six social indicators for which the range of years 2010-2015 is shown, the data refer to projections. When other ranges of years are shown, the data refer to the most recent year available within that range.

Organization of the Pocketbook

The country tables or profiles are presented alphabetically according to countries' names in English and contain the available data for the following broad categories:

- *General information:* includes each country's location by geographical region, currency, surface area, population and population density, capital city and population and United Nations membership date

- *Economic indicators:* includes national accounts (Gross domestic product (GDP), GDP growth rate, GDP per capita, gross national income per capita and gross fixed capital formation), exchange rates, balance of payments, consumer price index, production indices (industrial, agricultural and food), unemployment, employment, labour force participation, tourist arrivals, energy production, mobile-cellular telephone subscribers and internet users

- *Trade:* contains the value of total exports, imports and the trade balance as well as the countries' main trading partners

- *Social indicators:* includes population (growth rates, urban percentage, age groups and sex ratios), life expectancy, infant mortality rate, total fertility rate, contraceptive prevalence, international migrant stock, refugees, education (expenditure and enrolment), intentional homicide rate and female participation in national parliaments

- *Environmental indicators:* includes threatened species, forested area, proportion of terrestrial and marine areas protected, population using improved drinking water and improved sanitation, CO_2 emission estimates and energy supply per capita.

The complete set of indicators, listed by category and in the order in which they appear in the profiles, is shown at the beginning of the country profile section. Not all indicators are shown for each country or area due to different degrees of data availability.

For brevity the Pocketbook generally omits specific information on source or methodology present in the original source for individual data points.

The technical notes section, which follows the country profile pages, contains brief descriptions of the concepts and methodologies used in the compilation of the indicators as well as information on the statistical sources for the indicators. Readers interested in longer time-series data or more detailed descriptions of the concepts or methodologies should consult the primary sources of the data and the references listed in the section following the technical notes.

As noted above, the number of indicators actually shown for each country or area varies according to data availability.

Note

The present *World Statistics Pocketbook, 2015 edition* (Series V, No. 39) is an update of the previous edition which was released in 2014 and entitled *World Statistics Pocketbook 2014 edition* (Series V, No. 38).

* * *

The *World Statistics Pocketbook* is prepared annually by the Statistical Services Branch of the Statistics Division, Department of Economic and Social Affairs of the United Nations Secretariat. The programme manager is Francesca Perucci, the editor is Heather Page, and the software developer is Salomon Cameo. Thataw Batun, Jaspreet Doung, Tomas Kułaga and Bradford Neidkowski provided production assistance. Comments on this publication are welcome and may be sent by e-mail to statistics@un.org.

Symbols, abbreviations and conversion factors

The following symbols and abbreviations have been used in the *World Statistics Pocketbook*:

...	Data not available
−	Magnitude zero
<	Magnitude not zero, but less than half of the unit employed
−<	Magnitude not zero, but negative and less than half of the unit employed
000	Thousands
°C	Degrees Celsius
%	Percentage
60+	Aged sixty years and over
.	Decimal figures are always preceded by a period (.)
CFA	Coopération financière en Afrique centrale
CIF	Cost, Insurance and Freight
CO_2	Carbon dioxide
CPI	Consumer price index
est.	Estimated
f	Females
FOB	Free on board
GDP	Gross domestic product
GNI	Gross national income
ILO	International Labour Organization
ISIC	International Standard Industrial Classification
ISO	International Organization for Standardization
ITU	International Telecommunication Union
km	Kilometres
m	Males
mt	Metric tons
N & C Ame	North and Central America
Nes	Not elsewhere specified
pop.	Population
S.	South
S. America	South America
SAR	Special Administrative Region
sq km	Square kilometre
TT	Trinidad and Tobago
UAE	United Arab Emirates
UN	United Nations
UNESCO	United Nations Educational, Scientific and Cultural Organization
UNHCR	Office of the United Nations High Commissioner for Refugees
UNSD	United Nations Statistics Division
US$	United States dollars
WMO	World Meteorological Organization

The metric system of weights and measures has been employed in the *World Statistics Pocketbook*. The equivalents of the basic British Imperial and United States weights and measures are as follows:

Area	1 square kilometre	= 0.386102 square mile
Weight or mass	1 ton	= 1.102311 short tons or
		= 0.987207 long ton
	1 kilogram	= 35.273962 avoirdupois ounces
		= 2.204623 avoirdupois pounds
Distance	1 kilometre	= 0.621371 mile
	1 millimetre	= 0.039 inch
Temperature	°C	= (°F - 32) × 5/9

Country profile information and indicator list*

General information

Region	Surface area (sq km)
Population (est., 000)	Pop. density (per sq km)
Capital city	Capital city pop. (000)
Currency	UN membership date

Economic indicators

GDP: Gross domestic product (million current US$)
GDP: Growth rate at constant 2005 prices (annual %)
GDP per capita (current US$)
GNI: Gross national income per capita (current US$)
Gross fixed capital formation (% of GDP)
Exchange rates (national currency per US$)
Balance of payments, current account (million US$)
CPI: Consumer price index (2000=100)
Index of Industrial production (2010=100)
Agricultural production index (2004-2006=100)
Food production index (2004-2006=100)
Unemployment (% of labour force)
Employment in industrial sector (% of employed)
Employment in agricultural sector (% of employed)
Labour force participation, adult female population (%)
Labour force participation, adult male population (%)
Tourist arrivals at national borders (000)
Energy production, primary (Petajoules)
Mobile-cellular subscriptions (per 100 inhabitants)
Individuals using the Internet (%)

Trade

Total trade (exports, imports and balance, million US$)
Major trading partners (exports and imports, %)

Social indicators

Population growth rate (average annual %)
Urban population growth rate (average annual %)
Rural population growth rate (average annual %)
Urban population (%)
Population aged 0-14 years (%)
Population aged 60+ years (females and males, % of total)
Sex ratio (males per 100 females)
Life expectancy at birth (females and males, years)
Infant mortality rate (per 1 000 live births)
Fertility rate, total (live births per woman)
Contraceptive prevalence (ages 15-49, %)
International migrant stock (000 and % of total population)
Refugees and others of concern to UNHCR
Education: Government expenditure (% of GDP)
Education: Primary and secondary gross enrolment ratio (females and males per 100)
Education: Female third-level students (% of total)
Intentional homicide rate (per 100 000 population)
Seats held by women in national parliaments (%)

Environmental indicators

Threatened species
Forested area (% of land area)
Proportion of terrestrial and marine areas protected (%)
Population using improved drinking water sources (%)
Population using improved sanitation facilities (%)
CO_2 emission estimates (000 metric tons and metric tons per capita)
Energy supply per capita (Gigajoules)

---

* The complete set of information and indicators listed here may not be shown for each country or area depending upon data availability.

Country profiles

Afghanistan

Region	Southern Asia	Surface area (sq km)	652 864	
Population (est., 000)	31 281	Pop. density (per sq km)	48.0	
Capital city	Kabul	Capital city pop. (000)	4 436	
Currency	Afghani (AFN)	UN membership date	19 November 1946	

Economic indicators	2005	2010	2013
GDP: Gross domestic product (million current US$)	6 622	16 078	21 618
GDP: Growth rate at constant 2005 prices (annual %)	9.9	3.2	6.4
GDP per capita (current US$)	266.4	566.2	707.6
GNI: Gross national income per capita (current US$)	266.4	566.2	707.6
Gross fixed capital formation (% of GDP)	21.8	17.5	17.0
Exchange rates (national currency per US$)[a]	50.41	45.27	56.64
Balance of payments, current account (million US$)	−1 673[b]	−2 795	−6 706
Agricultural production index (2004-2006=100)	106	116	120
Food production index (2004-2006=100)	106	116	120
Unemployment (% of labour force)	8.5	8.5	8.0
Labour force participation, adult female pop. (%)	13.9	15.4	15.8
Labour force participation, adult male pop. (%)	80.7	80.1	79.5
Energy production, primary (Petajoules)	23	41	56[c]
Mobile-cellular subscriptions (per 100 inhabitants)	4.8	45.8[d]	70.0[d]
Individuals using the Internet (%)	1.2	4.0[d]	5.9[d]

Total trade		Major trading partners		2013
	(million US$)		(% of exports)	(% of imports)
Exports	515.0	Pakistan	38.5	...
Imports	8 554.4	Areas nes	27.4[e]	...
Balance	−8 039.4	India	20.0	...

Social indicators		
Population growth rate (average annual %)	2010-2015	2.4
Urban population growth rate (average annual %)	2010-2015	4.0
Rural population growth rate (average annual %)	2010-2015	1.9
Urban population (%)	2014	26.3
Population aged 0-14 years (%)	2014	45.8
Population aged 60+ years (females and males, % of total)	2014	4.3/3.6
Sex ratio (males per 100 females)	2014	102.8
Life expectancy at birth (females and males, years)	2010-2015	62.0/59.5
Infant mortality rate (per 1 000 live births)	2010-2015	67.3
Fertility rate, total (live births per woman)	2010-2015	5.0
Contraceptive prevalence (ages 15-49, %)	2007-2013	21.2
International migrant stock (000 and % of total population)	mid-2013	105.1/0.3
Refugees and others of concern to UNHCR	mid-2014	1 061 213
Education: Primary-secondary gross enrolment ratio (f/m per 100)	2007-2013	64.9/99.4
Education: Female third-level students (% of total)	2007-2013	24.3
Intentional homicide rate (per 100,000 population)	2008-2012	6.5
Seats held by women in national parliaments (%)	2015	27.7

Environmental indicators		
Threatened species	2014	37
Forested area (% of land area)	2012	2.1
Proportion of terrestrial and marine areas protected (%)	2014	0.5
Population using improved drinking water sources (%)	2012	64.0
Population using improved sanitation facilities (%)	2012	29.0
CO_2 emission estimates (000 metric tons and metric tons per capita)	2011	12 251/0.4
Energy supply per capita (Gigajoules)	2012	10.0

a Principal rate. b 2008. c 2012. d ITU estimate. e See technical notes.

Albania

Region	Southern Europe	Surface area (sq km)	28 748	
Population (est., 000)	3 185	Pop. density (per sq km)	110.8	
Capital city	Tirana	Capital city pop. (000)	445	
Currency	Lek (ALL)	UN membership date	14 December 1955	

Economic indicators	2005	2010	2013
GDP: Gross domestic product (million current US$)	8 094	11 927	12 904
GDP: Growth rate at constant 2005 prices (annual %)	5.8	3.7	1.3
GDP per capita (current US$)	2 532.4	3 786.2	4 066.4
GNI: Gross national income per capita (current US$)	2 583.1	3 748.3	4 077.9
Gross fixed capital formation (% of GDP)	34.7	28.4	24.2
Exchange rates (national currency per US$)[a]	103.58	104.00	101.86
Balance of payments, current account (million US$)	−571	−1 353	−1 378
CPI: Consumer price index (2000=100)	117	135	145
Index of industrial production (2010=100)[b]	50	100	174
Agricultural production index (2004-2006=100)	98	119	127
Food production index (2004-2006=100)	98	119	128
Unemployment (% of labour force)	12.5	14.2	16.0
Employment in industrial sector (% of employed)	13.5[c]	20.8[cde]	...
Employment in agricultural sector (% of employed)	58.5[c]	41.5[cde]	...
Labour force participation, adult female pop. (%)	48.3	45.2	44.9
Labour force participation, adult male pop. (%)	68.9	65.3	65.5
Tourist arrivals at national borders (000)[fgh]	748	2 417	3 256
Energy production, primary (Petajoules)	48	68	68[i]
Mobile-cellular subscriptions (per 100 inhabitants)	47.9	85.5[j]	116.2
Individuals using the Internet (%)	6.0	45.0	60.1[j]

Total trade		Major trading partners			2013
	(million US$)	(% of exports)			(% of imports)
Exports	2 331.5	Italy	46.3	Italy	33.1
Imports	4 880.6	Spain	9.8	Greece	8.9
Balance	−2 549.1	Serbia	7.5	China	6.8

Social indicators		
Population growth rate (average annual %)	2010-2015	0.3
Urban population growth rate (average annual %)	2010-2015	2.2
Rural population growth rate (average annual %)	2010-2015	−2.0
Urban population (%)	2014	56.4
Population aged 0-14 years (%)	2014	20.0
Population aged 60+ years (females and males, % of total)	2014	16.5/15.0
Sex ratio (males per 100 females)	2014	100.3
Life expectancy at birth (females and males, years)	2010-2015	80.5/74.5
Infant mortality rate (per 1 000 live births)	2010-2015	14.4
Fertility rate, total (live births per woman)	2010-2015	1.8
Contraceptive prevalence (ages 15-49, %)	2007-2013	69.3
International migrant stock (000 and % of total population)[k]	mid-2013	96.8/3.1
Refugees and others of concern to UNHCR	mid-2014	7 839
Education: Government expenditure (% of GDP)	2007-2013	3.3
Education: Primary-secondary gross enrolment ratio (f/m per 100)	2007-2013	79.0/81.1[l]
Education: Female third-level students (% of total)	2007-2013	55.5
Intentional homicide rate (per 100,000 population)	2008-2012	5.0
Seats held by women in national parliaments (%)	2015	20.7

Environmental indicators		
Threatened species	2014	109
Forested area (% of land area)	2012	28.3
Proportion of terrestrial and marine areas protected (%)	2014	1.9
Population using improved drinking water sources (%)	2012	96.0
Population using improved sanitation facilities (%)	2012	91.0
CO_2 emission estimates (000 metric tons and metric tons per capita)	2011	4 668/1.5
Energy supply per capita (Gigajoules)	2012	27.0

a Market rate. **b** ISIC Rev.4 (BCDE). **c** ISIC Rev.3. **d** Population aged 15-64. **e** Break in series. **f** Arrivals of non-resident visitors at national borders. **g** Excluding nationals residing abroad. **h** Including in-transit visitors. **i** 2012. **j** ITU estimate. **k** Refers to foreign citizens. **l** 2001.

Algeria

Region	Northern Africa	Surface area (sq km)	2 381 741
Population (est., 000)	39 929	Pop. density (per sq km)	16.8
Capital city	Algiers	Capital city pop. (000)	2 559[a]
Currency	Algerian Dinar (DZD)	UN membership date	8 October 1962

Economic indicators	2005	2010	2013
GDP: Gross domestic product (million current US$)	103 198	161 207	208 764
GDP: Growth rate at constant 2005 prices (annual %)	5.9	3.6	2.8
GDP per capita (current US$)	3 038.7	4 349.6	5 324.5
GNI: Gross national income per capita (current US$)	2 903.7	4 347.4	5 228.7
Gross fixed capital formation (% of GDP)	22.4	36.3	34.0
Exchange rates (national currency per US$)[b]	73.38	74.94	78.15
Balance of payments, current account (million US$)	21 180	12 308	869
CPI: Consumer price index (2000=100)	117	146	176
Index of industrial production (2010=100)[c]	103	100	103
Agricultural production index (2004-2006=100)	99	125	158
Food production index (2004-2006=100)	99	125	159
Unemployment (% of labour force)	15.3	10.0	9.8
Employment in industrial sector (% of employed)	26.0[def]	33.1[gh]	30.9[gi]
Employment in agricultural sector (% of employed)	20.7[def]	11.7[gh]	10.8[gi]
Labour force participation, adult female pop. (%)	12.9	14.6	15.2
Labour force participation, adult male pop. (%)	72.5	71.1	72.2
Tourist arrivals at national borders (000)[jk]	1 443	2 070	2 634[l]
Energy production, primary (Petajoules)	7 534	6 200	5 928[l]
Mobile-cellular subscriptions (per 100 inhabitants)	40.2	88.4	102.0
Individuals using the Internet (%)	5.8	12.5	16.5[m]

Total trade		Major trading partners			2013
	(million US$)		(% of exports)		(% of imports)
Exports	65 998.1	Spain	15.7	China	12.4
Imports	54 910.0	Italy	13.7	France	11.4
Balance	11 088.1	United Kingdom	10.9	Italy	10.3

Social indicators		
Population growth rate (average annual %)	2010-2015	1.8
Urban population growth rate (average annual %)	2010-2015	2.8
Rural population growth rate (average annual %)	2010-2015	−0.2
Urban population (%)	2014	70.1
Population aged 0-14 years (%)	2014	28.0
Population aged 60+ years (females and males, % of total)	2014	7.9/7.3
Sex ratio (males per 100 females)	2014	102.2
Life expectancy at birth (females and males, years)	2010-2015	72.6/69.4
Infant mortality rate (per 1 000 live births)	2010-2015	26.4
Fertility rate, total (live births per woman)	2010-2015	2.8
Contraceptive prevalence (ages 15-49, %)	2007-2013	61.4[n]
International migrant stock (000 and % of total population)[op]	mid-2013	270.4/0.7
Refugees and others of concern to UNHCR	mid-2014	98 038[q]
Education: Government expenditure (% of GDP)	2007-2013	4.3
Education: Primary-secondary gross enrolment ratio (f/m per 100)	2007-2013	104.2/104.7
Education: Female third-level students (% of total)	2007-2013	59.0
Intentional homicide rate (per 100,000 population)	2008-2012	0.7
Seats held by women in national parliaments (%)	2015	31.6

Environmental indicators		
Threatened species	2014	113
Forested area (% of land area)	2012	0.6
Proportion of terrestrial and marine areas protected (%)	2014	7.5
Population using improved drinking water sources (%)	2012	84.0
Population using improved sanitation facilities (%)	2012	95.0
CO_2 emission estimates (000 metric tons and metric tons per capita)	2011	121 755/3.2
Energy supply per capita (Gigajoules)	2012	50.0

a Refers to the Governorate of Grand Algiers. b Official rate. c ISIC Rev.3 (CDE). d 2004. e ISIC Rev.3. f September. g Fourth quarter. h Break in series. i 2011. j Arrivals of non-resident visitors at national borders. k Including nationals residing abroad. l 2012. m ITU estimate. n 2006. o Refers to foreign citizens. p Including refugees. q According to the Government of Algeria, there are an estimated 165,000 Sahrawi refugees in the Tindouf camps.

American Samoa

Region	Oceania-Polynesia	Surface area (sq km)	199	
Population (est., 000)	55	Pop. density (per sq km)	278.0	
Capital city	Pago Pago	Capital city pop. (000)	48	
Currency	U.S. Dollar (USD)			

Economic indicators	2005	2010	2013
CPI: Consumer price index (2000=100)[a]	122	156	168[b]
Agricultural production index (2004-2006=100)	107	106	106
Food production index (2004-2006=100)	107	106	106
Tourist arrivals at national borders (000)	24	23	22[c]
Mobile-cellular subscriptions (per 100 inhabitants)	3.8[d]	...	...

Social indicators		
Population growth rate (average annual %)	2010-2015	–<
Urban population growth rate (average annual %)	2010-2015	–0.1
Rural population growth rate (average annual %)	2010-2015	0.6
Urban population (%)	2014	87.3
Population aged 0-14 years (%)[efg]	2014	35.0[h]
Population aged 60+ years (females and males, % of total)[efg]	2014	6.9/6.6[h]
Sex ratio (males per 100 females)[efg]	2014	103.0[h]
Life expectancy at birth (females and males, years)[e]	2010-2015	76.2/68.5[i]
Infant mortality rate (per 1 000 live births)[j]	2010-2015	14.9[h]
Fertility rate, total (live births per woman)[j]	2010-2015	3.1[h]
International migrant stock (000 and % of total population)	mid-2013	41.8/75.9
Education: Female third-level students (% of total)	2007-2013	60.6

Environmental indicators		
Threatened species	2014	90
Forested area (% of land area)	2012	88.2
Proportion of terrestrial and marine areas protected (%)	2014	8.6

a Excluding rent. **b** 2011. **c** 2012. **d** 2004. **e** Data compiled by the United Nations Demographic Yearbook system. **f** Data refer to the latest available census. **g** Census, de jure, complete tabulation. **h** 2010. **i** 2006. **j** Data compiled by the Secretariat of the Pacific Community Demography Programme.

Andorra

Region	Southern Europe	Surface area (sq km)	468	
Population (est., 000)	80	Pop. density (per sq km)	171.3	
Capital city	Andorra la Vella	Capital city pop. (000)	23	
Currency	Euro (EUR)	UN membership date	28 July 1993	

Economic indicators	2005	2010	2013
GDP: Gross domestic product (million current US$)	3 248	3 346	3 249
GDP: Growth rate at constant 2005 prices (annual %)	7.8	−5.4	−0.1
GDP per capita (current US$)	39 990.3	42 952.7	41 014.7
GNI: Gross national income per capita (current US$)	39 990.3	42 952.7	41 014.7
Gross fixed capital formation (% of GDP)	29.9	23.0	18.5
Exchange rates (national currency per US$)[a]	0.84	0.76	0.72
CPI: Consumer price index (2000=100)[b]	113	126	132
Tourist arrivals at national borders (000)	2 418	1 808[c]	2 335
Energy production, primary (Petajoules)	0	1	0[de]
Mobile-cellular subscriptions (per 100 inhabitants)	79.5	84.1	80.7
Individuals using the Internet (%)	37.6	81.0	94.0[f]

Social indicators		
Population growth rate (average annual %)	2010-2015	0.8
Urban population growth rate (average annual %)	2010-2015	0.1
Rural population growth rate (average annual %)	2010-2015	4.8
Urban population (%)	2014	85.6
Population aged 0-14 years (%)[ghi]	2014	14.8[j]
Population aged 60+ years (females and males, % of total)[ghi]	2014	18.6/18.0[j]
Sex ratio (males per 100 females)[ghi]	2014	104.6[j]
Fertility rate, total (live births per woman)[g]	2010-2015	1.3[k]
International migrant stock (000 and % of total population)[l]	mid-2013	45.1/56.9
Education: Government expenditure (% of GDP)	2007-2013	3.1
Education: Female third-level students (% of total)	2007-2013	58.9
Intentional homicide rate (per 100,000 population)	2008-2012	1.3
Seats held by women in national parliaments (%)	2015	50.0

Environmental indicators		
Threatened species	2014	11
Forested area (% of land area)	2012	34.0
Proportion of terrestrial and marine areas protected (%)	2014	19.5
Population using improved drinking water sources (%)	2012	100.0
Population using improved sanitation facilities (%)	2012	100.0
CO_2 emission estimates (000 metric tons and metric tons per capita)	2011	491/6.3
Energy supply per capita (Gigajoules)	2012	116.0[e]

a UN operational exchange rate. b Index base 2001=100. c Methodology revised. d 2012. e UNSD estimate. f ITU estimate. g Data compiled by the United Nations Demographic Yearbook system. h Data refer to the latest available census. i De jure estimate. j 2011. k 2010. l Refers to foreign citizens.

Angola

Region	Middle Africa	Surface area (sq km)	1 246 700
Population (est., 000)	22 137	Pop. density (per sq km)	17.8
Capital city	Luanda	Capital city pop. (000)	5 288
Currency	Kwanza (AOA)	UN membership date	1 December 1976

Economic indicators	2005	2010	2013
GDP: Gross domestic product (million current US$)	32 811	82 513	121 692
GDP: Growth rate at constant 2005 prices (annual %)	20.5	3.5	5.1
GDP per capita (current US$)	1 983.2	4 220.8	5 667.6
GNI: Gross national income per capita (current US$)	1 739.6	3 807.1	5 040.6
Gross fixed capital formation (% of GDP)	8.3	15.3	14.1
Exchange rates (national currency per US$)[a]	80.78	92.64	97.56
Balance of payments, current account (million US$)	5 138	7 506	8 348
CPI: Consumer price index (2000=100)[b]	1 846	3 438[c]	4 680
Agricultural production index (2004-2006=100)	102	172	212
Food production index (2004-2006=100)	102	173	213
Unemployment (% of labour force)	6.8	6.9	6.8
Labour force participation, adult female pop. (%)	64.4	62.7	63.3
Labour force participation, adult male pop. (%)	76.3	77.0	76.9
Tourist arrivals at national borders (000)	210	425	650
Energy production, primary (Petajoules)	2 951	4 110	4 031[d]
Mobile-cellular subscriptions (per 100 inhabitants)	9.7	48.1[e]	61.9
Individuals using the Internet (%)	1.1	10.0[e]	19.1[e]

Social indicators		
Population growth rate (average annual %)	2010-2015	3.1
Urban population growth rate (average annual %)	2010-2015	5.0
Rural population growth rate (average annual %)	2010-2015	1.7
Urban population (%)	2014	43.3
Population aged 0-14 years (%)	2014	47.3
Population aged 60+ years (females and males, % of total)	2014	4.2/3.6
Sex ratio (males per 100 females)	2014	98.4
Life expectancy at birth (females and males, years)	2010-2015	53.2/50.2
Infant mortality rate (per 1 000 live births)	2010-2015	96.2
Fertility rate, total (live births per woman)	2010-2015	5.9
Contraceptive prevalence (ages 15-49, %)[f]	2007-2013	17.7
International migrant stock (000 and % of total population)[g]	mid-2013	87.4/0.4
Refugees and others of concern to UNHCR	mid-2014	44 466
Education: Government expenditure (% of GDP)	2007-2013	3.5
Education: Primary-secondary gross enrolment ratio (f/m per 100)	2007-2013	72.2/112.9
Education: Female third-level students (% of total)	2007-2013	27.4
Intentional homicide rate (per 100,000 population)	2008-2012	10.0
Seats held by women in national parliaments (%)	2015	36.8

Environmental indicators		
Threatened species	2014	130
Forested area (% of land area)	2012	46.7
Proportion of terrestrial and marine areas protected (%)	2014	5.0
Population using improved drinking water sources (%)	2012	54.0
Population using improved sanitation facilities (%)	2012	60.0
CO_2 emission estimates (000 metric tons and metric tons per capita)	2011	29 710/1.5
Energy supply per capita (Gigajoules)	2012	29.0

a Official rate. b Luanda. c Series linked to former series. d 2012. e ITU estimate. f Age group 12 to 49 years. g Including refugees.

Anguilla

Region	Caribbean	
Population (est., 000)	14	
Capital city	The Valley	
Currency	E.C. Dollar (XCD)	

		Surface area (sq km)	91
		Pop. density (per sq km)	158.9
		Capital city pop. (000)	1

Economic indicators	2005	2010	2013
GDP: Gross domestic product (million current US$)	229	268	284
GDP: Growth rate at constant 2005 prices (annual %)	13.1	-4.4	-0.9
GDP per capita (current US$)	18 121.0	19 477.8	19 886.2
GNI: Gross national income per capita (current US$)	18 435.4	19 673.6	19 732.5
Gross fixed capital formation (% of GDP)	35.0	24.1	19.9
Exchange rates (national currency per US$) [a]	2.70	2.70	2.70
Balance of payments, current account (million US$)	-52	-51	-48
CPI: Consumer price index (2000=100) [b]	114	138	149
Tourist arrivals at national borders (000) [c]	62	62	69
Energy production, primary (Petajoules) [d]	0	0	0[e]
Mobile-cellular subscriptions (per 100 inhabitants)	103.4	186.6	181.8[f]
Individuals using the Internet (%) [f]	29.0	49.6	64.8

Social indicators		
Population growth rate (average annual %)	2010-2015	1.2
Urban population growth rate (average annual %)	2010-2015	1.2
Urban population (%)	2014	100.0
Life expectancy at birth (females and males, years) [g]	2010-2015	81.1/76.5[h]
Contraceptive prevalence (ages 15-49, %) [i]	2007-2013	43.0[j]
International migrant stock (000 and % of total population)	mid-2013	6.5/45.6
Education: Government expenditure (% of GDP)	2007-2013	2.8
Education: Female third-level students (% of total)	2007-2013	83.3
Intentional homicide rate (per 100,000 population)	2008-2012	7.5

Environmental indicators		
Threatened species	2014	42
Forested area (% of land area)	2012	61.1
CO_2 emission estimates (000 metric tons and metric tons per capita)	2011	143/10.1
Energy supply per capita (Gigajoules)	2012	140.0[d]

a Official rate. b Index base 2001=100. c Excluding nationals residing abroad. d UNSD estimate. e 2012. f ITU estimate. g Data compiled by the United Nations Demographic Yearbook system. h 2000-2002. i Age group 15 to 45 years. j 2003.

Antigua and Barbuda

Region	Caribbean	Surface area (sq km)	442
Population (est., 000)	91	Pop. density (per sq km)	205.7
Capital city	St. John's	Capital city pop. (000)	22
Currency	E.C. Dollar (XCD)	UN membership date	11 November 1981

Economic indicators	2005	2010	2013
GDP: Gross domestic product (million current US$)	997	1 136	1 241
GDP: Growth rate at constant 2005 prices (annual %)	6.1	−7.2	1.5
GDP per capita (current US$)	12 079.9	13 017.3	13 789.7
GNI: Gross national income per capita (current US$)	11 570.7	12 656.3	13 205.4
Gross fixed capital formation (% of GDP)	27.6	28.4	24.6
Exchange rates (national currency per US$)[a]	2.70	2.70	2.70
Balance of payments, current account (million US$)	−171	−167	−204
CPI: Consumer price index (2000=100)	110	123	133
Agricultural production index (2004-2006=100)	95	89	89
Food production index (2004-2006=100)	95	89	89
Employment in industrial sector (% of employed)	15.6[b]	15.6[bc]	...
Employment in agricultural sector (% of employed)	2.8[b]	2.8[bc]	...
Tourist arrivals at national borders (000)[de]	245	230	244
Mobile-cellular subscriptions (per 100 inhabitants)	104.2	192.6	127.1
Individuals using the Internet (%)[f]	27.0	47.0	63.4

Total trade		Major trading partners			2013
	(million US$)	(% of exports)			(% of imports)
Exports	32.9	United States	27.1	United States	35.3
Imports	507.9	United Kingdom	20.7	Areas nes	32.5[g]
Balance	−475.0	Curaçao	7.3	China	3.9

Social indicators		
Population growth rate (average annual %)	2010-2015	1.0
Urban population growth rate (average annual %)	2010-2015	−1.0
Rural population growth rate (average annual %)	2010-2015	1.7
Urban population (%)	2014	24.2
Population aged 0-14 years (%)	2014	24.6
Population aged 60+ years (females and males, % of total)	2014	11.1/9.8
Sex ratio (males per 100 females)	2014	91.5
Life expectancy at birth (females and males, years)	2010-2015	78.2/73.4
Infant mortality rate (per 1 000 live births)	2010-2015	8.5
Fertility rate, total (live births per woman)	2010-2015	2.1
Contraceptive prevalence (ages 15-49, %)[h]	2007-2013	52.6[i]
International migrant stock (000 and % of total population)	mid-2013	28.7/31.9
Refugees and others of concern to UNHCR	mid-2014	0[j]
Education: Government expenditure (% of GDP)	2007-2013	2.6
Education: Primary-secondary gross enrolment ratio (f/m per 100)	2007-2013	102.3/99.9
Education: Female third-level students (% of total)	2007-2013	69.4
Intentional homicide rate (per 100,000 population)	2008-2012	11.2
Seats held by women in national parliaments (%)	2015	11.1

Environmental indicators		
Threatened species	2014	45
Forested area (% of land area)	2012	22.3
Proportion of terrestrial and marine areas protected (%)	2014	0.2
Population using improved drinking water sources (%)	2012	98.0
Population using improved sanitation facilities (%)	2012	91.0[k]
CO_2 emission estimates (000 metric tons and metric tons per capita)	2011	513/5.8
Energy supply per capita (Gigajoules)	2012	85.0[l]

a Official rate. b ISIC Rev.3. c 2008. d Excluding nationals residing abroad. e Arrivals by air. f ITU estimate. g See technical notes. h Age group 15 to 44 years. i 1988. j Value is zero, not available or not applicable. k 2010. l UNSD estimate.

Argentina

Region	South America	Surface area (sq km)	2 780 400	
Population (est., 000)	41 803	Pop. density (per sq km)	15.0	
Capital city	Buenos Aires	Capital city pop. (000)	15 024[a]	
Currency	Argentine Peso (ARS)	UN membership date	24 October 1945	

Economic indicators

	2005	2010	2013
GDP: Gross domestic product (million current US$)	222 911	464 616	611 726
GDP: Growth rate at constant 2005 prices (annual %)	9.2	9.1	2.9
GDP per capita (current US$)	5 767.7	11 507.8	14 759.5
GNI: Gross national income per capita (current US$)	5 578.7	11 227.1	14 503.6
Gross fixed capital formation (% of GDP)	18.3	17.9	17.0
Exchange rates (national currency per US$)[b]	3.01	3.96	6.50
Balance of payments, current account (million US$)	5 274	1 360	−4 813
CPI: Consumer price index (2000=100)[cd]	162	249	332
Agricultural production index (2004-2006=100)	103	115	120
Food production index (2004-2006=100)	103	115	120
Unemployment (% of labour force)	10.6	7.7	7.5
Employment in industrial sector (% of employed)	23.5[efgh]	23.2[eijk]	23.4[ijkl]
Employment in agricultural sector (% of employed)	1.1[efgh]	1.3[eijk]	0.6[ijkl]
Labour force participation, adult female pop. (%)	48.7	47.0	47.5
Labour force participation, adult male pop. (%)	76.5	74.9	75.0
Tourist arrivals at national borders (000)	3 823	5 325	5 571
Energy production, primary (Petajoules)	3 609	3 343	3 160[l]
Mobile-cellular subscriptions (per 100 inhabitants)	57.3	141.4	159.0
Individuals using the Internet (%)	17.7	45.0[m]	59.9[m]

Total trade

		Major trading partners			2013
	(million US$)		(% of exports)		(% of imports)
Exports	76 633.9	Brazil	21.2	Brazil	26.0
Imports	73 655.5	China	7.2	China	15.4
Balance	2 978.4	United States	5.6	United States	10.9

Social indicators

Population growth rate (average annual %)	2010-2015	0.9
Urban population growth rate (average annual %)	2010-2015	1.0
Rural population growth rate (average annual %)	2010-2015	−1.0
Urban population (%)	2014	91.6
Population aged 0-14 years (%)	2014	24.0
Population aged 60+ years (females and males, % of total)	2014	17.4/13.2
Sex ratio (males per 100 females)	2014	95.9
Life expectancy at birth (females and males, years)	2010-2015	79.8/72.5
Infant mortality rate (per 1 000 live births)	2010-2015	11.4
Fertility rate, total (live births per woman)	2010-2015	2.2
Contraceptive prevalence (ages 15-49, %)	2007-2013	78.9[n]
International migrant stock (000 and % of total population)	mid-2013	1 885.7/4.6
Refugees and others of concern to UNHCR	mid-2014	4 407
Education: Government expenditure (% of GDP)	2007-2013	5.1
Education: Primary-secondary gross enrolment ratio (f/m per 100)	2007-2013	117.4/113.5
Education: Female third-level students (% of total)	2007-2013	60.4
Intentional homicide rate (per 100,000 population)	2008-2012	5.5
Seats held by women in national parliaments (%)	2015	36.2

Environmental indicators

Threatened species	2014	243
Forested area (% of land area)	2012	10.6
Proportion of terrestrial and marine areas protected (%)	2014	5.4
Population using improved drinking water sources (%)	2012	99.0
Population using improved sanitation facilities (%)	2012	97.0
CO_2 emission estimates (000 metric tons and metric tons per capita)	2011	190 035/4.7
Energy supply per capita (Gigajoules)	2012	82.0

a Refers to Gran Buenos Aires. **b** Official rate. **c** Buenos Aires. **d** Metropolitan areas. **e** ISIC Rev.3. **f** Population aged 10 and over. **g** Second semester. **h** 28 urban agglomerations. **i** Average of quarterly estimates. **j** 31 urban agglomerations. **k** Break in series. **l** 2012. **m** ITU estimate. **n** 2004-2005.

Armenia

Region	Western Asia	Surface area (sq km)	29 743
Population (est., 000)	2 984	Pop. density (per sq km)	100.1
Capital city	Yerevan	Capital city pop. (000)	1 049
Currency	Dram (AMD)	UN membership date	2 March 1992

Economic indicators	2005	2010	2013
GDP: Gross domestic product (million current US$)	4 900	9 260	10 431
GDP: Growth rate at constant 2005 prices (annual %)	13.9	2.2	3.5
GDP per capita (current US$)	1 625.4	3 124.8	3 504.5
GNI: Gross national income per capita (current US$)	1 669.4	3 239.1	3 644.2
Gross fixed capital formation (% of GDP)	29.8	33.4	20.9
Exchange rates (national currency per US$)[a]	450.19	363.44	405.64
Balance of payments, current account (million US$)	−124	−1 318	−839
CPI: Consumer price index (2000=100)	117	154	179
Index of industrial production (2010=100)[b]	...	100	133
Agricultural production index (2004-2006=100)	103	102	128
Food production index (2004-2006=100)	103	102	128
Unemployment (% of labour force)	27.8	19.0	16.2
Employment in industrial sector (% of employed)	15.9[c]	17.4[d]	16.7[e]
Employment in agricultural sector (% of employed)	46.2[c]	38.6[d]	38.9[e]
Labour force participation, adult female pop. (%)	52.0	50.9	54.2
Labour force participation, adult male pop. (%)	69.6	72.3	72.6
Tourist arrivals at national borders (000)	319	684	1 084
Energy production, primary (Petajoules)	36	52	52[f]
Mobile-cellular subscriptions (per 100 inhabitants)	10.6	130.4	112.4
Individuals using the Internet (%)	5.3	25.0[g]	46.3[g]

Total trade		Major trading partners			2013
	(million US$)	(% of exports)		(% of imports)	
Exports	1 467.8	Russian Federation	22.6	Russian Federation	26.0
Imports	4 256.2	Bulgaria	10.4	China	9.0
Balance	−2 788.4	Belgium	8.9	Ukraine	5.3

Social indicators		
Population growth rate (average annual %)	2010-2015	0.2
Urban population growth rate (average annual %)	2010-2015	−0.1
Rural population growth rate (average annual %)	2010-2015	0.7
Urban population (%)	2014	62.8
Population aged 0-14 years (%)	2014	20.2
Population aged 60+ years (females and males, % of total)	2014	17.2/12.4
Sex ratio (males per 100 females)	2014	105.3
Life expectancy at birth (females and males, years)	2010-2015	77.9/71.2
Infant mortality rate (per 1 000 live births)	2010-2015	19.0
Fertility rate, total (live births per woman)	2010-2015	1.7
Contraceptive prevalence (ages 15-49, %)	2007-2013	54.9
International migrant stock (000 and % of total population)[h]	mid-2013	317.0/10.7
Refugees and others of concern to UNHCR	mid-2014	14 909
Education: Government expenditure (% of GDP)	2007-2013	2.3
Education: Primary-secondary gross enrolment ratio (f/m per 100)	2007-2013	105.6/92.1
Education: Female third-level students (% of total)	2007-2013	54.7
Intentional homicide rate (per 100,000 population)	2008-2012	1.8
Seats held by women in national parliaments (%)	2015	10.7

Environmental indicators		
Threatened species	2014	111
Forested area (% of land area)	2012	8.9
Proportion of terrestrial and marine areas protected (%)	2014	24.8
Population using improved drinking water sources (%)	2012	100.0
Population using improved sanitation facilities (%)	2012	91.0
CO_2 emission estimates (000 metric tons and metric tons per capita)	2011	4 961/1.7
Energy supply per capita (Gigajoules)	2012	49.0

a Official rate. b ISIC Rev.4 (BCDE). c ISIC Rev.3. d Break in series. e 2011. f 2012. g ITU estimate. h Including refugees.

Aruba

Region	Caribbean	Surface area (sq km)	180	
Population (est., 000)	103	Pop. density (per sq km)	574.6	
Capital city	Oranjestad	Capital city pop. (000)	29	
Currency	Aruban Guilder (AWG)			

Economic indicators	2005	2010	2013
GDP: Gross domestic product (million current US$)	2 331	2 391	2 589
GDP: Growth rate at constant 2005 prices (annual %)	1.2	−3.3	3.9
GDP per capita (current US$)	23 302.8	23 529.3	25 156.0
GNI: Gross national income per capita (current US$)	21 888.0	22 112.6	23 649.1
Gross fixed capital formation (% of GDP)	32.1	28.9	22.9
Exchange rates (national currency per US$)[a]	1.79	1.79	1.79
Balance of payments, current account (million US$)	105	−460	−269
CPI: Consumer price index (2000=100)	117	139	142
Tourist arrivals at national borders (000)	733	824	979
Energy production, primary (Petajoules)[b]	5	5	4[c]
Mobile-cellular subscriptions (per 100 inhabitants)	103.4	129.7[d]	134.9[d]
Individuals using the Internet (%)[d]	25.4	62.0	78.9

Total trade		Major trading partners			2013
	(million US$)		(% of exports)		(% of imports)
Exports	167.8	Colombia	36.8	United States	49.6
Imports	1 303.3	Curaçao	18.9	Areas nes	13.4[e]
Balance	−1 135.5	United States	12.8	Netherlands	11.1

Social indicators		
Population growth rate (average annual %)	2010-2015	0.5
Urban population growth rate (average annual %)	2010-2015	−0.3
Rural population growth rate (average annual %)	2010-2015	1.0
Urban population (%)	2014	41.8
Population aged 0-14 years (%)	2014	18.8
Population aged 60+ years (females and males, % of total)	2014	19.1/16.4
Sex ratio (males per 100 females)	2014	90.7
Life expectancy at birth (females and males, years)	2010-2015	77.8/72.9
Infant mortality rate (per 1 000 live births)	2010-2015	14.8
Fertility rate, total (live births per woman)	2010-2015	1.7
International migrant stock (000 and % of total population)	mid-2013	36.0/34.9
Refugees and others of concern to UNHCR	mid-2014	6
Education: Government expenditure (% of GDP)	2007-2013	6.0
Education: Primary-secondary gross enrolment ratio (f/m per 100)	2007-2013	104.4/100.0
Education: Female third-level students (% of total)	2007-2013	67.3
Intentional homicide rate (per 100,000 population)	2008-2012	3.9

Environmental indicators		
Threatened species	2014	23
Forested area (% of land area)	2012	2.3
Proportion of terrestrial and marine areas protected (%)	2014	0.5
CO_2 emission estimates (000 metric tons and metric tons per capita)	2011	2 439/23.9
Energy supply per capita (Gigajoules)	2012	162.0[b]

a Official rate. b UNSD estimate. c 2012. d ITU estimate. e See technical notes.

Australia

Region	Oceania	Surface area (sq km)	7 692 024 [a]
Population (est., 000)	23 630 [b]	Pop. density (per sq km)	3.1 [b]
Capital city	Canberra	Capital city pop. (000)	415
Currency	Australian Dollar (AUD)	UN membership date	1 November 1945

Economic indicators	2005	2010	2013
GDP: Gross domestic product (million current US$)	762 377	1 290 335	1 531 282
GDP: Growth rate at constant 2005 prices (annual %)	3.0	2.2	2.9
GDP per capita (current US$)	37 151.5	57 592.7	65 600.5
GNI: Gross national income per capita (current US$)	35 707.1	55 274.1	64 096.6
Gross fixed capital formation (% of GDP)	28.1	26.7	27.4
Exchange rates (national currency per US$) [c]	1.36	0.98	1.13
Balance of payments, current account (million US$)	–43 343	–44 714	–49 558
CPI: Consumer price index (2000=100)	116	134	145
Index of industrial production (2010=100) [de]	90	100	107
Agricultural production index (2004-2006=100)	108	100	116
Food production index (2004-2006=100)	108	102	115
Unemployment (% of labour force)	5.0	5.2	5.7
Employment in industrial sector (% of employed)	21.3 [fg]	21.1 [hij]	...
Employment in agricultural sector (% of employed)	3.6 [fg]	3.3 [hij]	...
Labour force participation, adult female pop. (%)	57.0	58.8	58.8
Labour force participation, adult male pop. (%)	72.2	72.5	71.8
Tourist arrivals at national borders (000) [kl]	5 499	5 790	6 382
Energy production, primary (Petajoules) [m]	11 586	12 928	13 374 [n]
Mobile-cellular subscriptions (per 100 inhabitants)	89.8	100.4	106.8
Individuals using the Internet (%)	63.0 [o]	76.0 [p]	83.0

Total trade		Major trading partners			2013
	(million US$)	(% of exports)			(% of imports)
Exports	252 155.1	China	34.6	China	19.3
Imports	232 481.3	Japan	12.4	United States	10.2
Balance	19 673.8	Areas nes	12.2 [q]	Japan	7.7

Social indicators		
Population growth rate (average annual %) [b]	2010-2015	1.3
Urban population growth rate (average annual %) [b]	2010-2015	1.5
Rural population growth rate (average annual %) [b]	2010-2015	0.1
Urban population (%) [b]	2014	89.3
Population aged 0-14 years (%) [b]	2014	19.1
Population aged 60+ years (females and males, % of total) [b]	2014	21.1/19.0
Sex ratio (males per 100 females) [b]	2014	99.0
Life expectancy at birth (females and males, years) [b]	2010-2015	84.7/80.2
Infant mortality rate (per 1 000 live births) [b]	2010-2015	3.9
Fertility rate, total (live births per woman) [b]	2010-2015	1.9
Contraceptive prevalence (ages 15-49, %) [r]	2007-2013	72.3 [s]
International migrant stock (000 and % of total population) [b]	mid-2013	6 468.6/27.7
Refugees and others of concern to UNHCR	mid-2014	48 726 [t]
Education: Government expenditure (% of GDP)	2007-2013	5.1
Education: Primary-secondary gross enrolment ratio (f/m per 100)	2007-2013	117.3/121.1
Education: Female third-level students (% of total)	2007-2013	56.7
Intentional homicide rate (per 100,000 population)	2008-2012	1.1
Seats held by women in national parliaments (%)	2015	26.7

Environmental indicators		
Threatened species [u]	2014	906
Forested area (% of land area)	2012	19.2
Proportion of terrestrial and marine areas protected (%)	2014	29.0
Population using improved drinking water sources (%)	2012	100.0
Population using improved sanitation facilities (%)	2012	100.0
CO_2 emission estimates (000 metric tons and metric tons per capita)	2011	369 040/16.2
Energy supply per capita (Gigajoules) [m]	2012	238.0

a Excluding Norfolk Island. **b** Including Christmas, Cocos (Keeling) and Norfolk Islands. **c** Market rate. **d** ISIC Rev.4 (BCDE). **e** Twelve months ending 30 June of the year stated. **f** ISIC Rev.3. **g** Average of February, May, August and November. **h** 2009. **i** Average of quarterly estimates. **j** Break in series. **k** Arrivals of non-resident visitors at national borders. **l** Excluding nationals residing abroad and crew members. **m** Excluding the overseas territories. **n** 2012. **o** Population aged 15 and over. **p** ITU estimate. **q** See technical notes. **r** Age group 18 to 44 years. **s** 2005. **t** Refugee population refers to the end of 2013. **u** Excluding Christmas and Cocos (Keeling) Islands.

Austria

Region	Western Europe	Surface area (sq km)		83 871
Population (est., 000)	8 526	Pop. density (per sq km)		101.7
Capital city	Vienna	Capital city pop. (000)		1 743
Currency	Euro (EUR)	UN membership date		14 December 1955

Economic indicators	2005	2010	2013
GDP: Gross domestic product (million current US$)	314 641	389 656	428 322
GDP: Growth rate at constant 2005 prices (annual %)	2.1	1.9	0.2
GDP per capita (current US$)	38 191.1	46 377.0	50 419.6
GNI: Gross national income per capita (current US$)	38 071.0	46 787.9	50 371.9
Gross fixed capital formation (% of GDP)	23.2	22.1	22.8
Exchange rates (national currency per US$) [a]	0.85	0.75	0.73
Balance of payments, current account (million US$)	6 245	13 149	4 439
CPI: Consumer price index (2000=100)	111	121	131
Index of industrial production (2010=100) [b]	91	100	108
Agricultural production index (2004-2006=100)	100	103	101
Food production index (2004-2006=100)	100	103	101
Unemployment (% of labour force)	5.2	4.4	4.9
Employment in industrial sector (% of employed)	27.5[cd]	24.9	26.2[e]
Employment in agricultural sector (% of employed)	5.5[cd]	5.2	4.9[e]
Labour force participation, adult female pop. (%)	51.2	53.9	54.6
Labour force participation, adult male pop. (%)	67.3	67.7	67.7
Tourist arrivals at national borders (000) [f]	19 952	22 004	24 813
Energy production, primary (Petajoules)	438	526	555[e]
Mobile-cellular subscriptions (per 100 inhabitants)	105.2	145.7	156.2
Individuals using the Internet (%)	58.0	75.2	80.6

Total trade		Major trading partners				2013
	(million US$)		(% of exports)			(% of imports)
Exports	166 271.4	Germany	29.4	Germany		36.8
Imports	173 357.5	Italy	6.3	Italy		6.0
Balance	−7 086.1	Switzerland	5.4	Switzerland		5.3

Social indicators		
Population growth rate (average annual %)	2010-2015	0.4
Urban population growth rate (average annual %)	2010-2015	0.4
Rural population growth rate (average annual %)	2010-2015	0.3
Urban population (%)	2014	65.9
Population aged 0-14 years (%)	2014	14.5
Population aged 60+ years (females and males, % of total)	2014	26.3/21.6
Sex ratio (males per 100 females)	2014	95.6
Life expectancy at birth (females and males, years)	2010-2015	83.5/78.5
Infant mortality rate (per 1 000 live births)	2010-2015	3.1
Fertility rate, total (live births per woman)	2010-2015	1.5
Contraceptive prevalence (ages 15-49, %) [g]	2007-2013	69.6
International migrant stock (000 and % of total population)	mid-2013	1 333.8/15.7
Refugees and others of concern to UNHCR	mid-2014	78 947[h]
Education: Government expenditure (% of GDP)	2007-2013	5.8
Education: Primary-secondary gross enrolment ratio (f/m per 100)	2007-2013	97.3/100.1
Education: Female third-level students (% of total)	2007-2013	53.4
Intentional homicide rate (per 100,000 population)	2008-2012	0.9
Seats held by women in national parliaments (%)	2015	30.6

Environmental indicators		
Threatened species	2014	107
Forested area (% of land area)	2012	47.3
Proportion of terrestrial and marine areas protected (%)	2014	28.4
Population using improved drinking water sources (%)	2012	100.0
Population using improved sanitation facilities (%)	2012	100.0
CO_2 emission estimates (000 metric tons and metric tons per capita)	2011	65 203/7.7
Energy supply per capita (Gigajoules)	2012	165.0

a Market rate. **b** ISIC Rev.4 (BCDE). **c** ISIC Rev.3. **d** Excluding conscripts. **e** 2012. **f** Arrivals of non-resident tourists in all types of accommodation establishments. **g** Age group 18 to 46 years. **h** Refugee population refers to the end of 2013.

Azerbaijan

Region	Western Asia	Surface area (sq km)	86 600
Population (est., 000)	9 515[a]	Pop. density (per sq km)	109.9[a]
Capital city	Baku	Capital city pop. (000)	2 317[b]
Currency	Azerbaijan Manat (AZN)	UN membership date	2 March 1992

Economic indicators	2005	2010	2013
GDP: Gross domestic product (million current US$)	13 246	52 906	73 557
GDP: Growth rate at constant 2005 prices (annual %)	28.0	4.6	6.0
GDP per capita (current US$)	1 546.8	5 817.2	7 814.0
GNI: Gross national income per capita (current US$)	1 370.3	5 468.9	7 376.4
Gross fixed capital formation (% of GDP)	41.3	18.2	24.6
Exchange rates (national currency per US$)[c]	0.92	0.80	0.78
Balance of payments, current account (million US$)	167	15 040	12 232
CPI: Consumer price index (2000=100)	125	204	...
Index of industrial production (2010=100)[d]	50	100	95
Agricultural production index (2004-2006=100)	104	118	137
Food production index (2004-2006=100)	103	122	142
Unemployment (% of labour force)	7.3	5.6	5.5
Employment in industrial sector (% of employed)	12.1[e]	13.7[fg]	14.3[fh]
Employment in agricultural sector (% of employed)	39.3[e]	38.2[fg]	37.7[fh]
Labour force participation, adult female pop. (%)	59.6	61.8	62.9
Labour force participation, adult male pop. (%)	69.2	67.4	69.6
Tourist arrivals at national borders (000)	693	1 280	2 130
Energy production, primary (Petajoules)	1 155	2 759	2 458[h]
Mobile-cellular subscriptions (per 100 inhabitants)	26.2	100.1	107.6
Individuals using the Internet (%)	8.0	46.0[i]	58.7[j]

Total trade		Major trading partners			2013
	(million US$)	(% of exports)			(% of imports)
Exports	23 904.1	Italy	25.1	Russian Federation	14.1
Imports	10 763.4	Indonesia	11.6	Turkey	13.8
Balance	13 140.7	Thailand	7.0	United Kingdom	12.3

Social indicators		
Population growth rate (average annual %)[a]	2010-2015	1.1
Urban population growth rate (average annual %)[a]	2010-2015	1.6
Rural population growth rate (average annual %)[a]	2010-2015	0.6
Urban population (%)[a]	2014	54.4
Population aged 0-14 years (%)[a]	2014	22.2
Population aged 60+ years (females and males, % of total)[a]	2014	10.0/7.7
Sex ratio (males per 100 females)[a]	2014	98.9
Life expectancy at birth (females and males, years)[a]	2010-2015	73.8/67.5
Infant mortality rate (per 1 000 live births)[a]	2010-2015	39.6
Fertility rate, total (live births per woman)[a]	2010-2015	1.9
Contraceptive prevalence (ages 15-49, %)	2007-2013	51.1[k]
International migrant stock (000 and % of total population)[al]	mid-2013	323.8/3.4
Refugees and others of concern to UNHCR	mid-2014	611 540
Education: Government expenditure (% of GDP)	2007-2013	2.4
Education: Primary-secondary gross enrolment ratio (f/m per 100)[m]	2007-2013	98.6/100.3
Education: Female third-level students (% of total)	2007-2013	50.0
Intentional homicide rate (per 100,000 population)	2008-2012	2.1
Seats held by women in national parliaments (%)	2015	15.6

Environmental indicators		
Threatened species	2014	92
Forested area (% of land area)	2012	11.3
Proportion of terrestrial and marine areas protected (%)	2014	14.0
Population using improved drinking water sources (%)	2012	80.0
Population using improved sanitation facilities (%)	2012	82.0
CO_2 emission estimates (000 metric tons and metric tons per capita)	2011	33 458/3.6
Energy supply per capita (Gigajoules)	2012	60.0

a Including Nagorno-Karabakh. **b** Including communities under the authority of the Town Council. **c** Official rate. **d** ISIC Rev.4 (BCDE). **e** ISIC Rev.3. **f** December. **g** Break in series. **h** 2012. **i** Population aged 7 and over. **j** ITU estimate. **k** 2006. **l** Including refugees. **m** National estimate.

Bahamas

Region	Caribbean	Surface area (sq km)	13 940
Population (est., 000)	383	Pop. density (per sq km)	27.6
Capital city	Nassau	Capital city pop. (000)	267
Currency	Bahamian Dollar (BSD)	UN membership date	18 September 1973

Economic indicators	2005	2010	2013
GDP: Gross domestic product (million current US$)	7 706	7 910	8 420
GDP: Growth rate at constant 2005 prices (annual %)	3.4	1.5	0.7
GDP per capita (current US$)	23 416.9	21 940.7	22 313.0
GNI: Gross national income per capita (current US$)	23 021.9	21 364.9	21 776.8
Gross fixed capital formation (% of GDP)	24.2	24.0	26.3
Balance of payments, current account (million US$)	−701	−814	−1 637
CPI: Consumer price index (2000=100)	110	125	132
Agricultural production index (2004-2006=100)	99	126	134
Food production index (2004-2006=100)	99	126	134
Unemployment (% of labour force)	10.2	14.7	13.6
Employment in industrial sector (% of employed)[a]	17.8[b]	16.0[bcd]	12.9[ef]
Employment in agricultural sector (% of employed)[a]	3.5[b]	2.9[bcd]	3.7[ef]
Labour force participation, adult female pop. (%)	67.7	69.2	69.3
Labour force participation, adult male pop. (%)	77.8	79.3	79.3
Tourist arrivals at national borders (000)	1 608	1 370	1 364
Energy production, primary (Petajoules)	0	0	0[g]
Mobile-cellular subscriptions (per 100 inhabitants)	69.2	118.8	76.1[h]
Individuals using the Internet (%)[h]	25.0	43.0	72.0

Total trade	Major trading partners				2013
(million US$)		(% of exports)			(% of imports)
Exports	811.5	United States	83.6	United States	89.3
Imports	3 365.3	United Kingdom	3.8	Trinidad and Tobago	2.4
Balance	−2 553.8	Canada	2.8	Japan	1.3

Social indicators		
Population growth rate (average annual %)	2010-2015	1.5
Urban population growth rate (average annual %)	2010-2015	1.5
Rural population growth rate (average annual %)	2010-2015	1.1
Urban population (%)	2014	82.8
Population aged 0-14 years (%)	2014	21.0
Population aged 60+ years (females and males, % of total)	2014	13.5/10.7
Sex ratio (males per 100 females)	2014	95.9
Life expectancy at birth (females and males, years)	2010-2015	78.1/72.0
Infant mortality rate (per 1 000 live births)	2010-2015	9.1
Fertility rate, total (live births per woman)	2010-2015	1.9
Contraceptive prevalence (ages 15-49, %)[i]	2007-2013	61.7[j]
International migrant stock (000 and % of total population)	mid-2013	61.3/16.3
Refugees and others of concern to UNHCR	mid-2014	30
Education: Government expenditure (% of GDP)[k]	2007-2013	2.9[l]
Education: Primary-secondary gross enrolment ratio (f/m per 100)	2007-2013	101.6/98.1
Intentional homicide rate (per 100,000 population)	2008-2012	29.8
Seats held by women in national parliaments (%)	2015	13.2

Environmental indicators		
Threatened species	2014	72
Forested area (% of land area)	2012	51.5
Proportion of terrestrial and marine areas protected (%)	2014	0.5
Population using improved drinking water sources (%)	2012	98.0
Population using improved sanitation facilities (%)	2012	92.0
CO_2 emission estimates (000 metric tons and metric tons per capita)	2011	1 907/5.2
Energy supply per capita (Gigajoules)	2012	75.0

a ISIC Rev.3. **b** April. **c** 2009. **d** Break in series. **e** 2011. **f** May. **g** 2012. **h** ITU estimate. **i** Age group 15 to 44 years. **j** 1988. **k** UNESCO estimate. **l** 2000.

Bahrain

Region	Western Asia	Surface area (sq km)	767
Population (est., 000)	1 344	Pop. density (per sq km)	1 936.8
Capital city	Manama	Capital city pop. (000)	398 [a]
Currency	Bahraini Dinar (BHD)	UN membership date	21 September 1971

Economic indicators	2005	2010	2013
GDP: Gross domestic product (million current US$)	15 969	25 713	32 898
GDP: Growth rate at constant 2005 prices (annual %)	6.8	4.3	5.3
GDP per capita (current US$)	18 155.9	20 545.8	24 694.9
GNI: Gross national income per capita (current US$)	17 686.0	18 649.5	21 477.4
Gross fixed capital formation (% of GDP)	25.7	26.1	15.6
Exchange rates (national currency per US$) [b]	0.38	0.38	0.38
Balance of payments, current account (million US$)	1 474	770	2 560
CPI: Consumer price index (2000=100)	105	120	127
Index of industrial production (2010=100) [c]	85	100	110
Agricultural production index (2004-2006=100)	92	115	207
Food production index (2004-2006=100)	92	115	207
Unemployment (% of labour force)	8.8	7.4	7.4
Employment in industrial sector (% of employed)	15.0 [def]	35.3 [ghi]	...
Employment in agricultural sector (% of employed)	0.8 [def]	1.1 [ghi]	...
Labour force participation, adult female pop. (%)	36.3	39.3	39.2
Labour force participation, adult male pop. (%)	83.4	87.2	86.9
Tourist arrivals at national borders (000) [j]	6 313	11 952	9 163
Energy production, primary (Petajoules)	672	840	825 [k]
Mobile-cellular subscriptions (per 100 inhabitants)	87.2	125.2	165.9
Individuals using the Internet (%)	21.3	55.0	90.0 [l]

Total trade		Major trading partners			2013
	(million US$) [m]	(% of exports) [m]		(% of imports) [m]	
Exports	22 561.9	...	Saudi Arabia	45.9	
Imports	17 643.3	...	China	7.7	
Balance	4 918.6	...	Brazil	7.1	

Social indicators		
Population growth rate (average annual %)	2010-2015	1.7
Urban population growth rate (average annual %)	2010-2015	1.7
Rural population growth rate (average annual %)	2010-2015	1.2
Urban population (%)	2014	88.7
Population aged 0-14 years (%)	2014	21.3
Population aged 60+ years (females and males, % of total)	2014	4.5/3.0
Sex ratio (males per 100 females)	2014	163.3
Life expectancy at birth (females and males, years)	2010-2015	77.4/75.8
Infant mortality rate (per 1 000 live births)	2010-2015	6.9
Fertility rate, total (live births per woman)	2010-2015	2.1
Contraceptive prevalence (ages 15-49, %)	2007-2013	61.8 [n]
International migrant stock (000 and % of total population) [o]	mid-2013	729.4/54.8
Refugees and others of concern to UNHCR	mid-2014	346
Education: Government expenditure (% of GDP)	2007-2013	2.7
Education: Primary-secondary gross enrolment ratio (f/m per 100)	2007-2013	101.6/99.7 [p]
Education: Female third-level students (% of total)	2007-2013	59.2
Intentional homicide rate (per 100,000 population)	2008-2012	0.5
Seats held by women in national parliaments (%)	2015	7.5

Environmental indicators		
Threatened species	2014	33
Forested area (% of land area)	2012	0.7
Proportion of terrestrial and marine areas protected (%)	2014	4.4
Population using improved drinking water sources (%)	2012	100.0
Population using improved sanitation facilities (%)	2012	99.0
CO_2 emission estimates (000 metric tons and metric tons per capita)	2011	23 439/18.1
Energy supply per capita (Gigajoules)	2012	400.0

a Refers to the urban area of the municipality of Al-Manamah. b Official rate. c ISIC Rev.3 (CDE). d 2004.
e ISIC Rev.3. f November. g Population census. h April. i Break in series. j Arrivals of non-resident visitors
at national borders. k 2012. l ITU estimate. m 2011. n 1995. o Refers to foreign citizens. p 1999.

Bangladesh

Region	Southern Asia	Surface area (sq km)	147 570	
Population (est., 000)	158 513	Pop. density (per sq km)	1 100.8	
Capital city	Dhaka	Capital city pop. (000)	16 982[a]	
Currency	Taka (BDT)	UN membership date	17 September 1974	

Economic indicators	2005	2010	2013
GDP: Gross domestic product (million current US$)	66 240	114 586	153 505
GDP: Growth rate at constant 2005 prices (annual %)	6.0	6.1	6.0
GDP per capita (current US$)	462.8	758.2	980.3
GNI: Gross national income per capita (current US$)	481.0	819.6	1 059.1
Gross fixed capital formation (% of GDP)	26.4	26.2	28.4
Exchange rates (national currency per US$)[b]	66.21	70.75	77.75
Balance of payments, current account (million US$)	508	1 168	2 366
CPI: Consumer price index (2000=100)[c]	127	183	247[d]
Index of industrial production (2010=100)[ef]	...	100	142
Agricultural production index (2004-2006=100)	103	129	136
Food production index (2004-2006=100)	103	130	136
Unemployment (% of labour force)	4.3	4.5	4.3
Employment in industrial sector (% of employed)	14.5[gh]	...	...
Employment in agricultural sector (% of employed)	48.1[gh]	...	...
Labour force participation, adult female pop. (%)	55.5	56.9	57.4
Labour force participation, adult male pop. (%)	85.0	84.2	84.1
Tourist arrivals at national borders (000)	208	303	148
Energy production, primary (Petajoules)	1 047	1 300	1 347[i]
Mobile-cellular subscriptions (per 100 inhabitants)	6.3	45.0	67.1
Individuals using the Internet (%)	0.2[j]	3.7[j]	6.5

Total trade		Major trading partners			2013
	(million US$)[k]		(% of exports)[k]		(% of imports)[k]
Exports	24 313.7	United States	21.0	Thailand	22.8
Imports	41 221.7	Germany	15.6	India	11.2
Balance	−16 908.0	United Kingdom	9.5	China	8.8

Social indicators		
Population growth rate (average annual %)	2010-2015	1.2
Urban population growth rate (average annual %)	2010-2015	3.6
Rural population growth rate (average annual %)	2010-2015	0.1
Urban population (%)	2014	33.5
Population aged 0-14 years (%)	2014	29.5
Population aged 60+ years (females and males, % of total)	2014	6.8/7.2
Sex ratio (males per 100 females)	2014	102.3
Life expectancy at birth (females and males, years)	2010-2015	71.3/69.8
Infant mortality rate (per 1 000 live births)	2010-2015	32.4
Fertility rate, total (live births per woman)	2010-2015	2.2
Contraceptive prevalence (ages 15-49, %)	2007-2013	61.2
International migrant stock (000 and % of total population)[l]	mid-2013	1 396.5/0.9
Refugees and others of concern to UNHCR	mid-2014	232 597[m]
Education: Government expenditure (% of GDP)	2007-2013	2.2
Education: Primary-secondary gross enrolment ratio (f/m per 100)[n]	2007-2013	80.8/73.7
Education: Female third-level students (% of total)	2007-2013	41.4
Intentional homicide rate (per 100,000 population)	2008-2012	2.7
Seats held by women in national parliaments (%)	2015	20.0

Environmental indicators		
Threatened species	2014	132
Forested area (% of land area)	2012	11.0
Proportion of terrestrial and marine areas protected (%)	2014	3.4
Population using improved drinking water sources (%)	2012	85.0
Population using improved sanitation facilities (%)	2012	57.0
CO_2 emission estimates (000 metric tons and metric tons per capita)	2011	57 070/0.4
Energy supply per capita (Gigajoules)	2012	10.0

a Mega city. b Principal rate. c Government officials. d Series linked to former series. e ISIC Rev.4 (BCD). f Twelve months ending 30 June of the year stated. g ISIC Rev.3. h Year ending in June of the year indicated. i 2012. j ITU estimate. k 2011. l Including refugees. m Including 200,000 persons originating from Myanmar in a refugee-like situation. n National estimate.

Barbados

Region	Caribbean	Surface area (sq km)	430	
Population (est., 000)	286	Pop. density (per sq km)	665.3	
Capital city	Bridgetown	Capital city pop. (000)	90	
Currency	Barbados Dollar (BBD)	UN membership date	9 December 1966	

Economic indicators	2005	2010	2013
GDP: Gross domestic product (million current US$)	3 892	4 434	4 228
GDP: Growth rate at constant 2005 prices (annual %)	4.0	0.3	−0.3
GDP per capita (current US$)	14 225.0	15 812.3	14 854.1
GNI: Gross national income per capita (current US$)	13 585.3	15 413.4	14 316.8
Gross fixed capital formation (% of GDP)	18.4	13.4	13.9
Exchange rates (national currency per US$)[a]	2.00	2.00	2.00
Balance of payments, current account (million US$)	−466	−218	...
CPI: Consumer price index (2000=100)	113	149	173
Index of industrial production (2010=100)[b]	114	100	92
Agricultural production index (2004-2006=100)	106	92	97
Food production index (2004-2006=100)	106	92	97
Unemployment (% of labour force)	9.1	10.8	12.2
Employment in industrial sector (% of employed)	17.3[cd]	19.6[ef]	19.4[eg]
Employment in agricultural sector (% of employed)	3.3[cd]	2.8[ef]	2.8[eg]
Labour force participation, adult female pop. (%)	65.0	65.9	65.9
Labour force participation, adult male pop. (%)	76.4	76.7	76.6
Tourist arrivals at national borders (000)	548	532	509
Energy production, primary (Petajoules)	5	4	3[g]
Mobile-cellular subscriptions (per 100 inhabitants)	75.4	124.9	108.1
Individuals using the Internet (%)[h]	52.5	68.1	75.0

Total trade		Major trading partners			2013
	(million US$)	(% of exports)			(% of imports)
Exports	467.4	Areas nes	27.4[i]	United States	33.0
Imports	1 768.7	United States	18.2	Trinidad and Tobago	26.2
Balance	−1 301.3	Trinidad and Tobago	11.5	Suriname	4.9

Social indicators		
Population growth rate (average annual %)	2010-2015	0.5
Urban population growth rate (average annual %)	2010-2015	0.1
Rural population growth rate (average annual %)	2010-2015	0.7
Urban population (%)	2014	31.6
Population aged 0-14 years (%)	2014	18.8
Population aged 60+ years (females and males, % of total)	2014	18.4/14.7
Sex ratio (males per 100 females)	2014	99.6
Life expectancy at birth (females and males, years)	2010-2015	77.7/72.9
Infant mortality rate (per 1 000 live births)	2010-2015	10.1
Fertility rate, total (live births per woman)	2010-2015	1.9
Contraceptive prevalence (ages 15-49, %)[j]	2007-2013	55.0[k]
International migrant stock (000 and % of total population)	mid-2013	32.3/11.3
Refugees and others of concern to UNHCR	mid-2014	1
Education: Government expenditure (% of GDP)	2007-2013	5.6
Education: Primary-secondary gross enrolment ratio (f/m per 100)[l]	2007-2013	107.5/102.7
Education: Female third-level students (% of total)	2007-2013	69.1
Intentional homicide rate (per 100,000 population)	2008-2012	7.4
Seats held by women in national parliaments (%)	2015	16.7

Environmental indicators		
Threatened species	2014	45
Forested area (% of land area)	2012	19.4
Population using improved drinking water sources (%)	2012	100.0
CO$_2$ emission estimates (000 metric tons and metric tons per capita)	2011	1 566/5.6
Energy supply per capita (Gigajoules)	2012	70.0

a Official rate. b ISIC Rev.3 (CDE). c 2004. d ISIC Rev.2. e Average of quarterly estimates. f Break in series. g 2012. h ITU estimate. i See technical notes. j Age group 15 to 44 years. k 1988. l National estimate.

Belarus

Region	Eastern Europe	Surface area (sq km)	207 600
Population (est., 000)	9 308	Pop. density (per sq km)	44.8
Capital city	Minsk	Capital city pop. (000)	1 905 [a]
Currency	Belarussian Ruble (BYR)	UN membership date	24 October 1945

Economic indicators	2005	2010	2013
GDP: Gross domestic product (million current US$)	30 210	55 221	71 710
GDP: Growth rate at constant 2005 prices (annual %)	9.4	7.7	0.9
GDP per capita (current US$)	3 125.8	5 818.2	7 664.0
GNI: Gross national income per capita (current US$)	3 131.6	5 695.7	7 374.5
Gross fixed capital formation (% of GDP)	26.5	39.3	36.9
Exchange rates (national currency per US$) [b]	2 152.00	3 000.00	9 510.00
Balance of payments, current account (million US$)	459	−8 280	−7 656
CPI: Consumer price index (2000=100)	384 [c]	623 [d]	...
Index of industrial production (2010=100) [e]	69	100	110
Agricultural production index (2004-2006=100)	98	117	116
Food production index (2004-2006=100)	98	117	116
Unemployment (% of labour force)	6.3	6.1	5.8
Employment in industrial sector (% of employed)	...	33.7 [fgh]	...
Employment in agricultural sector (% of employed)	...	10.5 [fgh]	...
Labour force participation, adult female pop. (%)	50.8	49.5	50.1
Labour force participation, adult male pop. (%)	62.8	61.7	63.1
Tourist arrivals at national borders (000) [i]	91	120	137
Energy production, primary (Petajoules)	159	173	172 [j]
Mobile-cellular subscriptions (per 100 inhabitants)	42.4	108.9	118.8
Individuals using the Internet (%)	16.2 [kl]	31.8 [l]	54.2 [m]

Total trade		Major trading partners			2013
	(million US$)		(% of exports)		(% of imports)
Exports	37 203.0	Russian Federation	45.0	Russian Federation	52.5
Imports	43 022.7	Ukraine	11.3	Germany	7.1
Balance	−5 819.7	Netherlands	9.0	China	6.6

Social indicators		
Population growth rate (average annual %)	2010-2015	−0.5
Urban population growth rate (average annual %)	2010-2015	0.1
Rural population growth rate (average annual %)	2010-2015	−2.2
Urban population (%)	2014	76.3
Population aged 0-14 years (%)	2014	15.5
Population aged 60+ years (females and males, % of total)	2014	24.0/14.7
Sex ratio (males per 100 females)	2014	86.5
Life expectancy at birth (females and males, years)	2010-2015	75.7/64.1
Infant mortality rate (per 1 000 live births)	2010-2015	5.6
Fertility rate, total (live births per woman)	2010-2015	1.5
Contraceptive prevalence (ages 15-49, %)	2007-2013	63.1
International migrant stock (000 and % of total population)	mid-2013	1 085.4/11.6
Refugees and others of concern to UNHCR	mid-2014	7 442
Education: Government expenditure (% of GDP)	2007-2013	5.1
Education: Primary-secondary gross enrolment ratio (f/m per 100)	2007-2013	101.7/103.2
Education: Female third-level students (% of total)	2007-2013	56.1
Intentional homicide rate (per 100,000 population)	2008-2012	5.1
Seats held by women in national parliaments (%)	2015	27.3

Environmental indicators		
Threatened species	2014	22
Forested area (% of land area)	2012	42.9
Proportion of terrestrial and marine areas protected (%)	2014	8.6
Population using improved drinking water sources (%)	2012	100.0
Population using improved sanitation facilities (%)	2012	94.0
CO_2 emission estimates (000 metric tons and metric tons per capita)	2011	63 303/6.7
Energy supply per capita (Gigajoules)	2012	136.0

a Including communities under the authority of the Town Council. b Official rate. c Annual average is the weighted mean of monthly data. d Series linked to former series. e ISIC Rev.3 (CDE). f 2009. g Population census. h ISIC Rev.3. i Organized tourism. j 2012. k 2006. l Population aged 16 and over. m Population aged 6 and over.

Belgium

Region	Western Europe	Surface area (sq km)	30 528
Population (est., 000)	11 144	Pop. density (per sq km)	365.1
Capital city	Brussels	Capital city pop. (000)	2 029 [a]
Currency	Euro (EUR)	UN membership date	27 December 1945

Economic indicators	2005	2010	2013
GDP: Gross domestic product (million current US$)	386 945	484 404	524 806
GDP: Growth rate at constant 2005 prices (annual %)	1.9	2.5	0.3
GDP per capita (current US$)	36 823.6	44 273.1	47 260.7
GNI: Gross national income per capita (current US$)	37 156.8	45 097.7	46 784.7
Gross fixed capital formation (% of GDP)	22.2	22.3	22.3
Exchange rates (national currency per US$) [b]	0.85	0.75	0.73
Balance of payments, current account (million US$)	7 703	8 468	−18 481
CPI: Consumer price index (2000=100)	111	123	132
Index of industrial production (2010=100) [c]	85	100	102
Agricultural production index (2004-2006=100)	100	100	101
Food production index (2004-2006=100)	100	100	101
Unemployment (% of labour force)	8.4	8.3	8.4
Employment in industrial sector (% of employed)	24.7 [d]	23.4	21.8 [e]
Employment in agricultural sector (% of employed)	2.0 [d]	1.4	1.2 [e]
Labour force participation, adult female pop. (%)	45.6	47.6	47.5
Labour force participation, adult male pop. (%)	61.3	60.6	59.3
Tourist arrivals at national borders (000) [f]	6 747	7 186	7 684
Energy production, primary (Petajoules)	577	635	660 [e]
Mobile-cellular subscriptions (per 100 inhabitants)	91.4	111.1 [gh]	110.9
Individuals using the Internet (%)	55.8 [i]	75.0	82.2

Total trade		Major trading partners			2013
	(million US$)	(% of exports)			(% of imports)
Exports	511 492.5	Germany	16.9	Netherlands	20.4
Imports	488 442.1	France	15.6	Germany	13.6
Balance	23 050.4	Netherlands	12.2	France	10.5

Social indicators		
Population growth rate (average annual %)	2010-2015	0.4
Urban population growth rate (average annual %)	2010-2015	0.5
Rural population growth rate (average annual %)	2010-2015	−1.5
Urban population (%)	2014	97.8
Population aged 0-14 years (%)	2014	17.1
Population aged 60+ years (females and males, % of total)	2014	26.4/22.1
Sex ratio (males per 100 females)	2014	96.4
Life expectancy at birth (females and males, years)	2010-2015	83.0/77.9
Infant mortality rate (per 1 000 live births)	2010-2015	3.2
Fertility rate, total (live births per woman)	2010-2015	1.9
Contraceptive prevalence (ages 15-49, %) [j]	2007-2013	70.4
International migrant stock (000 and % of total population) [k]	mid-2013	1 159.8/10.4
Refugees and others of concern to UNHCR	mid-2014	42 005
Education: Government expenditure (% of GDP)	2007-2013	6.6
Education: Primary-secondary gross enrolment ratio (f/m per 100)	2007-2013	104.5/102.6
Education: Female third-level students (% of total)	2007-2013	55.5
Intentional homicide rate (per 100,000 population)	2008-2012	1.6
Seats held by women in national parliaments (%)	2015	39.3

Environmental indicators		
Threatened species	2014	31
Forested area (% of land area)	2012	22.5
Proportion of terrestrial and marine areas protected (%)	2014	24.3
Population using improved drinking water sources (%)	2012	100.0
Population using improved sanitation facilities (%)	2012	100.0
CO_2 emission estimates (000 metric tons and metric tons per capita)	2011	97 766/8.9
Energy supply per capita (Gigajoules)	2012	210.0

a Refers to the population of Brussels-Capital Region and 'communes' of the agglomeration and suburbs. b Market rate. c ISIC Rev.4 (BCDE). d ISIC Rev.3. e 2012. f Arrivals of non-resident tourists in all types of accommodation establishments. g Number of active clients. h Including mobile virtual network operator. i ITU estimate. j Age group 18 to 49 years. k Refers to foreign citizens.

Belize

Region	Central America	Surface area (sq km)	22 966
Population (est., 000)	340	Pop. density (per sq km)	14.8
Capital city	Belmopan	Capital city pop. (000)	17
Currency	Belize Dollar (BZD)	UN membership date	25 September 1981

Economic indicators	2005	2010	2013
GDP: Gross domestic product (million current US$)	1 114	1 397	1 624
GDP: Growth rate at constant 2005 prices (annual %)	2.6	3.3	1.5
GDP per capita (current US$)	4 097.5	4 527.3	4 893.9
GNI: Gross national income per capita (current US$)	3 648.4	4 300.7	4 730.7
Gross fixed capital formation (% of GDP)	18.5	15.3	17.9
Exchange rates (national currency per US$) [a]	2.00	2.00	2.00
Balance of payments, current account (million US$)	−151	−46	−72
CPI: Consumer price index (2000=100)	113	128	133
Agricultural production index (2004-2006=100)	97	93	105
Food production index (2004-2006=100)	97	93	105
Unemployment (% of labour force)	11.0	10.7	14.6
Employment in industrial sector (% of employed)	17.9[bcd]	...	...
Employment in agricultural sector (% of employed)	19.5[bcd]	...	...
Labour force participation, adult female pop. (%)	44.8	48.8	49.2
Labour force participation, adult male pop. (%)	80.8	82.1	82.3
Tourist arrivals at national borders (000)	237	242	294
Energy production, primary (Petajoules)	4	14	11[ef]
Mobile-cellular subscriptions (per 100 inhabitants)	35.3[g]	62.9[h]	52.9[g]
Individuals using the Internet (%)	9.2	14.0[g]	31.7[g]

Total trade		Major trading partners			2013
	(million US$)		(% of exports)		(% of imports)
Exports	411.4	United States	39.1	United States	32.1
Imports	931.2	United Kingdom	21.0	Curaçao	12.5
Balance	−519.8	Netherlands	5.6	Mexico	11.4

Social indicators		
Population growth rate (average annual %)	2010-2015	2.4
Urban population growth rate (average annual %)	2010-2015	1.9
Rural population growth rate (average annual %)	2010-2015	2.7
Urban population (%)	2014	44.1
Population aged 0-14 years (%)	2014	33.4
Population aged 60+ years (females and males, % of total)	2014	6.3/5.5
Sex ratio (males per 100 females)	2014	99.8
Life expectancy at birth (females and males, years)	2010-2015	77.0/70.8
Infant mortality rate (per 1 000 live births)	2010-2015	12.9
Fertility rate, total (live births per woman)	2010-2015	2.7
Contraceptive prevalence (ages 15-49, %)	2007-2013	55.2
International migrant stock (000 and % of total population) [i]	mid-2013	50.9/15.3
Refugees and others of concern to UNHCR	mid-2014	72
Education: Government expenditure (% of GDP)	2007-2013	6.6
Education: Primary-secondary gross enrolment ratio (f/m per 100)	2007-2013	102.3/102.2
Education: Female third-level students (% of total)	2007-2013	62.2
Intentional homicide rate (per 100,000 population)	2008-2012	44.7
Seats held by women in national parliaments (%)	2015	3.1

Environmental indicators		
Threatened species	2014	105
Forested area (% of land area)	2012	60.2
Proportion of terrestrial and marine areas protected (%)	2014	18.6
Population using improved drinking water sources (%)	2012	99.0
Population using improved sanitation facilities (%)	2012	91.0
CO_2 emission estimates (000 metric tons and metric tons per capita)	2011	550/1.8
Energy supply per capita (Gigajoules)	2012	43.0[f]

a Official rate. b ISIC Rev.3. c Population aged 14 and over. d April. e 2012. f UNSD estimate. g ITU estimate. h Including Mobile GSM, AMPS Post and Pre Mobile Base. i Including refugees.

Benin

Region	Western Africa	Surface area (sq km)	114 763	
Population (est., 000)	10 600	Pop. density (per sq km)	94.1	
Capital city	Porto-Novo[a]	Capital city pop. (000)	268	
Currency	CFA Franc (XOF)	UN membership date	20 September 1960	

Economic indicators	2005	2010	2013
GDP: Gross domestic product (million current US$)	4 358	6 558	8 307
GDP: Growth rate at constant 2005 prices (annual %)	2.9	2.6	5.6
GDP per capita (current US$)	532.6	689.6	804.7
GNI: Gross national income per capita (current US$)	530.4	684.0	800.9
Gross fixed capital formation (% of GDP)	19.4	20.5	26.3
Exchange rates (national currency per US$)[b]	556.04	490.91	475.64
Balance of payments, current account (million US$)	−226	−530	−577[c]
CPI: Consumer price index (2000=100)[d]	115	134[e]	148
Index of industrial production (2010=100)[f]	77	100	114
Agricultural production index (2004-2006=100)	102	115	145
Food production index (2004-2006=100)	102	122	150
Unemployment (% of labour force)	1.3	1.0	1.0
Labour force participation, adult female pop. (%)	66.2	67.3	67.6
Labour force participation, adult male pop. (%)	78.7	78.4	78.3
Tourist arrivals at national borders (000)	176	199	231
Energy production, primary (Petajoules)	70	86	91[c]
Mobile-cellular subscriptions (per 100 inhabitants)	7.3	74.4	93.3
Individuals using the Internet (%)	1.3	3.1	4.9[g]

Total trade		Major trading partners			2013
	(million US$)	(% of exports)			(% of imports)
Exports	639.3	China	18.8	United States	27.9
Imports	3 780.7	India	11.1	France	8.9
Balance	−3 141.4	Nigeria	11.0	India	8.8

Social indicators		
Population growth rate (average annual %)	2010-2015	2.7
Urban population growth rate (average annual %)	2010-2015	3.7
Rural population growth rate (average annual %)	2010-2015	2.0
Urban population (%)	2014	43.5
Population aged 0-14 years (%)	2014	42.5
Population aged 60+ years (females and males, % of total)	2014	5.2/4.0
Sex ratio (males per 100 females)	2014	99.4
Life expectancy at birth (females and males, years)	2010-2015	60.6/57.8
Infant mortality rate (per 1 000 live births)	2010-2015	68.7
Fertility rate, total (live births per woman)	2010-2015	4.9
Contraceptive prevalence (ages 15-49, %)	2007-2013	12.9
International migrant stock (000 and % of total population)[hi]	mid-2013	234.2/2.3
Refugees and others of concern to UNHCR	mid-2014	298
Education: Government expenditure (% of GDP)	2007-2013	5.4
Education: Primary-secondary gross enrolment ratio (f/m per 100)	2007-2013	81.0/98.6
Education: Female third-level students (% of total)	2007-2013	21.2
Intentional homicide rate (per 100,000 population)	2008-2012	8.4
Seats held by women in national parliaments (%)	2015	8.4

Environmental indicators		
Threatened species	2014	74
Forested area (% of land area)	2012	39.6
Proportion of terrestrial and marine areas protected (%)	2014	22.3
Population using improved drinking water sources (%)	2012	76.0
Population using improved sanitation facilities (%)	2012	14.0
CO_2 emission estimates (000 metric tons and metric tons per capita)	2011	4 987/0.5
Energy supply per capita (Gigajoules)	2012	16.0

a Porto-Novo is the constitutional capital and Cotonou is the economic capital. b Official rate. c 2012.
d Cotonou. e Series linked to former series. f ISIC Rev.3 (CDE). g ITU estimate. h Refers to foreign-born
and foreign citizens. i Including refugees.

Bermuda

Region	Northern America	Surface area (sq km)	53	
Population (est., 000)	65	Pop. density (per sq km)	1 235.1	
Capital city	Hamilton	Capital city pop. (000)	10	
Currency	Bermuda Dollar (BMD)			

Economic indicators	2005	2010	2013
GDP: Gross domestic product (million current US$)	4 868	5 744	5 574
GDP: Growth rate at constant 2005 prices (annual %)	1.7	−2.1	−2.5
GDP per capita (current US$)	75 902.1	88 442.3	85 301.9
GNI: Gross national income per capita (current US$)	93 848.1	110 297.0	108 456.6
Gross fixed capital formation (% of GDP)	19.6	13.3	11.7
Balance of payments, current account (million US$)	1 252[a]	696	841
CPI: Consumer price index (2000=100)	116	136	145
Agricultural production index (2004-2006=100)	98	116	120
Food production index (2004-2006=100)	98	116	120
Employment in industrial sector (% of employed)	12.1[bcd]	...	...
Employment in agricultural sector (% of employed)	1.7[bc]	...	...
Tourist arrivals at national borders (000)[e]	270	232	236
Energy production, primary (Petajoules)	...	1[f]	1[fg]
Mobile-cellular subscriptions (per 100 inhabitants)	82.2	135.8[h]	144.3[h]
Individuals using the Internet (%)	65.5	84.2[h]	95.3[h]

Total trade		Major trading partners			2013
	(million US$)		(% of exports)		(% of imports)
Exports	21.7	United Kingdom	68.2	United States	68.8
Imports	994.6	United States	29.0	Canada	12.2
Balance	−972.9	Areas nes	0.9[i]	Bahamas	6.2

Social indicators		
Population growth rate (average annual %)	2010-2015	0.2
Urban population growth rate (average annual %)	2010-2015	0.2
Urban population (%)	2014	100.0
Population aged 0-14 years (%)[ikl]	2014	17.0[g]
Population aged 60+ years (females and males, % of total)[ikl]	2014	21.4/17.5[g]
Sex ratio (males per 100 females)[ikl]	2014	90.6[g]
Life expectancy at birth (females and males, years)[j]	2010-2015	82.4/77.2[g]
Fertility rate, total (live births per woman)[j]	2010-2015	1.8[g]
International migrant stock (000 and % of total population)	mid-2013	19.1/29.2
Education: Government expenditure (% of GDP)	2007-2013	2.6
Education: Primary-secondary gross enrolment ratio (f/m per 100)	2007-2013	83.3/78.6
Education: Female third-level students (% of total)	2007-2013	64.8
Intentional homicide rate (per 100,000 population)	2008-2012	7.7

Environmental indicators		
Threatened species	2014	60
Forested area (% of land area)	2012	20.0
Proportion of terrestrial and marine areas protected (%)	2014	5.1
CO$_2$ emission estimates (000 metric tons and metric tons per capita)	2011	392/6.1
Energy supply per capita (Gigajoules)	2012	158.0[f]

a 2006. b 2004. c ISIC Rev.2. d Excluding mining and quarrying. e Arrivals by air. f UNSD estimate. g 2012. h ITU estimate. i See technical notes. j Data compiled by the United Nations Demographic Yearbook system. k Data refer to the latest available census. l De jure estimate.

Bhutan

Region	Southern Asia	Surface area (sq km)		38 394
Population (est., 000)	766	Pop. density (per sq km)		16.3
Capital city	Thimphu	Capital city pop. (000)		152
Currency	Ngultrum (BTN)	UN membership date		21 September 1971

Economic indicators	2005	2010	2013
GDP: Gross domestic product (million current US$)	819	1 585	1 781
GDP: Growth rate at constant 2005 prices (annual %)	7.1	11.7	2.1
GDP per capita (current US$)	1 259.0	2 211.4	2 362.6
GNI: Gross national income per capita (current US$)	1 241.2	2 088.7	2 208.8
Gross fixed capital formation (% of GDP)	53.4	61.7	47.3
Exchange rates (national currency per US$)[a]	45.06	44.81	61.90
Balance of payments, current account (million US$)	−38[b]	−323	−509
CPI: Consumer price index (2000=100)	117	156	205[c]
Agricultural production index (2004-2006=100)	106	95	97
Food production index (2004-2006=100)	106	94	97
Unemployment (% of labour force)	3.1	3.3	2.1
Employment in industrial sector (% of employed)[d]	17.2[ef]	6.7[gh]	8.6[gi]
Employment in agricultural sector (% of employed)[d]	43.6[ef]	59.5[gh]	62.2[gi]
Labour force participation, adult female pop. (%)	63.5	65.9	66.7
Labour force participation, adult male pop. (%)	77.6	76.0	77.2
Tourist arrivals at national borders (000)	14	41[j]	116[j]
Energy production, primary (Petajoules)	53	73	72[i]
Mobile-cellular subscriptions (per 100 inhabitants)	5.5	55.0	72.2
Individuals using the Internet (%)	3.9	13.6[k]	29.9[l]

Total trade		Major trading partners			2013
	(million US$)[i]	(% of exports)[i]		(% of imports)[i]	
Exports	531.2	India	93.7	India	78.8
Imports	991.7	Bangladesh	4.1	Republic of Korea	3.1
Balance	−460.5	Italy	0.4	China	2.5

Social indicators		
Population growth rate (average annual %)	2010-2015	1.6
Urban population growth rate (average annual %)	2010-2015	3.7
Rural population growth rate (average annual %)	2010-2015	0.4
Urban population (%)	2014	37.9
Population aged 0-14 years (%)	2014	27.6
Population aged 60+ years (females and males, % of total)	2014	6.7/7.4
Sex ratio (males per 100 females)	2014	116.1
Life expectancy at birth (females and males, years)	2010-2015	68.4/67.7
Infant mortality rate (per 1 000 live births)	2010-2015	30.7
Fertility rate, total (live births per woman)	2010-2015	2.3
Contraceptive prevalence (ages 15-49, %)	2007-2013	65.6
International migrant stock (000 and % of total population)	mid-2013	50.9/6.8
Education: Government expenditure (% of GDP)	2007-2013	5.5
Education: Primary-secondary gross enrolment ratio (f/m per 100)	2007-2013	94.5/91.3
Education: Female third-level students (% of total)	2007-2013	40.0
Intentional homicide rate (per 100,000 population)	2008-2012	1.7
Seats held by women in national parliaments (%)	2015	8.5

Environmental indicators		
Threatened species	2014	65
Forested area (% of land area)	2012	85.8
Proportion of terrestrial and marine areas protected (%)	2014	47.3
Population using improved drinking water sources (%)	2012	98.0
Population using improved sanitation facilities (%)	2012	47.0
CO_2 emission estimates (000 metric tons and metric tons per capita)	2011	561/0.8
Energy supply per capita (Gigajoules)	2012	83.0

a Official rate. **b** 2006. **c** Series linked to former series. **d** ISIC Rev.3. **e** Population census. **f** May. **g** March to April. **h** Break in series. **i** 2012. **j** Including regional high end tourists. **k** Country estimate. **l** ITU estimate.

Bolivia (Plurinational State of)

Region	South America	Surface area (sq km)	1 098 581 [a]
Population (est., 000)	10 848	Pop. density (per sq km)	9.9
Capital city	Sucre [b]	Capital city pop. (000)	358
Currency	Boliviano (BOB)	UN membership date	14 November 1945

Economic indicators	2005	2010	2013
GDP: Gross domestic product (million current US$)	9 549	19 650	30 601
GDP: Growth rate at constant 2005 prices (annual %)	4.4	4.1	6.8
GDP per capita (current US$)	1 020.8	1 934.7	2 867.6
GNI: Gross national income per capita (current US$)	989.0	1 849.4	2 687.6
Gross fixed capital formation (% of GDP)	13.0	16.6	19.1
Exchange rates (national currency per US$) [c]	8.04	6.99	6.91
Balance of payments, current account (million US$)	622	874	1 173
CPI: Consumer price index (2000=100) [d]	117	160	194
Agricultural production index (2004-2006=100)	100	120	134
Food production index (2004-2006=100)	100	120	134
Unemployment (% of labour force)	5.4	3.3	2.6
Employment in industrial sector (% of employed)	19.4[ef]	20.0[fghi]	...
Employment in agricultural sector (% of employed)	38.6[ef]	32.1[fghi]	...
Labour force participation, adult female pop. (%)	61.1	63.7	64.2
Labour force participation, adult male pop. (%)	81.5	80.9	80.9
Tourist arrivals at national borders (000)	524	679	798
Energy production, primary (Petajoules)	595	659	802[j]
Mobile-cellular subscriptions (per 100 inhabitants)	25.9	70.7	97.7
Individuals using the Internet (%)	5.2	22.4[k]	39.5[k]

Total trade		Major trading partners			2013
	(million US$)		(% of exports)		(% of imports)
Exports	12 207.5	Brazil	33.0	Brazil	15.7
Imports	10 388.3	Argentina	20.6	United States	13.5
Balance	1 819.2	United States	10.0	China	12.1

Social indicators		
Population growth rate (average annual %)	2010-2015	1.6
Urban population growth rate (average annual %)	2010-2015	2.3
Rural population growth rate (average annual %)	2010-2015	0.4
Urban population (%)	2014	68.1
Population aged 0-14 years (%)	2014	34.5
Population aged 60+ years (females and males, % of total)	2014	8.2/6.8
Sex ratio (males per 100 females)	2014	99.8
Life expectancy at birth (females and males, years)	2010-2015	69.3/64.9
Infant mortality rate (per 1 000 live births)	2010-2015	39.1
Fertility rate, total (live births per woman)	2010-2015	3.3
Contraceptive prevalence (ages 15-49, %)	2007-2013	60.5
International migrant stock (000 and % of total population)	mid-2013	154.3/1.5
Refugees and others of concern to UNHCR	mid-2014	756
Education: Government expenditure (% of GDP)	2007-2013	6.4
Education: Primary-secondary gross enrolment ratio (f/m per 100)	2007-2013	85.0/86.3
Education: Female third-level students (% of total) [l]	2007-2013	45.0
Intentional homicide rate (per 100,000 population)	2008-2012	12.1
Seats held by women in national parliaments (%)	2015	53.1

Environmental indicators		
Threatened species	2014	216
Forested area (% of land area)	2012	52.2
Proportion of terrestrial and marine areas protected (%)	2014	24.8
Population using improved drinking water sources (%)	2012	88.0
Population using improved sanitation facilities (%)	2012	46.0
CO$_2$ emission estimates (000 metric tons and metric tons per capita)	2011	16 120/1.6
Energy supply per capita (Gigajoules)	2012	30.0

a Interior waters correspond to natural or artificial bodies of water or snow. b La Paz is the seat of government and Sucre is the constitutional capital. c Market rate. d Urban areas. e ISIC Rev.3. f Population aged 10 and over. g 2009. h ISIC Rev.2. i Break in series. j 2012. k ITU estimate. l National estimate.

Bosnia and Herzegovina

Region	Southern Europe	Surface area (sq km)	51 209	
Population (est., 000)	3 825	Pop. density (per sq km)	74.7	
Capital city	Sarajevo	Capital city pop. (000)	322	
Currency	Convertible Mark (BAM)	UN membership date	22 May 1992	

Economic indicators	2005	2010	2013
GDP: Gross domestic product (million current US$)	10 904	16 847	17 852
GDP: Growth rate at constant 2005 prices (annual %)	3.9	0.8	2.5
GDP per capita (current US$)	2 810.3	4 380.5	4 661.9
GNI: Gross national income per capita (current US$)	2 930.9	4 453.1	4 705.2
Gross fixed capital formation (% of GDP)	27.9	17.3	17.9
Exchange rates (national currency per US$)[a]	1.66	1.46	1.42
Balance of payments, current account (million US$)	−1 844	−1 031	−1 062
CPI: Consumer price index (2000=100)[b]	100	118	124
Index of industrial production (2010=100)[c]	...	100	103
Agricultural production index (2004-2006=100)	98	107	113
Food production index (2004-2006=100)	98	108	114
Unemployment (% of labour force)	25.6	27.2	28.4
Employment in industrial sector (% of employed)[de]	30.7[f]	31.0	30.3[g]
Employment in agricultural sector (% of employed)[de]	20.6[f]	19.7	20.5[g]
Labour force participation, adult female pop. (%)	31.7	34.0	34.1
Labour force participation, adult male pop. (%)	56.5	57.2	57.3
Tourist arrivals at national borders (000)[h]	217	365	529
Energy production, primary (Petajoules)	152	182	188[g]
Mobile-cellular subscriptions (per 100 inhabitants)	41.1	80.9	91.2
Individuals using the Internet (%)	21.3	52.0	67.9[i]

Total trade		Major trading partners			2013
	(million US$)		(% of exports)		(% of imports)
Exports	5 687.5	Germany	15.6	Croatia	12.9
Imports	10 295.2	Croatia	14.3	Germany	11.4
Balance	−4 607.7	Italy	12.0	Russian Federation	9.9

Social indicators		
Population growth rate (average annual %)	2010-2015	−0.1
Urban population growth rate (average annual %)	2010-2015	0.1
Rural population growth rate (average annual %)	2010-2015	−0.3
Urban population (%)	2014	39.6
Population aged 0-14 years (%)	2014	15.2
Population aged 60+ years (females and males, % of total)	2014	23.6/18.9
Sex ratio (males per 100 females)	2014	95.3
Life expectancy at birth (females and males, years)	2010-2015	78.8/73.7
Infant mortality rate (per 1 000 live births)	2010-2015	7.6
Fertility rate, total (live births per woman)	2010-2015	1.3
Contraceptive prevalence (ages 15-49, %)	2007-2013	45.8
International migrant stock (000 and % of total population)[jk]	mid-2013	23.2/0.6
Refugees and others of concern to UNHCR	mid-2014	144 793
Education: Female third-level students (% of total)	2007-2013	55.3
Intentional homicide rate (per 100,000 population)	2008-2012	1.3
Seats held by women in national parliaments (%)	2015	21.4

Environmental indicators		
Threatened species	2014	83
Forested area (% of land area)	2012	42.8
Proportion of terrestrial and marine areas protected (%)	2014	1.3
Population using improved drinking water sources (%)	2012	100.0
Population using improved sanitation facilities (%)	2012	95.0
CO_2 emission estimates (000 metric tons and metric tons per capita)	2011	23 747/6.2
Energy supply per capita (Gigajoules)	2012	73.0

a Market rate. **b** Index base 2005=100. **c** ISIC Rev.4 (BCD). **d** April. **e** ISIC Rev.3. **f** 2006. **g** 2012. **h** Arrivals of non-resident tourists in all types of accommodation establishments. **i** ITU estimate. **j** Estimate. **k** Including refugees.

Botswana

Region	Southern Africa	
Population (est., 000)	2 039	
Capital city	Gaborone	
Currency	Pula (BWP)	

Surface area (sq km)	582 000
Pop. density (per sq km)	3.5
Capital city pop. (000)	247
UN membership date	17 October 1966

Economic indicators	2005	2010	2013
GDP: Gross domestic product (million current US$)	9 931	13 747	14 778
GDP: Growth rate at constant 2005 prices (annual %)	4.6	8.6	6.5
GDP per capita (current US$)	5 294.4	6 980.4	7 311.9
GNI: Gross national income per capita (current US$)	4 848.9	6 699.0	7 228.9
Gross fixed capital formation (% of GDP)	25.3	31.3	33.9
Exchange rates (national currency per US$)[a]	5.51	6.44	8.72
Balance of payments, current account (million US$)	1 634	−825	1 769
CPI: Consumer price index (2000=100)	146	227	281
Agricultural production index (2004-2006=100)	101	124	130
Food production index (2004-2006=100)	101	124	130
Unemployment (% of labour force)	22.0	17.9	18.4
Employment in industrial sector (% of employed)	15.2[bcde]	...	...
Employment in agricultural sector (% of employed)	29.9[bcde]	...	...
Labour force participation, adult female pop. (%)	71.1	71.7	71.9
Labour force participation, adult male pop. (%)	80.9	81.3	81.6
Tourist arrivals at national borders (000)	1 474	2 145	...
Energy production, primary (Petajoules)	29	30	41[f]
Mobile-cellular subscriptions (per 100 inhabitants)	30.1	120.0	160.6[g]
Individuals using the Internet (%)	3.3[h]	6.0	15.0[h]

Total trade		Major trading partners			2013
	(million US$)	(% of exports)			(% of imports)
Exports	7 573.3	United Kingdom	49.0	South Africa	65.8
Imports	7 433.5	Belgium	12.9	United Kingdom	7.3
Balance	139.8	South Africa	10.6	Namibia	6.9

Social indicators

Population growth rate (average annual %)	2010-2015	0.9
Urban population growth rate (average annual %)	2010-2015	1.3
Rural population growth rate (average annual %)	2010-2015	0.3
Urban population (%)	2014	57.2
Population aged 0-14 years (%)	2014	33.3
Population aged 60+ years (females and males, % of total)	2014	7.1/5.0
Sex ratio (males per 100 females)	2014	101.5
Life expectancy at birth (females and males, years)	2010-2015	46.5/48.0
Infant mortality rate (per 1 000 live births)	2010-2015	31.8
Fertility rate, total (live births per woman)	2010-2015	2.6
Contraceptive prevalence (ages 15-49, %)[i]	2007-2013	52.8
International migrant stock (000 and % of total population)[j]	mid-2013	146.5/7.3
Refugees and others of concern to UNHCR	mid-2014	3 029
Education: Government expenditure (% of GDP)	2007-2013	9.5
Education: Primary-secondary gross enrolment ratio (f/m per 100)[k]	2007-2013	95.3/94.9
Education: Female third-level students (% of total)	2007-2013	56.7
Intentional homicide rate (per 100,000 population)	2008-2012	18.4
Seats held by women in national parliaments (%)	2015	9.5

Environmental indicators

Threatened species	2014	24
Forested area (% of land area)	2012	19.6
Proportion of terrestrial and marine areas protected (%)	2014	29.2
Population using improved drinking water sources (%)	2012	97.0
Population using improved sanitation facilities (%)	2012	64.0
CO_2 emission estimates (000 metric tons and metric tons per capita)	2011	4 855/2.5
Energy supply per capita (Gigajoules)	2012	38.0

a Official rate. **b** 2006. **c** ISIC Rev.3. **d** Population aged 12 and over. **e** Excluding conscripts. **f** 2012. **g** December. **h** ITU estimate. **i** Age group 12 to 49 years. **j** Refers to foreign citizens. **k** UNESCO estimate.

Brazil

Region	South America	Surface area (sq km)	8 514 877
Population (est., 000)	202 034	Pop. density (per sq km)	23.7
Capital city	Brasília	Capital city pop. (000)	4 074 [a]
Currency	Real (BRL)	UN membership date	24 October 1945

Economic indicators	2005	2010	2013
GDP: Gross domestic product (million current US$)	882 044	2 143 035	2 243 854
GDP: Growth rate at constant 2005 prices (annual %)	3.2	7.5	2.5
GDP per capita (current US$)	4 738.5	10 978.1	11 199.0
GNI: Gross national income per capita (current US$)	4 602.6	10 780.0	11 002.9
Gross fixed capital formation (% of GDP)	15.9	19.5	18.4
Exchange rates (national currency per US$) [b]	2.34	1.69	2.35
Balance of payments, current account (million US$)	13 985	−47 273	−81 063
CPI: Consumer price index (2000=100)	151	190	227
Index of industrial production (2010=100) [c]	87	100	100
Agricultural production index (2004-2006=100)	99	122	135
Food production index (2004-2006=100)	99	123	136
Unemployment (% of labour force)	9.3	7.9	5.9
Employment in industrial sector (% of employed)	21.4[def]	22.1[deghi]	21.9[ijk]
Employment in agricultural sector (% of employed)	20.5[def]	17.0[deghi]	15.3[ijk]
Labour force participation, adult female pop. (%)	58.9	59.4	59.4
Labour force participation, adult male pop. (%)	82.1	81.1	80.8
Tourist arrivals at national borders (000)	5 358	5 161	5 813
Energy production, primary (Petajoules)	8 359	10 074	10 331[l]
Mobile-cellular subscriptions (per 100 inhabitants)	46.3	100.9[m]	135.3
Individuals using the Internet (%)	21.0[n]	40.7[n]	51.6[o]

Total trade		Major trading partners			2013
	(million US$)	(% of exports)			(% of imports)
Exports	242 178.1	China	19.0	China	15.6
Imports	239 620.9	United States	10.3	United States	15.1
Balance	2 557.2	Argentina	8.1	Argentina	6.9

Social indicators		
Population growth rate (average annual %)	2010-2015	0.9
Urban population growth rate (average annual %)	2010-2015	1.2
Rural population growth rate (average annual %)	2010-2015	−1.0
Urban population (%)	2014	85.4
Population aged 0-14 years (%)	2014	23.6
Population aged 60+ years (females and males, % of total)	2014	12.6/10.4
Sex ratio (males per 100 females)	2014	96.7
Life expectancy at birth (females and males, years)	2010-2015	77.5/70.2
Infant mortality rate (per 1 000 live births)	2010-2015	19.5
Fertility rate, total (live births per woman)	2010-2015	1.8
Contraceptive prevalence (ages 15-49, %)	2007-2013	80.3[p]
International migrant stock (000 and % of total population)	mid-2013	599.7/0.3
Refugees and others of concern to UNHCR	mid-2014	46 237
Education: Government expenditure (% of GDP)	2007-2013	5.8
Education: Primary-secondary gross enrolment ratio (f/m per 100)	2007-2013	118.5/115.1[q]
Education: Female third-level students (% of total)	2007-2013	57.1
Intentional homicide rate (per 100,000 population)	2008-2012	25.2
Seats held by women in national parliaments (%)	2015	9.0

Environmental indicators		
Threatened species	2014	965
Forested area (% of land area)	2012	61.6
Proportion of terrestrial and marine areas protected (%)	2014	20.4
Population using improved drinking water sources (%)	2012	98.0
Population using improved sanitation facilities (%)	2012	81.0
CO_2 emission estimates (000 metric tons and metric tons per capita)	2011	439 413/2.2
Energy supply per capita (Gigajoules)	2012	59.0

a Refers to the 'Região Integrada de Desenvolvimento do Distrito Federal e Entorno'. **b** Market rate. **c** ISIC Rev.4 (BCDE). **d** ISIC Rev.3. **e** Population aged 10 and over. **f** September. **g** 2009. **h** August. **i** Break in series. **j** 2011. **k** ISIC Rev.2. **l** 2012. **m** Methodology revised. **n** Population aged 10 and over using the Internet in the last 3 months. **o** ITU estimate. **p** 2006. **q** 2005.

British Virgin Islands

Region	Caribbean	Surface area (sq km)	151
Population (est., 000)	29	Pop. density (per sq km)	189.2
Capital city	Road Town	Capital city pop. (000)	13
Currency	U.S. Dollar (USD)		

Economic indicators	2005	2010	2013
GDP: Gross domestic product (million current US$)	870	894	916
GDP: Growth rate at constant 2005 prices (annual %)	14.3	1.3	−0.3
GDP per capita (current US$)	37 550.2	32 839.9	32 306.6
GNI: Gross national income per capita (current US$)	34 701.5	30 011.4	29 563.5
Gross fixed capital formation (% of GDP)	24.0	23.9	23.9
CPI: Consumer price index (2000=100)	110	...	...
Agricultural production index (2004-2006=100)	100	102	104
Food production index (2004-2006=100)	100	102	104
Tourist arrivals at national borders (000)	337	330	366
Energy production, primary (Petajoules)	0	0	0[a]
Mobile-cellular subscriptions (per 100 inhabitants)	83.4[b]	174.6	188.4
Individuals using the Internet (%)	...	37.0	32.5[c]

Social indicators		
Population growth rate (average annual %)	2010-2015	1.1
Urban population growth rate (average annual %)	2010-2015	1.8
Rural population growth rate (average annual %)	2010-2015	0.6
Urban population (%)	2014	45.9
Life expectancy at birth (females and males, years)[d]	2010-2015	78.5/69.9[e]
International migrant stock (000 and % of total population)	mid-2013	9.1/32.3
Refugees and others of concern to UNHCR	mid-2014	3
Education: Government expenditure (% of GDP)	2007-2013	4.4
Education: Primary-secondary gross enrolment ratio (f/m per 100)[f]	2007-2013	103.7/105.2
Education: Female third-level students (% of total)	2007-2013	64.7
Intentional homicide rate (per 100,000 population)	2008-2012	8.4[g]

Environmental indicators		
Threatened species	2014	53
Forested area (% of land area)	2012	24.3
Proportion of terrestrial and marine areas protected (%)	2014	0.1
CO$_2$ emission estimates (000 metric tons and metric tons per capita)	2011	176/6.3
Energy supply per capita (Gigajoules)	2012	88.0[h]

a 2012. b 2007. c ITU estimate. d Data compiled by the United Nations Demographic Yearbook system.
e 2004. f UNESCO estimate. g 2006. h UNSD estimate.

Brunei Darussalam

Region	South-Eastern Asia	Surface area (sq km)	5 765	
Population (est., 000)	423	Pop. density (per sq km)	73.4	
Capital city	Bandar Seri Begawan	Capital city pop. (000)	14	
Currency	Brunei Dollar (BND)	UN membership date	21 September 1984	

Economic indicators	2005	2010	2013
GDP: Gross domestic product (million current US$)	9 531	12 371	16 111
GDP: Growth rate at constant 2005 prices (annual %)	0.4	2.6	−1.8
GDP per capita (current US$)	25 913.7	30 882.3	38 563.3
GNI: Gross national income per capita (current US$)	25 913.7	31 032.3	38 750.5
Gross fixed capital formation (% of GDP)	11.4	15.9	15.3
Exchange rates (national currency per US$)[a]	1.66	1.29	1.27
Balance of payments, current account (million US$)	4 033	3 977[b]	5 684[c]
CPI: Consumer price index (2000=100)	101	105[d]	106[d]
Index of industrial production (2010=100)[e]	114	100	94
Agricultural production index (2004-2006=100)	75	139	167
Food production index (2004-2006=100)	75	140	167
Unemployment (% of labour force)	3.2	3.7	3.8
Labour force participation, adult female pop. (%)	55.1	53.5	52.6
Labour force participation, adult male pop. (%)	77.8	76.1	75.3
Tourist arrivals at national borders (000)[f]	126	214	225
Energy production, primary (Petajoules)	853	775	773[c]
Mobile-cellular subscriptions (per 100 inhabitants)	63.3	108.6	112.2
Individuals using the Internet (%)	36.5	53.0[g]	64.5[g]

Total trade		Major trading partners				2013
	(million US$)	(% of exports)				(% of imports)
Exports	11 447.2	Japan	39.8	Malaysia		21.9
Imports	3 612.4	Republic of Korea	16.3	Singapore		19.1
Balance	7 834.8	India	7.5	United States		11.9

Social indicators		
Population growth rate (average annual %)	2010-2015	1.4
Urban population growth rate (average annual %)	2010-2015	1.8
Rural population growth rate (average annual %)	2010-2015	−0.1
Urban population (%)	2014	76.9
Population aged 0-14 years (%)	2014	24.9
Population aged 60+ years (females and males, % of total)	2014	8.1/8.0
Sex ratio (males per 100 females)	2014	102.6
Life expectancy at birth (females and males, years)	2010-2015	80.4/76.6
Infant mortality rate (per 1 000 live births)	2010-2015	4.2
Fertility rate, total (live births per woman)	2010-2015	2.0
International migrant stock (000 and % of total population)	mid-2013	206.2/49.4
Refugees and others of concern to UNHCR	mid-2014	20 524
Education: Government expenditure (% of GDP)	2007-2013	3.8
Education: Primary-secondary gross enrolment ratio (f/m per 100)	2007-2013	100.7/100.2
Education: Female third-level students (% of total)	2007-2013	61.9
Intentional homicide rate (per 100,000 population)	2008-2012	2.0

Environmental indicators		
Threatened species	2014	187
Forested area (% of land area)	2012	71.4
Proportion of terrestrial and marine areas protected (%)	2014	29.7
CO_2 emission estimates (000 metric tons and metric tons per capita)	2011	9 743/24.0
Energy supply per capita (Gigajoules)	2012	392.0

a Market rate. **b** 2009. **c** 2012. **d** Series linked to former series. **e** ISIC Rev.3 (CDE). **f** Arrivals by air. **g** ITU estimate.

Bulgaria

Region	Eastern Europe	Surface area (sq km)	110 900
Population (est., 000)	7 168	Pop. density (per sq km)	64.6
Capital city	Sofia	Capital city pop. (000)	1 222
Currency	Lev (BGN)	UN membership date	14 December 1955

Economic indicators	2005	2010	2013
GDP: Gross domestic product (million current US$)	29 300	48 669	54 481
GDP: Growth rate at constant 2005 prices (annual %)	6.0	0.7	1.1
GDP per capita (current US$)	3 813.5	6 586.6	7 542.8
GNI: Gross national income per capita (current US$)	3 812.6	6 424.2	7 408.8
Gross fixed capital formation (% of GDP)	26.0	22.9	21.3
Exchange rates (national currency per US$) [a]	1.66	1.47	1.42
Balance of payments, current account (million US$)	−3 347	−796	963
CPI: Consumer price index (2000=100)	130	178	193
Index of industrial production (2010=100) [b]	103	100	105
Agricultural production index (2004-2006=100)	91	106	116
Food production index (2004-2006=100)	91	107	118
Unemployment (% of labour force)	10.1	10.2	12.9
Employment in industrial sector (% of employed)	34.2[c]	33.3	31.3[de]
Employment in agricultural sector (% of employed)	8.9[c]	6.8	6.4[de]
Labour force participation, adult female pop. (%)	44.6	47.5	47.9
Labour force participation, adult male pop. (%)	56.3	59.5	59.0
Tourist arrivals at national borders (000)	4 837	6 047	6 898
Energy production, primary (Petajoules)	444	442	491[d]
Mobile-cellular subscriptions (per 100 inhabitants)	81.3	138.0	145.2
Individuals using the Internet (%)	20.0	46.2	53.1

Total trade		Major trading partners			2013
	(million US$)		(% of exports)		(% of imports)
Exports	29 512.3	Germany	12.3	Russian Federation	18.5
Imports	34 306.8	Turkey	9.0	Germany	10.8
Balance	−4 794.5	Italy	8.7	Italy	7.5

Social indicators		
Population growth rate (average annual %)	2010-2015	−0.8
Urban population growth rate (average annual %)	2010-2015	−0.3
Rural population growth rate (average annual %)	2010-2015	−2.0
Urban population (%)	2014	73.6
Population aged 0-14 years (%)	2014	13.8
Population aged 60+ years (females and males, % of total)	2014	30.1/22.9
Sex ratio (males per 100 females)	2014	94.4
Life expectancy at birth (females and males, years)	2010-2015	77.2/69.9
Infant mortality rate (per 1 000 live births)	2010-2015	9.0
Fertility rate, total (live births per woman)	2010-2015	1.5
Contraceptive prevalence (ages 15-49, %) [f]	2007-2013	69.2
International migrant stock (000 and % of total population)	mid-2013	84.1/1.2
Refugees and others of concern to UNHCR	mid-2014	6 368[g]
Education: Government expenditure (% of GDP)	2007-2013	3.8
Education: Primary-secondary gross enrolment ratio (f/m per 100)	2007-2013	93.6/96.6
Education: Female third-level students (% of total)	2007-2013	54.6
Intentional homicide rate (per 100,000 population)	2008-2012	1.9
Seats held by women in national parliaments (%)	2015	20.4

Environmental indicators		
Threatened species	2014	86
Forested area (% of land area)	2012	37.2
Proportion of terrestrial and marine areas protected (%)	2014	31.5
Population using improved drinking water sources (%)	2012	99.0
Population using improved sanitation facilities (%)	2012	100.0
CO_2 emission estimates (000 metric tons and metric tons per capita)	2011	49 339/6.7
Energy supply per capita (Gigajoules)	2012	105.0

a Market rate. b ISIC Rev.4 (BCD). c ISIC Rev.3. d 2012. e Break in series. f Age group 20 to 49 years. g Refugee population refers to the end of 2013.

Burkina Faso

Region	Western Africa	Surface area (sq km)	272 967	
Population (est., 000)	17 420	Pop. density (per sq km)	63.6	
Capital city	Ouagadougou	Capital city pop. (000)	2 565	
Currency	CFA Franc (XOF)	UN membership date	20 September 1960	

Economic indicators	2005	2010	2013
GDP: Gross domestic product (million current US$)	5 463	8 993	12 547
GDP: Growth rate at constant 2005 prices (annual %)	8.7	8.5	6.7
GDP per capita (current US$)	407.0	578.7	740.9
GNI: Gross national income per capita (current US$)	403.8	563.5	728.1
Gross fixed capital formation (% of GDP)	19.7	22.8	17.0
Exchange rates (national currency per US$)[a]	556.04	490.91	475.64
Balance of payments, current account (million US$)	−634	−181	...
CPI: Consumer price index (2000=100)[b]	116	131[c]	141
Agricultural production index (2004-2006=100)	103	116	123
Food production index (2004-2006=100)	103	123	124
Unemployment (% of labour force)	2.7	3.3	3.1
Employment in industrial sector (% of employed)	3.1[de]	...	...
Employment in agricultural sector (% of employed)	84.8[de]	...	...
Labour force participation, adult female pop. (%)	76.9	77.2	77.1
Labour force participation, adult male pop. (%)	90.4	90.3	90.0
Tourist arrivals at national borders (000)[f]	245	274	218
Energy production, primary (Petajoules)	98	118	121[g]
Mobile-cellular subscriptions (per 100 inhabitants)	4.7	36.7	66.4
Individuals using the Internet (%)	0.5	2.4[h]	4.4[h]

Total trade		Major trading partners			2013
	(million US$)		(% of exports)		(% of imports)
Exports	2 650.5	Switzerland	52.2	China	9.7
Imports	4 365.4	Mali	6.6	Côte d'Ivoire	8.9
Balance	−1 714.9	South Africa	5.4	France	8.6

Social indicators		
Population growth rate (average annual %)	2010-2015	2.8
Urban population growth rate (average annual %)	2010-2015	5.9
Rural population growth rate (average annual %)	2010-2015	1.7
Urban population (%)	2014	29.0
Population aged 0-14 years (%)	2014	45.3
Population aged 60+ years (females and males, % of total)	2014	4.6/3.1
Sex ratio (males per 100 females)	2014	99.0
Life expectancy at birth (females and males, years)	2010-2015	56.7/55.5
Infant mortality rate (per 1 000 live births)	2010-2015	69.8
Fertility rate, total (live births per woman)	2010-2015	5.7
Contraceptive prevalence (ages 15-49, %)	2007-2013	16.2
International migrant stock (000 and % of total population)[i]	mid-2013	697.0/4.1
Refugees and others of concern to UNHCR	mid-2014	33 363
Education: Government expenditure (% of GDP)	2007-2013	3.4
Education: Primary-secondary gross enrolment ratio (f/m per 100)	2007-2013	56.5/60.3
Education: Female third-level students (% of total)	2007-2013	32.4
Intentional homicide rate (per 100,000 population)	2008-2012	8.0
Seats held by women in national parliaments (%)	2015	13.3

Environmental indicators		
Threatened species	2014	29
Forested area (% of land area)	2012	20.2
Proportion of terrestrial and marine areas protected (%)	2014	15.5
Population using improved drinking water sources (%)	2012	82.0
Population using improved sanitation facilities (%)	2012	19.0
CO_2 emission estimates (000 metric tons and metric tons per capita)	2011	1 933/0.1
Energy supply per capita (Gigajoules)	2012	9.0

a Official rate. b Ouagadougou. c Series linked to former series. d Core Welfare Indicators Questionnaire (World Bank). e ISIC Rev.3. f Arrivals of non-resident tourists in hotels and similar establishments. g 2012. h ITU estimate. i Including refugees.

Burundi

Region	Eastern Africa	Surface area (sq km)	27 834
Population (est., 000)	10 483	Pop. density (per sq km)	376.6
Capital city	Bujumbura	Capital city pop. (000)	707
Currency	Burundi Franc (BIF)	UN membership date	18 September 1962

Economic indicators	2005	2010	2013
GDP: Gross domestic product (million current US$)	1 117	2 032	2 549
GDP: Growth rate at constant 2005 prices (annual %)	−0.9	15.7	4.6
GDP per capita (current US$)	143.7	220.1	250.8
GNI: Gross national income per capita (current US$)	141.5	218.9	251.0
Gross fixed capital formation (% of GDP)	18.4	15.9	28.9
Exchange rates (national currency per US$) [a]	997.78	1 232.50	1 541.99
Balance of payments, current account (million US$)	−6	−301	−253
CPI: Consumer price index (2000=100) [b]	145	236	332
Agricultural production index (2004-2006=100)	92	108	129
Food production index (2004-2006=100)	100	114	145
Unemployment (% of labour force)	7.3	7.1	6.9
Labour force participation, adult female pop. (%)	83.4	83.0	83.3
Labour force participation, adult male pop. (%)	81.9	81.5	82.0
Tourist arrivals at national borders (000) [c]	148	142 [d]	...
Energy production, primary (Petajoules)	79	86	88 [e]
Mobile-cellular subscriptions (per 100 inhabitants)	2.0	18.2 [f]	25.0
Individuals using the Internet (%)	0.5	1.0 [f]	1.3 [f]

Total trade		Major trading partners			2013
	(million US$)	(% of exports)			(% of imports)
Exports	205.7	United Arab Emirates	58.3	Saudi Arabia	12.1
Imports	721.7	Switzerland	7.4	India	10.7
Balance	−516.0	Kenya	6.5	China	8.7

Social indicators		
Population growth rate (average annual %)	2010-2015	3.2
Urban population growth rate (average annual %)	2010-2015	5.7
Rural population growth rate (average annual %)	2010-2015	2.8
Urban population (%)	2014	11.8
Population aged 0-14 years (%)	2014	44.8
Population aged 60+ years (females and males, % of total)	2014	4.1/3.8
Sex ratio (males per 100 females)	2014	97.6
Life expectancy at birth (females and males, years)	2010-2015	55.8/52.0
Infant mortality rate (per 1 000 live births)	2010-2015	87.0
Fertility rate, total (live births per woman)	2010-2015	6.1
Contraceptive prevalence (ages 15-49, %)	2007-2013	21.9
International migrant stock (000 and % of total population) [g]	mid-2013	254.5/2.5
Refugees and others of concern to UNHCR	mid-2014	138 545
Education: Government expenditure (% of GDP)	2007-2013	5.8
Education: Primary-secondary gross enrolment ratio (f/m per 100)	2007-2013	81.7/85.9
Education: Female third-level students (% of total)	2007-2013	35.4
Intentional homicide rate (per 100,000 population)	2008-2012	8.0
Seats held by women in national parliaments (%)	2015	30.5

Environmental indicators		
Threatened species	2014	60
Forested area (% of land area)	2012	6.6
Proportion of terrestrial and marine areas protected (%)	2014	6.9
Population using improved drinking water sources (%)	2012	75.0
Population using improved sanitation facilities (%)	2012	47.0
CO$_2$ emission estimates (000 metric tons and metric tons per capita)	2011	209/0.0
Energy supply per capita (Gigajoules)	2012	9.0

a Official rate. b Bujumbura. c Including nationals residing abroad. d Break in series. e 2012. f ITU estimate.
g Including refugees.

Cabo Verde

Region	Western Africa	Surface area (sq km)	4 033
Population (est., 000)	504	Pop. density (per sq km)	124.9
Capital city	Praia	Capital city pop. (000)	145
Currency	Cabo Verde Escudo (CVE)	UN membership date	16 September 1975

Economic indicators	2005	2010	2013
GDP: Gross domestic product (million current US$)	1 105	1 664	1 861
GDP: Growth rate at constant 2005 prices (annual %)	6.5	1.5	0.5
GDP per capita (current US$)	2 309.4	3 413.3	3 730.9
GNI: Gross national income per capita (current US$)	2 229.4	3 263.2	3 616.4
Gross fixed capital formation (% of GDP)	34.1	45.2	34.1
Exchange rates (national currency per US$)[a]	93.47	82.53	79.96
Balance of payments, current account (million US$)	−41	−223	−74
CPI: Consumer price index (2000=100)	105	127	138
Agricultural production index (2004-2006=100)	98	113	90
Food production index (2004-2006=100)	98	113	90
Unemployment (% of labour force)	7.2	7.0	7.0
Labour force participation, adult female pop. (%)	48.0	50.4	51.5
Labour force participation, adult male pop. (%)	83.0	83.1	83.7
Tourist arrivals at national borders (000)[b]	198	336	503
Energy production, primary (Petajoules)	2	2	2[c]
Mobile-cellular subscriptions (per 100 inhabitants)	17.1	76.3	100.1
Individuals using the Internet (%)	6.1	30.0[d]	37.5[d]

Total trade		Major trading partners			2013
	(million US$)	(% of exports)			(% of imports)
Exports	69.2	Spain	66.8	Portugal	40.2
Imports	726.4	Portugal	16.5	Netherlands	20.0
Balance	−657.2	Italy	5.5	Spain	7.9

Social indicators		
Population growth rate (average annual %)	2010-2015	0.8
Urban population growth rate (average annual %)	2010-2015	2.0
Rural population growth rate (average annual %)	2010-2015	−1.2
Urban population (%)	2014	64.8
Population aged 0-14 years (%)	2014	28.9
Population aged 60+ years (females and males, % of total)	2014	9.0/5.9
Sex ratio (males per 100 females)	2014	99.5
Life expectancy at birth (females and males, years)	2010-2015	78.7/70.9
Infant mortality rate (per 1 000 live births)	2010-2015	17.2
Fertility rate, total (live births per woman)	2010-2015	2.3
Contraceptive prevalence (ages 15-49, %)	2007-2013	61.3[e]
International migrant stock (000 and % of total population)	mid-2013	14.9/3.0
Refugees and others of concern to UNHCR	mid-2014	0[f]
Education: Government expenditure (% of GDP)	2007-2013	5.0
Education: Primary-secondary gross enrolment ratio (f/m per 100)	2007-2013	103.4/100.6
Education: Female third-level students (% of total)	2007-2013	58.6
Intentional homicide rate (per 100,000 population)	2008-2012	10.3
Seats held by women in national parliaments (%)	2015	20.8

Environmental indicators		
Threatened species	2014	51
Forested area (% of land area)	2012	21.3
Proportion of terrestrial and marine areas protected (%)	2014	0.0
Population using improved drinking water sources (%)	2012	89.0
Population using improved sanitation facilities (%)	2012	65.0
CO_2 emission estimates (000 metric tons and metric tons per capita)	2011	425/0.9
Energy supply per capita (Gigajoules)	2012	13.0

a Official rate. b Arrivals of non-resident tourists in hotels and similar establishments. c 2012. d ITU estimate. e 2005. f Value is zero, not available or not applicable.

Cambodia

Region	South-Eastern Asia	Surface area (sq km)	181 035
Population (est., 000)	15 408	Pop. density (per sq km)	85.1
Capital city	Phnom Penh	Capital city pop. (000)	1 684[a]
Currency	Riel (KHR)	UN membership date	14 December 1955

Economic indicators	2005	2010	2013
GDP: Gross domestic product (million current US$)	6 293	11 242	15 250
GDP: Growth rate at constant 2005 prices (annual %)	13.3	6.0	7.5
GDP per capita (current US$)	471.2	782.6	1 007.6
GNI: Gross national income per capita (current US$)	403.4	745.6	884.8
Gross fixed capital formation (% of GDP)	18.9	16.2	17.7
Exchange rates (national currency per US$)[b]	4 112.00	4 051.00	3 995.00
Balance of payments, current account (million US$)	−321	−410	−1 607
CPI: Consumer price index (2000=100)[c]	114	165	185
Agricultural production index (2004-2006=100)	105	148	177
Food production index (2004-2006=100)	105	148	177
Unemployment (% of labour force)	1.3	0.4	0.3
Employment in industrial sector (% of employed)	...	16.2[de]	18.6[def]
Employment in agricultural sector (% of employed)	...	54.2[de]	51.0[def]
Labour force participation, adult female pop. (%)	76.1	79.0	78.8
Labour force participation, adult male pop. (%)	85.8	86.3	86.5
Tourist arrivals at national borders (000)[g]	1 422	2 508	4 210
Energy production, primary (Petajoules)	105	152	165[f]
Mobile-cellular subscriptions (per 100 inhabitants)	8.0	56.7	133.9
Individuals using the Internet (%)	0.3	1.3	6.0

Total trade		Major trading partners			2013
	(million US$)	(% of exports)			(% of imports)
Exports	9 248.1	United States	23.5	China	32.6
Imports	9 227.4	China, Hong Kong SAR	17.2	United States	12.2
Balance	20.7	Singapore	8.6	Thailand	11.9

Social indicators

Population growth rate (average annual %)	2010-2015	1.8
Urban population growth rate (average annual %)	2010-2015	2.7
Rural population growth rate (average annual %)	2010-2015	1.5
Urban population (%)	2014	20.5
Population aged 0-14 years (%)	2014	31.1
Population aged 60+ years (females and males, % of total)	2014	9.3/6.9
Sex ratio (males per 100 females)	2014	95.4
Life expectancy at birth (females and males, years)	2010-2015	74.2/68.8
Infant mortality rate (per 1 000 live births)	2010-2015	40.6
Fertility rate, total (live births per woman)	2010-2015	2.9
Contraceptive prevalence (ages 15-49, %)	2007-2013	50.5
International migrant stock (000 and % of total population)	mid-2013	75.6/0.5
Refugees and others of concern to UNHCR	mid-2014	92
Education: Government expenditure (% of GDP)	2007-2013	2.6
Education: Primary-secondary gross enrolment ratio (f/m per 100)[h]	2007-2013	81.1/88.6
Education: Female third-level students (% of total)	2007-2013	37.6
Intentional homicide rate (per 100,000 population)	2008-2012	6.5
Seats held by women in national parliaments (%)	2015	20.3

Environmental indicators

Threatened species	2014	237
Forested area (% of land area)	2012	55.7
Proportion of terrestrial and marine areas protected (%)	2014	20.6
Population using improved drinking water sources (%)	2012	71.0
Population using improved sanitation facilities (%)	2012	37.0
CO_2 emission estimates (000 metric tons and metric tons per capita)	2011	4 496/0.3
Energy supply per capita (Gigajoules)	2012	15.0

a Refers to the municipality of Phnon Penh including suburban areas. **b** Market rate. **c** Phnom Penh. **d** Socio-economic survey. **e** Population aged 15-64. **f** 2012. **g** Arrivals by all means of transport. **h** UNESCO estimate.

Cameroon

Region	Middle Africa	Surface area (sq km)	475 650	
Population (est., 000)	22 819	Pop. density (per sq km)	48.0	
Capital city	Yaoundé	Capital city pop. (000)	2 930	
Currency	CFA Franc (XAF)	UN membership date	20 September 1960	

Economic indicators	2005	2010	2013
GDP: Gross domestic product (million current US$)	16 588	23 622	29 568
GDP: Growth rate at constant 2005 prices (annual %)	2.3	3.3	5.6
GDP per capita (current US$)	914.6	1 145.4	1 328.6
GNI: Gross national income per capita (current US$)	880.4	1 140.3	1 274.3
Gross fixed capital formation (% of GDP)	17.7	19.0	19.4
Exchange rates (national currency per US$)[a]	556.04	490.91	475.64
Balance of payments, current account (million US$)	−495	−856	−1 128
CPI: Consumer price index (2000=100)	111	129	138
Index of industrial production (2010=100)[b]	98	100	116
Agricultural production index (2004-2006=100)	103	139	154
Food production index (2004-2006=100)	102	143	159
Unemployment (% of labour force)	4.4	3.8	4.0
Employment in industrial sector (% of employed)	14.1[c]	12.6[c]	...
Employment in agricultural sector (% of employed)	55.7[c]	53.3[c]	...
Labour force participation, adult female pop. (%)	62.1	63.3	63.8
Labour force participation, adult male pop. (%)	76.2	76.5	76.8
Tourist arrivals at national borders (000)[d]	451[e]	573	912
Energy production, primary (Petajoules)	442	351	328[f]
Mobile-cellular subscriptions (per 100 inhabitants)	12.4	41.9	70.4
Individuals using the Internet (%)	1.4	4.3[g]	6.4[g]

Total trade		Major trading partners			2013
	(million US$)		(% of exports)		(% of imports)
Exports	4 520.9	Portugal	25.5	China	14.2
Imports	6 657.2	Spain	12.8	Nigeria	13.8
Balance	−2 136.3	Netherlands	10.5	France	12.3

Social indicators		
Population growth rate (average annual %)	2010-2015	2.5
Urban population growth rate (average annual %)	2010-2015	3.6
Rural population growth rate (average annual %)	2010-2015	1.3
Urban population (%)	2014	53.8
Population aged 0-14 years (%)	2014	42.8
Population aged 60+ years (females and males, % of total)	2014	5.2/4.5
Sex ratio (males per 100 females)	2014	100.0
Life expectancy at birth (females and males, years)	2010-2015	56.0/53.7
Infant mortality rate (per 1 000 live births)	2010-2015	73.5
Fertility rate, total (live births per woman)	2010-2015	4.8
Contraceptive prevalence (ages 15-49, %)	2007-2013	23.4
International migrant stock (000 and % of total population)	mid-2013	291.8/1.3
Refugees and others of concern to UNHCR	mid-2014	240 459
Education: Government expenditure (% of GDP)	2007-2013	3.0
Education: Primary-secondary gross enrolment ratio (f/m per 100)	2007-2013	75.2/86.5
Education: Female third-level students (% of total)	2007-2013	42.2
Intentional homicide rate (per 100,000 population)	2008-2012	7.6
Seats held by women in national parliaments (%)	2015	31.1

Environmental indicators		
Threatened species	2014	688
Forested area (% of land area)	2012	41.2
Proportion of terrestrial and marine areas protected (%)	2014	10.7
Population using improved drinking water sources (%)	2012	74.0
Population using improved sanitation facilities (%)	2012	45.0
CO_2 emission estimates (000 metric tons and metric tons per capita)	2011	5 662/0.3
Energy supply per capita (Gigajoules)	2012	13.0

a Official rate. **b** ISIC Rev.4 (CDE). **c** Population aged 10 and over. **d** Arrivals of non-resident visitors at national borders. **e** 2006. **f** 2012. **g** ITU estimate.

Canada

Region	Northern America	Surface area (sq km)	9 984 670
Population (est., 000)	35 525	Pop. density (per sq km)	3.6
Capital city	Ottawa-Gatineau [a]	Capital city pop. (000)	1 306 [b]
Currency	Canadian Dollar (CAD)	UN membership date	9 November 1945

Economic indicators	2005	2010	2013
GDP: Gross domestic product (million current US$)	1 164 179	1 614 072	1 838 964
GDP: Growth rate at constant 2005 prices (annual %)	3.2	3.3	1.6
GDP per capita (current US$)	36 095.1	47 297.1	52 270.5
GNI: Gross national income per capita (current US$)	35 352.6	46 379.7	51 158.6
Gross fixed capital formation (% of GDP)	22.0	23.3	23.9
Exchange rates (national currency per US$) [c]	1.16	1.00	1.06
Balance of payments, current account (million US$)	21 910	−56 626	−58 584
CPI: Consumer price index (2000=100)	112	122	129
Index of industrial production (2010=100) [d]	...	100	107
Agricultural production index (2004-2006=100)	102	102	115
Food production index (2004-2006=100)	102	103	115
Unemployment (% of labour force)	6.7	8.0	7.1
Employment in industrial sector (% of employed)	22.0[ef]	21.5[efg]	...
Employment in agricultural sector (% of employed)	2.7[ef]	2.4[efg]	...
Labour force participation, adult female pop. (%)	60.9	61.8	61.6
Labour force participation, adult male pop. (%)	72.6	71.5	71.0
Tourist arrivals at national borders (000)	18 771	16 219	16 590
Energy production, primary (Petajoules)	16 658	16 256	17 227[h]
Mobile-cellular subscriptions (per 100 inhabitants)	52.8	75.7	78.4[i]
Individuals using the Internet (%)	71.7[j]	80.3[j]	85.8[i]

Total trade		Major trading partners			2013
	(million US$)		(% of exports)		(% of imports)
Exports	456 395.3	United States	75.8	United States	52.1
Imports	461 799.5	China	4.4	China	11.1
Balance	−5 404.2	United Kingdom	3.0	Mexico	5.6

Social indicators		
Population growth rate (average annual %)	2010-2015	1.0
Urban population growth rate (average annual %)	2010-2015	1.2
Rural population growth rate (average annual %)	2010-2015	<
Urban population (%)	2014	81.7
Population aged 0-14 years (%)	2014	16.5
Population aged 60+ years (females and males, % of total)	2014	23.2/20.2
Sex ratio (males per 100 females)	2014	98.5
Life expectancy at birth (females and males, years)	2010-2015	83.5/79.3
Infant mortality rate (per 1 000 live births)	2010-2015	4.4
Fertility rate, total (live births per woman)	2010-2015	1.7
Contraceptive prevalence (ages 15-49, %) [k]	2007-2013	74.0[l]
International migrant stock (000 and % of total population)	mid-2013	7 284.1/20.7
Refugees and others of concern to UNHCR	mid-2014	177 747[m]
Education: Government expenditure (% of GDP)	2007-2013	5.3
Education: Primary-secondary gross enrolment ratio (f/m per 100)	2007-2013	100.6/101.4
Education: Female third-level students (% of total)	2007-2013	56.0[n]
Intentional homicide rate (per 100,000 population)	2008-2012	1.6
Seats held by women in national parliaments (%)	2015	25.2

Environmental indicators		
Threatened species	2014	93
Forested area (% of land area)	2012	34.1
Proportion of terrestrial and marine areas protected (%)	2014	6.2
Population using improved drinking water sources (%)	2012	100.0
Population using improved sanitation facilities (%)	2012	100.0
CO_2 emission estimates (000 metric tons and metric tons per capita)	2011	485 463/14.1
Energy supply per capita (Gigajoules)	2012	297.0

a The capital is Ottawa. b Refers to the Census Metropolitan Area. The capital is Ottawa. c Market rate.
d ISIC Rev.4 (BCDE). e ISIC Rev.3. f Excluding residents of the Territories and indigenous persons living
on reserves. g 2008. h 2012. i ITU estimate. j Population aged 16 and over. k Age group 18 to 44 years.
l 2002. m Refugee population refers to the end of 2013. n 2000.

Cayman Islands

Region	Caribbean	Surface area (sq km)	264	
Population (est., 000)	59	Pop. density (per sq km)	224.3	
Capital city	George Town	Capital city pop. (000)	31	
Currency	Cayman Islands Dollar (KYD)			

Economic indicators	2005	2010	2013
GDP: Gross domestic product (million current US$)	3 042	3 267	3 474
GDP: Growth rate at constant 2005 prices (annual %)	6.5	-2.7	1.4
GDP per capita (current US$)	62 558.1	58 856.7	59 447.8
GNI: Gross national income per capita (current US$)	56 667.9	53 315.0	53 850.4
Gross fixed capital formation (% of GDP)	22.4	22.4	22.4
Exchange rates (national currency per US$)[a]	...	...	0.82[b]
CPI: Consumer price index (2000=100)	117	125	130
Agricultural production index (2004-2006=100)	94	105	113
Food production index (2004-2006=100)	94	105	113
Employment in industrial sector (% of employed)	22.2[cd]	19.1[cde]	...
Employment in agricultural sector (% of employed)	1.7[cd]	1.9[cde]	...
Tourist arrivals at national borders (000)[f]	168	288	345
Mobile-cellular subscriptions (per 100 inhabitants)[g]	166.5	181.2	167.8
Individuals using the Internet (%)	38.0	66.0[h]	74.1[h]

Total trade		Major trading partners		2013
	(million US$)	(% of exports)		(% of imports)
Imports	929.3	...	United States	41.7
		...	Jamaica	9.0
		...	Panama	5.2

Social indicators		
Population growth rate (average annual %)	2010-2015	1.5
Urban population growth rate (average annual %)	2010-2015	1.5
Urban population (%)	2014	100.0
Population aged 0-14 years (%)[ijk]	2014	18.3[l]
Population aged 60+ years (females and males, % of total)[ijkm]	2014	6.6/5.2[l]
Sex ratio (males per 100 females)[ijk]	2014	95.8[l]
Life expectancy at birth (females and males, years)[in]	2010-2015	83.8/76.3[o]
International migrant stock (000 and % of total population)	mid-2013	33.7/57.6
Refugees and others of concern to UNHCR	mid-2014	8
Education: Female third-level students (% of total)	2007-2013	68.9
Intentional homicide rate (per 100,000 population)	2008-2012	14.7

Environmental indicators		
Threatened species	2014	61
Forested area (% of land area)	2012	52.9
Proportion of terrestrial and marine areas protected (%)	2014	1.5
CO_2 emission estimates (000 metric tons and metric tons per capita)	2011	583/10.3
Energy supply per capita (Gigajoules)	2012	133.0

a UN operational exchange rate. b August 2012. c ISIC Rev.3. d October. e 2008. f Arrivals by air. g Year-end mobile handsets in operation. h ITU estimate. i Data compiled by the United Nations Demographic Yearbook system. j Data refer to the latest available census. k De jure estimate. l 2012. m Population aged 65 and over. n Data are based on a small number of deaths. o 2006.

Central African Republic

Region	Middle Africa	Surface area (sq km)	622 984	
Population (est., 000)	4 709	Pop. density (per sq km)	7.6	
Capital city	Bangui	Capital city pop. (000)	781	
Currency	CFA Franc (XAF)	UN membership date	20 September 1960	

Economic indicators

	2005	2010	2013
GDP: Gross domestic product (million current US$)	1 413	2 034	1 585
GDP: Growth rate at constant 2005 prices (annual %)	2.4	3.6	−36.0
GDP per capita (current US$)	356.7	467.6	343.4
GNI: Gross national income per capita (current US$)	354.3	469.2	342.8
Gross fixed capital formation (% of GDP)	11.0	13.5	8.1
Exchange rates (national currency per US$)[a]	556.04	490.91	475.64
CPI: Consumer price index (2000=100)[bc]	112	138	150
Index of industrial production (2010=100)[d]	79	100	68
Agricultural production index (2004-2006=100)	99	114	123
Food production index (2004-2006=100)	99	113	121
Unemployment (% of labour force)	7.0	6.9	7.6
Labour force participation, adult female pop. (%)	71.5	72.5	72.6
Labour force participation, adult male pop. (%)	85.4	85.2	85.1
Tourist arrivals at national borders (000)[e]	12	54	71[f]
Energy production, primary (Petajoules)	19	19	19[f]
Mobile-cellular subscriptions (per 100 inhabitants)	2.5	22.5	29.5[g]
Individuals using the Internet (%)[g]	0.3	2.0	3.5

Total trade / Major trading partners

Total trade		Major trading partners			2013
	(million US$)		(% of exports)		(% of imports)
Exports	48.5	Belgium	33.2	France	24.7
Imports	129.7	China	18.4	United States	9.8
Balance	−81.2	Germany	14.8	Netherlands	8.9

Social indicators

Population growth rate (average annual %)	2010-2015	2.0
Urban population growth rate (average annual %)	2010-2015	2.6
Rural population growth rate (average annual %)	2010-2015	1.6
Urban population (%)	2014	39.8
Population aged 0-14 years (%)	2014	39.5
Population aged 60+ years (females and males, % of total)	2014	6.3/5.1
Sex ratio (males per 100 females)	2014	96.9
Life expectancy at birth (females and males, years)	2010-2015	51.8/48.0
Infant mortality rate (per 1 000 live births)	2010-2015	93.3
Fertility rate, total (live births per woman)	2010-2015	4.4
Contraceptive prevalence (ages 15-49, %)	2007-2013	15.2
International migrant stock (000 and % of total population)[h]	mid-2013	134.2/2.9
Refugees and others of concern to UNHCR	mid-2014	911 706
Education: Government expenditure (% of GDP)	2007-2013	1.2
Education: Primary-secondary gross enrolment ratio (f/m per 100)	2007-2013	46.4/66.1
Education: Female third-level students (% of total)	2007-2013	26.9
Intentional homicide rate (per 100,000 population)	2008-2012	11.8

Environmental indicators

Threatened species	2014	53
Forested area (% of land area)	2012	36.2
Proportion of terrestrial and marine areas protected (%)	2014	18.1
Population using improved drinking water sources (%)	2012	68.0
Population using improved sanitation facilities (%)	2012	22.0
CO_2 emission estimates (000 metric tons and metric tons per capita)	2011	286/0.1
Energy supply per capita (Gigajoules)	2012	5.0

a Official rate. b Bangui. c Excluding rent. d ISIC Rev.3 (CDE). e Arrivals by air to Bangui only. f 2012. g ITU estimate. h Refers to foreign citizens.

Chad

Region	Middle Africa	Surface area (sq km)		1 284 000
Population (est., 000)	13 211	Pop. density (per sq km)		10.3
Capital city	N'Djaména	Capital city pop. (000)		1 212
Currency	CFA Franc (XAF)	UN membership date		20 September 1960

Economic indicators	2005	2010	2013
GDP: Gross domestic product (million current US$)	5 873	8 630	10 460
GDP: Growth rate at constant 2005 prices (annual %)	7.9	13.2	3.4
GDP per capita (current US$)	586.5	736.3	815.6
GNI: Gross national income per capita (current US$)	330.4	404.2	449.5
Gross fixed capital formation (% of GDP)	20.3	19.3	21.7
Exchange rates (national currency per US$)[a]	556.04	490.91	475.64
CPI: Consumer price index (2000=100)[b]	126	147	161
Index of industrial production (2010=100)[c]	127	100	83
Agricultural production index (2004-2006=100)	104	104	115
Food production index (2004-2006=100)	104	110	120
Unemployment (% of labour force)	7.0	7.0	7.0
Labour force participation, adult female pop. (%)	64.2	64.1	64.0
Labour force participation, adult male pop. (%)	79.4	79.2	79.2
Tourist arrivals at national borders (000)[d]	29	14[e]	32
Energy production, primary (Petajoules)	433	324	288[f]
Mobile-cellular subscriptions (per 100 inhabitants)	2.1	24.5	35.6
Individuals using the Internet (%)	0.4	1.7[g]	2.3[g]

Social indicators		
Population growth rate (average annual %)	2010-2015	3.0
Urban population growth rate (average annual %)	2010-2015	3.4
Rural population growth rate (average annual %)	2010-2015	2.9
Urban population (%)	2014	22.3
Population aged 0-14 years (%)	2014	48.2
Population aged 60+ years (females and males, % of total)	2014	4.1/3.5
Sex ratio (males per 100 females)	2014	100.4
Life expectancy at birth (females and males, years)	2010-2015	51.9/50.1
Infant mortality rate (per 1 000 live births)	2010-2015	95.8
Fertility rate, total (live births per woman)	2010-2015	6.3
Contraceptive prevalence (ages 15-49, %)	2007-2013	4.8
International migrant stock (000 and % of total population)[h]	mid-2013	439.1/3.4
Refugees and others of concern to UNHCR	mid-2014	476 500
Education: Government expenditure (% of GDP)	2007-2013	2.3
Education: Primary-secondary gross enrolment ratio (f/m per 100)	2007-2013	49.8/71.4
Education: Female third-level students (% of total)	2007-2013	19.1
Intentional homicide rate (per 100,000 population)	2008-2012	7.3
Seats held by women in national parliaments (%)	2015	14.9

Environmental indicators		
Threatened species	2014	38
Forested area (% of land area)	2012	9.0
Proportion of terrestrial and marine areas protected (%)	2014	17.8
Population using improved drinking water sources (%)	2012	51.0
Population using improved sanitation facilities (%)	2012	12.0
CO_2 emission estimates (000 metric tons and metric tons per capita)	2011	539/0.0
Energy supply per capita (Gigajoules)	2012	6.0

a Official rate. b N'Djamena. c ISIC Rev.3 (CDE). d Arrivals of non-resident tourists in hotels and similar establishments. e Partial data. f 2012. g ITU estimate. h Including refugees.

Region	South America	Surface area (sq km)	756 102
Population (est., 000)	17 773	Pop. density (per sq km)	23.5
Capital city	Santiago	Capital city pop. (000)	6 472
Currency	Chilean Peso (CLP)	UN membership date	24 October 1945

Economic indicators	2005	2010	2013
GDP: Gross domestic product (million current US$)	123 056	217 556	277 043
GDP: Growth rate at constant 2005 prices (annual %)	6.2	5.8	4.1
GDP per capita (current US$)	7 532.0	12 684.9	15 723.5
GNI: Gross national income per capita (current US$)	6 902.4	11 831.8	15 092.6
Gross fixed capital formation (% of GDP)	21.5	21.1	23.6
Exchange rates (national currency per US$) [a]	514.21	468.37	523.76
Balance of payments, current account (million US$)	1 449	3 581	−9 486
CPI: Consumer price index (2000=100) [b]	114	101[c]	110[c]
Agricultural production index (2004-2006=100)	100	109	117
Food production index (2004-2006=100)	100	109	117
Unemployment (% of labour force)	8.0	8.1	6.0
Employment in industrial sector (% of employed) [d]	23.0[e]	23.0[f]	23.4[fg]
Employment in agricultural sector (% of employed) [d]	13.2[e]	10.6[f]	10.3[fg]
Labour force participation, adult female pop. (%)	38.3	46.8	49.2
Labour force participation, adult male pop. (%)	73.0	74.3	74.8
Tourist arrivals at national borders (000)	2 027	2 801	3 576
Energy production, primary (Petajoules)	390	385	545[h]
Mobile-cellular subscriptions (per 100 inhabitants)	64.7	115.8	134.3
Individuals using the Internet (%) [i]	31.2	45.0[j]	66.5

Total trade		Major trading partners			2013
	(million US$)	China	(% of exports)		(% of imports)
Exports	76 684.1	China	24.9	United States	20.3
Imports	79 172.8	United States	12.8	China	19.7
Balance	−2 488.7	Japan	9.9	Brazil	6.5

Social indicators		
Population growth rate (average annual %)	2010-2015	0.9
Urban population growth rate (average annual %)	2010-2015	1.1
Rural population growth rate (average annual %)	2010-2015	−0.8
Urban population (%)	2014	89.4
Population aged 0-14 years (%)	2014	20.8
Population aged 60+ years (females and males, % of total)	2014	16.0/13.2
Sex ratio (males per 100 females)	2014	97.9
Life expectancy at birth (females and males, years)	2010-2015	82.6/77.0
Infant mortality rate (per 1 000 live births)	2010-2015	5.9
Fertility rate, total (live births per woman)	2010-2015	1.8
Contraceptive prevalence (ages 15-49, %) [k]	2007-2013	64.2[l]
International migrant stock (000 and % of total population)	mid-2013	398.3/2.3
Refugees and others of concern to UNHCR	mid-2014	2 252
Education: Government expenditure (% of GDP)	2007-2013	4.6
Education: Primary-secondary gross enrolment ratio (f/m per 100)	2007-2013	94.9/94.8
Education: Female third-level students (% of total)	2007-2013	52.0
Intentional homicide rate (per 100,000 population)	2008-2012	3.1
Seats held by women in national parliaments (%)	2015	15.8

Environmental indicators		
Threatened species	2014	182
Forested area (% of land area)	2012	21.9
Proportion of terrestrial and marine areas protected (%)	2014	6.9
Population using improved drinking water sources (%)	2012	99.0
Population using improved sanitation facilities (%)	2012	99.0
CO_2 emission estimates (000 metric tons and metric tons per capita)	2011	79 409/4.6
Energy supply per capita (Gigajoules)	2012	89.0

a Principal rate. b Santiago. c Index base 2009=100. d ISIC Rev.2. e Fourth quarter. f Break in series. g 2011. h 2012. i ITU estimate. j Population aged 5 and over. k Age group 15 to 44 years. l 2006.

China[a]

Region	Eastern Asia	Surface area (sq km)	9 596 961
Population (est., 000)	1 393 784	Pop. density (per sq km)	145.2
Capital city	Beijing	Capital city pop. (000)	19 520
Currency	Yuan Renminbi (CNY)	UN membership date	24 October 1945

Economic indicators	2005	2010	2013
GDP: Gross domestic product (million current US$)	2 287 237	5 949 785	9 181 204
GDP: Growth rate at constant 2005 prices (annual %)	11.3	10.4	7.7
GDP per capita (current US$)	1 735.2	4 375.4	6 626.3
GNI: Gross national income per capita (current US$)	1 699.9	4 342.2	6 594.7
Gross fixed capital formation (% of GDP)	39.6	45.6	45.9
Exchange rates (national currency per US$)[b]	8.07	6.62	6.10
Balance of payments, current account (million US$)	132 378	237 810	182 807
CPI: Consumer price index (2000=100)[c]	107	124	137
Agricultural production index (2004-2006=100)	100	120	131
Food production index (2004-2006=100)	100	120	131
Unemployment (% of labour force)	4.1	4.2	4.6
Employment in industrial sector (% of employed)[de]	23.8	28.7	29.5[f]
Employment in agricultural sector (% of employed)[de]	44.8	36.7	34.8[f]
Labour force participation, adult female pop. (%)	66.5	63.5	63.9
Labour force participation, adult male pop. (%)	79.5	77.6	78.3
Tourist arrivals at national borders (000)	46 809	55 664	55 686
Energy production, primary (Petajoules)	62 586	85 079	93 752[g]
Mobile-cellular subscriptions (per 100 inhabitants)	29.8	63.2	88.7
Individuals using the Internet (%)	8.5	34.3	45.8[h]

Total trade		Major trading partners			2013
	(million US$)	(% of exports)		(% of imports)	
Exports	2 209 007.3	China, Hong Kong SAR	17.4	Republic of Korea	9.4
Imports	1 949 992.3	United States	16.7	Japan	8.3
Balance	259 015.0	Japan	6.8	China	8.1[i]

Social indicators		
Population growth rate (average annual %)	2010-2015	0.6
Urban population growth rate (average annual %)	2010-2015	3.1
Rural population growth rate (average annual %)	2010-2015	−2.1
Urban population (%)	2014	54.4
Population aged 0-14 years (%)	2014	18.1
Population aged 60+ years (females and males, % of total)	2014	15.2/13.8
Sex ratio (males per 100 females)	2014	107.6
Life expectancy at birth (females and males, years)	2010-2015	76.6/74.0
Infant mortality rate (per 1 000 live births)	2010-2015	13.0
Fertility rate, total (live births per woman)	2010-2015	1.7
Contraceptive prevalence (ages 15-49, %)	2007-2013	84.6[j]
International migrant stock (000 and % of total population)[k]	mid-2013	848.5/0.1
Refugees and others of concern to UNHCR	mid-2014	301 442[l]
Education: Government expenditure (% of GDP)	2007-2013	1.9[m]
Education: Primary-secondary gross enrolment ratio (f/m per 100)	2007-2013	105.8/105.0
Education: Female third-level students (% of total)	2007-2013	50.4
Intentional homicide rate (per 100,000 population)	2008-2012	1.0
Seats held by women in national parliaments (%)	2015	23.6

Environmental indicators		
Threatened species	2014	995
Forested area (% of land area)	2012	22.6
Proportion of terrestrial and marine areas protected (%)	2014	15.6
Population using improved drinking water sources (%)	2012	92.0
Population using improved sanitation facilities (%)	2012	65.0
CO_2 emission estimates (000 metric tons and metric tons per capita)	2011	9 019 518/6.6
Energy supply per capita (Gigajoules)	2012	79.0

a For statistical purposes, the data for China do not include Hong Kong SAR, Macao SAR or Taiwan Province of China, unless otherwise indicated. **b** Principal rate. **c** Index base 2000=100. **d** December. **e** Population aged 16 and over. **f** 2011. **g** 2012. **h** ITU estimate. **i** Data refer to returned goods or goods resulting from outward processing, i.e. minor processing or, in general, operations which do not change the country of origin. When these goods come back they are recorded as re-imports and the country of origin is the country itself. **j** 2006. **k** Estimate. **l** The 300,000 Vietnamese refugees are well integrated and in practice receive protection from the Government of China. **m** 1999.

China, Hong Kong SAR

Region	Eastern Asia	Surface area (sq km)	1 104
Population (est., 000)	7 260	Pop. density (per sq km)	6 605.6
Capital city	Hong Kong	Capital city pop. (000)	7 260[a]
Currency	Hong Kong Dollar (HKD)		

Economic indicators	2005	2010	2013
GDP: Gross domestic product (million current US$)	181 569	228 639	274 027
GDP: Growth rate at constant 2005 prices (annual %)	7.4	6.8	2.9
GDP per capita (current US$)	26 327.0	32 433.3	38 039.0
GNI: Gross national income per capita (current US$)	26 466.2	33 119.7	38 793.8
Gross fixed capital formation (% of GDP)	21.4	21.8	23.9
Exchange rates (national currency per US$)[b]	7.75	7.77	7.75
Balance of payments, current account (million US$)	21 575	16 012	5 097
CPI: Consumer price index (2000=100)	94	104	119
Agricultural production index (2004-2006=100)	99	56	60
Food production index (2004-2006=100)	99	56	60
Unemployment (% of labour force)	5.6	4.3	3.3
Employment in industrial sector (% of employed)	15.1[cd]	11.4[efg]	11.6[efh]
Employment in agricultural sector (% of employed)	0.3[cd]	0.0[efg]	0.0[efh]
Labour force participation, adult female pop. (%)	51.7	51.8	51.3
Labour force participation, adult male pop. (%)	71.2	68.4	67.8
Tourist arrivals at national borders (000)	14 773	20 085	25 661
Energy production, primary (Petajoules)	...	0[i]	0[hi]
Mobile-cellular subscriptions (per 100 inhabitants)	123.9	195.7	238.7
Individuals using the Internet (%)[j]	56.9	72.0	74.2

Total trade		Major trading partners			2013
	(million US$)	(% of exports)			(% of imports)
Exports	535 186.7	China	59.9	China	42.9
Imports	621 416.9	United States	8.0	Switzerland	8.2
Balance	−86 230.2	Japan	3.3	Japan	6.2

Social indicators		
Population growth rate (average annual %)	2010-2015	0.7
Urban population growth rate (average annual %)	2010-2015	0.7
Urban population (%)	2014	100.0
Population aged 0-14 years (%)	2014	11.7
Population aged 60+ years (females and males, % of total)	2014	20.6/21.1
Sex ratio (males per 100 females)	2014	88.0
Life expectancy at birth (females and males, years)	2010-2015	86.4/80.3
Infant mortality rate (per 1 000 live births)	2010-2015	1.9
Fertility rate, total (live births per woman)	2010-2015	1.1
Contraceptive prevalence (ages 15-49, %)	2007-2013	79.5
International migrant stock (000 and % of total population)	mid-2013	2 804.8/38.9
Refugees and others of concern to UNHCR	mid-2014	2 405
Education: Government expenditure (% of GDP)	2007-2013	3.8
Education: Primary-secondary gross enrolment ratio (f/m per 100)	2007-2013	100.2/102.7
Education: Female third-level students (% of total)	2007-2013	52.1
Intentional homicide rate (per 100,000 population)	2008-2012	19.4

Environmental indicators		
Threatened species	2014	59
Proportion of terrestrial and marine areas protected (%)	2014	41.8
CO$_2$ emission estimates (000 metric tons and metric tons per capita)	2011	40 275/5.7
Energy supply per capita (Gigajoules)	2012	79.0

a Consists of the population of Hong Kong Island, New Kowloon the new towns in New Territories and the marine areas. b Market rate. c ISIC Rev.2. d Excluding marine and institutional populations. e Average of quarterly estimates. f Excluding institutional population. g Break in series. h 2012. i UNSD estimate. j Population aged 10 and over.

China, Macao SAR

Region	Eastern Asia	Surface area (sq km)	30	
Population (est., 000)	575	Pop. density (per sq km)	22 133.9	
Capital city	Macao	Capital city pop. (000)	575	
Currency	Pataca (MOP)			

Economic indicators	2005	2010	2013
GDP: Gross domestic product (million current US$)	11 793	28 360	51 753
GDP: Growth rate at constant 2005 prices (annual %)	8.6	27.5	11.9
GDP per capita (current US$)	25 189.8	53 046.0	91 376.5
GNI: Gross national income per capita (current US$)	23 584.1	47 340.6	81 847.9
Gross fixed capital formation (% of GDP)	25.8	12.5	12.8
Exchange rates (national currency per US$)[a]	7.99	8.02	7.99
Balance of payments, current account (million US$)	2 965	12 130	20 762
CPI: Consumer price index (2000=100)	99	124	147
Index of industrial production (2010=100)[b]	...	100	87
Agricultural production index (2004-2006=100)	100	95	88
Food production index (2004-2006=100)	100	95	88
Unemployment (% of labour force)	4.2	2.8	1.8
Employment in industrial sector (% of employed)[c]	25.0[d]	13.7[ef]	12.8[eg]
Employment in agricultural sector (% of employed)[c]	0.1[d]	0.2[efh]	0.2[egh]
Labour force participation, adult female pop. (%)	59.0	65.7	66.0
Labour force participation, adult male pop. (%)	74.3	77.2	77.6
Tourist arrivals at national borders (000)[i]	9 014	11 926[j]	14 268[j]
Energy production, primary (Petajoules)[k]	2	2	2[g]
Mobile-cellular subscriptions (per 100 inhabitants)	113.8	209.9	304.1
Individuals using the Internet (%)	34.9	55.2[l]	65.8[l]

Total trade		Major trading partners			2013
	(million US$)[g]	(% of exports)[g]		(% of imports)[g]	
Exports	1 020.5	China, Hong Kong SAR	39.7	China	32.3
Imports	8 982.1	Areas nes	36.4[m]	China, Hong Kong SAR	11.4
Balance	−7 961.6	China	11.0	France	8.7

Social indicators		
Population growth rate (average annual %)	2010-2015	1.8
Urban population growth rate (average annual %)	2010-2015	1.8
Urban population (%)	2014	100.0
Population aged 0-14 years (%)	2014	12.4
Population aged 60+ years (females and males, % of total)	2014	14.0/14.3
Sex ratio (males per 100 females)	2014	92.7
Life expectancy at birth (females and males, years)	2010-2015	82.5/78.1
Infant mortality rate (per 1 000 live births)	2010-2015	4.1
Fertility rate, total (live births per woman)	2010-2015	1.1
International migrant stock (000 and % of total population)	mid-2013	333.3/58.8
Refugees and others of concern to UNHCR	mid-2014	6
Education: Government expenditure (% of GDP)	2007-2013	3.3
Education: Primary-secondary gross enrolment ratio (f/m per 100)	2007-2013	90.9/90.2[n]
Education: Female third-level students (% of total)	2007-2013	56.4
Intentional homicide rate (per 100,000 population)	2008-2012	13.3

Environmental indicators		
Threatened species	2014	11
CO$_2$ emission estimates (000 metric tons and metric tons per capita)	2011	1 166/2.1
Energy supply per capita (Gigajoules)	2012	55.0[k]

a Market rate. b ISIC Rev.4 (CD). c ISIC Rev.3. d Population aged 14 and over. e Population aged 16 and over. f Break in series. g 2012. h Including mining and quarrying. i Country estimates. j Excluding other non-residents (workers, students, etc.). k UNSD estimate. l Population aged 3 and over. m See technical notes. n 1999.

Colombia

Region	South America	Surface area (sq km)	1 141 748
Population (est., 000)	48 930	Pop. density (per sq km)	43.0
Capital city	Bogotá	Capital city pop. (000)	9 558 [a]
Currency	Colombian Peso (COP)	UN membership date	5 November 1945

Economic indicators	2005	2010	2013
GDP: Gross domestic product (million current US$)	146 566	287 018	378 148
GDP: Growth rate at constant 2005 prices (annual %)	4.7	4.0	4.3
GDP per capita (current US$)	3 394.0	6 179.8	7 825.7
GNI: Gross national income per capita (current US$)	3 309.2	5 959.9	7 522.5
Gross fixed capital formation (% of GDP)	19.7	21.9	24.1
Exchange rates (national currency per US$) [b]	2 284.22	1 989.88	1 922.56
Balance of payments, current account (million US$)	−1 892	−8 666	−12 276
CPI: Consumer price index (2000=100) [c]	140	177	194
Agricultural production index (2004-2006=100)	99	101	114
Food production index (2004-2006=100)	99	103	115
Unemployment (% of labour force)	12.0	12.0	10.5
Employment in industrial sector (% of employed) [de]	20.3	19.6	20.9 [f]
Employment in agricultural sector (% of employed) [de]	21.4	18.4	16.9 [f]
Labour force participation, adult female pop. (%)	53.0	55.3	55.8
Labour force participation, adult male pop. (%)	81.0	79.7	79.7
Tourist arrivals at national borders (000)	933	1 405	2 288
Energy production, primary (Petajoules)	3 335	4 565	5 216 [f]
Mobile-cellular subscriptions (per 100 inhabitants)	50.6	95.8	104.1
Individuals using the Internet (%)	11.0	36.5 [g]	51.7 [g]

Total trade		Major trading partners			2013
	(million US$)	(% of exports)		(% of imports)	
Exports	58 821.9	United States	31.8	United States	27.7
Imports	59 381.2	China	8.7	China	17.5
Balance	−559.3	Panama	5.5	Mexico	9.3

Social indicators

Population growth rate (average annual %)	2010-2015	1.3
Urban population growth rate (average annual %)	2010-2015	1.7
Rural population growth rate (average annual %)	2010-2015	0.1
Urban population (%)	2014	76.2
Population aged 0-14 years (%)	2014	27.3
Population aged 60+ years (females and males, % of total)	2014	10.7/8.9
Sex ratio (males per 100 females)	2014	96.7
Life expectancy at birth (females and males, years)	2010-2015	77.6/70.3
Infant mortality rate (per 1 000 live births)	2010-2015	16.3
Fertility rate, total (live births per woman)	2010-2015	2.3
Contraceptive prevalence (ages 15-49, %)	2007-2013	79.1
International migrant stock (000 and % of total population)	mid-2013	129.6/0.3
Refugees and others of concern to UNHCR	mid-2014	5 700 789
Education: Government expenditure (% of GDP)	2007-2013	4.9
Education: Primary-secondary gross enrolment ratio (f/m per 100)	2007-2013	106.6/102.7
Education: Female third-level students (% of total)	2007-2013	52.6
Intentional homicide rate (per 100,000 population)	2008-2012	30.8
Seats held by women in national parliaments (%)	2015	19.9

Environmental indicators

Threatened species	2014	741
Forested area (% of land area)	2012	54.4
Proportion of terrestrial and marine areas protected (%)	2014	17.4
Population using improved drinking water sources (%)	2012	91.0
Population using improved sanitation facilities (%)	2012	80.0
CO_2 emission estimates (000 metric tons and metric tons per capita)	2011	72 423/1.5
Energy supply per capita (Gigajoules)	2012	29.0

a Refers to the nuclei of Santa Fe de Bogotá, Soacha, Chia and Funza. **b** Official rate. **c** Low income group. **d** ISIC Rev.2. **e** Population aged 12 and over. **f** 2012. **g** Population aged 5 and over.

Comoros

Region	Eastern Africa	Surface area (sq km)	2 235
Population (est., 000)	752	Pop. density (per sq km)	404.3
Capital city	Moroni	Capital city pop. (000)	56
Currency	Comoros Franc (KMF)	UN membership date	12 November 1975

Economic indicators	2005	2010	2013
GDP: Gross domestic product (million current US$)	387	533	622
GDP: Growth rate at constant 2005 prices (annual %)	4.2	2.0	3.6
GDP per capita (current US$)	644.3	780.8	846.4
GNI: Gross national income per capita (current US$)	642.5	792.1	877.9
Gross fixed capital formation (% of GDP)	9.3	11.0	1.4
Exchange rates (national currency per US$)[a]	417.03	368.18	356.73
Balance of payments, current account (million US$)	−27	−39	−41[b]
Agricultural production index (2004-2006=100)	96	114	114
Food production index (2004-2006=100)	96	114	113
Unemployment (% of labour force)	6.7	6.5	6.5
Labour force participation, adult female pop. (%)	32.5	34.6	35.2
Labour force participation, adult male pop. (%)	79.6	80.2	80.1
Tourist arrivals at national borders (000)	26	15	....
Energy production, primary (Petajoules)	2	2	3[b]
Mobile-cellular subscriptions (per 100 inhabitants)	2.6	24.2	47.3[c]
Individuals using the Internet (%)[c]	2.0	5.1	6.5

Social indicators		
Population growth rate (average annual %)	2010-2015	2.4
Urban population growth rate (average annual %)	2010-2015	2.7
Rural population growth rate (average annual %)	2010-2015	2.3
Urban population (%)	2014	28.2
Population aged 0-14 years (%)	2014	41.9
Population aged 60+ years (females and males, % of total)	2014	5.0/4.3
Sex ratio (males per 100 females)	2014	101.6
Life expectancy at birth (females and males, years)	2010-2015	62.2/59.4
Infant mortality rate (per 1 000 live births)	2010-2015	67.2
Fertility rate, total (live births per woman)	2010-2015	4.7
Contraceptive prevalence (ages 15-49, %)	2007-2013	19.4
International migrant stock (000 and % of total population)	mid-2013	12.5/1.7
Refugees and others of concern to UNHCR	mid-2014	0[d]
Education: Government expenditure (% of GDP)	2007-2013	7.6
Education: Primary-secondary gross enrolment ratio (f/m per 100)	2007-2013	83.3/85.4
Education: Female third-level students (% of total)	2007-2013	45.7
Intentional homicide rate (per 100,000 population)	2008-2012	10.0

Environmental indicators		
Threatened species	2014	106
Forested area (% of land area)	2012	1.2
Proportion of terrestrial and marine areas protected (%)	2014	2.4
Population using improved drinking water sources (%)	2012	95.0[e]
Population using improved sanitation facilities (%)	2012	35.0[e]
CO$_2$ emission estimates (000 metric tons and metric tons per capita)	2011	158/0.2
Energy supply per capita (Gigajoules)	2012	7.0[f]

a Official rate. b 2012. c ITU estimate. d Value is zero, not available or not applicable. e 2010. f UNSD estimate.

Congo

Region	Middle Africa	Surface area (sq km)	342 000	
Population (est., 000)	4 559	Pop. density (per sq km)	13.3	
Capital city	Brazzaville	Capital city pop. (000)	1 827	
Currency	CFA Franc (XAF)	UN membership date	20 September 1960	

Economic indicators

	2005	2010	2013
GDP: Gross domestic product (million current US$)	6 087	12 281	14 022
GDP: Growth rate at constant 2005 prices (annual %)	7.7	8.7	3.3
GDP per capita (current US$)	1 718.1	2 986.8	3 152.6
GNI: Gross national income per capita (current US$)	1 246.1	2 365.3	2 751.1
Gross fixed capital formation (% of GDP)	24.2	29.7	44.5
Exchange rates (national currency per US$) [a]	556.04	490.91	475.64
Balance of payments, current account (million US$)	696	−2 181[b]	...
CPI: Consumer price index (2000=100) [cd]	110	139[e]	154
Agricultural production index (2004-2006=100)	100	123	136
Food production index (2004-2006=100)	100	123	136
Unemployment (% of labour force)	6.6	6.5	6.5
Employment in industrial sector (% of employed)	20.6[fgh]	...	...
Employment in agricultural sector (% of employed)	35.4[fgh]	...	...
Labour force participation, adult female pop. (%)	67.5	68.3	68.5
Labour force participation, adult male pop. (%)	71.7	72.8	73.0
Tourist arrivals at national borders (000) [i]	35	194	297
Energy production, primary (Petajoules)	563	718	649[j]
Mobile-cellular subscriptions (per 100 inhabitants)	15.8	90.4	104.8
Individuals using the Internet (%) [k]	1.5	5.0	6.6

Total trade

Total trade		Major trading partners			2013
	(million US$)	(% of exports)			(% of imports)
Exports	10 453.1	China	40.4	Angola	15.1
Imports	8 371.6	Angola	8.5	Gabon	12.2
Balance	2 081.5	Australia	7.8	France	9.1

Social indicators

Population growth rate (average annual %)	2010-2015	2.6
Urban population growth rate (average annual %)	2010-2015	3.2
Rural population growth rate (average annual %)	2010-2015	1.4
Urban population (%)	2014	65.0
Population aged 0-14 years (%)	2014	42.5
Population aged 60+ years (females and males, % of total)	2014	5.5/4.8
Sex ratio (males per 100 females)	2014	100.0
Life expectancy at birth (females and males, years)	2010-2015	60.1/57.2
Infant mortality rate (per 1 000 live births)	2010-2015	63.6
Fertility rate, total (live births per woman)	2010-2015	5.0
Contraceptive prevalence (ages 15-49, %)	2007-2013	44.7
International migrant stock (000 and % of total population)	mid-2013	431.5/9.7
Refugees and others of concern to UNHCR	mid-2014	52 859
Education: Government expenditure (% of GDP)	2007-2013	6.2
Education: Primary-secondary gross enrolment ratio (f/m per 100)	2007-2013	82.5/82.2
Education: Female third-level students (% of total)	2007-2013	42.8
Intentional homicide rate (per 100,000 population)	2008-2012	12.5
Seats held by women in national parliaments (%)	2015	7.4

Environmental indicators

Threatened species	2014	118
Forested area (% of land area)	2012	65.6
Proportion of terrestrial and marine areas protected (%)	2014	31.8
Population using improved drinking water sources (%)	2012	75.0
Population using improved sanitation facilities (%)	2012	15.0
CO_2 emission estimates (000 metric tons and metric tons per capita)	2011	2 248/0.5
Energy supply per capita (Gigajoules)	2012	16.0

a Official rate. b 2007. c Brazzaville. d African population. e Series linked to former series. f Core Welfare Indicators Questionnaire (World Bank). g ISIC Rev.2. h June to August. i Arrivals of non-resident tourists in hotels and similar establishments. j 2012. k ITU estimate.

Cook Islands

Region	Oceania-Polynesia	Surface area (sq km)	236[a]
Population (est., 000)	21	Pop. density (per sq km)	87.9
Capital city	Avarua[b]	Capital city pop. (000)	5[c]
Currency	New Zealand Dollar (NZD)		

Economic indicators	2005	2010	2013
GDP: Gross domestic product (million current US$)	183	257	330
GDP: Growth rate at constant 2005 prices (annual %)	−1.1	−3.0	3.2
GDP per capita (current US$)	9 410.7	12 653.0	16 001.8
GNI: Gross national income per capita (current US$)	9 410.7	12 653.0	16 001.8
Gross fixed capital formation (% of GDP)	13.1	12.1	12.4
Exchange rates (national currency per US$)[d]	1.46	1.31	1.22
CPI: Consumer price index (2000=100)[e]	118	144	154
Agricultural production index (2004-2006=100)	100	104	97
Food production index (2004-2006=100)	100	104	97
Tourist arrivals at national borders (000)	88	104	121

Total trade		Major trading partners			2013
	(million US$)[c]	(% of exports)[c]			(% of imports)[c]
Exports	3.1	Japan	58.1	New Zealand	77.1
Imports	109.3	China	16.1	Fiji	10.0
Balance	−106.2	United States	6.5	Australia	5.3

Social indicators

Population growth rate (average annual %)	2010-2015	0.5
Urban population growth rate (average annual %)	2010-2015	0.9
Rural population growth rate (average annual %)	2010-2015	−0.4
Urban population (%)	2014	74.3
Population aged 0-14 years (%)[fg]	2014	28.5
Population aged 60+ years (females and males, % of total)[hij]	2014	11.5/10.8[k]
Sex ratio (males per 100 females)[fg]	2014	100.0
Life expectancy at birth (females and males, years)[fg]	2010-2015	79.8/73.6[lm]
Infant mortality rate (per 1 000 live births)[fg]	2010-2015	7.0[lm]
Fertility rate, total (live births per woman)[fg]	2010-2015	2.8[cm]
Contraceptive prevalence (ages 15-49, %)	2007-2013	43.2[n]
International migrant stock (000 and % of total population)	mid-2013	3.2/15.7
Education: Government expenditure (% of GDP)	2007-2013	3.1
Education: Primary-secondary gross enrolment ratio (f/m per 100)[o]	2007-2013	97.2/96.3
Education: Female third-level students (% of total)	2007-2013	52.8
Intentional homicide rate (per 100,000 population)	2008-2012	3.1

Environmental indicators

Threatened species	2014	73
Forested area (% of land area)	2012	64.6
Population using improved drinking water sources (%)	2012	100.0
Population using improved sanitation facilities (%)	2012	97.0
CO_2 emission estimates (000 metric tons and metric tons per capita)	2011	70/3.5
Energy supply per capita (Gigajoules)	2012	49.0[p]

a Excluding Niue. b Refers to the island of Rarotonga. c 2011. d UN operational exchange rate. e Rarotonga. f Data compiled by the Secretariat of the Pacific Community Demography Programme. g Resident population only. h Data compiled by the United Nations Demographic Yearbook system. i Data refer to the latest available census. j Census, de jure, complete tabulation. k 2006. l 2006-2012. m Preliminary. n 1999. o National estimate. p UNSD estimate.

Costa Rica

Region	Central America	Surface area (sq km)	51 100
Population (est., 000)	4 938	Pop. density (per sq km)	96.6
Capital city	San José	Capital city pop. (000)	1 160 [a]
Currency	Costa Rica Colon (CRC)	UN membership date	2 November 1945

Economic indicators	2005	2010	2013
GDP: Gross domestic product (million current US$)	19 965	36 298	49 621
GDP: Growth rate at constant 2005 prices (annual %)	5.9	5.0	3.5
GDP per capita (current US$)	4 621.4	7 773.2	10 184.6
GNI: Gross national income per capita (current US$)	4 440.6	7 563.1	9 884.9
Gross fixed capital formation (% of GDP)	18.7	19.8	21.0
Exchange rates (national currency per US$) [b]	496.68	512.97	501.40
Balance of payments, current account (million US$)	−981	−1 281	−2 522
CPI: Consumer price index (2000=100) [c]	170	268	309
Agricultural production index (2004-2006=100)	98	113	122
Food production index (2004-2006=100)	98	115	125
Unemployment (% of labour force)	6.6	7.3	7.6
Employment in industrial sector (% of employed)	21.6[def]	19.5[de]	19.5[fgh]
Employment in agricultural sector (% of employed)	15.2[def]	15.0[de]	13.4[fgh]
Labour force participation, adult female pop. (%)	44.0	46.1	46.6
Labour force participation, adult male pop. (%)	80.5	78.9	79.0
Tourist arrivals at national borders (000)	1 679	2 100	2 428
Energy production, primary (Petajoules)	93	104	106[g]
Mobile-cellular subscriptions (per 100 inhabitants)	25.5	67.0	146.0
Individuals using the Internet (%)	22.1[i]	36.5[j]	46.0[k]

Total trade		Major trading partners			2013
(million US$)		(% of exports)			(% of imports)
Exports	11 472.1	United States	38.3	United States	50.0
Imports	18 124.5	Netherlands	7.2	China	9.6
Balance	−6 652.4	China, Hong Kong SAR	5.6	Mexico	6.4

Social indicators		
Population growth rate (average annual %)	2010-2015	1.4
Urban population growth rate (average annual %)	2010-2015	2.7
Rural population growth rate (average annual %)	2010-2015	−2.6
Urban population (%)	2014	75.9
Population aged 0-14 years (%)	2014	23.1
Population aged 60+ years (females and males, % of total)	2014	11.6/10.3
Sex ratio (males per 100 females)	2014	103.1
Life expectancy at birth (females and males, years)	2010-2015	82.1/77.7
Infant mortality rate (per 1 000 live births)	2010-2015	8.5
Fertility rate, total (live births per woman)	2010-2015	1.8
Contraceptive prevalence (ages 15-49, %)	2007-2013	76.2
International migrant stock (000 and % of total population) [l]	mid-2013	419.6/8.6
Refugees and others of concern to UNHCR	mid-2014	22 229
Education: Government expenditure (% of GDP)	2007-2013	6.9
Education: Primary-secondary gross enrolment ratio (f/m per 100)	2007-2013	107.6/104.4
Education: Female third-level students (% of total)	2007-2013	54.0
Intentional homicide rate (per 100,000 population)	2008-2012	8.5
Seats held by women in national parliaments (%)	2015	33.3

Environmental indicators		
Threatened species	2014	317
Forested area (% of land area)	2012	51.9
Proportion of terrestrial and marine areas protected (%)	2014	3.1
Population using improved drinking water sources (%)	2012	97.0
Population using improved sanitation facilities (%)	2012	94.0
CO_2 emission estimates (000 metric tons and metric tons per capita)	2011	7 844/1.7
Energy supply per capita (Gigajoules)	2012	43.0

a Refers to the urban population of cantons. **b** Market rate. **c** Central area. **d** ISIC Rev.2. **e** Population aged 12 and over. **f** July. **g** 2012. **h** Break in series. **i** Population aged 5 and over. **j** Population aged 5 and over using the Internet within the last 3 months. **k** Total population in the last 3 months. **l** Including refugees.

Côte d'Ivoire

Region	Western Africa	Surface area (sq km)	322 463	
Population (est., 000)	20 805	Pop. density (per sq km)	64.5	
Capital city	Yamoussoukro[a]	Capital city pop. (000)	259	
Currency	CFA Franc (XOF)	UN membership date	20 September 1960	

Economic indicators	2005	2010	2013
GDP: Gross domestic product (million current US$)	17 085	22 921	28 593
GDP: Growth rate at constant 2005 prices (annual %)	1.7	2.4	9.0
GDP per capita (current US$)	982.2	1 207.9	1 407.4
GNI: Gross national income per capita (current US$)	914.3	1 163.2	1 355.4
Gross fixed capital formation (% of GDP)	9.2	9.0	17.5
Exchange rates (national currency per US$)[b]	556.04	490.91	475.64
Balance of payments, current account (million US$)	40	465	...
CPI: Consumer price index (2000=100)[cd]	117	133[e]	145
Index of industrial production (2010=100)[f]	97	100	130
Agricultural production index (2004-2006=100)	100	107	123
Food production index (2004-2006=100)	98	109	124
Unemployment (% of labour force)	4.1	4.1	4.0
Labour force participation, adult female pop. (%)	50.6	52.0	52.4
Labour force participation, adult male pop. (%)	82.2	81.7	81.4
Tourist arrivals at national borders (000)[g]	182[h]	252	289[i]
Energy production, primary (Petajoules)	451	467	523[i]
Mobile-cellular subscriptions (per 100 inhabitants)	13.5	82.2	95.5
Individuals using the Internet (%)	1.0	2.1[j]	2.6[j]

Total trade		Major trading partners				2013
	(million US$)	(% of exports)				(% of imports)
Exports	12 083.8	Ghana	15.3	Nigeria		23.1
Imports	12 483.0	Netherlands	8.0	Bahamas		11.7
Balance	−399.2	Nigeria	7.1	China		11.4

Social indicators		
Population growth rate (average annual %)	2010-2015	2.3
Urban population growth rate (average annual %)	2010-2015	3.7
Rural population growth rate (average annual %)	2010-2015	0.8
Urban population (%)	2014	53.5
Population aged 0-14 years (%)	2014	41.2
Population aged 60+ years (females and males, % of total)	2014	4.7/5.5
Sex ratio (males per 100 females)	2014	103.8
Life expectancy at birth (females and males, years)	2010-2015	51.4/49.7
Infant mortality rate (per 1 000 live births)	2010-2015	75.3
Fertility rate, total (live births per woman)	2010-2015	4.9
Contraceptive prevalence (ages 15-49, %)	2007-2013	18.2
International migrant stock (000 and % of total population)[k]	mid-2013	2 446.2/12.0
Refugees and others of concern to UNHCR	mid-2014	739 909
Education: Government expenditure (% of GDP)	2007-2013	4.6
Education: Primary-secondary gross enrolment ratio (f/m per 100)	2007-2013	60.3/74.6
Education: Female third-level students (% of total)	2007-2013	38.0
Intentional homicide rate (per 100,000 population)	2008-2012	13.6
Seats held by women in national parliaments (%)	2015	9.2

Environmental indicators		
Threatened species	2014	226
Forested area (% of land area)	2012	32.7
Proportion of terrestrial and marine areas protected (%)	2014	14.9
Population using improved drinking water sources (%)	2012	80.0
Population using improved sanitation facilities (%)	2012	22.0
CO$_2$ emission estimates (000 metric tons and metric tons per capita)	2011	6 447/0.3
Energy supply per capita (Gigajoules)	2012	27.0

a Yamoussoukro is the capital and Abidjan is the administrative capital. b Official rate. c Abidjan. d African population. e Series linked to former series. f ISIC Rev.3 (CDE). g Arrivals of non-resident visitors at national borders. h 2007. i 2012. j ITU estimate. k Refers to foreign-born and foreign citizens.

Croatia

Region	Southern Europe	Surface area (sq km)	56 594	
Population (est., 000)	4 272	Pop. density (per sq km)	75.6	
Capital city	Zagreb	Capital city pop. (000)	687 [a]	
Currency	Kuna (HRK)	UN membership date	22 May 1992	

Economic indicators	2005	2010	2013
GDP: Gross domestic product (million current US$)	45 416	59 665	57 869
GDP: Growth rate at constant 2005 prices (annual %)	4.2	−1.7	−0.9
GDP per capita (current US$)	10 348.1	13 754.0	13 490.2
GNI: Gross national income per capita (current US$)	9 996.0	13 190.2	13 017.1
Gross fixed capital formation (% of GDP)	25.4	21.3	19.3
Exchange rates (national currency per US$) [b]	6.23	5.57	5.55
Balance of payments, current account (million US$)	−2 460	−900	716
CPI: Consumer price index (2000=100)	114	133	144 [c]
Index of industrial production (2010=100) [d]	101	100	92
Agricultural production index (2004-2006=100)	98	100	96
Food production index (2004-2006=100)	98	100	96
Unemployment (% of labour force)	12.6	11.8	17.7
Employment in industrial sector (% of employed)	28.6 [ef]	27.3	27.4 [g]
Employment in agricultural sector (% of employed)	17.3 [ef]	14.9	13.7 [g]
Labour force participation, adult female pop. (%)	46.3	45.7	44.7
Labour force participation, adult male pop. (%)	61.3	59.1	58.4
Tourist arrivals at national borders (000) [hi]	7 743	9 111	10 955
Energy production, primary (Petajoules)	159	176	144 [g]
Mobile-cellular subscriptions (per 100 inhabitants)	83.2	113.6 [j]	114.5
Individuals using the Internet (%)	33.1	56.6	66.8

Total trade		Major trading partners			2013
	(million US$)		(% of exports)		(% of imports)
Exports	12 741.6	Italy	14.5	Germany	14.0
Imports	21 932.0	Bosnia-Herzegovina	12.3	Italy	13.1
Balance	−9 190.4	Germany	11.7	Slovenia	11.5

Social indicators		
Population growth rate (average annual %)	2010-2015	−0.4
Urban population growth rate (average annual %)	2010-2015	0.1
Rural population growth rate (average annual %)	2010-2015	−1.1
Urban population (%)	2014	58.7
Population aged 0-14 years (%)	2014	14.7
Population aged 60+ years (females and males, % of total)	2014	28.8/22.1
Sex ratio (males per 100 females)	2014	93.2
Life expectancy at birth (females and males, years)	2010-2015	80.3/73.6
Infant mortality rate (per 1 000 live births)	2010-2015	5.1
Fertility rate, total (live births per woman)	2010-2015	1.5
Contraceptive prevalence (ages 15-49, %) [k]	2007-2013	58.0 [l]
International migrant stock (000 and % of total population) [m]	mid-2013	757.0/17.7
Refugees and others of concern to UNHCR	mid-2014	19 752
Education: Government expenditure (% of GDP)	2007-2013	4.2
Education: Primary-secondary gross enrolment ratio (f/m per 100)	2007-2013	99.2/96.8
Education: Female third-level students (% of total)	2007-2013	56.7
Intentional homicide rate (per 100,000 population)	2008-2012	1.2
Seats held by women in national parliaments (%)	2015	25.8

Environmental indicators		
Threatened species	2014	158
Forested area (% of land area)	2012	34.4
Proportion of terrestrial and marine areas protected (%)	2014	23.7
Population using improved drinking water sources (%)	2012	99.0
Population using improved sanitation facilities (%)	2012	98.0
CO_2 emission estimates (000 metric tons and metric tons per capita)	2011	20 554/4.8
Energy supply per capita (Gigajoules)	2012	77.0

a Refers to the settlement of Zagreb. b Market rate. c Series linked to former series. d ISIC Rev.4 (BCD). e ISIC Rev.3. f Excluding conscripts. g 2012. h Arrivals of non-resident tourists in all types of accommodation establishments. i Excluding nautical ports. j ITU estimate. k Age group 15 to 44 years. l 1970. m Including refugees.

Cuba

Region	Caribbean	Surface area (sq km)	109 884
Population (est., 000)	11 259	Pop. density (per sq km)	101.6
Capital city	Havana	Capital city pop. (000)	2 146
Currency	Cuban Peso (CUP)[a]	UN membership date	24 October 1945

Economic indicators	2005	2010	2013
GDP: Gross domestic product (million current US$)	42 644	64 328	78 694
GDP: Growth rate at constant 2005 prices (annual %)	11.2	2.4	2.7
GDP per capita (current US$)	3 776.5	5 702.0	6 985.3
GNI: Gross national income per capita (current US$)	3 720.4	5 618.7	6 883.6
Gross fixed capital formation (% of GDP)	9.0	10.6	9.6
CPI: Consumer price index (2000=100)	109	125[b]	...
Agricultural production index (2004-2006=100)	97	88	100
Food production index (2004-2006=100)	97	88	101
Unemployment (% of labour force)	1.9	2.5	3.2
Employment in industrial sector (% of employed)[c]	19.1[de]	17.0[fg]	17.1[fh]
Employment in agricultural sector (% of employed)[c]	20.2[de]	18.5[fg]	19.7[fh]
Labour force participation, adult female pop. (%)	38.7	43.1	43.4
Labour force participation, adult male pop. (%)	67.2	70.1	70.0
Tourist arrivals at national borders (000)[i]	2 261	2 507	2 829
Energy production, primary (Petajoules)	205	200	206[j]
Mobile-cellular subscriptions (per 100 inhabitants)	1.2	8.9	17.7
Individuals using the Internet (%)	9.7[k]	15.9[k]	25.7[l]

Social indicators		
Population growth rate (average annual %)	2010-2015	−0.1
Urban population growth rate (average annual %)	2010-2015	0.1
Rural population growth rate (average annual %)	2010-2015	−0.5
Urban population (%)	2014	77.0
Population aged 0-14 years (%)	2014	15.9
Population aged 60+ years (females and males, % of total)	2014	20.2/17.9
Sex ratio (males per 100 females)	2014	101.0
Life expectancy at birth (females and males, years)	2010-2015	81.2/77.2
Infant mortality rate (per 1 000 live births)	2010-2015	4.5
Fertility rate, total (live births per woman)	2010-2015	1.5
Contraceptive prevalence (ages 15-49, %)	2007-2013	74.3
International migrant stock (000 and % of total population)	mid-2013	16.2/0.1
Refugees and others of concern to UNHCR	mid-2014	372
Education: Government expenditure (% of GDP)	2007-2013	12.8
Education: Primary-secondary gross enrolment ratio (f/m per 100)	2007-2013	94.4/95.0
Education: Female third-level students (% of total)	2007-2013	60.9
Intentional homicide rate (per 100,000 population)	2008-2012	4.2
Seats held by women in national parliaments (%)	2015	48.9

Environmental indicators		
Threatened species	2014	332
Forested area (% of land area)	2012	27.6
Proportion of terrestrial and marine areas protected (%)	2014	5.0
Population using improved drinking water sources (%)	2012	94.0
Population using improved sanitation facilities (%)	2012	93.0
CO_2 emission estimates (000 metric tons and metric tons per capita)	2011	35 922/3.2
Energy supply per capita (Gigajoules)	2012	48.0

a The national currency of Cuba is the Cuban Peso (CUP). The convertible peso (CUC) is used by foreigners and tourists in Cuba. **b** 2008. **c** ISIC Rev.2. **d** Population aged 17-60. **e** December. **f** Population aged 17-59. **g** Break in series. **h** 2011. **i** Arrivals by air. **j** 2012. **k** Including users of the international network and also those having access only to the Cuban network. **l** Population aged 6 and over.

Curaçao

Region	Caribbean	Surface area (sq km)	444
Population (est., 000)	162	Pop. density (per sq km)	364.5
Capital city	Willemstad	Capital city pop. (000)	145 [a]

Economic indicators	2005	2010	2013
GDP: Gross domestic product (million current US$)	2 345	2 951	3 148
GDP: Growth rate at constant 2005 prices (annual %)	4.1	2.8	1.3
GDP per capita (current US$)	18 119.6	20 001.0	19 830.4
GNI: Gross national income per capita (current US$)	18 420.5	19 928.7	19 758.7
Gross fixed capital formation (% of GDP)	34.4	38.5	35.2
Balance of payments, current account (million US$)	...	−830 [b]	−663
CPI: Consumer price index (2000=100)	110	130	139
Tourist arrivals at national borders (000) [c]	222	342	441

Social indicators		
Population growth rate (average annual %)	2010-2015	2.2
Urban population growth rate (average annual %)	2010-2015	2.0
Rural population growth rate (average annual %)	2010-2015	3.3
Urban population (%)	2014	89.4
Population aged 0-14 years (%)	2014	19.2
Population aged 60+ years (females and males, % of total)	2014	21.5/19.4
Sex ratio (males per 100 females)	2014	82.4
Life expectancy at birth (females and males, years)	2010-2015	80.1/73.6
Infant mortality rate (per 1 000 live births)	2010-2015	11.2
Fertility rate, total (live births per woman)	2010-2015	1.9
International migrant stock (000 and % of total population)	mid-2013	36.9/23.2
Refugees and others of concern to UNHCR	mid-2014	68

Environmental indicators		
Threatened species	2014	42

a Total population of Curaçao excluding some neighborhoods (see source). b 2011. c Arrivals by air.

Cyprus[a]

Region	Western Asia	Surface area (sq km)	9 251
Population (est., 000)	1 153[b]	Pop. density (per sq km)	124.6[b]
Capital city	Nicosia	Capital city pop. (000)	251
Currency	Euro (EUR)	UN membership date	20 September 1960

Economic indicators

	2005	2010	2013
GDP: Gross domestic product (million current US$)	18 528	25 247	24 057
GDP: Growth rate at constant 2005 prices (annual %)	3.9	1.4	−5.4
GDP per capita (current US$)	24 443.7	31 410.4	27 662.5
GNI: Gross national income per capita (current US$)	23 161.4	30 234.5	26 814.5
Gross fixed capital formation (% of GDP)	21.6	21.8	13.4
Exchange rates (national currency per US$)	0.48[cd]	0.75[ef]	0.73[ef]
Balance of payments, current account (million US$)	−971	−2 309	−423
CPI: Consumer price index (2000=100)	115	129	136
Index of industrial production (2010=100)[gh]	100	100	73
Agricultural production index (2004-2006=100)	98	83	81
Food production index (2004-2006=100)	98	84	81
Unemployment (% of labour force)	5.3	6.3	15.8
Employment in industrial sector (% of employed)	24.1[i]	20.4[j]	20.2[k]
Employment in agricultural sector (% of employed)	4.6[i]	3.8[j]	2.9[k]
Labour force participation, adult female pop. (%)	53.6	57.1	56.0
Labour force participation, adult male pop. (%)	73.1	71.3	71.1
Tourist arrivals at national borders (000)	2 470	2 173	2 405
Energy production, primary (Petajoules)	0	4	4[k]
Mobile-cellular subscriptions (per 100 inhabitants)	75.8	93.7	95.2
Individuals using the Internet (%)	32.8	53.0	65.5

Total trade

Total trade		Major trading partners			2013
	(million US$)	(% of exports)			(% of imports)
Exports	2 134.4	Greece	16.6	Greece	23.2
Imports	6 418.2	Bunkers	15.8[l]	Israel	13.5
Balance	−4 283.8	United Kingdom	13.0	Italy	7.0

Social indicators

Population growth rate (average annual %)[b]	2010-2015	1.1
Urban population growth rate (average annual %)	2010-2015	0.9
Rural population growth rate (average annual %)	2010-2015	1.5
Urban population (%)	2014	67.0
Population aged 0-14 years (%)[b]	2014	16.8
Population aged 60+ years (females and males, % of total)[b]	2014	19.2/16.0
Sex ratio (males per 100 females)[b]	2014	104.3
Life expectancy at birth (females and males, years)[b]	2010-2015	81.8/77.8
Infant mortality rate (per 1 000 live births)[b]	2010-2015	3.7
Fertility rate, total (live births per woman)[b]	2010-2015	1.5
International migrant stock (000 and % of total population)[b]	mid-2013	207.3/18.2
Refugees and others of concern to UNHCR	mid-2014	7 111
Education: Government expenditure (% of GDP)	2007-2013	7.2
Education: Primary-secondary gross enrolment ratio (f/m per 100)[m]	2007-2013	97.9/97.1
Education: Female third-level students (% of total)	2007-2013	53.1
Intentional homicide rate (per 100,000 population)	2008-2012	2.0
Seats held by women in national parliaments (%)	2015	12.5

Environmental indicators

Threatened species	2014	58
Forested area (% of land area)	2012	18.8
Proportion of terrestrial and marine areas protected (%)	2014	2.0
Population using improved drinking water sources (%)	2012	100.0
Population using improved sanitation facilities (%)	2012	100.0
CO_2 emission estimates (000 metric tons and metric tons per capita)	2011	7 521/6.8
Energy supply per capita (Gigajoules)	2012	83.0

a Data generally refer to the government-controlled area unless otherwise indicated. b Including Northern Cyprus. c Official rate. d Cyprus Pound (CYP). e Market rate. f Euro. g ISIC Rev.4 (BCDE). h For government controlled areas. i ISIC Rev.3. j Break in series. k 2012. l See technical notes. m National estimate.

Czech Republic

Region	Eastern Europe	Surface area (sq km)	78 866	
Population (est., 000)	10 740	Pop. density (per sq km)	136.2	
Capital city	Prague	Capital city pop. (000)	1 303	
Currency	Czech Koruna (CZK)	UN membership date	19 January 1993	

Economic indicators	2005	2010	2013
GDP: Gross domestic product (million current US$)	135 990	207 016	208 796
GDP: Growth rate at constant 2005 prices (annual %)	6.4	2.3	−0.7
GDP per capita (current US$)	13 292.4	19 615.5	19 509.6
GNI: Gross national income per capita (current US$)	12 732.1	18 141.2	18 217.6
Gross fixed capital formation (% of GDP)	28.4	27.1	25.1
Exchange rates (national currency per US$)[a]	24.59	18.75	19.89
Balance of payments, current account (million US$)	−1 210	−7 602	−2 853
CPI: Consumer price index (2000=100)	112	129	137
Index of industrial production (2010=100)[b]	91	100	105
Agricultural production index (2004-2006=100)	100	91	93
Food production index (2004-2006=100)	100	91	93
Unemployment (% of labour force)	7.9	7.3	6.9
Employment in industrial sector (% of employed)	39.5[c]	38.0	38.1[de]
Employment in agricultural sector (% of employed)	4.0[c]	3.1	3.1[de]
Labour force participation, adult female pop. (%)	50.6	49.2	51.1
Labour force participation, adult male pop. (%)	68.7	68.0	68.3
Tourist arrivals at national borders (000)	9 404	8 185	9 004
Energy production, primary (Petajoules)	1 374	1 342	1 357[d]
Mobile-cellular subscriptions (per 100 inhabitants)	115.1	122.6	131.3[f]
Individuals using the Internet (%)	35.3	68.8	74.1

Total trade		Major trading partners			2013
	(million US$)		(% of exports)		(% of imports)
Exports	161 524.2	Germany	31.3	Germany	25.9
Imports	142 525.8	Slovakia	8.9	China	10.9
Balance	18 998.4	Poland	6.0	Poland	7.5

Social indicators		
Population growth rate (average annual %)	2010-2015	0.4
Urban population growth rate (average annual %)	2010-2015	0.4
Rural population growth rate (average annual %)	2010-2015	0.6
Urban population (%)	2014	73.0
Population aged 0-14 years (%)	2014	15.1
Population aged 60+ years (females and males, % of total)	2014	26.9/21.0
Sex ratio (males per 100 females)	2014	97.0
Life expectancy at birth (females and males, years)	2010-2015	80.6/74.5
Infant mortality rate (per 1 000 live births)	2010-2015	2.6
Fertility rate, total (live births per woman)	2010-2015	1.6
Contraceptive prevalence (ages 15-49, %)[g]	2007-2013	86.3
International migrant stock (000 and % of total population)[h]	mid-2013	432.8/4.0
Refugees and others of concern to UNHCR	mid-2014	4 856[i]
Education: Government expenditure (% of GDP)	2007-2013	4.5
Education: Primary-secondary gross enrolment ratio (f/m per 100)	2007-2013	98.1/97.8
Education: Female third-level students (% of total)	2007-2013	57.3
Intentional homicide rate (per 100,000 population)	2008-2012	1.0
Seats held by women in national parliaments (%)	2015	19.0

Environmental indicators		
Threatened species	2014	46
Forested area (% of land area)	2012	34.5
Proportion of terrestrial and marine areas protected (%)	2014	21.1
Population using improved drinking water sources (%)	2012	100.0
Population using improved sanitation facilities (%)	2012	100.0
CO$_2$ emission estimates (000 metric tons and metric tons per capita)	2011	109 486/10.3
Energy supply per capita (Gigajoules)	2012	167.0

a Official rate. b ISIC Rev.4 (BCD). c ISIC Rev.3. d 2012. e Break in series. f Estimate. g Age group 18 to 49 years. h Refers to foreign citizens. i Refugee population refers to the end of 2013.

Democratic People's Republic of Korea

Region	Eastern Asia	Surface area (sq km)		120 538
Population (est., 000)	25 027	Pop. density (per sq km)		207.6
Capital city	P'yongyang	Capital city pop. (000)		2 856
Currency	North Korean Won (KPW)	UN membership date		17 September 1991

Economic indicators	2005	2010	2013
GDP: Gross domestic product (million current US$)	13 031	13 945	15 454
GDP: Growth rate at constant 2005 prices (annual %)	3.8	−0.5	0.8
GDP per capita (current US$)	547.9	569.8	621.5
GNI: Gross national income per capita (current US$)	546.6	570.4	622.3
Exchange rates (national currency per US$)[a]	141.00	98.10[b]	97.79
Agricultural production index (2004-2006=100)	101	98	103
Food production index (2004-2006=100)	101	98	102
Unemployment (% of labour force)	4.6	4.5	4.6
Labour force participation, adult female pop. (%)	73.5	72.5	72.2
Labour force participation, adult male pop. (%)	86.1	84.3	84.2
Energy production, primary (Petajoules)	923	872	848[c]
Mobile-cellular subscriptions (per 100 inhabitants)	...	1.8	9.7[d]

Social indicators		
Population growth rate (average annual %)	2010-2015	0.5
Urban population growth rate (average annual %)	2010-2015	0.8
Rural population growth rate (average annual %)	2010-2015	0.2
Urban population (%)	2014	60.7
Population aged 0-14 years (%)	2014	21.4
Population aged 60+ years (females and males, % of total)	2014	15.1/9.6
Sex ratio (males per 100 females)	2014	95.6
Life expectancy at birth (females and males, years)	2010-2015	73.3/66.3
Infant mortality rate (per 1 000 live births)	2010-2015	22.0
Fertility rate, total (live births per woman)	2010-2015	2.0
Contraceptive prevalence (ages 15-49, %)[e]	2007-2013	70.6
International migrant stock (000 and % of total population)[f]	mid-2013	46.8/0.2
Seats held by women in national parliaments (%)	2015	16.3

Environmental indicators		
Threatened species	2014	63
Forested area (% of land area)	2012	45.0
Proportion of terrestrial and marine areas protected (%)	2014	1.3
Population using improved drinking water sources (%)	2012	98.0
Population using improved sanitation facilities (%)	2012	82.0
CO_2 emission estimates (000 metric tons and metric tons per capita)	2011	73 578/3.0
Energy supply per capita (Gigajoules)	2012	24.0

a UN operational exchange rate. b December 2010. c 2012. d ITU estimate. e Age group 20 to 49 years. f Estimate.

Democratic Republic of the Congo

Region	Middle Africa	Surface area (sq km)	2 344 858
Population (est., 000)	69 360	Pop. density (per sq km)	29.6
Capital city	Kinshasa	Capital city pop. (000)	11 116
Currency	Congo Franc (CDF)	UN membership date	20 September 1960

Economic indicators	2005	2010	2013
GDP: Gross domestic product (million current US$)	11 965	21 562	32 691
GDP: Growth rate at constant 2005 prices (annual %)	6.1	7.1	8.5
GDP per capita (current US$)	221.5	346.7	484.2
GNI: Gross national income per capita (current US$)	220.4	327.6	439.8
Gross fixed capital formation (% of GDP)	11.7	20.6	20.6
Exchange rates (national currency per US$) [a]	431.28	915.13	925.50
Balance of payments, current account (million US$)	−389	−2 174	−2 863
Agricultural production index (2004-2006=100)	100	106	117
Food production index (2004-2006=100)	100	107	117
Labour force participation, adult female pop. (%)	71.0	70.7	70.7
Labour force participation, adult male pop. (%)	73.1	73.1	73.2
Tourist arrivals at national borders (000)	61	81[b]	191[c]
Energy production, primary (Petajoules)	866	855	877[d]
Mobile-cellular subscriptions (per 100 inhabitants)	5.1[e]	19.0	43.7
Individuals using the Internet (%)	0.2[f]	0.7[g]	2.2[f]

Social indicators		
Population growth rate (average annual %)	2010-2015	2.7
Urban population growth rate (average annual %)	2010-2015	4.0
Rural population growth rate (average annual %)	2010-2015	1.9
Urban population (%)	2014	42.0
Population aged 0-14 years (%)	2014	44.8
Population aged 60+ years (females and males, % of total)	2014	4.9/4.1
Sex ratio (males per 100 females)	2014	98.7
Life expectancy at birth (females and males, years)	2010-2015	51.6/48.1
Infant mortality rate (per 1 000 live births)	2010-2015	108.6
Fertility rate, total (live births per woman)	2010-2015	6.0
Contraceptive prevalence (ages 15-49, %)	2007-2013	17.7
International migrant stock (000 and % of total population)[h]	mid-2013	446.9/0.7
Refugees and others of concern to UNHCR	mid-2014	3 045 232
Education: Government expenditure (% of GDP)	2007-2013	1.6
Education: Primary-secondary gross enrolment ratio (f/m per 100)	2007-2013	71.2/89.3
Education: Female third-level students (% of total)	2007-2013	35.4
Intentional homicide rate (per 100,000 population)	2008-2012	28.3
Seats held by women in national parliaments (%)	2015	8.9

Environmental indicators		
Threatened species	2014	332
Forested area (% of land area)	2012	67.7
Proportion of terrestrial and marine areas protected (%)	2014	12.1
Population using improved drinking water sources (%)	2012	46.0
Population using improved sanitation facilities (%)	2012	31.0
CO_2 emission estimates (000 metric tons and metric tons per capita)	2011	3 425/0.0
Energy supply per capita (Gigajoules)	2012	13.0

a Market rate. b Arrivals by air only. c Including only three border posts. d 2012. e Including inactive subscriptions. f ITU estimate. g Country estimate. h Including refugees.

Denmark

Region	Northern Europe	Surface area (sq km)	43 094 [a]	
Population (est., 000)	5 640	Pop. density (per sq km)	130.9	
Capital city	Copenhagen	Capital city pop. (000)	1 255 [b]	
Currency	Danish Krone (DKK)	UN membership date	24 October 1945	

Economic indicators	2005	2010	2013
GDP: Gross domestic product (million current US$)	264 559	319 812	336 701
GDP: Growth rate at constant 2005 prices (annual %)	2.4	1.6	−0.1
GDP per capita (current US$)	48 832.4	57 613.9	59 920.9
GNI: Gross national income per capita (current US$)	49 203.8	58 562.7	61 840.6
Gross fixed capital formation (% of GDP)	21.2	18.4	18.5
Exchange rates (national currency per US$) [c]	6.32	5.61	5.41
Balance of payments, current account (million US$)	11 104	18 183	23 911
CPI: Consumer price index (2000=100)	110	122	130
Index of industrial production (2010=100) [d]	116	100	103
Agricultural production index (2004-2006=100)	101	101	100
Food production index (2004-2006=100)	101	101	100
Unemployment (% of labour force)	4.8	7.5	7.0
Employment in industrial sector (% of employed) [e]	23.4 [f]	19.6	19.7 [g]
Employment in agricultural sector (% of employed) [e]	2.8 [f]	2.4	2.6 [g]
Labour force participation, adult female pop. (%)	60.5	59.8	58.7
Labour force participation, adult male pop. (%)	71.4	69.1	66.4
Tourist arrivals at national borders (000) [h]	9 178 [i]	8 744	8 557 [i]
Energy production, primary (Petajoules) [a]	1 298	968	787 [g]
Mobile-cellular subscriptions (per 100 inhabitants)	100.6	115.7 [i]	127.5
Individuals using the Internet (%)	82.7	88.7	94.6

Total trade		Major trading partners				2013
	(million US$) [a]	(% of exports) [a]			(% of imports) [a]	
Exports	110 416.1	Germany	15.3	Germany	20.5	
Imports	97 589.9	Sweden	11.7	Sweden	12.3	
Balance	12 826.2	Areas nes	9.6 [k]	Netherlands	7.4	

Social indicators		
Population growth rate (average annual %)	2010-2015	0.4
Urban population growth rate (average annual %)	2010-2015	0.6
Rural population growth rate (average annual %)	2010-2015	−1.0
Urban population (%)	2014	87.5
Population aged 0-14 years (%)	2014	17.4
Population aged 60+ years (females and males, % of total)	2014	25.9/22.8
Sex ratio (males per 100 females)	2014	98.5
Life expectancy at birth (females and males, years)	2010-2015	81.4/77.2
Infant mortality rate (per 1 000 live births)	2010-2015	3.4
Fertility rate, total (live births per woman)	2010-2015	1.9
Contraceptive prevalence (ages 15-49, %)	2007-2013	76.5 [i]
International migrant stock (000 and % of total population)	mid-2013	556.8/9.9
Refugees and others of concern to UNHCR	mid-2014	20 098 [m]
Education: Government expenditure (% of GDP)	2007-2013	8.8
Education: Primary-secondary gross enrolment ratio (f/m per 100)	2007-2013	112.4/112.4
Education: Female third-level students (% of total)	2007-2013	57.4
Intentional homicide rate (per 100,000 population)	2008-2012	0.8
Seats held by women in national parliaments (%)	2015	38.0

Environmental indicators		
Threatened species	2014	36
Forested area (% of land area)	2012	12.9
Proportion of terrestrial and marine areas protected (%)	2014	18.0
Population using improved drinking water sources (%)	2012	100.0
Population using improved sanitation facilities (%)	2012	100.0
CO_2 emission estimates (000 metric tons and metric tons per capita)	2011	40 377/7.3
Energy supply per capita (Gigajoules) [a]	2012	129.0

a Excluding Faeroe Islands and Greenland. **b** Refers to the Greater Copenhagen Region, consisting of (parts of) 16 municipalities. **c** Market rate. **d** ISIC Rev.4 (BCD). **e** Population aged 15-74. **f** ISIC Rev.3. **g** 2012. **h** Arrivals of non-resident tourists in all types of accommodation establishments. **i** Methodology revised. **j** Break in comparability. **k** See technical notes. **l** 1991-1993. **m** Refugee population refers to the end of 2013.

Djibouti

Region	Eastern Africa	Surface area (sq km)	23 200	
Population (est., 000)	886	Pop. density (per sq km)	38.2	
Capital city	Djibouti	Capital city pop. (000)	522[a]	
Currency	Djibouti Franc (DJF)	UN membership date	20 September 1977	

Economic indicators	2005	2010	2013
GDP: Gross domestic product (million current US$)	709	1 129	1 456
GDP: Growth rate at constant 2005 prices (annual %)	3.2	4.5	5.0
GDP per capita (current US$)	912.5	1 353.2	1 667.7
GNI: Gross national income per capita (current US$)	999.0	1 444.8	1 780.6
Gross fixed capital formation (% of GDP)	16.6	17.5	18.3
Exchange rates (national currency per US$)[b]	177.72	177.72	177.72
Balance of payments, current account (million US$)	20	50	−309
Agricultural production index (2004-2006=100)	95	119	134
Food production index (2004-2006=100)	95	119	134
Labour force participation, adult female pop. (%)	33.3	35.6	36.3
Labour force participation, adult male pop. (%)	66.1	66.7	67.7
Tourist arrivals at national borders (000)[c]	30	51	63
Energy production, primary (Petajoules)	3	3	3[d]
Mobile-cellular subscriptions (per 100 inhabitants)	5.7	19.9	28.0
Individuals using the Internet (%)	1.0	6.5[e]	9.5[e]

Social indicators		
Population growth rate (average annual %)	2010-2015	1.5
Urban population growth rate (average annual %)	2010-2015	1.6
Rural population growth rate (average annual %)	2010-2015	1.2
Urban population (%)	2014	77.3
Population aged 0-14 years (%)	2014	33.6
Population aged 60+ years (females and males, % of total)	2014	6.5/5.7
Sex ratio (males per 100 females)	2014	100.9
Life expectancy at birth (females and males, years)	2010-2015	63.2/60.0
Infant mortality rate (per 1 000 live births)	2010-2015	55.3
Fertility rate, total (live births per woman)	2010-2015	3.4
Contraceptive prevalence (ages 15-49, %)	2007-2013	19.0
International migrant stock (000 and % of total population)[f]	mid-2013	123.5/14.2
Refugees and others of concern to UNHCR	mid-2014	24 509
Education: Government expenditure (% of GDP)	2007-2013	4.5
Education: Primary-secondary gross enrolment ratio (f/m per 100)	2007-2013	51.6/61.3
Education: Female third-level students (% of total)	2007-2013	39.9
Intentional homicide rate (per 100,000 population)	2008-2012	10.1
Seats held by women in national parliaments (%)	2015	12.7

Environmental indicators		
Threatened species	2014	94
Forested area (% of land area)	2012	<
Proportion of terrestrial and marine areas protected (%)	2014	1.1
Population using improved drinking water sources (%)	2012	92.0
Population using improved sanitation facilities (%)	2012	61.0
CO_2 emission estimates (000 metric tons and metric tons per capita)	2011	473/0.6
Energy supply per capita (Gigajoules)	2012	13.0[g]

a Refers to the population of the 'cercle'. **b** Official rate. **c** Arrivals of non-resident tourists in hotels and similar establishments. **d** 2012. **e** ITU estimate. **f** Including refugees. **g** UNSD estimate.

Dominica

Region	Caribbean	Surface area (sq km)	751	
Population (est., 000)	72	Pop. density (per sq km)	96.3	
Capital city	Roseau	Capital city pop. (000)	15	
Currency	E.C. Dollar (XCD)	UN membership date	18 December 1978	

Economic indicators	2005	2010	2013
GDP: Gross domestic product (million current US$)	356	475	498
GDP: Growth rate at constant 2005 prices (annual %)	-0.3	1.2	-0.9
GDP per capita (current US$)	5 049.4	6 676.5	6 915.4
GNI: Gross national income per capita (current US$)	4 638.6	6 543.8	6 727.9
Gross fixed capital formation (% of GDP)	20.6	21.4	12.0
Exchange rates (national currency per US$)[a]	2.70	2.70	2.70
Balance of payments, current account (million US$)	-76	-80	-72
CPI: Consumer price index (2000=100)[b]	106	122[c]	126
Agricultural production index (2004-2006=100)	95	111	113
Food production index (2004-2006=100)	95	112	114
Tourist arrivals at national borders (000)	79	77	78
Energy production, primary (Petajoules)	0	0	0[d]
Mobile-cellular subscriptions (per 100 inhabitants)	73.7	148.3[e]	130.0
Individuals using the Internet (%)	38.5[f]	47.5	59.0[f]

Total trade		Major trading partners			2013
	(million US$)[d]	(% of exports)[d]		(% of imports)[d]	
Exports	37.0	Trinidad and Tobago	18.6	United States	36.8
Imports	211.9	Jamaica	16.2	Trinidad and Tobago	17.0
Balance	-174.9	Saint Kitts and Nevis	14.3	Areas nes	8.6[g]

Social indicators		
Population growth rate (average annual %)	2010-2015	0.4
Urban population growth rate (average annual %)	2010-2015	0.8
Rural population growth rate (average annual %)	2010-2015	-0.5
Urban population (%)	2014	69.3
Population aged 0-14 years (%)[hij]	2014	29.5[k]
Population aged 60+ years (females and males, % of total)[hij]	2014	15.1/11.7[k]
Sex ratio (males per 100 females)[hij]	2014	103.7[k]
Life expectancy at birth (females and males, years)[h]	2010-2015	78.2/73.8[l]
Contraceptive prevalence (ages 15-49, %)[m]	2007-2013	49.8[n]
International migrant stock (000 and % of total population)	mid-2013	6.4/8.9
Refugees and others of concern to UNHCR	mid-2014	0[o]
Education: Government expenditure (% of GDP)[p]	2007-2013	5.0[q]
Education: Primary-secondary gross enrolment ratio (f/m per 100)	2007-2013	107.0/104.3
Intentional homicide rate (per 100,000 population)	2008-2012	21.1
Seats held by women in national parliaments (%)	2015	21.9

Environmental indicators		
Threatened species	2014	55
Forested area (% of land area)	2012	58.8
Proportion of terrestrial and marine areas protected (%)	2014	0.6
CO$_2$ emission estimates (000 metric tons and metric tons per capita)	2011	125/1.8
Energy supply per capita (Gigajoules)	2012	29.0[r]

a Official rate. b Index base 2001=100. c Series linked to former series. d 2012. e Estimate. f ITU estimate.
g See technical notes. h Data compiled by the United Nations Demographic Yearbook system. i Data refer
to the latest available census. j De facto estimate. k 2006. l 2008. m Age group 15 to 44 years. n 1987.
o Value is zero, not available or not applicable. p UNESCO estimate. q 1999. r UNSD estimate.

Dominican Republic

Region	Caribbean	Surface area (sq km)	48 192
Population (est., 000)	10 529	Pop. density (per sq km)	217.0
Capital city	Santo Domingo	Capital city pop. (000)	2 873
Currency	Dominican Peso (DOP)	UN membership date	24 October 1945

Economic indicators	2005	2010	2013
GDP: Gross domestic product (million current US$)	33 431	50 980	60 612
GDP: Growth rate at constant 2005 prices (annual %)	9.3	7.8	4.1
GDP per capita (current US$)	3 578.1	5 089.5	5 826.0
GNI: Gross national income per capita (current US$)	3 377.9	4 923.6	5 556.1
Gross fixed capital formation (% of GDP)	16.4	16.3	14.4
Exchange rates (national currency per US$)[a]	34.88	37.93	42.85
Balance of payments, current account (million US$)	−473	−4 006	−2 467
CPI: Consumer price index (2000=100)	230	314	370
Index of industrial production (2010=100)[b]	88	100	113
Agricultural production index (2004-2006=100)	99	128	133
Food production index (2004-2006=100)	99	130	136
Unemployment (% of labour force)	18.0	12.4	14.9
Employment in industrial sector (% of employed)[c]	22.3[d]	14.9[d]	17.8[efg]
Employment in agricultural sector (% of employed)[c]	14.6[d]	12.0[d]	14.5[efg]
Labour force participation, adult female pop. (%)	49.0	51.0	51.3
Labour force participation, adult male pop. (%)	80.5	78.9	78.6
Tourist arrivals at national borders (000)[hi]	3 691	4 125	4 690
Energy production, primary (Petajoules)	24	36	38[j]
Mobile-cellular subscriptions (per 100 inhabitants)	38.8	88.8	88.4
Individuals using the Internet (%)	11.5	31.4[k]	45.9[l]

Total trade		Major trading partners			2013
	(million US$)	(% of exports)			(% of imports)
Exports	7 961.0	United States	51.1	United States	38.2
Imports	17 845.0	Haiti	13.1	China	10.5
Balance	−9 884.0	Canada	12.2	Venezuela	7.1

Social indicators		
Population growth rate (average annual %)	2010-2015	1.2
Urban population growth rate (average annual %)	2010-2015	2.6
Rural population growth rate (average annual %)	2010-2015	−3.2
Urban population (%)	2014	78.1
Population aged 0-14 years (%)	2014	29.9
Population aged 60+ years (females and males, % of total)	2014	9.7/9.1
Sex ratio (males per 100 females)	2014	100.0
Life expectancy at birth (females and males, years)	2010-2015	76.6/70.3
Infant mortality rate (per 1 000 live births)	2010-2015	25.6
Fertility rate, total (live births per woman)	2010-2015	2.5
Contraceptive prevalence (ages 15-49, %)	2007-2013	73.0
International migrant stock (000 and % of total population)	mid-2013	402.5/3.9
Refugees and others of concern to UNHCR	mid-2014	211 434[m]
Education: Government expenditure (% of GDP)	2007-2013	3.8
Education: Primary-secondary gross enrolment ratio (f/m per 100)	2007-2013	89.0/90.1
Education: Female third-level students (% of total)	2007-2013	61.3
Intentional homicide rate (per 100,000 population)	2008-2012	22.1
Seats held by women in national parliaments (%)	2015	20.8

Environmental indicators		
Threatened species	2014	147
Forested area (% of land area)	2012	40.8
Proportion of terrestrial and marine areas protected (%)	2014	11.2
Population using improved drinking water sources (%)	2012	81.0
Population using improved sanitation facilities (%)	2012	82.0
CO_2 emission estimates (000 metric tons and metric tons per capita)	2011	21 888/2.2
Energy supply per capita (Gigajoules)	2012	32.0

a Principal rate. b ISIC Rev.3 (CDE). c ISIC Rev.2. d Population aged 10 and over. e 2011. f April to June. g Break in series. h Arrivals by air. i Including nationals residing abroad. j 2012. k ITU estimate. l Population aged 12 and over. m Including an estimated number of individuals resident in the country who belong to the first generation born on Dominican territory to Haitian migrant parents. No population data is currently available on subsequent generations born in the Dominican Republic.

Ecuador

Region	South America	Surface area (sq km)	257 217
Population (est., 000)	15 983	Pop. density (per sq km)	56.4
Capital city	Quito	Capital city pop. (000)	1 699
Currency	U.S. Dollar (USD)	UN membership date	21 December 1945

Economic indicators	2005	2010	2013
GDP: Gross domestic product (million current US$)	41 507	69 555	94 473
GDP: Growth rate at constant 2005 prices (annual %)	5.3	3.5	4.6
GDP per capita (current US$)	3 012.8	4 636.7	6 002.9
GNI: Gross national income per capita (current US$)	2 863.0	4 571.0	5 810.4
Gross fixed capital formation (% of GDP)	20.4	24.6	27.9
Balance of payments, current account (million US$)	474	−1 607	−1 290
CPI: Consumer price index (2000=100)	175[a]	219	247
Agricultural production index (2004-2006=100)	98	121	116
Food production index (2004-2006=100)	98	123	117
Unemployment (% of labour force)	6.6	5.0	4.2
Employment in industrial sector (% of employed)[bc]	17.2[d]	18.6	17.8[e]
Employment in agricultural sector (% of employed)[bc]	31.5[d]	28.2	27.8[e]
Labour force participation, adult female pop. (%)	55.3	53.7	54.7
Labour force participation, adult male pop. (%)	84.7	82.5	82.7
Tourist arrivals at national borders (000)[fg]	860	1 047	1 364
Energy production, primary (Petajoules)	1 281	1 185	1 245[e]
Mobile-cellular subscriptions (per 100 inhabitants)	45.3	98.5	111.5
Individuals using the Internet (%)	6.0[h]	29.0[i]	40.4[i]

Total trade		Major trading partners			2013
	(million US$)	(% of exports)			(% of imports)
Exports	24 957.6	United States	44.6	United States	25.2
Imports	27 064.5	Chile	9.9	China	16.7
Balance	−2 106.9	Peru	7.5	Colombia	8.0

Social indicators		
Population growth rate (average annual %)	2010-2015	1.6
Urban population growth rate (average annual %)	2010-2015	1.9
Rural population growth rate (average annual %)	2010-2015	1.0
Urban population (%)	2014	63.5
Population aged 0-14 years (%)	2014	29.6
Population aged 60+ years (females and males, % of total)	2014	10.3/9.2
Sex ratio (males per 100 females)	2014	99.9
Life expectancy at birth (females and males, years)	2010-2015	79.3/73.6
Infant mortality rate (per 1 000 live births)	2010-2015	17.0
Fertility rate, total (live births per woman)	2010-2015	2.6
Contraceptive prevalence (ages 15-49, %)	2007-2013	72.7[j]
International migrant stock (000 and % of total population)[k]	mid-2013	359.3/2.3
Refugees and others of concern to UNHCR	mid-2014	134 716[l]
Education: Government expenditure (% of GDP)	2007-2013	4.4
Education: Primary-secondary gross enrolment ratio (f/m per 100)	2007-2013	109.3/106.7
Education: Female third-level students (% of total)	2007-2013	56.0
Intentional homicide rate (per 100,000 population)	2008-2012	12.4
Seats held by women in national parliaments (%)	2015	41.6

Environmental indicators		
Threatened species	2014	2 299
Forested area (% of land area)	2012	38.1
Proportion of terrestrial and marine areas protected (%)	2014	15.4
Population using improved drinking water sources (%)	2012	86.0
Population using improved sanitation facilities (%)	2012	83.0
CO_2 emission estimates (000 metric tons and metric tons per capita)	2011	35 728/2.4
Energy supply per capita (Gigajoules)	2012	41.0

a Series linked to former series. b Population aged 10 and over. c ISIC Rev.2. d Fourth quarter. e 2012. f Arrivals of non-resident visitors at national borders. g Excluding nationals residing abroad. h ITU estimate. i Population aged 5 and over. j 2004. k Including refugees. l Refers to the end of 2013.

Egypt

Region	Northern Africa	Surface area (sq km)	1 002 000
Population (est., 000)	83 387	Pop. density (per sq km)	83.3
Capital city	Cairo	Capital city pop. (000)	18 419
Currency	Egyptian Pound (EGP)	UN membership date	24 October 1945

Economic indicators	2005	2010	2013
GDP: Gross domestic product (million current US$)	94 456	214 630	255 199
GDP: Growth rate at constant 2005 prices (annual %)	4.5	5.1	2.1
GDP per capita (current US$)	1 316.0	2 749.0	3 110.0
GNI: Gross national income per capita (current US$)	1 301.9	2 734.5	3 079.1
Gross fixed capital formation (% of GDP)	16.9	19.2	13.8
Exchange rates (national currency per US$)[a]	5.73	5.79	6.94
Balance of payments, current account (million US$)	2 103	−4 504	−6 972[b]
CPI: Consumer price index (2000=100)	134	232[c]	299
Agricultural production index (2004-2006=100)	99	109	118
Food production index (2004-2006=100)	99	110	120
Unemployment (% of labour force)	11.2	9.0	12.7
Employment in industrial sector (% of employed)	21.5[def]	25.3[g]	23.5[h]
Employment in agricultural sector (% of employed)	30.9[def]	28.2[g]	29.2[h]
Labour force participation, adult female pop. (%)	20.2	23.3	23.7
Labour force participation, adult male pop. (%)	75.5	74.1	74.8
Tourist arrivals at national borders (000)	8 244	14 051	9 174
Energy production, primary (Petajoules)	3 383	3 694	3 670[b]
Mobile-cellular subscriptions (per 100 inhabitants)	19.0	90.5	121.5
Individuals using the Internet (%)	12.8	31.4	49.6[i]

Total trade		Major trading partners			2013
	(million US$)		(% of exports)		(% of imports)
Exports	28 779.4	Italy	9.4	China	10.5
Imports	66 666.4	India	7.4	Germany	7.9
Balance	−37 887.0	Saudi Arabia	6.9	United States	7.8

Social indicators

Population growth rate (average annual %)	2010-2015	1.6
Urban population growth rate (average annual %)	2010-2015	1.7
Rural population growth rate (average annual %)	2010-2015	1.6
Urban population (%)	2014	43.1
Population aged 0-14 years (%)	2014	31.0
Population aged 60+ years (females and males, % of total)	2014	9.7/7.8
Sex ratio (males per 100 females)	2014	100.9
Life expectancy at birth (females and males, years)	2010-2015	73.5/68.7
Infant mortality rate (per 1 000 live births)	2010-2015	18.9
Fertility rate, total (live births per woman)	2010-2015	2.8
Contraceptive prevalence (ages 15-49, %)	2007-2013	60.3
International migrant stock (000 and % of total population)[j]	mid-2013	297.5/0.4
Refugees and others of concern to UNHCR	mid-2014	262 333
Education: Government expenditure (% of GDP)	2007-2013	3.8
Education: Primary-secondary gross enrolment ratio (f/m per 100)	2007-2013	98.6/101.8
Education: Female third-level students (% of total)	2007-2013	48.2
Intentional homicide rate (per 100,000 population)	2008-2012	3.4

Environmental indicators

Threatened species	2014	139
Forested area (% of land area)	2012	<
Proportion of terrestrial and marine areas protected (%)	2014	9.6
Population using improved drinking water sources (%)	2012	99.0
Population using improved sanitation facilities (%)	2012	96.0
CO_2 emission estimates (000 metric tons and metric tons per capita)	2011	220 790/2.8
Energy supply per capita (Gigajoules)	2012	43.0

a Principal rate. b 2012. c Series linked to former series. d ISIC Rev.3. e Population aged 15-64. f Average of May and November. g Break in series. h 2011. i Population aged 6 and over. j Including refugees.

El Salvador

Region	Central America	Surface area (sq km)	21 041 [a]	
Population (est., 000)	6 384	Pop. density (per sq km)	303.4	
Capital city	San Salvador	Capital city pop. (000)	1 097 [b]	
Currency	El Salvador Colon (SVC)	UN membership date	24 October 1945	

Economic indicators	2005	2010	2013
GDP: Gross domestic product (million current US$)	17 094	21 418	24 259
GDP: Growth rate at constant 2005 prices (annual %)	3.6	1.4	1.7
GDP per capita (current US$)	2 814.9	3 444.5	3 826.1
GNI: Gross national income per capita (current US$)	2 734.2	3 357.9	3 673.8
Gross fixed capital formation (% of GDP)	15.3	13.3	15.1
Exchange rates (national currency per US$) [c]	8.75	8.75	8.75
Balance of payments, current account (million US$)	−622	−533	−1 577
CPI: Consumer price index (2000=100) [d]	118	140[e]	151
Index of industrial production (2010=100) [f]	95	100	106
Agricultural production index (2004-2006=100)	99	108	110
Food production index (2004-2006=100)	99	106	118
Unemployment (% of labour force)	7.2	7.0	6.3
Employment in industrial sector (% of employed) [g]	22.2[hi]	21.4[jkl]	21.1[jkm]
Employment in agricultural sector (% of employed) [g]	20.0[hi]	20.8[jkl]	21.0[jkm]
Labour force participation, adult female pop. (%)	44.7	47.2	47.8
Labour force participation, adult male pop. (%)	77.7	79.2	79.0
Tourist arrivals at national borders (000)	1 127	1 150	1 283
Energy production, primary (Petajoules)	104	95	96[m]
Mobile-cellular subscriptions (per 100 inhabitants)	39.7	123.8[n]	136.2
Individuals using the Internet (%) [h]	4.2[o]	15.9	23.1

Total trade		Major trading partners			2013
	(million US$)	(% of exports)		(% of imports)	
Exports	5 491.1	United States	45.8	United States	38.9
Imports	10 772.0	Honduras	14.4	Guatemala	8.7
Balance	−5 280.9	Guatemala	13.1	Mexico	6.9

Social indicators		
Population growth rate (average annual %)	2010-2015	0.7
Urban population growth rate (average annual %)	2010-2015	1.4
Rural population growth rate (average annual %)	2010-2015	−0.8
Urban population (%)	2014	66.3
Population aged 0-14 years (%)	2014	29.3
Population aged 60+ years (females and males, % of total)	2014	10.7/9.0
Sex ratio (males per 100 females)	2014	89.9
Life expectancy at birth (females and males, years)	2010-2015	77.0/67.7
Infant mortality rate (per 1 000 live births)	2010-2015	17.3
Fertility rate, total (live births per woman)	2010-2015	2.2
Contraceptive prevalence (ages 15-49, %) [p]	2007-2013	72.3
International migrant stock (000 and % of total population) [q]	mid-2013	41.6/0.7
Refugees and others of concern to UNHCR	mid-2014	43
Education: Government expenditure (% of GDP)	2007-2013	3.4
Education: Primary-secondary gross enrolment ratio (f/m per 100)	2007-2013	87.6/89.6
Education: Female third-level students (% of total)	2007-2013	53.3
Intentional homicide rate (per 100,000 population)	2008-2012	41.2
Seats held by women in national parliaments (%)	2015	27.4

Environmental indicators		
Threatened species	2014	83
Forested area (% of land area)	2012	13.4
Proportion of terrestrial and marine areas protected (%)	2014	2.1
Population using improved drinking water sources (%)	2012	90.0
Population using improved sanitation facilities (%)	2012	70.0
CO$_2$ emission estimates (000 metric tons and metric tons per capita)	2011	6 685/1.1
Energy supply per capita (Gigajoules)	2012	30.0

a The total surface is 21040.79 square kilometres, without taking into account the last ruling of The Hague. b Refers to the urban parts of the municipalities San Salvador, Mejicanos, Soyapango, Delgado, Ilopango, Cuscatancingo, Ayutuxtepeque and San Marcos. c Principal rate. d Urban areas. e Series linked to former series. f ISIC Rev.3 (CDE). g ISIC Rev.3. h Population aged 10 and over. i December. j Population aged 16 and over. k January to December. l Break in series. m 2012. n Estimate. o ITU estimate. p Age group 15 to 44 years. q Including refugees.

Equatorial Guinea

Region	Middle Africa	Surface area (sq km)	28 051
Population (est., 000)	778	Pop. density (per sq km)	27.7
Capital city	Malabo	Capital city pop. (000)	145
Currency	CFA Franc (XAF)	UN membership date	12 November 1968

Economic indicators	2005	2010	2013
GDP: Gross domestic product (million current US$)	7 206	13 392	18 532
GDP: Growth rate at constant 2005 prices (annual %)	8.9	1.3	−4.8
GDP per capita (current US$)	11 936.6	19 236.7	24 479.7
GNI: Gross national income per capita (current US$)	6 061.7	10 644.3	16 874.9
Gross fixed capital formation (% of GDP)	21.7	47.4	37.1
Exchange rates (national currency per US$)[a]	556.04	490.91	475.64
CPI: Consumer price index (2000=100)[b]	145[c]	...	...
Agricultural production index (2004-2006=100)	100	111	117
Food production index (2004-2006=100)	101	113	118
Unemployment (% of labour force)	6.8	7.0	8.0
Labour force participation, adult female pop. (%)	80.3	80.5	80.7
Labour force participation, adult male pop. (%)	92.5	92.3	92.2
Energy production, primary (Petajoules)	822	849	889[de]
Mobile-cellular subscriptions (per 100 inhabitants)	16.1	57.4	67.5
Individuals using the Internet (%)	1.2	6.0	16.4[f]

Social indicators		
Population growth rate (average annual %)	2010-2015	2.8
Urban population growth rate (average annual %)	2010-2015	3.1
Rural population growth rate (average annual %)	2010-2015	2.5
Urban population (%)	2014	39.8
Population aged 0-14 years (%)	2014	38.7
Population aged 60+ years (females and males, % of total)	2014	4.6/5.0
Sex ratio (males per 100 females)	2014	104.9
Life expectancy at birth (females and males, years)	2010-2015	54.5/51.5
Infant mortality rate (per 1 000 live births)	2010-2015	88.9
Fertility rate, total (live births per woman)	2010-2015	4.9
Contraceptive prevalence (ages 15-49, %)	2007-2013	12.6
International migrant stock (000 and % of total population)[g]	mid-2013	10.1/1.3
Refugees and others of concern to UNHCR	mid-2014	0[h]
Education: Government expenditure (% of GDP)	2007-2013	0.7[i]
Education: Primary-secondary gross enrolment ratio (f/m per 100)	2007-2013	57.5/64.7[j]
Education: Female third-level students (% of total)	2007-2013	30.3[k]
Intentional homicide rate (per 100,000 population)	2008-2012	19.3
Seats held by women in national parliaments (%)	2015	24.0

Environmental indicators		
Threatened species	2014	151
Forested area (% of land area)	2012	57.1
Proportion of terrestrial and marine areas protected (%)	2014	2.1
CO₂ emission estimates (000 metric tons and metric tons per capita)	2011	6 689/9.4
Energy supply per capita (Gigajoules)	2012	120.0[e]

a Official rate. **b** Malabo. **c** 2006. **d** 2012. **e** UNSD estimate. **f** ITU estimate. **g** Refers to foreign citizens. **h** Value is zero, not available or not applicable. **i** 2002. **j** 2005. **k** 2000.

Eritrea

Region	Eastern Africa	Surface area (sq km)	117 600
Population (est., 000)	6 536	Pop. density (per sq km)	55.6
Capital city	Asmara	Capital city pop. (000)	775
Currency	Nakfa (ERN)	UN membership date	28 May 1993

Economic indicators	2005	2010	2013
GDP: Gross domestic product (million current US$)	1 098	2 117	3 438
GDP: Growth rate at constant 2005 prices (annual %)	2.6	2.2	1.1
GDP per capita (current US$)	226.3	368.8	542.8
GNI: Gross national income per capita (current US$)	224.4	365.3	537.9
Gross fixed capital formation (% of GDP)	20.3	9.3	8.8
Exchange rates (national currency per US$)[a]	15.38	15.38	15.38
Agricultural production index (2004-2006=100)	106	106	110
Food production index (2004-2006=100)	106	106	110
Unemployment (% of labour force)	7.5	7.3	7.2
Labour force participation, adult female pop. (%)	78.1	79.6	80.0
Labour force participation, adult male pop. (%)	89.4	89.7	89.8
Tourist arrivals at national borders (000)[bc]	83	84	...
Energy production, primary (Petajoules)	21	24	26[d]
Mobile-cellular subscriptions (per 100 inhabitants)	0.8	3.2	5.6
Individuals using the Internet (%)[e]	0.4[f]	0.6	0.9

Social indicators		
Population growth rate (average annual %)	2010-2015	3.2
Urban population growth rate (average annual %)	2010-2015	5.1
Rural population growth rate (average annual %)	2010-2015	2.7
Urban population (%)	2014	22.2
Population aged 0-14 years (%)	2014	43.1
Population aged 60+ years (females and males, % of total)	2014	4.4/3.1
Sex ratio (males per 100 females)	2014	99.7
Life expectancy at birth (females and males, years)	2010-2015	64.9/60.2
Infant mortality rate (per 1 000 live births)	2010-2015	41.8
Fertility rate, total (live births per woman)	2010-2015	4.7
Contraceptive prevalence (ages 15-49, %)	2007-2013	8.0[g]
International migrant stock (000 and % of total population)[h]	mid-2013	15.8/0.3
Refugees and others of concern to UNHCR	mid-2014	3 243
Education: Government expenditure (% of GDP)	2007-2013	2.1[i]
Education: Female third-level students (% of total)	2007-2013	32.8
Intentional homicide rate (per 100,000 population)	2008-2012	7.1
Seats held by women in national parliaments (%)	2015	22.0

Environmental indicators		
Threatened species	2014	113
Forested area (% of land area)	2012	15.1
Proportion of terrestrial and marine areas protected (%)	2014	3.1
CO_2 emission estimates (000 metric tons and metric tons per capita)	2011	521/0.1
Energy supply per capita (Gigajoules)	2012	5.0

a Official rate. b Arrivals of non-resident visitors at national borders. c Including nationals residing abroad. d 2012. e ITU estimate. f 2007. g 2002. h Estimate. i 2006.

Estonia

Region	Northern Europe	Surface area (sq km)	45 227
Population (est., 000)	1 284	Pop. density (per sq km)	28.5
Capital city	Tallinn	Capital city pop. (000)	392
Currency	Euro (EUR)	UN membership date	17 September 1991

Economic indicators	2005	2010	2013
GDP: Gross domestic product (million current US$)	14 001	19 491	24 880
GDP: Growth rate at constant 2005 prices (annual %)	9.5	2.5	1.6
GDP per capita (current US$)	10 565.8	15 009.7	19 328.2
GNI: Gross national income per capita (current US$)	10 154.0	14 232.9	18 841.1
Gross fixed capital formation (% of GDP)	32.9	21.3	27.3
Exchange rates (national currency per US$)	13.22[ab]	11.71[ab]	0.73[cd]
Balance of payments, current account (million US$)	−1 386	391	−300
CPI: Consumer price index (2000=100)	119	151	169
Index of industrial production (2010=100)[e]	96	100	125
Agricultural production index (2004-2006=100)	103	110	127
Food production index (2004-2006=100)	103	110	127
Unemployment (% of labour force)	7.9	16.9	8.8
Employment in industrial sector (% of employed)[f]	33.8[g]	30.5	31.1[h]
Employment in agricultural sector (% of employed)[f]	5.2[g]	4.2	4.7[h]
Labour force participation, adult female pop. (%)	53.3	56.2	56.2
Labour force participation, adult male pop. (%)	65.4	67.6	68.9
Tourist arrivals at national borders (000)	1 917	2 372	2 868
Energy production, primary (Petajoules)	163	204	213[h]
Mobile-cellular subscriptions (per 100 inhabitants)	109.1	127.3[i]	159.7
Individuals using the Internet (%)	61.5	74.1[j]	80.0

Total trade		Major trading partners			2013
	(million US$)		(% of exports)		(% of imports)
Exports	18 288.2	Russian Federation	17.8	Finland	9.9
Imports	20 058.3	Sweden	14.9	Germany	9.9
Balance	−1 770.1	Finland	14.4	Russian Federation	9.3

Social indicators		
Population growth rate (average annual %)	2010-2015	−0.3
Urban population growth rate (average annual %)	2010-2015	−0.5
Rural population growth rate (average annual %)	2010-2015	0.1
Urban population (%)	2014	67.6
Population aged 0-14 years (%)	2014	16.0
Population aged 60+ years (females and males, % of total)	2014	29.3/18.8
Sex ratio (males per 100 females)	2014	86.5
Life expectancy at birth (females and males, years)	2010-2015	79.5/68.9
Infant mortality rate (per 1 000 live births)	2010-2015	4.2
Fertility rate, total (live births per woman)	2010-2015	1.6
Contraceptive prevalence (ages 15-49, %)[k]	2007-2013	63.4[l]
International migrant stock (000 and % of total population)	mid-2013	210.0/16.3
Refugees and others of concern to UNHCR	mid-2014	89 658[m]
Education: Government expenditure (% of GDP)	2007-2013	5.2
Education: Primary-secondary gross enrolment ratio (f/m per 100)	2007-2013	102.6/102.8
Education: Female third-level students (% of total)	2007-2013	59.2
Intentional homicide rate (per 100,000 population)	2008-2012	5.0
Seats held by women in national parliaments (%)	2015	19.8

Environmental indicators		
Threatened species	2014	17
Forested area (% of land area)	2012	51.8
Proportion of terrestrial and marine areas protected (%)	2014	19.9
Population using improved drinking water sources (%)	2012	99.0
Population using improved sanitation facilities (%)	2012	95.0
CO_2 emission estimates (000 metric tons and metric tons per capita)	2011	18 650/14.4
Energy supply per capita (Gigajoules)	2012	181.0

a Official rate. b Estonian Kroon (EEK). c Market rate. d Euro. e ISIC Rev.4 (BCD). f Population aged 15-74.
g Excluding conscripts. h 2012. i Excluding 1,890,000 prepaid cards that are used to provide Travel SIM service. j Population aged 16 to 74 using the Internet in the last 3 months. k Age group 18 to 49 years. l 2004-2005. m Almost all people recorded as being stateless have permanent residence.

Ethiopia

Region	Eastern Africa	Surface area (sq km)	1 104 300
Population (est., 000)	96 506	Pop. density (per sq km)	87.4
Capital city	Addis Ababa	Capital city pop. (000)	3 168
Currency	Birr (ETB)	UN membership date	13 November 1945

Economic indicators	2005	2010	2013
GDP: Gross domestic product (million current US$)	12 164	26 311	46 017
GDP: Growth rate at constant 2005 prices (annual %)	11.8	12.6	10.4
GDP per capita (current US$)	159.7	302.1	489.0
GNI: Gross national income per capita (current US$)	159.9	301.5	488.0
Gross fixed capital formation (% of GDP)	26.0	27.0	33.0
Exchange rates (national currency per US$)[a]	8.68	16.55	18.18[b]
Balance of payments, current account (million US$)	−1 568	−425	−2 985[b]
CPI: Consumer price index (2000=100)[c]	138	313	559
Index of industrial production (2010=100)[de]	63	100	152
Agricultural production index (2004-2006=100)	102	137	147
Food production index (2004-2006=100)	103	137	148
Unemployment (% of labour force)	5.4	5.4	5.7
Employment in industrial sector (% of employed)	6.6[fgh]	...	...
Employment in agricultural sector (% of employed)	79.3[fgh]	...	...
Labour force participation, adult female pop. (%)	78.4	78.2	78.2
Labour force participation, adult male pop. (%)	90.9	89.7	89.3
Tourist arrivals at national borders (000)[ij]	227	468	681
Energy production, primary (Petajoules)	1 030	1 205	1 249[b]
Mobile-cellular subscriptions (per 100 inhabitants)	0.5	7.9	27.3
Individuals using the Internet (%)	0.2	0.8[k]	1.9[k]

Total trade		Major trading partners			2013
	(million US$)	(% of exports)			(% of imports)
Exports	4 076.9	Somalia	16.0	China	21.8
Imports	14 899.1	Netherlands	11.5	Areas nes	16.4[l]
Balance	−10 822.2	Saudi Arabia	9.7	India	8.8

Social indicators		
Population growth rate (average annual %)	2010-2015	2.6
Urban population growth rate (average annual %)	2010-2015	4.9
Rural population growth rate (average annual %)	2010-2015	2.0
Urban population (%)	2014	19.0
Population aged 0-14 years (%)	2014	42.1
Population aged 60+ years (females and males, % of total)	2014	5.5/4.9
Sex ratio (males per 100 females)	2014	100.1
Life expectancy at birth (females and males, years)	2010-2015	65.0/61.7
Infant mortality rate (per 1 000 live births)	2010-2015	49.7
Fertility rate, total (live births per woman)	2010-2015	4.6
Contraceptive prevalence (ages 15-49, %)	2007-2013	28.6
International migrant stock (000 and % of total population)[m]	mid-2013	718.2/0.8
Refugees and others of concern to UNHCR	mid-2014	590 071
Education: Government expenditure (% of GDP)	2007-2013	4.7
Education: Primary-secondary gross enrolment ratio (f/m per 100)	2007-2013	54.2/67.3[n]
Education: Female third-level students (% of total)	2007-2013	31.5
Intentional homicide rate (per 100,000 population)	2008-2012	12.0
Seats held by women in national parliaments (%)	2015	27.8

Environmental indicators		
Threatened species	2014	144
Forested area (% of land area)	2012	12.0
Proportion of terrestrial and marine areas protected (%)	2014	18.4
Population using improved drinking water sources (%)	2012	52.0
Population using improved sanitation facilities (%)	2012	24.0
CO_2 emission estimates (000 metric tons and metric tons per capita)	2011	7 543/0.1
Energy supply per capita (Gigajoules)	2012	15.0

a Official rate. b 2012. c Index base 2001=100. d ISIC Rev.3 (CDE). e Twelve months ending 30 June of the year stated. f ISIC Rev.3. g Population aged 10 and over. h March. i Arrivals through all ports of entry. j Including nationals residing abroad. k ITU estimate. l See technical notes. m Including refugees. n 2006.

Faeroe Islands

Region	Northern Europe	Surface area (sq km)	1 393
Population (est., 000)	49	Pop. density (per sq km)	35.4
Capital city	Tórshavn	Capital city pop. (000)	21
Currency	Danish Krone (DKK)		

Economic indicators	2005	2010	2013
Balance of payments, current account (million US$)	31	144	194[a]
CPI: Consumer price index (2000=100)	109	121	126
Agricultural production index (2004-2006=100)	100	102	104
Food production index (2004-2006=100)	100	102	104
Employment in industrial sector (% of employed)	22.2[bcd]	...	...
Employment in agricultural sector (% of employed)	11.1[bcd]	...	...
Energy production, primary (Petajoules)	0	0	0[e]
Mobile-cellular subscriptions (per 100 inhabitants)	85.5	119.9	120.7[f]
Individuals using the Internet (%)	67.9[f]	75.2	90.0[f]

Social indicators		
Population growth rate (average annual %)	2010-2015	-<
Urban population growth rate (average annual %)	2010-2015	0.5
Rural population growth rate (average annual %)	2010-2015	-0.4
Urban population (%)	2014	41.7
Population aged 0-14 years (%)[ghi]	2014	22.0[j]
Population aged 60+ years (females and males, % of total)[ghi]	2014	20.5/18.1[j]
Sex ratio (males per 100 females)[ghi]	2014	108.2[j]
Life expectancy at birth (females and males, years)[g]	2010-2015	82.3/76.8[j]
International migrant stock (000 and % of total population)	mid-2013	3.6/7.4

Environmental indicators		
Threatened species	2014	13
Forested area (% of land area)	2012	<
CO$_2$ emission estimates (000 metric tons and metric tons per capita)	2011	568/11.5
Energy supply per capita (Gigajoules)	2012	173.0[k]

a 2011. b ISIC Rev.2. c Population aged 16 and over. d September. e 2012. f ITU estimate. g Data compiled by the United Nations Demographic Yearbook system. h Data refer to the latest available census. i De jure estimate. j 2008. k UNSD estimate.

Fiji

Region	Oceania-Melanesia	Surface area (sq km)	18 272
Population (est., 000)	887	Pop. density (per sq km)	48.5
Capital city	Suva	Capital city pop. (000)	176
Currency	Fiji Dollar (FJD)	UN membership date	13 October 1970

Economic indicators	2005	2010	2013
GDP: Gross domestic product (million current US$)	3 007	3 140	4 034
GDP: Growth rate at constant 2005 prices (annual %)	0.7	−0.2	4.6
GDP per capita (current US$)	3 655.5	3 649.3	4 578.5
GNI: Gross national income per capita (current US$)	3 579.3	3 571.0	4 303.3
Gross fixed capital formation (% of GDP)	18.1	12.9	25.9
Exchange rates (national currency per US$)[a]	1.74	1.82	1.90
Balance of payments, current account (million US$)	−212	−142	−561
CPI: Consumer price index (2000=100)	115	146	169
Index of industrial production (2010=100)[b]	99	100	...
Agricultural production index (2004-2006=100)	99	82	86
Food production index (2004-2006=100)	99	82	86
Unemployment (% of labour force)	4.6	8.4	8.1
Labour force participation, adult female pop. (%)	38.1	37.4	37.5
Labour force participation, adult male pop. (%)	73.8	72.0	72.0
Tourist arrivals at national borders (000)[c]	545	632	658
Energy production, primary (Petajoules)	9	6	6[d]
Mobile-cellular subscriptions (per 100 inhabitants)	24.9[e]	81.1[f]	101.1
Individuals using the Internet (%)	8.5	20.0[g]	37.1[g]

Total trade		Major trading partners			2013
	(million US$)	(% of exports)			(% of imports)
Exports	1 108.0	Areas nes	19.7[h]	Singapore	21.0
Imports	2 825.7	Australia	13.6	France	14.6
Balance	−1 717.7	United States	13.3	Australia	13.6

Social indicators		
Population growth rate (average annual %)	2010-2015	0.7
Urban population growth rate (average annual %)	2010-2015	1.5
Rural population growth rate (average annual %)	2010-2015	−0.1
Urban population (%)	2014	53.4
Population aged 0-14 years (%)	2014	28.8
Population aged 60+ years (females and males, % of total)	2014	9.6/8.3
Sex ratio (males per 100 females)	2014	103.6
Life expectancy at birth (females and males, years)	2010-2015	72.9/66.9
Infant mortality rate (per 1 000 live births)	2010-2015	16.0
Fertility rate, total (live births per woman)	2010-2015	2.6
Contraceptive prevalence (ages 15-49, %)	2007-2013	40.9[i]
International migrant stock (000 and % of total population)	mid-2013	22.8/2.6
Refugees and others of concern to UNHCR	mid-2014	18
Education: Government expenditure (% of GDP)	2007-2013	4.2
Education: Primary-secondary gross enrolment ratio (f/m per 100)	2007-2013	98.7/93.5
Education: Female third-level students (% of total)[j]	2007-2013	53.1[k]
Intentional homicide rate (per 100,000 population)	2008-2012	4.0
Seats held by women in national parliaments (%)	2015	14.0

Environmental indicators		
Threatened species	2014	278
Forested area (% of land area)	2012	55.9
Proportion of terrestrial and marine areas protected (%)	2014	1.0
Population using improved drinking water sources (%)	2012	96.0
Population using improved sanitation facilities (%)	2012	87.0
CO_2 emission estimates (000 metric tons and metric tons per capita)	2011	1 236/1.4
Energy supply per capita (Gigajoules)	2012	26.0[l]

a Official rate. **b** ISIC Rev.3 (CDE). **c** Excluding nationals residing abroad. **d** 2012. **e** Data refer to March of the following year. **f** June 2011. **g** ITU estimate. **h** See technical notes. **i** 1974. **j** UNESCO estimate. **k** 2005. **l** UNSD estimate.

Finland

Region	Northern Europe	Surface area (sq km)	336 855 [a]
Population (est., 000)	5 444 [b]	Pop. density (per sq km)	16.1 [b]
Capital city	Helsinki	Capital city pop. (000)	1 170
Currency	Euro (EUR)	UN membership date	14 December 1955

Economic indicators	2005	2010	2013
GDP: Gross domestic product (million current US$)	204 431	247 800	267 329
GDP: Growth rate at constant 2005 prices (annual %)	2.8	3.0	−1.2
GDP per capita (current US$)	38 966.2	46 165.1	49 265.2
GNI: Gross national income per capita (current US$)	39 121.2	46 781.7	49 413.7
Gross fixed capital formation (% of GDP)	23.0	21.9	21.2
Exchange rates (national currency per US$) [c]	0.85	0.75	0.73
Balance of payments, current account (million US$)	7 788	5 944	−2 466
CPI: Consumer price index (2000=100)	106 [d]	116	126
Index of industrial production (2010=100) [e]	100	100	96
Agricultural production index (2004-2006=100)	102	94	99
Food production index (2004-2006=100)	102	94	99
Unemployment (% of labour force)	8.4	8.4	8.2
Employment in industrial sector (% of employed) [f]	25.6 [g]	23.2	22.7 [h]
Employment in agricultural sector (% of employed) [f]	4.8 [g]	4.4	4.1 [h]
Labour force participation, adult female pop. (%)	56.8	56.2	55.7
Labour force participation, adult male pop. (%)	65.4	64.6	64.0
Tourist arrivals at national borders (000) [i]	2 080	2 319	2 797
Energy production, primary (Petajoules)	615	724	717 [h]
Mobile-cellular subscriptions (per 100 inhabitants)	100.5	156.3	171.7
Individuals using the Internet (%)	74.5	86.9	91.5

Total trade		Major trading partners			2013
	(million US$)	(% of exports)			(% of imports)
Exports	74 445.4	Sweden	11.5	Russian Federation	18.0
Imports	77 587.0	Russian Federation	9.4	Germany	12.3
Balance	−3 141.6	Germany	9.3	Sweden	11.3

Social indicators		
Population growth rate (average annual %) [b]	2010-2015	0.3
Urban population growth rate (average annual %) [b]	2010-2015	0.5
Rural population growth rate (average annual %) [b]	2010-2015	−0.5
Urban population (%) [b]	2014	84.1
Population aged 0-14 years (%) [b]	2014	16.5
Population aged 60+ years (females and males, % of total) [b]	2014	29.2/24.2
Sex ratio (males per 100 females) [b]	2014	96.7
Life expectancy at birth (females and males, years) [b]	2010-2015	83.6/77.3
Infant mortality rate (per 1 000 live births) [b]	2010-2015	2.3
Fertility rate, total (live births per woman) [b]	2010-2015	1.9
Contraceptive prevalence (ages 15-49, %) [j]	2007-2013	77.4 [k]
International migrant stock (000 and % of total population) [b]	mid-2013	293.2/5.4
Refugees and others of concern to UNHCR	mid-2014	14 432 [l]
Education: Government expenditure (% of GDP)	2007-2013	6.8
Education: Primary-secondary gross enrolment ratio (f/m per 100)	2007-2013	105.3/103.0
Education: Female third-level students (% of total)	2007-2013	53.7
Intentional homicide rate (per 100,000 population)	2008-2012	1.6
Seats held by women in national parliaments (%)	2015	42.5

Environmental indicators		
Threatened species	2014	25
Forested area (% of land area)	2012	72.9
Proportion of terrestrial and marine areas protected (%)	2014	14.1
Population using improved drinking water sources (%)	2012	100.0
Population using improved sanitation facilities (%)	2012	100.0
CO_2 emission estimates (000 metric tons and metric tons per capita)	2011	54 767/10.2
Energy supply per capita (Gigajoules)	2012	257.0

a Excluding Åland Islands. b Including Åland Islands. c Market rate. d Series linked to former series. e ISIC Rev.4 (BCDE). f Population aged 15-74. g ISIC Rev.3. h 2012. i Arrivals of non-resident tourists in all types of accommodation establishments. j Age group 25 to 49 years. k 1989-1990. l Refugee population refers to the end of 2013.

France

Region	Western Europe	Surface area (sq km)	551 500	
Population (est., 000)	64 641	Pop. density (per sq km)	117.2	
Capital city	Paris	Capital city pop. (000)	10 764	
Currency	Euro (EUR)	UN membership date	24 October 1945	

Economic indicators	2005	2010	2013
GDP: Gross domestic product (million current US$)	2 203 626	2 646 836	2 806 432
GDP: Growth rate at constant 2005 prices (annual %)	1.6	2.0	0.3
GDP per capita (current US$)	34 824.5	40 616.8	42 338.6
GNI: Gross national income per capita (current US$)	35 433.4	41 446.0	43 073.4
Gross fixed capital formation (% of GDP)	21.8	22.1	22.1
Exchange rates (national currency per US$)[a]	0.85	0.75	0.73
Balance of payments, current account (million US$)	−10 260	−33 734	−40 227
CPI: Consumer price index (2000=100)	110	119	124
Index of industrial production (2010=100)[bc]	112	100	99
Agricultural production index (2004-2006=100)	100	97	97
Food production index (2004-2006=100)	100	97	97
Unemployment (% of labour force)	8.9	9.3	10.4
Employment in industrial sector (% of employed)	23.7[d]	22.2	21.7[e]
Employment in agricultural sector (% of employed)	3.6[d]	2.9	2.9[e]
Labour force participation, adult female pop. (%)	49.9	50.9	50.7
Labour force participation, adult male pop. (%)	62.4	62.0	61.6
Tourist arrivals at national borders (000)	74 988	77 648	84 726
Energy production, primary (Petajoules)[fg]	5 682	5 619	5 583[e]
Mobile-cellular subscriptions (per 100 inhabitants)	78.3	91.4	98.5
Individuals using the Internet (%)	42.9[h]	77.3	81.9

Total trade		Major trading partners				2013
	(million US$)[g]	(% of exports)[g]			(% of imports)[g]	
Exports	566 879.0	Germany	16.4	Germany		17.1
Imports	668 658.1	Belgium	7.7	China		8.1
Balance	−101 779.1	Italy	7.1	Belgium		7.8

Social indicators		
Population growth rate (average annual %)	2010-2015	0.6
Urban population growth rate (average annual %)	2010-2015	0.8
Rural population growth rate (average annual %)	2010-2015	−0.6
Urban population (%)	2014	79.3
Population aged 0-14 years (%)	2014	18.2
Population aged 60+ years (females and males, % of total)	2014	26.9/21.9
Sex ratio (males per 100 females)	2014	93.9
Life expectancy at birth (females and males, years)	2010-2015	85.1/78.2
Infant mortality rate (per 1 000 live births)	2010-2015	3.2
Fertility rate, total (live births per woman)	2010-2015	2.0
Contraceptive prevalence (ages 15-49, %)[i]	2007-2013	76.4
International migrant stock (000 and % of total population)	mid-2013	7 439.1/11.6
Refugees and others of concern to UNHCR	mid-2014	298 828
Education: Government expenditure (% of GDP)	2007-2013	5.7
Education: Primary-secondary gross enrolment ratio (f/m per 100)	2007-2013	109.0/108.5
Education: Female third-level students (% of total)	2007-2013	54.8
Intentional homicide rate (per 100,000 population)	2008-2012	1.0
Seats held by women in national parliaments (%)	2015	26.2

Environmental indicators		
Threatened species	2014	234
Forested area (% of land area)	2012	29.3
Proportion of terrestrial and marine areas protected (%)	2014	25.7
Population using improved drinking water sources (%)	2012	100.0
Population using improved sanitation facilities (%)	2012	100.0
CO_2 emission estimates (000 metric tons and metric tons per capita)[g]	2011	338 805/5.3
Energy supply per capita (Gigajoules)[fg]	2012	165.0

a Market rate. b ISIC Rev.4 (BCDE). c Excluding the Overseas Department (French Guiana, Guadeloupe, Martinique, Mayotte and Réunion). d ISIC Rev.3. e 2012. f Excluding Guadeloupe, French Guiana, Martinique, New Caledonia, French Polynesia, Réunion and St. Pierre Miquelon. g Including Monaco. h Population aged 11 and over using the Internet in the last month. i Age group 20 to 49 years.

French Guiana

Region	South America	Surface area (sq km)	83 534
Population (est., 000)	255	Pop. density (per sq km)	2.8
Capital city	Cayenne	Capital city pop. (000)	58
Currency	Euro (EUR)		

Economic indicators	2005	2010	2013
Exchange rates (national currency per US$)[a]	0.84	0.76	0.72
CPI: Consumer price index (2000=100)	108	119	125
Agricultural production index (2004-2006=100)	96	90	89
Food production index (2004-2006=100)	96	90	89
Employment in industrial sector (% of employed)	...	14.1[bc]	14.9[bcd]
Labour force participation, adult female pop. (%)	45.6	47.1	48.7
Labour force participation, adult male pop. (%)	61.5	60.0	60.6
Tourist arrivals at national borders (000)	95	83[e]	...
Energy production, primary (Petajoules)	3[f]	3[f]	3[d]

Social indicators		
Population growth rate (average annual %)	2010-2015	2.5
Urban population growth rate (average annual %)	2010-2015	2.8
Rural population growth rate (average annual %)	2010-2015	0.7
Urban population (%)	2014	84.1
Population aged 0-14 years (%)	2014	31.9
Population aged 60+ years (females and males, % of total)	2014	8.3/8.3
Sex ratio (males per 100 females)	2014	100.0
Life expectancy at birth (females and males, years)	2010-2015	80.8/73.8
Infant mortality rate (per 1 000 live births)	2010-2015	12.2
Fertility rate, total (live births per woman)	2010-2015	3.1
International migrant stock (000 and % of total population)	mid-2013	104.3/41.9
Intentional homicide rate (per 100,000 population)	2008-2012	13.3

Environmental indicators		
Threatened species	2014	66
Forested area (% of land area)	2012	98.2
Proportion of terrestrial and marine areas protected (%)	2014	48.8
CO_2 emission estimates (000 metric tons and metric tons per capita)	2011	719/3.0
Energy supply per capita (Gigajoules)	2012	53.0[f]

a UN operational exchange rate. b March to June. c Excluding institutional population. d 2012. e 2009.
f UNSD estimate.

French Polynesia

Region	Oceania-Polynesia	Surface area (sq km)	4 000
Population (est., 000)	280	Pop. density (per sq km)	70.0
Capital city	Papeete	Capital city pop. (000)	133[a]
Currency	CFP Franc (XPF)		

Economic indicators	2005	2010	2013
GDP: Gross domestic product (million current US$)	5 703	6 322	6 412
GDP: Growth rate at constant 2005 prices (annual %)	1.4	0.6	−0.2
GDP per capita (current US$)	22 374.0	23 583.4	23 161.7
GNI: Gross national income per capita (current US$)	22 374.0	23 583.4	23 161.7
Gross fixed capital formation (% of GDP)	24.0	23.3	23.6
Exchange rates (national currency per US$)[b]	100.84	90.81	86.46
Balance of payments, current account (million US$)	9	77	255[c]
CPI: Consumer price index (2000=100)	106	116	121
Agricultural production index (2004-2006=100)	104	99	105
Food production index (2004-2006=100)	104	99	105
Employment in industrial sector (% of employed)[d]	8.8	8.3[e]	8.3[f]
Employment in agricultural sector (% of employed)	4.3[d]	3.4[de]	...
Labour force participation, adult female pop. (%)	47.2	47.0	47.1
Labour force participation, adult male pop. (%)	65.8	64.0	64.2
Tourist arrivals at national borders (000)[g]	208	154	164
Energy production, primary (Petajoules)	1	1	1[ch]
Mobile-cellular subscriptions (per 100 inhabitants)	47.1	80.5	85.6[i]
Individuals using the Internet (%)	21.5	49.0	56.8[i]

Total trade		Major trading partners			2013
	(million US$)	(% of exports)			(% of imports)
Exports	151.5	Japan	29.4	France	24.7
Imports	1 814.8	China, Hong Kong SAR	27.5	Republic of Korea	10.9
Balance	−1 663.3	United States	14.5	China	9.8

Social indicators		
Population growth rate (average annual %)	2010-2015	1.1
Urban population growth rate (average annual %)	2010-2015	0.9
Rural population growth rate (average annual %)	2010-2015	1.3
Urban population (%)	2014	56.0
Population aged 0-14 years (%)	2014	22.5
Population aged 60+ years (females and males, % of total)	2014	11.5/10.9
Sex ratio (males per 100 females)	2014	104.4
Life expectancy at birth (females and males, years)	2010-2015	78.6/74.0
Infant mortality rate (per 1 000 live births)	2010-2015	6.9
Fertility rate, total (live births per woman)	2010-2015	2.1
International migrant stock (000 and % of total population)	mid-2013	34.8/12.6
Intentional homicide rate (per 100,000 population)	2008-2012	0.4

Environmental indicators		
Threatened species	2014	175
Forested area (% of land area)	2012	45.1
Proportion of terrestrial and marine areas protected (%)	2014	0.0
CO_2 emission estimates (000 metric tons and metric tons per capita)	2011	858/3.2
Energy supply per capita (Gigajoules)	2012	46.0

a Refers to the total population in the communes of Arue, Faaa, Mahina, Papara, Papeete, Pirae and Punaauia. b UN operational exchange rate. c 2012. d Administrative records and related sources. e Break in series. f 2011. g Excluding nationals residing abroad. h UNSD estimate. i ITU estimate.

Gabon

Region	Middle Africa	Surface area (sq km)	267 668
Population (est., 000)	1 711	Pop. density (per sq km)	6.4
Capital city	Libreville	Capital city pop. (000)	695
Currency	CFA Franc (XAF)	UN membership date	20 September 1960

Economic indicators	2005	2010	2013
GDP: Gross domestic product (million current US$)	9 579	12 882	16 970
GDP: Growth rate at constant 2005 prices (annual %)	1.1	6.9	5.6
GDP per capita (current US$)	6 944.0	8 277.7	10 151.3
GNI: Gross national income per capita (current US$)	6 176.7	7 311.9	9 078.0
Gross fixed capital formation (% of GDP)	21.0	31.3	31.1
Exchange rates (national currency per US$)[a]	556.04	490.91	475.64
Balance of payments, current account (million US$)	1 983	...	...
CPI: Consumer price index (2000=100)[bc]	105	123	128
Index of industrial production (2010=100)[d]	85	100	...
Agricultural production index (2004-2006=100)	100	117	122
Food production index (2004-2006=100)	100	115	120
Unemployment (% of labour force)	21.0	20.4	19.6
Employment in industrial sector (% of employed)	11.8[ef]	...	...
Employment in agricultural sector (% of employed)	24.2[ef]	...	...
Labour force participation, adult female pop. (%)	54.4	55.5	56.2
Labour force participation, adult male pop. (%)	64.1	64.7	65.4
Tourist arrivals at national borders (000)[g]	269	...	...
Energy production, primary (Petajoules)	622	602	585[h]
Mobile-cellular subscriptions (per 100 inhabitants)	53.4[i]	103.5	214.8[i]
Individuals using the Internet (%)	4.9	7.2[j]	9.2[j]

Social indicators		
Population growth rate (average annual %)	2010-2015	2.4
Urban population growth rate (average annual %)	2010-2015	2.7
Rural population growth rate (average annual %)	2010-2015	0.2
Urban population (%)	2014	86.9
Population aged 0-14 years (%)	2014	38.4
Population aged 60+ years (females and males, % of total)	2014	7.9/6.6
Sex ratio (males per 100 females)	2014	101.1
Life expectancy at birth (females and males, years)	2010-2015	64.3/62.3
Infant mortality rate (per 1 000 live births)	2010-2015	43.3
Fertility rate, total (live births per woman)	2010-2015	4.1
Contraceptive prevalence (ages 15-49, %)	2007-2013	31.1
International migrant stock (000 and % of total population)[k]	mid-2013	395.0/23.6
Refugees and others of concern to UNHCR	mid-2014	2 875
Education: Government expenditure (% of GDP)[l]	2007-2013	3.8[m]
Education: Primary-secondary gross enrolment ratio (f/m per 100)	2007-2013	95.1/98.0[n]
Education: Female third-level students (% of total)	2007-2013	36.3[o]
Intentional homicide rate (per 100,000 population)	2008-2012	9.1
Seats held by women in national parliaments (%)	2015	14.2

Environmental indicators		
Threatened species	2014	227
Forested area (% of land area)	2012	85.4
Proportion of terrestrial and marine areas protected (%)	2014	12.3
Population using improved drinking water sources (%)	2012	92.0
Population using improved sanitation facilities (%)	2012	41.0
CO_2 emission estimates (000 metric tons and metric tons per capita)	2011	2 237/1.4
Energy supply per capita (Gigajoules)	2012	57.0

a Official rate. **b** Libreville. **c** African population. **d** ISIC Rev.3 (DE). **e** Core Welfare Indicators Questionnaire (World Bank). **f** ISIC Rev.2. **g** Arrivals of non-resident tourists at Libreville Airport. **h** 2012. **i** Including inactive subscriptions. **j** ITU estimate. **k** Refers to foreign citizens. **l** UNESCO estimate. **m** 2000. **n** 1999. **o** 2003.

Gambia

Region	Western Africa	Surface area (sq km)	11 295
Population (est., 000)	1 909	Pop. density (per sq km)	169.0
Capital city	Banjul	Capital city pop. (000)	489[a]
Currency	Dalasi (GMD)	UN membership date	21 September 1965

Economic indicators	2005	2010	2013
GDP: Gross domestic product (million current US$)	624	952	902
GDP: Growth rate at constant 2005 prices (annual %)	−0.9	6.5	5.7
GDP per capita (current US$)	434.5	566.4	487.7
GNI: Gross national income per capita (current US$)	418.9	548.6	468.9
Gross fixed capital formation (% of GDP)	29.5	18.4	21.1
Exchange rates (national currency per US$)[b]	28.13	28.39	37.91
Balance of payments, current account (million US$)	−43	56	58[c]
CPI: Consumer price index (2000=100)[d]	157	193	223
Agricultural production index (2004-2006=100)	94	134	98
Food production index (2004-2006=100)	94	134	98
Unemployment (% of labour force)	7.2	7.0	7.0
Labour force participation, adult female pop. (%)	71.7	72.2	72.2
Labour force participation, adult male pop. (%)	83.5	83.2	82.9
Tourist arrivals at national borders (000)[e]	108	91	171
Energy production, primary (Petajoules)	6	6	7[c]
Mobile-cellular subscriptions (per 100 inhabitants)	17.2	88.0	100.0
Individuals using the Internet (%)	3.8[f]	9.2	14.0[f]

Total trade		Major trading partners			2013
	(million US$)		(% of exports)		(% of imports)
Exports	106.2	Mali	36.2	Côte d'Ivoire	22.9
Imports	350.2	Guinea	32.3	Brazil	11.0
Balance	−244.0	Senegal	17.2	China	6.9

Social indicators		
Population growth rate (average annual %)	2010-2015	3.2
Urban population growth rate (average annual %)	2010-2015	4.3
Rural population growth rate (average annual %)	2010-2015	1.6
Urban population (%)	2014	59.0
Population aged 0-14 years (%)	2014	45.8
Population aged 60+ years (females and males, % of total)	2014	3.6/3.9
Sex ratio (males per 100 females)	2014	97.9
Life expectancy at birth (females and males, years)	2010-2015	60.1/57.4
Infant mortality rate (per 1 000 live births)	2010-2015	55.3
Fertility rate, total (live births per woman)	2010-2015	5.8
Contraceptive prevalence (ages 15-49, %)	2007-2013	9.0
International migrant stock (000 and % of total population)	mid-2013	162.9/8.8
Refugees and others of concern to UNHCR	mid-2014	11 946
Education: Government expenditure (% of GDP)	2007-2013	4.1
Education: Primary-secondary gross enrolment ratio (f/m per 100)[g]	2007-2013	72.7/73.0
Intentional homicide rate (per 100,000 population)	2008-2012	10.2
Seats held by women in national parliaments (%)	2015	9.4

Environmental indicators		
Threatened species	2014	55
Forested area (% of land area)	2012	47.8
Proportion of terrestrial and marine areas protected (%)	2014	1.4
Population using improved drinking water sources (%)	2012	90.0
Population using improved sanitation facilities (%)	2012	60.0
CO_2 emission estimates (000 metric tons and metric tons per capita)	2011	422/0.3
Energy supply per capita (Gigajoules)	2012	7.0[h]

a Refers to the local government areas of Banjul and Kanifing. b Market rate. c 2012. d Banjul and Kombo St. Mary only. e Charter tourists only. f ITU estimate. g UNESCO estimate. h UNSD estimate.

Georgia

Region	Western Asia	Surface area (sq km)	69 700
Population (est., 000)	4 323 [a]	Pop. density (per sq km)	62.0 [a]
Capital city	Tbilisi	Capital city pop. (000)	1 150
Currency	Lari (GEL)	UN membership date	31 July 1992

Economic indicators	2005	2010	2013
GDP: Gross domestic product (million current US$)	6 411	11 638	16 127
GDP: Growth rate at constant 2005 prices (annual %)	9.6	6.3	3.2
GDP per capita (current US$)	1 432.5	2 651.9	3 715.1
GNI: Gross national income per capita (current US$)	1 453.6	2 570.0	3 649.3
Gross fixed capital formation (% of GDP)	28.1	19.3	22.0
Exchange rates (national currency per US$) [b]	1.79	1.77	1.74
Balance of payments, current account (million US$)	−695	−1 196	−923
CPI: Consumer price index (2000=100)	132 [c]	189 [c]	...
Index of industrial production (2010=100) [d]	73	100	131
Agricultural production index (2004-2006=100)	121	67	86
Food production index (2004-2006=100)	121	68	88
Unemployment (% of labour force)	13.8	16.3	14.3
Employment in industrial sector (% of employed)	9.3 [e]	10.4 [ef]	...
Employment in agricultural sector (% of employed)	54.3 [e]	53.4 [ef]	...
Labour force participation, adult female pop. (%)	55.4	55.6	56.5
Labour force participation, adult male pop. (%)	73.3	73.9	75.1
Tourist arrivals at national borders (000) [g]	560	2 032	5 392
Energy production, primary (Petajoules)	53	58	53 [h]
Mobile-cellular subscriptions (per 100 inhabitants)	26.2	90.7 [ij]	115.0
Individuals using the Internet (%)	6.1 [k]	26.9	43.1 [l]

Total trade		Major trading partners			2013
	(million US$)		(% of exports)		(% of imports)
Exports	2 909.3	Azerbaijan	24.4	Turkey	17.1
Imports	7 874.0	Armenia	10.9	Azerbaijan	8.1
Balance	−4 964.7	Ukraine	6.6	Ukraine	7.7

Social indicators		
Population growth rate (average annual %) [a]	2010-2015	−0.4
Urban population growth rate (average annual %) [a]	2010-2015	−0.1
Rural population growth rate (average annual %) [a]	2010-2015	−0.7
Urban population (%) [a]	2014	53.5
Population aged 0-14 years (%) [a]	2014	18.2
Population aged 60+ years (females and males, % of total) [a]	2014	22.8/17.0
Sex ratio (males per 100 females) [a]	2014	89.2
Life expectancy at birth (females and males, years) [a]	2010-2015	77.7/70.5
Infant mortality rate (per 1 000 live births) [a]	2010-2015	19.4
Fertility rate, total (live births per woman) [a]	2010-2015	1.8
Contraceptive prevalence (ages 15-49, %) [m]	2007-2013	53.4
International migrant stock (000 and % of total population) [a]	mid-2013	189.9/4.4
Refugees and others of concern to UNHCR	mid-2014	258 970
Education: Government expenditure (% of GDP)	2007-2013	2.0
Education: Primary-secondary gross enrolment ratio (f/m per 100)	2007-2013	102.3/101.5
Education: Female third-level students (% of total)	2007-2013	55.9
Intentional homicide rate (per 100,000 population)	2008-2012	4.3
Seats held by women in national parliaments (%)	2015	11.3

Environmental indicators		
Threatened species	2014	115
Forested area (% of land area)	2012	39.4
Proportion of terrestrial and marine areas protected (%)	2014	6.5
Population using improved drinking water sources (%)	2012	99.0
Population using improved sanitation facilities (%)	2012	93.0
CO_2 emission estimates (000 metric tons and metric tons per capita)	2011	7 932/1.8
Energy supply per capita (Gigajoules)	2012	39.0

a Including Abkhazia and South Ossetia. b Official rate. c 5 cities. d ISIC Rev.3 (CDE). e ISIC Rev.3. f 2007. g Arrivals of non-resident visitors at national borders. h 2012. i Methodology revised. j Active subscriptions in the last quarter. k ITU estimate. l Population aged 6 and over. m Age group 15 to 44 years.

Germany

Region	Western Europe	Surface area (sq km)	357 137
Population (est., 000)	82 652	Pop. density (per sq km)	231.5
Capital city	Berlin	Capital city pop. (000)	3 547
Currency	Euro (EUR)	UN membership date	18 September 1973

Economic indicators	2005	2010	2013
GDP: Gross domestic product (million current US$)	2 857 559	3 412 009	3 730 261
GDP: Growth rate at constant 2005 prices (annual %)	0.7	4.1	0.1
GDP per capita (current US$)	34 085.1	41 099.9	45 091.4
GNI: Gross national income per capita (current US$)	34 425.0	41 964.3	46 253.1
Gross fixed capital formation (% of GDP)	19.1	19.4	19.8
Exchange rates (national currency per US$)[a]	0.85	0.75	0.73
Balance of payments, current account (million US$)	133 770	195 389	256 022
CPI: Consumer price index (2000=100)	108	117	124[b]
Index of industrial production (2010=100)[c]	96	100	106
Agricultural production index (2004-2006=100)	100	102	105
Food production index (2004-2006=100)	100	102	105
Unemployment (% of labour force)	11.1	7.1	5.3
Employment in industrial sector (% of employed)	29.8[d]	28.4	28.2[e]
Employment in agricultural sector (% of employed)	2.4[d]	1.6	1.5[e]
Labour force participation, adult female pop. (%)	50.6	52.7	53.6
Labour force participation, adult male pop. (%)	66.6	66.3	66.4
Tourist arrivals at national borders (000)[f]	21 500	26 875	31 545
Energy production, primary (Petajoules)	5 704	5 407	5 161[e]
Mobile-cellular subscriptions (per 100 inhabitants)	94.6	106.5	119.0[g]
Individuals using the Internet (%)	68.7	82.0	84.0

Total trade		Major trading partners			2013
	(million US$)		(% of exports)		(% of imports)
Exports	1 458 647.0	France	9.0	Netherlands	8.9
Imports	1 194 482.6	United States	8.1	China	8.3
Balance	264 164.4	United Kingdom	6.5	France	7.1

Social indicators		
Population growth rate (average annual %)	2010-2015	−0.1
Urban population growth rate (average annual %)	2010-2015	0.2
Rural population growth rate (average annual %)	2010-2015	−0.9
Urban population (%)	2014	75.1
Population aged 0-14 years (%)	2014	13.0
Population aged 60+ years (females and males, % of total)	2014	30.0/25.0
Sex ratio (males per 100 females)	2014	96.5
Life expectancy at birth (females and males, years)	2010-2015	83.1/78.2
Infant mortality rate (per 1 000 live births)	2010-2015	3.1
Fertility rate, total (live births per woman)	2010-2015	1.4
Contraceptive prevalence (ages 15-49, %)[h]	2007-2013	66.2[i]
International migrant stock (000 and % of total population)	mid-2013	9 845.2/11.9
Refugees and others of concern to UNHCR	mid-2014	374 327
Education: Government expenditure (% of GDP)	2007-2013	5.0
Education: Primary-secondary gross enrolment ratio (f/m per 100)	2007-2013	99.0/103.0
Education: Female third-level students (% of total)	2007-2013	50.1
Intentional homicide rate (per 100,000 population)	2008-2012	0.8
Seats held by women in national parliaments (%)	2015	36.5

Environmental indicators		
Threatened species	2014	110
Forested area (% of land area)	2012	31.8
Proportion of terrestrial and marine areas protected (%)	2014	38.5
Population using improved drinking water sources (%)	2012	100.0
Population using improved sanitation facilities (%)	2012	100.0
CO$_2$ emission estimates (000 metric tons and metric tons per capita)	2011	729 458/8.8
Energy supply per capita (Gigajoules)	2012	157.0

a Market rate. **b** Series linked to former series. **c** ISIC Rev.4 (BCD). **d** ISIC Rev.3. **e** 2012. **f** Arrivals of non-resident tourists in all types of accommodation establishments. **g** ITU estimate. **h** Age group 18 to 49 years. **i** 2005.

Ghana

Region	Western Africa	Surface area (sq km)	238 533	
Population (est., 000)	26 442	Pop. density (per sq km)	110.9	
Capital city	Accra	Capital city pop. (000)	2 242	
Currency	Cedi (GHS)	UN membership date	8 March 1957	

Economic indicators	2005	2010	2013
GDP: Gross domestic product (million current US$)	17 199	32 174	47 830
GDP: Growth rate at constant 2005 prices (annual %)	6.2	7.3	7.1
GDP per capita (current US$)	804.3	1 326.1	1 846.4
GNI: Gross national income per capita (current US$)	794.5	1 304.1	1 798.2
Gross fixed capital formation (% of GDP)	20.6	24.7	22.8
Exchange rates (national currency per US$) [a]	0.91	1.47	2.20
Balance of payments, current account (million US$)	−1 105	−2 747	−5 685
CPI: Consumer price index (2000=100)	251	511	678
Index of industrial production (2010=100) [b]	...	100	182
Agricultural production index (2004-2006=100)	100	125	143
Food production index (2004-2006=100)	100	125	143
Unemployment (% of labour force)	3.8	4.2	4.6
Employment in industrial sector (% of employed)	13.6[cdefg]	15.4[hij]	...
Employment in agricultural sector (% of employed)	57.2[cdefg]	41.5[hij]	...
Labour force participation, adult female pop. (%)	67.6	66.9	67.3
Labour force participation, adult male pop. (%)	71.7	70.9	71.4
Tourist arrivals at national borders (000) [k]	429	931	...
Energy production, primary (Petajoules)	164	148	347[l]
Mobile-cellular subscriptions (per 100 inhabitants)	13.4	71.9	108.2
Individuals using the Internet (%)	1.8	7.8[mn]	12.3

Total trade		Major trading partners			2013
	(million US$)	(% of exports)			(% of imports)
Exports	12 643.9	South Africa	22.4	China	17.8
Imports	12 787.2	United Arab Emirates	13.1	United States	9.8
Balance	−143.3	Switzerland	9.3	Belgium	7.2

Social indicators		
Population growth rate (average annual %)	2010-2015	2.1
Urban population growth rate (average annual %)	2010-2015	3.4
Rural population growth rate (average annual %)	2010-2015	0.7
Urban population (%)	2014	53.4
Population aged 0-14 years (%)	2014	38.3
Population aged 60+ years (females and males, % of total)	2014	5.8/4.9
Sex ratio (males per 100 females)	2014	98.6
Life expectancy at birth (females and males, years)	2010-2015	61.9/60.0
Infant mortality rate (per 1 000 live births)	2010-2015	51.1
Fertility rate, total (live births per woman)	2010-2015	3.9
Contraceptive prevalence (ages 15-49, %)	2007-2013	19.5
International migrant stock (000 and % of total population)	mid-2013	358.8/1.4
Refugees and others of concern to UNHCR	mid-2014	20 971
Education: Government expenditure (% of GDP)	2007-2013	8.1
Education: Primary-secondary gross enrolment ratio (f/m per 100)	2007-2013	87.3/89.3
Education: Female third-level students (% of total)	2007-2013	37.7
Intentional homicide rate (per 100,000 population)	2008-2012	6.1
Seats held by women in national parliaments (%)	2015	10.9

Environmental indicators		
Threatened species	2014	223
Forested area (% of land area)	2012	20.7
Proportion of terrestrial and marine areas protected (%)	2014	7.8
Population using improved drinking water sources (%)	2012	87.0
Population using improved sanitation facilities (%)	2012	14.0
CO_2 emission estimates (000 metric tons and metric tons per capita)	2011	10 081/0.4
Energy supply per capita (Gigajoules)	2012	13.0

a Principal rate. b ISIC Rev.4 (BCDE). c 2006. d Living standards survey. e ISIC Rev.3. f Population aged 15-64. g September of the preceding year to September of the current year. h Population census. i September. j Break in series. k Including nationals residing abroad. l 2012. m Break in comparability. n Population aged 12 years and over.

Greece

Region	Southern Europe	
Population (est., 000)	11 128	
Capital city	Athens	
Currency	Euro (EUR)	

Surface area (sq km)	131 957
Pop. density (per sq km)	84.3
Capital city pop. (000)	3 060 [a]
UN membership date	25 October 1945

Economic indicators	2005	2010	2013
GDP: Gross domestic product (million current US$)	247 666	299 598	242 230
GDP: Growth rate at constant 2005 prices (annual %)	0.9	−5.5	−3.3
GDP per capita (current US$)	22 430.2	26 966.5	21 767.7
GNI: Gross national income per capita (current US$)	22 440.8	26 413.5	21 761.0
Gross fixed capital formation (% of GDP)	20.7	17.3	11.2
Exchange rates (national currency per US$) [b]	0.85	0.75	0.73
Balance of payments, current account (million US$)	−18 233	−30 274	1 409
CPI: Consumer price index (2000=100)	118 [c]	139	144
Index of industrial production (2010=100) [d]	118	100	90
Agricultural production index (2004-2006=100)	103	83	86
Food production index (2004-2006=100)	103	87	88
Unemployment (% of labour force)	9.8	12.5	27.3
Employment in industrial sector (% of employed)	22.4 [e]	19.7	16.7 [f]
Employment in agricultural sector (% of employed)	12.4 [e]	12.5	13.0 [f]
Labour force participation, adult female pop. (%)	42.1	44.1	44.2
Labour force participation, adult male pop. (%)	64.7	64.4	62.5
Tourist arrivals at national borders (000)	14 765 [g]	15 007 [h]	17 920 [h]
Energy production, primary (Petajoules)	432	396	437 [f]
Mobile-cellular subscriptions (per 100 inhabitants)	92.9	110.7	116.8
Individuals using the Internet (%)	24.0	44.4	59.9

Total trade		Major trading partners			2013
	(million US$)		(% of exports)		(% of imports)
Exports	36 261.6	Turkey	11.7	Russian Federation	14.4
Imports	61 148.1	Italy	8.9	Germany	9.6
Balance	−24 886.5	Germany	6.5	Iraq	7.8

Social indicators		
Population growth rate (average annual %)	2010-2015	<
Urban population growth rate (average annual %)	2010-2015	0.5
Rural population growth rate (average annual %)	2010-2015	−1.5
Urban population (%)	2014	77.7
Population aged 0-14 years (%)	2014	14.7
Population aged 60+ years (females and males, % of total)	2014	28.3/23.6
Sex ratio (males per 100 females)	2014	97.5
Life expectancy at birth (females and males, years)	2010-2015	83.0/78.3
Infant mortality rate (per 1 000 live births)	2010-2015	3.6
Fertility rate, total (live births per woman)	2010-2015	1.5
Contraceptive prevalence (ages 15-49, %) [i]	2007-2013	76.2 [j]
International migrant stock (000 and % of total population) [k]	mid-2013	988.2/8.9
Refugees and others of concern to UNHCR	mid-2014	59 085 [l]
Education: Government expenditure (% of GDP)	2007-2013	4.1 [m]
Education: Primary-secondary gross enrolment ratio (f/m per 100)	2007-2013	104.6/106.0
Education: Female third-level students (% of total)	2007-2013	49.1
Intentional homicide rate (per 100,000 population)	2008-2012	1.7
Seats held by women in national parliaments (%)	2015	23.0

Environmental indicators		
Threatened species	2014	286
Forested area (% of land area)	2012	30.8
Proportion of terrestrial and marine areas protected (%)	2014	8.6
Population using improved drinking water sources (%)	2012	100.0
Population using improved sanitation facilities (%)	2012	99.0
CO_2 emission estimates (000 metric tons and metric tons per capita)	2011	84 048/7.6
Energy supply per capita (Gigajoules)	2012	101.0

a Refers to the localities of Calithèa, Peristérion and Piraeus, among others. b Market rate. c Series linked to former series. d ISIC Rev.4 (BCDE). e ISIC Rev.3. f 2012. g Information based on administrative data. h Information based on border survey. i Age group 16 to 45 years. j 2001. k Refers to foreign citizens. l Refugee population refers to the end of 2013. m 2005.

Greenland

Region	Northern America	Surface area (sq km)	2 166 086
Population (est., 000)	57	Pop. density (per sq km)	<
Capital city	Nuuk	Capital city pop. (000)	17
Currency	Danish Krone (DKK)		

Economic indicators	2005	2010	2013
GDP: Gross domestic product (million current US$)	1 650	2 287	2 418
GDP: Growth rate at constant 2005 prices (annual %)	3.7	2.5	−1.9
GDP per capita (current US$)	28 977.4	40 447.3	42 437.2
GNI: Gross national income per capita (current US$)	28 290.6	39 503.8	41 433.7
Gross fixed capital formation (% of GDP)	24.8	53.7	53.3
Exchange rates (national currency per US$)[a]	6.30	5.68	5.41
CPI: Consumer price index (2000=100)	113	132	142
Agricultural production index (2004-2006=100)	100	99	99
Food production index (2004-2006=100)	99	99	99
Energy production, primary (Petajoules)	1	1	1[bc]
Mobile-cellular subscriptions (per 100 inhabitants)	81.6	101.4	106.0[d]
Individuals using the Internet (%)	57.7	63.0	65.8[d]

Total trade		Major trading partners			2013
	(million US$)		(% of exports)		(% of imports)
Exports	490.1	Denmark	85.5	Denmark	62.5
Imports	822.1	Areas nes	5.3[e]	Sweden	23.2
Balance	−332.0	Portugal	4.6	China	2.7

Social indicators		
Population growth rate (average annual %)	2010-2015	0.3
Urban population growth rate (average annual %)	2010-2015	0.7
Rural population growth rate (average annual %)	2010-2015	−2.6
Urban population (%)	2014	86.1
Population aged 0-14 years (%)[fgh]	2014	21.7[b]
Population aged 60+ years (females and males, % of total)[fgh]	2014	11.1/11.7[b]
Sex ratio (males per 100 females)[fgh]	2014	112.8[b]
Life expectancy at birth (females and males, years)[f]	2010-2015	72.9/68.2[i]
Fertility rate, total (live births per woman)[f]	2010-2015	2.1[i]
International migrant stock (000 and % of total population)	mid-2013	5.7/10.0

Environmental indicators		
Threatened species	2014	17
Forested area (% of land area)	2012	0.0
Proportion of terrestrial and marine areas protected (%)	2014	22.4
CO2 emission estimates (000 metric tons and metric tons per capita)	2011	708/12.5
Energy supply per capita (Gigajoules)	2012	162.0

a UN operational exchange rate. **b** 2012. **c** UNSD estimate. **d** ITU estimate. **e** See technical notes. **f** Data compiled by the United Nations Demographic Yearbook system. **g** Data refer to the latest available census. **h** De jure estimate. **i** 2007-2011. **j** 2011.

Grenada

Region	Caribbean	Surface area (sq km)	344
Population (est., 000)	106	Pop. density (per sq km)	309.0
Capital city	St.George's	Capital city pop. (000)	38
Currency	E.C. Dollar (XCD)	UN membership date	17 September 1974

Economic indicators	2005	2010	2013
GDP: Gross domestic product (million current US$)	695	771	831
GDP: Growth rate at constant 2005 prices (annual %)	13.3	−0.5	1.6
GDP per capita (current US$)	6 754.4	7 365.6	7 842.8
GNI: Gross national income per capita (current US$)	6 479.7	6 984.7	7 647.9
Gross fixed capital formation (% of GDP)	46.3	22.0	18.6
Exchange rates (national currency per US$)[a]	2.70	2.70	2.70
Balance of payments, current account (million US$)	−193	−204	−213
CPI: Consumer price index (2000=100)	112	136[b]	142
Agricultural production index (2004-2006=100)	77	90	97
Food production index (2004-2006=100)	77	90	97
Tourist arrivals at national borders (000)	99	110	116
Energy production, primary (Petajoules)	0	0	0[c]
Mobile-cellular subscriptions (per 100 inhabitants)	45.5	116.5	125.6
Individuals using the Internet (%)[d]	20.5	27.0	35.0

Social indicators		
Population growth rate (average annual %)	2010-2015	0.4
Urban population growth rate (average annual %)	2010-2015	0.3
Rural population growth rate (average annual %)	2010-2015	0.4
Urban population (%)	2014	35.6
Population aged 0-14 years (%)	2014	26.6
Population aged 60+ years (females and males, % of total)	2014	11.3/8.6
Sex ratio (males per 100 females)	2014	100.5
Life expectancy at birth (females and males, years)	2010-2015	75.2/70.2
Infant mortality rate (per 1 000 live births)	2010-2015	8.9
Fertility rate, total (live births per woman)	2010-2015	2.2
Contraceptive prevalence (ages 15-49, %)[e]	2007-2013	54.3[f]
International migrant stock (000 and % of total population)	mid-2013	11.4/10.7
Refugees and others of concern to UNHCR	mid-2014	0[g]
Education: Government expenditure (% of GDP)	2007-2013	3.9[h]
Education: Primary-secondary gross enrolment ratio (f/m per 100)	2007-2013	105.1/105.6
Education: Female third-level students (% of total)	2007-2013	57.1
Seats held by women in national parliaments (%)	2015	33.3

Environmental indicators		
Threatened species	2014	45
Forested area (% of land area)	2012	50.0
Proportion of terrestrial and marine areas protected (%)	2014	0.1
Population using improved drinking water sources (%)	2012	97.0
Population using improved sanitation facilities (%)	2012	98.0
CO$_2$ emission estimates (000 metric tons and metric tons per capita)	2011	253/2.4
Energy supply per capita (Gigajoules)	2012	39.0

a Official rate. b Series linked to former series. c 2012. d ITU estimate. e Age group 15 to 44 years. f 1990. g Value is zero, not available or not applicable. h 2003.

Guadeloupe

Region	Caribbean	Surface area (sq km)	1 705
Population (est., 000)	468 [a]	Pop. density (per sq km)	274.5 [a]
Capital city	Basse-Terre	Capital city pop. (000)	55
Currency	Euro (EUR)		

Economic indicators	2005	2010	2013
Exchange rates (national currency per US$) [b]	0.84	0.76	0.72
CPI: Consumer price index (2000=100)	112	122	129
Agricultural production index (2004-2006=100)	103	89	100
Food production index (2004-2006=100)	103	89	100
Unemployment (% of labour force)	25.9	23.8	23.6
Employment in industrial sector (% of employed)	...	13.8 [cd]	13.5 [cde]
Employment in agricultural sector (% of employed)	...	0.0 [cd]	3.3 [cde]
Labour force participation, adult female pop. (%)	48.6	51.4	50.0
Labour force participation, adult male pop. (%)	56.1	57.5	57.2
Tourist arrivals at national borders (000) [fg]	372 [h]	392	487 [i]
Energy production, primary (Petajoules) [j]	2	2	3 [e]

Social indicators		
Population growth rate (average annual %) [a]	2010-2015	0.5
Urban population growth rate (average annual %) [a]	2010-2015	0.5
Rural population growth rate (average annual %) [a]	2010-2015	0.2
Urban population (%) [a]	2014	98.4
Population aged 0-14 years (%) [a]	2014	21.2
Population aged 60+ years (females and males, % of total) [a]	2014	20.3/17.5
Sex ratio (males per 100 females) [a]	2014	89.0
Life expectancy at birth (females and males, years) [a]	2010-2015	84.0/77.4
Infant mortality rate (per 1 000 live births) [a]	2010-2015	5.6
Fertility rate, total (live births per woman) [a]	2010-2015	2.1
Contraceptive prevalence (ages 15-49, %)	2007-2013	29.4 [k]
International migrant stock (000 and % of total population) [a]	mid-2013	97.1/20.8
Intentional homicide rate (per 100,000 population)	2008-2012	7.9

Environmental indicators		
Threatened species	2014	62
Forested area (% of land area)	2012	38.0
Proportion of terrestrial and marine areas protected (%)	2014	2.6
CO_2 emission estimates (000 metric tons and metric tons per capita)	2011	1 775/3.9
Energy supply per capita (Gigajoules)	2012	67.0 [j]

a Including Saint-Barthélemy and Saint-Martin (French part). b UN operational exchange rate. c March to June. d Excluding institutional population. e 2012. f Arrivals by air. g Excluding the north islands (Saint Martin and Saint Barthelemy). h Information based on survey conducted at Guadeloupe Airport. i Including residents and non-residents. j UNSD estimate. k 1976.

Guam

Region	Oceania-Micronesia	Surface area (sq km)	549	
Population (est., 000)	168	Pop. density (per sq km)	305.2	
Capital city	Hagåtña	Capital city pop. (000)	143	
Currency	U.S. Dollar (USD)			

Economic indicators	2005	2010	2013
CPI: Consumer price index (2000=100)	116	154	164
Agricultural production index (2004-2006=100)	100	97	97
Food production index (2004-2006=100)	100	97	97
Employment in industrial sector (% of employed)	...	14.0[a]	...
Employment in agricultural sector (% of employed)	...	0.3[a]	...
Labour force participation, adult female pop. (%)	56.1	54.8	55.7
Labour force participation, adult male pop. (%)	69.7	70.1	69.4
Tourist arrivals at national borders (000)	1 228	1 196	1 334
Individuals using the Internet (%)	38.6	54.0[b]	65.4[b]

Social indicators		
Population growth rate (average annual %)	2010-2015	1.3
Urban population growth rate (average annual %)	2010-2015	1.4
Rural population growth rate (average annual %)	2010-2015	−0.2
Urban population (%)	2014	94.4
Population aged 0-14 years (%)	2014	25.9
Population aged 60+ years (females and males, % of total)	2014	13.6/11.7
Sex ratio (males per 100 females)	2014	103.0
Life expectancy at birth (females and males, years)	2010-2015	81.5/76.1
Infant mortality rate (per 1 000 live births)	2010-2015	9.7
Fertility rate, total (live births per woman)	2010-2015	2.4
Contraceptive prevalence (ages 15-49, %)[c]	2007-2013	66.6[d]
International migrant stock (000 and % of total population)	mid-2013	80.8/48.9
Intentional homicide rate (per 100,000 population)	2008-2012	2.5

Environmental indicators		
Threatened species	2014	95
Forested area (% of land area)	2012	47.9
Proportion of terrestrial and marine areas protected (%)	2014	5.2

a Population census. b ITU estimate. c Age group 18 to 44 years. d 2002.

Guatemala

Region	Central America	Surface area (sq km)	108 889	
Population (est., 000)	15 860	Pop. density (per sq km)	145.7	
Capital city	Guatemala City	Capital city pop. (000)	2 847	
Currency	Quetzal (GTQ)	UN membership date	21 November 1945	

Economic indicators	2005	2010	2013
GDP: Gross domestic product (million current US$)	27 211	41 338	53 797
GDP: Growth rate at constant 2005 prices (annual %)	3.3	2.9	3.7
GDP per capita (current US$)	2 146.2	2 882.4	3 477.9
GNI: Gross national income per capita (current US$)	2 119.7	2 797.7	3 388.2
Gross fixed capital formation (% of GDP)	18.3	14.8	14.3
Exchange rates (national currency per US$) [a]	7.61	8.02	7.85
Balance of payments, current account (million US$)	−1 241	−563	−1 465
CPI: Consumer price index (2000=100)	144	193	222
Index of industrial production (2010=100) [b]	89	100	111
Agricultural production index (2004-2006=100)	98	128	147
Food production index (2004-2006=100)	98	131	150
Unemployment (% of labour force)	2.5	3.7	2.8
Employment in industrial sector (% of employed) [c]	22.8[de]	21.8[f]	19.5[fg]
Employment in agricultural sector (% of employed) [c]	33.2[de]	33.5[f]	32.3[fg]
Labour force participation, adult female pop. (%)	44.9	48.8	49.3
Labour force participation, adult male pop. (%)	87.4	88.2	88.2
Tourist arrivals at national borders (000) [h]	1 316	1 876	2 000
Energy production, primary (Petajoules)	256	314	345[g]
Mobile-cellular subscriptions (per 100 inhabitants)	35.6	126.0	140.4
Individuals using the Internet (%)	5.7	10.5[i]	19.7[i]

Total trade		Major trading partners			2013
	(million US$)		(% of exports)		(% of imports)
Exports	10 065.3	United States	38.4	United States	37.2
Imports	17 504.0	El Salvador	11.0	Mexico	10.6
Balance	−7 438.7	Honduras	7.9	China	8.2

Social indicators		
Population growth rate (average annual %)	2010-2015	2.5
Urban population growth rate (average annual %)	2010-2015	3.4
Rural population growth rate (average annual %)	2010-2015	1.6
Urban population (%)	2014	51.1
Population aged 0-14 years (%)	2014	40.1
Population aged 60+ years (females and males, % of total)	2014	6.9/6.4
Sex ratio (males per 100 females)	2014	95.3
Life expectancy at birth (females and males, years)	2010-2015	75.5/68.4
Infant mortality rate (per 1 000 live births)	2010-2015	23.5
Fertility rate, total (live births per woman)	2010-2015	3.8
Contraceptive prevalence (ages 15-49, %)	2007-2013	54.1
International migrant stock (000 and % of total population) [j]	mid-2013	72.8/0.5
Refugees and others of concern to UNHCR	mid-2014	222
Education: Government expenditure (% of GDP)	2007-2013	2.9
Education: Primary-secondary gross enrolment ratio (f/m per 100)	2007-2013	87.4/92.2
Education: Female third-level students (% of total)	2007-2013	51.3
Intentional homicide rate (per 100,000 population)	2008-2012	39.9
Seats held by women in national parliaments (%)	2015	13.3

Environmental indicators		
Threatened species	2014	271
Forested area (% of land area)	2012	33.1
Proportion of terrestrial and marine areas protected (%)	2014	15.7
Population using improved drinking water sources (%)	2012	94.0
Population using improved sanitation facilities (%)	2012	80.0
CO$_2$ emission estimates (000 metric tons and metric tons per capita)	2011	11 258/0.8
Energy supply per capita (Gigajoules)	2012	31.0

a Market rate. **b** ISIC Rev.3 (CDE). **c** ISIC Rev.3. **d** 2006. **e** Population aged 10 and over. **f** Break in series. **g** 2012. **h** Arrivals of non-resident visitors at national borders. **i** ITU estimate. **j** Including refugees.

Guinea

Region	Western Africa	Surface area (sq km)	245 857
Population (est., 000)	12 044	Pop. density (per sq km)	49.0
Capital city	Conakry	Capital city pop. (000)	1 886
Currency	Guinean Franc (GNF)	UN membership date	12 December 1958

Economic indicators	2005	2010	2013
GDP: Gross domestic product (million current US$)	2 935	5 233	7 219
GDP: Growth rate at constant 2005 prices (annual %)	3.0	1.9	2.5
GDP per capita (current US$)	306.5	481.1	614.6
GNI: Gross national income per capita (current US$)	301.4	474.1	570.2
Gross fixed capital formation (% of GDP)	27.6	30.0	33.1
Exchange rates (national currency per US$)[a]	4 500.00	6 083.95	7 005.83
Balance of payments, current account (million US$)	−160	−327	−1 161
CPI: Consumer price index (2000=100)[b]	185	439	686
Agricultural production index (2004-2006=100)	101	113	123
Food production index (2004-2006=100)	101	113	123
Unemployment (% of labour force)	1.9	1.6	1.8
Labour force participation, adult female pop. (%)	63.8	65.3	65.6
Labour force participation, adult male pop. (%)	78.3	78.3	78.3
Tourist arrivals at national borders (000)[c]	45	12	56
Energy production, primary (Petajoules)	109	112	112[d]
Mobile-cellular subscriptions (per 100 inhabitants)	2.0	36.8	63.3
Individuals using the Internet (%)	0.5	1.0[e]	1.6[e]

Social indicators		
Population growth rate (average annual %)	2010-2015	2.5
Urban population growth rate (average annual %)	2010-2015	3.8
Rural population growth rate (average annual %)	2010-2015	1.8
Urban population (%)	2014	36.7
Population aged 0-14 years (%)	2014	42.1
Population aged 60+ years (females and males, % of total)	2014	5.5/4.8
Sex ratio (males per 100 females)	2014	100.4
Life expectancy at birth (females and males, years)	2010-2015	56.7/55.2
Infant mortality rate (per 1 000 live births)	2010-2015	73.6
Fertility rate, total (live births per woman)	2010-2015	5.0
Contraceptive prevalence (ages 15-49, %)	2007-2013	5.6
International migrant stock (000 and % of total population)[fg]	mid-2013	378.5/3.2
Refugees and others of concern to UNHCR	mid-2014	8 862
Education: Government expenditure (% of GDP)	2007-2013	2.5
Education: Primary-secondary gross enrolment ratio (f/m per 100)	2007-2013	56.1/71.7
Education: Female third-level students (% of total)[h]	2007-2013	26.7
Intentional homicide rate (per 100,000 population)	2008-2012	8.9
Seats held by women in national parliaments (%)	2015	21.9

Environmental indicators		
Threatened species	2014	163
Forested area (% of land area)	2012	26.3
Proportion of terrestrial and marine areas protected (%)	2014	20.3
Population using improved drinking water sources (%)	2012	75.0
Population using improved sanitation facilities (%)	2012	19.0
CO_2 emission estimates (000 metric tons and metric tons per capita)	2011	2 596/0.2
Energy supply per capita (Gigajoules)	2012	13.0

a Market rate. b Conakry. c Arrivals by air at Conakry Airport. d 2012. e ITU estimate. f Refers to foreign citizens. g Including refugees. h UNESCO estimate.

Guinea-Bissau

Region	Western Africa	Surface area (sq km)	36 125
Population (est., 000)	1 746	Pop. density (per sq km)	48.3
Capital city	Bissau	Capital city pop. (000)	473
Currency	CFA Franc (XOF)	UN membership date	17 September 1974

Economic indicators	2005	2010	2013
GDP: Gross domestic product (million current US$)	587	845	1 036
GDP: Growth rate at constant 2005 prices (annual %)	6.5	4.5	0.3
GDP per capita (current US$)	412.8	532.6	608.1
GNI: Gross national income per capita (current US$)	404.6	532.0	604.3
Gross fixed capital formation (% of GDP)	6.1	6.6	5.5
Exchange rates (national currency per US$)[a]	556.04	490.91	475.64
Balance of payments, current account (million US$)	−10	−71	−83[b]
CPI: Consumer price index (2000=100)[c]	104[d]	122[de]	...
Agricultural production index (2004-2006=100)	99	122	140
Food production index (2004-2006=100)	99	122	141
Unemployment (% of labour force)	6.9	6.8	7.1
Labour force participation, adult female pop. (%)	66.2	68.0	68.2
Labour force participation, adult male pop. (%)	78.5	78.4	78.5
Tourist arrivals at national borders (000)[f]	5	...	...
Energy production, primary (Petajoules)	22	24	24[b]
Mobile-cellular subscriptions (per 100 inhabitants)	7.0	42.7	74.1[g]
Individuals using the Internet (%)	1.9	2.5[g]	3.1[g]

Social indicators		
Population growth rate (average annual %)	2010-2015	2.4
Urban population growth rate (average annual %)	2010-2015	4.1
Rural population growth rate (average annual %)	2010-2015	0.8
Urban population (%)	2014	48.6
Population aged 0-14 years (%)	2014	41.3
Population aged 60+ years (females and males, % of total)	2014	5.8/5.2
Sex ratio (males per 100 females)	2014	98.9
Life expectancy at birth (females and males, years)	2010-2015	55.7/52.7
Infant mortality rate (per 1 000 live births)	2010-2015	93.9
Fertility rate, total (live births per woman)	2010-2015	5.0
Contraceptive prevalence (ages 15-49, %)	2007-2013	14.2
International migrant stock (000 and % of total population)[h]	mid-2013	18.0/1.1
Refugees and others of concern to UNHCR	mid-2014	8 686
Education: Government expenditure (% of GDP)	2007-2013	5.3[i]
Education: Primary-secondary gross enrolment ratio (f/m per 100)	2007-2013	40.6/62.4[j]
Intentional homicide rate (per 100,000 population)	2008-2012	8.4
Seats held by women in national parliaments (%)	2015	13.7

Environmental indicators		
Threatened species	2014	66
Forested area (% of land area)	2012	71.2
Proportion of terrestrial and marine areas protected (%)	2014	10.4
Population using improved drinking water sources (%)	2012	74.0
Population using improved sanitation facilities (%)	2012	20.0
CO_2 emission estimates (000 metric tons and metric tons per capita)	2011	246/0.2
Energy supply per capita (Gigajoules)	2012	17.0

a Official rate. b 2012. c Bissau. d Index base 2003=100. e Series linked to former series. f Arrivals by air. g ITU estimate. h Including refugees. i 1999. j 2000.

Guyana

Region	South America	Surface area (sq km)	214 969
Population (est., 000)	804	Pop. density (per sq km)	3.7
Capital city	Georgetown	Capital city pop. (000)	124
Currency	Guyana Dollar (GYD)	UN membership date	20 September 1966

Economic indicators	2005	2010	2013
GDP: Gross domestic product (million current US$)	1 315	2 259	2 990
GDP: Growth rate at constant 2005 prices (annual %)	−2.0	4.4	5.3
GDP per capita (current US$)	1 728.9	2 874.0	3 739.5
GNI: Gross national income per capita (current US$)	1 717.8	2 890.2	3 775.2
Gross fixed capital formation (% of GDP)	20.3	25.4	18.6
Exchange rates (national currency per US$)[a]	200.25	203.50	206.25
Balance of payments, current account (million US$)	−96	−155	−426
CPI: Consumer price index (2000=100)[b]	128	177[c]	186[d]
Agricultural production index (2004-2006=100)	94	108	129
Food production index (2004-2006=100)	94	108	129
Unemployment (% of labour force)	12.6	11.4	11.1
Labour force participation, adult female pop. (%)	39.4	41.6	42.6
Labour force participation, adult male pop. (%)	81.8	81.4	80.5
Tourist arrivals at national borders (000)[e]	117	152	177[f]
Energy production, primary (Petajoules)	9	8	8[f]
Mobile-cellular subscriptions (per 100 inhabitants)	37.0	71.3	69.4
Individuals using the Internet (%)	...	29.9	33.0[g]

Total trade		Major trading partners			2013
	(million US$)		(% of exports)		(% of imports)
Exports	1 375.9	Canada	30.1	United States	21.7
Imports	1 866.3	United States	26.3	Trinidad and Tobago	19.3
Balance	−490.4	Venezuela	11.9	Venezuela	11.7

Social indicators		
Population growth rate (average annual %)	2010-2015	0.5
Urban population growth rate (average annual %)	2010-2015	0.8
Rural population growth rate (average annual %)	2010-2015	0.5
Urban population (%)	2014	28.5
Population aged 0-14 years (%)	2014	35.3
Population aged 60+ years (females and males, % of total)	2014	6.7/4.3
Sex ratio (males per 100 females)	2014	103.3
Life expectancy at birth (females and males, years)	2010-2015	68.9/63.5
Infant mortality rate (per 1 000 live births)	2010-2015	28.5
Fertility rate, total (live births per woman)	2010-2015	2.6
Contraceptive prevalence (ages 15-49, %)	2007-2013	42.5
International migrant stock (000 and % of total population)	mid-2013	14.8/1.9
Refugees and others of concern to UNHCR	mid-2014	12
Education: Government expenditure (% of GDP)	2007-2013	3.2
Education: Primary-secondary gross enrolment ratio (f/m per 100)	2007-2013	91.8/80.2
Education: Female third-level students (% of total)	2007-2013	66.8
Intentional homicide rate (per 100,000 population)	2008-2012	17.0
Seats held by women in national parliaments (%)	2015	31.3

Environmental indicators		
Threatened species	2014	86
Forested area (% of land area)	2012	77.2
Proportion of terrestrial and marine areas protected (%)	2014	5.3
Population using improved drinking water sources (%)	2012	98.0
Population using improved sanitation facilities (%)	2012	84.0
CO_2 emission estimates (000 metric tons and metric tons per capita)	2011	1 782/2.2
Energy supply per capita (Gigajoules)	2012	45.0

a Principal rate. b Georgetown. c Series linked to former series. d 2011. e Arrivals to Timehri Airport only. f 2012. g ITU estimate.

Haiti

Region	Caribbean	Surface area (sq km)	27 750
Population (est., 000)	10 461	Pop. density (per sq km)	377.0
Capital city	Port-au-Prince	Capital city pop. (000)	2 376
Currency	Gourde (HTG)	UN membership date	24 October 1945

Economic indicators	2005	2010	2013
GDP: Gross domestic product (million current US$)	3 807	6 147	7 691
GDP: Growth rate at constant 2005 prices (annual %)	1.8	−5.5	4.3
GDP per capita (current US$)	411.1	621.1	745.5
GNI: Gross national income per capita (current US$)	418.3	623.2	750.9
Gross fixed capital formation (% of GDP)	14.3	13.3	15.7
Exchange rates (national currency per US$)[a]	43.00	39.88	43.88
Balance of payments, current account (million US$)	7	−102	−543
CPI: Consumer price index (2000=100)	252[b]	375	457
Agricultural production index (2004-2006=100)	102	111	118
Food production index (2004-2006=100)	102	113	121
Unemployment (% of labour force)	7.4	8.0	7.0
Labour force participation, adult female pop. (%)	58.4	60.1	60.9
Labour force participation, adult male pop. (%)	69.5	70.5	71.0
Tourist arrivals at national borders (000)[c]	112	255[d]	295[def]
Energy production, primary (Petajoules)	115	131	140[e]
Mobile-cellular subscriptions (per 100 inhabitants)	5.4[g]	40.4	69.4[g]
Individuals using the Internet (%)[g]	6.4	8.4	10.6

Social indicators		
Population growth rate (average annual %)	2010-2015	1.4
Urban population growth rate (average annual %)	2010-2015	3.8
Rural population growth rate (average annual %)	2010-2015	−1.6
Urban population (%)	2014	57.4
Population aged 0-14 years (%)	2014	34.6
Population aged 60+ years (females and males, % of total)	2014	7.4/6.4
Sex ratio (males per 100 females)	2014	97.7
Life expectancy at birth (females and males, years)	2010-2015	64.9/61.1
Infant mortality rate (per 1 000 live births)	2010-2015	40.2
Fertility rate, total (live births per woman)	2010-2015	3.2
Contraceptive prevalence (ages 15-49, %)	2007-2013	34.5
International migrant stock (000 and % of total population)	mid-2013	38.1/0.4
Refugees and others of concern to UNHCR	mid-2014	7
Seats held by women in national parliaments (%)	2015	4.2

Environmental indicators		
Threatened species	2014	159
Forested area (% of land area)	2012	3.6
Proportion of terrestrial and marine areas protected (%)	2014	0.1
Population using improved drinking water sources (%)	2012	62.0
Population using improved sanitation facilities (%)	2012	24.0
CO_2 emission estimates (000 metric tons and metric tons per capita)	2011	2 211/0.2
Energy supply per capita (Gigajoules)	2012	17.0

a Principal rate. b Series linked to former series. c Arrivals by air. d Including nationals residing abroad. e 2012. f Including data for only 10 months; data for September and October are not available. g ITU estimate.

Honduras

Region	Central America	Surface area (sq km)	112 492
Population (est., 000)	8 261	Pop. density (per sq km)	73.7
Capital city	Tegucigalpa	Capital city pop. (000)	1 101
Currency	Lempira (HNL)	UN membership date	17 December 1945

Economic indicators	2005	2010	2013
GDP: Gross domestic product (million current US$)	9 757	15 839	18 569
GDP: Growth rate at constant 2005 prices (annual %)	6.1	3.7	2.6
GDP per capita (current US$)	1 414.3	2 078.3	2 293.1
GNI: Gross national income per capita (current US$)	1 348.1	1 982.7	2 131.1
Gross fixed capital formation (% of GDP)	24.9	21.6	24.5
Exchange rates (national currency per US$)[a]	18.90	18.90	20.60
Balance of payments, current account (million US$)	−304	−682	−1 655
CPI: Consumer price index (2000=100)	150	208	245
Index of industrial production (2010=100)[b]	89	100	114
Agricultural production index (2004-2006=100)	103	111	121
Food production index (2004-2006=100)	104	109	118
Unemployment (% of labour force)	4.2	4.8	4.2
Employment in industrial sector (% of employed)[c]	20.9[de]	19.5[d]	19.8[fgh]
Employment in agricultural sector (% of employed)[c]	39.2[de]	36.0[d]	35.3[fgh]
Labour force participation, adult female pop. (%)	39.6	41.9	42.8
Labour force participation, adult male pop. (%)	83.7	82.9	82.9
Tourist arrivals at national borders (000)	673	863	863
Energy production, primary (Petajoules)	77	93	103[i]
Mobile-cellular subscriptions (per 100 inhabitants)	18.6	124.7	95.9
Individuals using the Internet (%)	6.5[jk]	11.1	17.8

Total trade		Major trading partners			2013
	(million US$)	(% of exports)		(% of imports)	
Exports	3 648.8	United States	36.9	United States	39.7
Imports	8 566.1	El Salvador	8.3	China	9.8
Balance	−4 917.3	Germany	7.8	Guatemala	7.2

Social indicators		
Population growth rate (average annual %)	2010-2015	2.0
Urban population growth rate (average annual %)	2010-2015	3.1
Rural population growth rate (average annual %)	2010-2015	0.7
Urban population (%)	2014	54.1
Population aged 0-14 years (%)	2014	34.8
Population aged 60+ years (females and males, % of total)	2014	7.0/6.4
Sex ratio (males per 100 females)	2014	100.2
Life expectancy at birth (females and males, years)	2010-2015	76.2/71.3
Infant mortality rate (per 1 000 live births)	2010-2015	22.3
Fertility rate, total (live births per woman)	2010-2015	3.0
Contraceptive prevalence (ages 15-49, %)	2007-2013	73.2
International migrant stock (000 and % of total population)[l]	mid-2013	27.5/0.3
Refugees and others of concern to UNHCR	mid-2014	41
Education: Primary-secondary gross enrolment ratio (f/m per 100)	2007-2013	92.9/87.3
Education: Female third-level students (% of total)	2007-2013	57.2
Intentional homicide rate (per 100,000 population)	2008-2012	90.4
Seats held by women in national parliaments (%)	2015	25.8

Environmental indicators		
Threatened species	2014	284
Forested area (% of land area)	2012	44.3
Proportion of terrestrial and marine areas protected (%)	2014	7.8
Population using improved drinking water sources (%)	2012	90.0
Population using improved sanitation facilities (%)	2012	80.0
CO_2 emission estimates (000 metric tons and metric tons per capita)	2011	8 412/1.1
Energy supply per capita (Gigajoules)	2012	27.0

a Principal rate. b ISIC Rev.3 (CDE). c ISIC Rev.2. d Population aged 10 and over. e September. f 2011. g May. h Break in series. i 2012. j Population aged 5 and over. k ITU estimate. l Including refugees.

Hungary

Region	Eastern Europe	Surface area (sq km)	93 024	
Population (est., 000)	9 933	Pop. density (per sq km)	106.8	
Capital city	Budapest	Capital city pop. (000)	1 717	
Currency	Forint (HUF)	UN membership date	14 December 1955	

Economic indicators	2005	2010	2013
GDP: Gross domestic product (million current US$)	111 890	129 583	133 424
GDP: Growth rate at constant 2005 prices (annual %)	4.3	0.8	1.5
GDP per capita (current US$)	11 082.7	12 939.4	13 402.8
GNI: Gross national income per capita (current US$)	10 517.5	12 335.4	13 014.1
Gross fixed capital formation (% of GDP)	23.9	20.4	19.9
Exchange rates (national currency per US$)[a]	213.58	208.65	215.67
Balance of payments, current account (million US$)	−7 883	346	5 497
CPI: Consumer price index (2000=100)	133	173	193
Index of industrial production (2010=100)[b]	93	100	105
Agricultural production index (2004-2006=100)	97	80	88
Food production index (2004-2006=100)	96	80	88
Unemployment (% of labour force)	7.2	11.2	10.2
Employment in industrial sector (% of employed)[c]	32.4[de]	30.7	29.8[f]
Employment in agricultural sector (% of employed)[c]	5.0[de]	4.5	5.2[f]
Labour force participation, adult female pop. (%)	42.9	43.7	44.8
Labour force participation, adult male pop. (%)	58.3	58.3	60.0
Tourist arrivals at national borders (000)	9 979	9 510	10 675
Energy production, primary (Petajoules)	434	461	442[f]
Mobile-cellular subscriptions (per 100 inhabitants)	92.3	119.9	116.4
Individuals using the Internet (%)	39.0	65.0	72.6

Total trade		Major trading partners			2013
	(million US$)		(% of exports)		(% of imports)
Exports	107 730.0	Germany	25.8	Germany	25.0
Imports	98 661.8	Romania	5.7	Russian Federation	8.7
Balance	9 068.2	Austria	5.6	Austria	6.7

Social indicators		
Population growth rate (average annual %)	2010-2015	−0.2
Urban population growth rate (average annual %)	2010-2015	0.5
Rural population growth rate (average annual %)	2010-2015	−1.8
Urban population (%)	2014	70.8
Population aged 0-14 years (%)	2014	14.7
Population aged 60+ years (females and males, % of total)	2014	28.2/20.0
Sex ratio (males per 100 females)	2014	90.6
Life expectancy at birth (females and males, years)	2010-2015	78.5/70.4
Infant mortality rate (per 1 000 live births)	2010-2015	4.8
Fertility rate, total (live births per woman)	2010-2015	1.4
Contraceptive prevalence (ages 15-49, %)[g]	2007-2013	80.6[h]
International migrant stock (000 and % of total population)[i]	mid-2013	472.8/4.8
Refugees and others of concern to UNHCR	mid-2014	4 214
Education: Government expenditure (% of GDP)	2007-2013	4.7
Education: Primary-secondary gross enrolment ratio (f/m per 100)	2007-2013	100.3/102.1
Education: Female third-level students (% of total)	2007-2013	55.5
Intentional homicide rate (per 100,000 population)	2008-2012	1.3
Seats held by women in national parliaments (%)	2015	10.1

Environmental indicators		
Threatened species	2014	68
Forested area (% of land area)	2012	22.6
Proportion of terrestrial and marine areas protected (%)	2014	22.6
Population using improved drinking water sources (%)	2012	100.0
Population using improved sanitation facilities (%)	2012	100.0
CO$_2$ emission estimates (000 metric tons and metric tons per capita)	2011	48 492/4.8
Energy supply per capita (Gigajoules)	2012	99.0

a Official rate. b ISIC Rev.4 (BCD). c Population aged 15-74. d ISIC Rev.3. e Excluding conscripts. f 2012. g Age group 18 to 41 years. h 1992-1993. i Including refugees.

Iceland

Region	Northern Europe	Surface area (sq km)		103 000
Population (est., 000)	333	Pop. density (per sq km)		3.2
Capital city	Reykjavík	Capital city pop. (000)		184
Currency	Iceland Krona (ISK)	UN membership date		19 November 1946

Economic indicators	2005	2010	2013
GDP: Gross domestic product (million current US$)	16 799	13 261	15 330
GDP: Growth rate at constant 2005 prices (annual %)	6.0	−2.9	3.5
GDP per capita (current US$)	56 609.2	41 695.9	46 520.3
GNI: Gross national income per capita (current US$)	54 340.4	34 939.5	45 661.5
Gross fixed capital formation (% of GDP)	29.7	14.3	15.5
Exchange rates (national currency per US$)[a]	62.98	115.05	115.55
Balance of payments, current account (million US$)	−2 334	−272	1 378
CPI: Consumer price index (2000=100)[b]	122	182	207
Agricultural production index (2004-2006=100)	99	110	114
Food production index (2004-2006=100)	99	110	114
Unemployment (% of labour force)	2.6	7.6	5.6
Employment in industrial sector (% of employed)[c]	21.7[d]	18.3	18.2[e]
Employment in agricultural sector (% of employed)[c]	6.5[d]	5.5	5.5[e]
Labour force participation, adult female pop. (%)	70.8	70.4	70.5
Labour force participation, adult male pop. (%)	80.2	78.6	77.4
Tourist arrivals at national borders (000)	374	489	800
Energy production, primary (Petajoules)	124	243	272[e]
Mobile-cellular subscriptions (per 100 inhabitants)	95.4	107.2	108.1
Individuals using the Internet (%)	87.0	93.4[f]	96.6

Total trade		Major trading partners			2013
	(million US$)	(% of exports)			(% of imports)
Exports	4 997.7	Netherlands	30.0	Norway	15.1
Imports	5 019.2	Germany	12.1	United States	9.6
Balance	−21.5	United Kingdom	9.5	Denmark	8.3

Social indicators		
Population growth rate (average annual %)	2010-2015	1.1
Urban population growth rate (average annual %)	2010-2015	1.3
Rural population growth rate (average annual %)	2010-2015	−0.5
Urban population (%)	2014	94.0
Population aged 0-14 years (%)	2014	20.6
Population aged 60+ years (females and males, % of total)	2014	19.3/17.4
Sex ratio (males per 100 females)	2014	101.4
Life expectancy at birth (females and males, years)	2010-2015	83.8/80.2
Infant mortality rate (per 1 000 live births)	2010-2015	1.8
Fertility rate, total (live births per woman)	2010-2015	2.1
International migrant stock (000 and % of total population)	mid-2013	34.4/10.4
Refugees and others of concern to UNHCR	mid-2014	349[g]
Education: Government expenditure (% of GDP)	2007-2013	7.4
Education: Primary-secondary gross enrolment ratio (f/m per 100)	2007-2013	105.1/105.5
Education: Female third-level students (% of total)	2007-2013	62.5
Intentional homicide rate (per 100,000 population)	2008-2012	0.3
Seats held by women in national parliaments (%)	2015	41.3

Environmental indicators		
Threatened species	2014	19
Forested area (% of land area)	2012	<
Proportion of terrestrial and marine areas protected (%)	2014	2.3
Population using improved drinking water sources (%)	2012	100.0
Population using improved sanitation facilities (%)	2012	100.0
CO_2 emission estimates (000 metric tons and metric tons per capita)	2011	1 881/5.8
Energy supply per capita (Gigajoules)	2012	910.0

a Official rate. b Annual averages are based on the months February to December and January of the following year. c Population aged 16-74. d ISIC Rev.3. e 2012. f Population aged 16 to 74 using the Internet in the last 3 months. g Refugee population refers to the end of 2013.

India

Region	Southern Asia	Surface area (sq km)	3 287 263
Population (est., 000)	1 267 402	Pop. density (per sq km)	385.6
Capital city	New Delhi	Capital city pop. (000)	250 [a]
Currency	Indian Rupee (INR)	UN membership date	30 October 1945

Economic indicators	2005	2010	2013
GDP: Gross domestic product (million current US$)	837 499	1 704 795	1 937 797
GDP: Growth rate at constant 2005 prices (annual %)	9.3	10.6	5.0
GDP per capita (current US$)	743.0	1 414.0	1 547.6
GNI: Gross national income per capita (current US$)	737.8	1 399.2	1 409.9
Gross fixed capital formation (% of GDP)	31.5	33.8	29.8
Exchange rates (national currency per US$) [b]	45.06	44.81	61.90
Balance of payments, current account (million US$)	−10 284	−54 516	−49 226
CPI: Consumer price index (2000=100) [c]	122	183	241
Index of industrial production (2010=100) [de]	66	100	104
Agricultural production index (2004-2006=100)	100	125	140
Food production index (2004-2006=100)	100	123	139
Unemployment (% of labour force)	4.4	3.5	3.6
Employment in industrial sector (% of employed) [fg]	19.0	22.4	24.7[h]
Employment in agricultural sector (% of employed) [fg]	55.8	51.1	47.2[h]
Labour force participation, adult female pop. (%)	36.9	28.6	27.0
Labour force participation, adult male pop. (%)	83.3	80.8	79.9
Tourist arrivals at national borders (000) [i]	3 919	5 776	6 968
Energy production, primary (Petajoules)	20 522	25 386	26 206[h]
Mobile-cellular subscriptions (per 100 inhabitants)	8.0	62.4[j]	70.8[j]
Individuals using the Internet (%) [k]	2.4	7.5	15.1

Total trade		Major trading partners			2013
	(million US$)	(% of exports)			(% of imports)
Exports	336 611.4	United States	12.5	China	11.1
Imports	466 045.6	United Arab Emirates	10.1	Saudi Arabia	7.9
Balance	−129 434.2	China	4.9	United Arab Emirates	7.1

Social indicators		
Population growth rate (average annual %)	2010-2015	1.2
Urban population growth rate (average annual %)	2010-2015	2.4
Rural population growth rate (average annual %)	2010-2015	0.7
Urban population (%)	2014	32.4
Population aged 0-14 years (%)	2014	28.8
Population aged 60+ years (females and males, % of total)	2014	9.3/7.9
Sex ratio (males per 100 females)	2014	107.0
Life expectancy at birth (females and males, years)	2010-2015	68.1/64.6
Infant mortality rate (per 1 000 live births)	2010-2015	43.8
Fertility rate, total (live births per woman)	2010-2015	2.5
Contraceptive prevalence (ages 15-49, %)	2007-2013	54.8
International migrant stock (000 and % of total population) [l]	mid-2013	5 338.5/0.4
Refugees and others of concern to UNHCR	mid-2014	203 383
Education: Government expenditure (% of GDP)	2007-2013	3.8
Education: Primary-secondary gross enrolment ratio (f/m per 100)	2007-2013	86.5/87.9
Education: Female third-level students (% of total)	2007-2013	41.8
Intentional homicide rate (per 100,000 population)	2008-2012	3.5
Seats held by women in national parliaments (%)	2015	12.0

Environmental indicators		
Threatened species	2014	988
Forested area (% of land area)	2012	23.1
Proportion of terrestrial and marine areas protected (%)	2014	3.1
Population using improved drinking water sources (%)	2012	93.0
Population using improved sanitation facilities (%)	2012	36.0
CO_2 emission estimates (000 metric tons and metric tons per capita)	2011	2 074 345/1.7
Energy supply per capita (Gigajoules)	2012	28.0

a 2011. b Market rate. c Industrial workers. d ISIC Rev.3 (CDE). e Twelve months beginning 1 April of the year stated. f July of the preceding year to June of the current year. g Excluding Leh and Kargil of Jammu and Kashmir districts, some villages in Nagaland, Andaman and Nicobar Islands. h 2012. i Excluding nationals residing abroad. j December. k ITU estimate. l Including refugees.

Indonesia

Region	South-Eastern Asia	Surface area (sq km)	1 910 931
Population (est., 000)	252 812	Pop. density (per sq km)	132.7
Capital city	Jakarta	Capital city pop. (000)	10 176[a]
Currency	Rupiah (IDR)	UN membership date	28 September 1950

Economic indicators	2005	2010	2013
GDP: Gross domestic product (million current US$)	285 869	709 191	868 346
GDP: Growth rate at constant 2005 prices (annual %)	5.7	6.2	5.8
GDP per capita (current US$)	1 273.5	2 946.7	3 475.3
GNI: Gross national income per capita (current US$)	1 211.5	2 863.9	3 367.7
Gross fixed capital formation (% of GDP)	23.6	32.0	31.7
Exchange rates (national currency per US$)[b]	9 830.00	8 991.00	12 189.00
Balance of payments, current account (million US$)	278	5 144	−29 130
CPI: Consumer price index (2000=100)	156	227	267
Agricultural production index (2004-2006=100)	98	123	137
Food production index (2004-2006=100)	98	124	138
Unemployment (% of labour force)	11.2	7.1	6.3
Employment in industrial sector (% of employed)[c]	18.7[d]	19.3[ef]	20.6[eg]
Employment in agricultural sector (% of employed)[c]	44.0[d]	38.3[ef]	35.9[eg]
Labour force participation, adult female pop. (%)	50.0	51.2	51.4
Labour force participation, adult male pop. (%)	85.4	84.5	84.2
Tourist arrivals at national borders (000)	5 002	7 003	8 802
Energy production, primary (Petajoules)	11 348	16 799	18 358[h]
Mobile-cellular subscriptions (per 100 inhabitants)	20.9	87.8	121.5[i]
Individuals using the Internet (%)	3.6	10.9	15.8

Total trade		Major trading partners			2013
	(million US$)	(% of exports)		(% of imports)	
Exports	182 551.8	Japan	14.8	China	16.0
Imports	186 628.6	China	12.4	Singapore	13.7
Balance	−4 076.8	Singapore	9.1	Japan	10.3

Social indicators		
Population growth rate (average annual %)	2010-2015	1.2
Urban population growth rate (average annual %)	2010-2015	2.7
Rural population growth rate (average annual %)	2010-2015	−0.4
Urban population (%)	2014	53.0
Population aged 0-14 years (%)	2014	28.5
Population aged 60+ years (females and males, % of total)	2014	9.0/7.7
Sex ratio (males per 100 females)	2014	101.2
Life expectancy at birth (females and males, years)	2010-2015	72.8/68.7
Infant mortality rate (per 1 000 live births)	2010-2015	25.6
Fertility rate, total (live births per woman)	2010-2015	2.4
Contraceptive prevalence (ages 15-49, %)	2007-2013	61.9
International migrant stock (000 and % of total population)[jk]	mid-2013	295.4/0.1
Refugees and others of concern to UNHCR	mid-2014	10 116
Education: Government expenditure (% of GDP)	2007-2013	3.6
Education: Primary-secondary gross enrolment ratio (f/m per 100)	2007-2013	96.7/95.5
Education: Female third-level students (% of total)	2007-2013	50.8
Intentional homicide rate (per 100,000 population)	2008-2012	0.6
Seats held by women in national parliaments (%)	2015	17.1

Environmental indicators		
Threatened species	2014	1 225
Forested area (% of land area)	2012	51.4
Proportion of terrestrial and marine areas protected (%)	2014	6.0
Population using improved drinking water sources (%)	2012	85.0
Population using improved sanitation facilities (%)	2012	59.0
CO_2 emission estimates (000 metric tons and metric tons per capita)	2011	563 985/2.3
Energy supply per capita (Gigajoules)	2012	41.0

a Refers to the functional urban area. **b** Market rate. **c** August. **d** ISIC Rev.3. **e** ISIC Rev.2. **f** Break in series. **g** 2011. **h** 2012. **i** ITU estimate. **j** Refers to foreign citizens. **k** Including refugees.

Iran (Islamic Republic of)

Region	Southern Asia	Surface area (sq km)	1 628 750 [a]
Population (est., 000)	78 470	Pop. density (per sq km)	47.6
Capital city	Tehran	Capital city pop. (000)	8 353
Currency	Iranian Rial (IRR)	UN membership date	24 October 1945

Economic indicators	2005	2010	2013
GDP: Gross domestic product (million current US$)	205 587	421 716	492 783
GDP: Growth rate at constant 2005 prices (annual %)	5.3	5.8	-1.9
GDP per capita (current US$)	2 930.6	5 663.5	6 362.8
GNI: Gross national income per capita (current US$)	2 885.5	5 620.8	6 321.5
Gross fixed capital formation (% of GDP)	25.8	26.5	27.0
Exchange rates (national currency per US$) [b]	9 091.00	10 353.00	24 774.00
CPI: Consumer price index (2000=100)	193	386	779 [c]
Agricultural production index (2004-2006=100)	103	108	113
Food production index (2004-2006=100)	103	108	114
Unemployment (% of labour force)	12.1	13.5	13.2
Employment in industrial sector (% of employed)	30.3 [de]	32.2 [def]	...
Employment in agricultural sector (% of employed)	24.7 [de]	21.2 [def]	...
Labour force participation, adult female pop. (%)	19.4	16.0	16.6
Labour force participation, adult male pop. (%)	74.4	71.9	73.6
Tourist arrivals at national borders (000) [g]	1 889	2 938	4 769
Energy production, primary (Petajoules)	13 004	15 644	13 471 [h]
Mobile-cellular subscriptions (per 100 inhabitants)	12.1 [i]	72.6	84.3
Individuals using the Internet (%)	8.1 [i]	14.7 [k]	31.4

Total trade		Major trading partners			2013
	(million US$) [l]	(% of exports) [lm]		(% of imports) [l]	
Exports	130 544.0	Asia nes	47.0	United Arab Emirates	26.6
Imports	68 319.0	Europe nes	18.9	Areas nes	14.7 [m]
Balance	62 225.0	Areas nes	7.1	China	10.3

Social indicators

Population growth rate (average annual %)	2010-2015	1.3
Urban population growth rate (average annual %)	2010-2015	2.1
Rural population growth rate (average annual %)	2010-2015	-0.7
Urban population (%)	2014	72.9
Population aged 0-14 years (%)	2014	23.9
Population aged 60+ years (females and males, % of total)	2014	8.7/8.1
Sex ratio (males per 100 females)	2014	101.0
Life expectancy at birth (females and males, years)	2010-2015	75.9/72.1
Infant mortality rate (per 1 000 live births)	2010-2015	15.7
Fertility rate, total (live births per woman)	2010-2015	1.9
Contraceptive prevalence (ages 15-49, %)	2007-2013	77.4
International migrant stock (000 and % of total population) [n]	mid-2013	2 649.5/3.4
Refugees and others of concern to UNHCR	mid-2014	982 123
Education: Government expenditure (% of GDP)	2007-2013	3.7
Education: Primary-secondary gross enrolment ratio (f/m per 100)	2007-2013	92.1/96.0
Education: Female third-level students (% of total)	2007-2013	49.8
Intentional homicide rate (per 100,000 population)	2008-2012	4.1
Seats held by women in national parliaments (%)	2015	3.1

Environmental indicators

Threatened species	2014	121
Forested area (% of land area)	2012	6.8
Proportion of terrestrial and marine areas protected (%)	2014	6.7
Population using improved drinking water sources (%)	2012	96.0
Population using improved sanitation facilities (%)	2012	89.0
CO_2 emission estimates (000 metric tons and metric tons per capita)	2011	586 599/7.8
Energy supply per capita (Gigajoules)	2012	127.0

a Land area only. **b** Official rate. **c** Series linked to former series. **d** ISIC Rev.3. **e** Population aged 10 and over. **f** 2008. **g** Arrivals of non-resident visitors at national borders. **h** 2012. **i** October. **j** ITU estimate. **k** Refers to total population. **l** 2011. **m** See technical notes. **n** Including refugees.

Iraq

Region	Western Asia	Surface area (sq km)	435 052
Population (est., 000)	34 769	Pop. density (per sq km)	79.3
Capital city	Baghdad	Capital city pop. (000)	6 483
Currency	Iraqi Dinar (IQD)	UN membership date	21 December 1945

Economic indicators	2005	2010	2013
GDP: Gross domestic product (million current US$)	36 268	117 138	195 517
GDP: Growth rate at constant 2005 prices (annual %)	4.4	5.5	4.2
GDP per capita (current US$)	1 324.8	3 783.2	5 790.5
GNI: Gross national income per capita (current US$)	1 351.8	3 834.6	5 921.4
Gross fixed capital formation (% of GDP)	19.1	19.2	20.0
Exchange rates (national currency per US$)[a]	1 487.00	1 170.00	1 166.00
Balance of payments, current account (million US$)	−3 335	6 488	29 541[b]
CPI: Consumer price index (2000=100)	323	660[c]	753
Agricultural production index (2004-2006=100)	104	104	129
Food production index (2004-2006=100)	104	104	129
Unemployment (% of labour force)	18.0	15.2	16.0
Employment in industrial sector (% of employed)	17.7[de]	18.2[ef]	...
Employment in agricultural sector (% of employed)	29.7[de]	23.4[ef]	...
Labour force participation, adult female pop. (%)	13.6	14.5	14.9
Labour force participation, adult male pop. (%)	69.1	69.5	69.8
Tourist arrivals at national borders (000)[g]	...	1 518	892
Energy production, primary (Petajoules)	4 147	5 273	6 420[b]
Mobile-cellular subscriptions (per 100 inhabitants)	5.6	75.1	96.1[h]
Individuals using the Internet (%)	0.9[h]	2.5	9.2[h]

Social indicators		
Population growth rate (average annual %)	2010-2015	2.9
Urban population growth rate (average annual %)	2010-2015	3.0
Rural population growth rate (average annual %)	2010-2015	2.6
Urban population (%)	2014	69.4
Population aged 0-14 years (%)	2014	39.7
Population aged 60+ years (females and males, % of total)	2014	5.7/4.6
Sex ratio (males per 100 females)	2014	102.2
Life expectancy at birth (females and males, years)	2010-2015	73.1/66.0
Infant mortality rate (per 1 000 live births)	2010-2015	28.1
Fertility rate, total (live births per woman)	2010-2015	4.1
Contraceptive prevalence (ages 15-49, %)	2007-2013	52.5
International migrant stock (000 and % of total population)[ij]	mid-2013	95.8/0.3
Refugees and others of concern to UNHCR	mid-2014	2 329 610[k]
Education: Primary-secondary gross enrolment ratio (f/m per 100)	2007-2013	73.9/90.8
Education: Female third-level students (% of total)[l]	2007-2013	36.2[m]
Intentional homicide rate (per 100,000 population)	2008-2012	8.0
Seats held by women in national parliaments (%)	2015	26.5

Environmental indicators		
Threatened species	2014	69
Forested area (% of land area)	2012	1.9
Proportion of terrestrial and marine areas protected (%)	2014	0.4
Population using improved drinking water sources (%)	2012	85.0
Population using improved sanitation facilities (%)	2012	85.0
CO_2 emission estimates (000 metric tons and metric tons per capita)	2011	133 655/4.2
Energy supply per capita (Gigajoules)	2012	57.0

a Principal rate. b 2012. c Series linked to former series. d 2006. e ISIC Rev.3. f 2008. g Arrivals of non-resident visitors at national borders. h ITU estimate. i Refers to foreign citizens. j Including refugees. k Including an estimate for stateless persons population. l UNESCO estimate. m 2005.

Ireland

Region	Northern Europe	Surface area (sq km)	69 825
Population (est., 000)	4 677	Pop. density (per sq km)	66.6
Capital city	Dublin	Capital city pop. (000)	1 155
Currency	Euro (EUR)	UN membership date	14 December 1955

Economic indicators	2005	2010	2013
GDP: Gross domestic product (million current US$)	210 358	218 435	232 077
GDP: Growth rate at constant 2005 prices (annual %)	5.7	−0.3	0.2
GDP per capita (current US$)	50 591.1	48 893.5	50 155.3
GNI: Gross national income per capita (current US$)	43 398.1	41 110.1	42 671.2
Gross fixed capital formation (% of GDP)	28.9	15.8	15.2
Exchange rates (national currency per US$)[a]	0.85	0.75	0.73
Balance of payments, current account (million US$)	−7 150	2 319	14 438
CPI: Consumer price index (2000=100)	119	128	134
Index of industrial production (2010=100)[b]	92	100	98
Agricultural production index (2004-2006=100)	99	100	99
Food production index (2004-2006=100)	99	100	99
Unemployment (% of labour force)	4.3	13.9	13.1
Employment in industrial sector (% of employed)	27.9[cd]	19.5[e]	18.3[f]
Employment in agricultural sector (% of employed)	5.9[cd]	4.5[e]	4.7[f]
Labour force participation, adult female pop. (%)	51.9	53.1	53.1
Labour force participation, adult male pop. (%)	72.5	69.0	68.1
Tourist arrivals at national borders (000)[g]	7 333	7 134[h]	8 260
Energy production, primary (Petajoules)	69	78	54[f]
Mobile-cellular subscriptions (per 100 inhabitants)	102.7	105.2	102.8
Individuals using the Internet (%)	41.6	69.9	78.3

Total trade		Major trading partners			2013
	(million US$)		(% of exports)		(% of imports)
Exports	115 323.5	United States	21.2	United Kingdom	33.6
Imports	65 950.7	United Kingdom	16.1	United States	10.5
Balance	49 372.8	Belgium	12.9	Germany	8.2

Social indicators		
Population growth rate (average annual %)	2010-2015	1.1
Urban population growth rate (average annual %)	2010-2015	1.6
Rural population growth rate (average annual %)	2010-2015	0.4
Urban population (%)	2014	63.0
Population aged 0-14 years (%)	2014	21.6
Population aged 60+ years (females and males, % of total)	2014	18.1/16.3
Sex ratio (males per 100 females)	2014	98.8
Life expectancy at birth (females and males, years)	2010-2015	82.7/78.4
Infant mortality rate (per 1 000 live births)	2010-2015	2.9
Fertility rate, total (live births per woman)	2010-2015	2.0
Contraceptive prevalence (ages 15-49, %)[i]	2007-2013	64.8[j]
International migrant stock (000 and % of total population)	mid-2013	735.5/15.9
Refugees and others of concern to UNHCR	mid-2014	11 233[k]
Education: Government expenditure (% of GDP)	2007-2013	6.2
Education: Primary-secondary gross enrolment ratio (f/m per 100)	2007-2013	110.3/109.3
Education: Female third-level students (% of total)	2007-2013	50.9
Intentional homicide rate (per 100,000 population)	2008-2012	1.2
Seats held by women in national parliaments (%)	2015	16.3

Environmental indicators		
Threatened species	2014	38
Forested area (% of land area)	2012	11.0
Proportion of terrestrial and marine areas protected (%)	2014	3.5
Population using improved drinking water sources (%)	2012	100.0
Population using improved sanitation facilities (%)	2012	99.0
CO_2 emission estimates (000 metric tons and metric tons per capita)	2011	36 069/8.0
Energy supply per capita (Gigajoules)	2012	121.0

a Market rate. b ISIC Rev.4 (BCD). c ISIC Rev.3. d Second quarter. e Break in series. f 2012. g Including tourists from North Ireland. h Methodology revised. i Age group 18 to 49 years. j 2004-2005. k Refugee population refers to the end of 2013.

Israel

Region	Western Asia	Surface area (sq km)	22 072
Population (est., 000)	7 822	Pop. density (per sq km)	353.2
Capital city	Jerusalem[a]	Capital city pop. (000)	829[a]
Currency	New Sheqel (NIS)	UN membership date	11 May 1949

Economic indicators	2005	2010	2013
GDP: Gross domestic product (million current US$)	139 082	231 676	291 567
GDP: Growth rate at constant 2005 prices (annual %)	4.9	5.7	3.3
GDP per capita (current US$)	21 061.3	31 221.6	37 703.5
GNI: Gross national income per capita (current US$)	20 852.8	30 532.7	36 990.6
Gross fixed capital formation (% of GDP)	18.0	18.5	19.6
Exchange rates (national currency per US$)[b]	4.60	3.55	3.47
Balance of payments, current account (million US$)	4 043	7 855	6 893
CPI: Consumer price index (2000=100)	0	124	132[c]
Index of industrial production (2010=100)[d]	79	100	107
Agricultural production index (2004-2006=100)	100	104	110
Food production index (2004-2006=100)	100	105	111
Unemployment (% of labour force)	9.0	6.6	6.3
Employment in industrial sector (% of employed)	21.4[e]	20.4[efgh]	...
Employment in agricultural sector (% of employed)	2.0[e]	1.7[efh]	...
Labour force participation, adult female pop. (%)	50.1	52.6	57.9
Labour force participation, adult male pop. (%)	60.7	62.3	69.1
Tourist arrivals at national borders (000)[i]	1 903	2 803	2 962
Energy production, primary (Petajoules)	88	162	137[j]
Mobile-cellular subscriptions (per 100 inhabitants)	117.5	122.8[k]	122.9
Individuals using the Internet (%)	25.2	67.5[l]	70.8[l]

Total trade		Major trading partners			2013
	(million US$)	(% of exports)			(% of imports)
Exports	66 781.2	United States	26.2	Areas nes	19.9[m]
Imports	71 995.0	China, Hong Kong SAR	8.1	United States	11.3
Balance	−5 213.8	United Kingdom	5.8	China	7.9

Social indicators		
Population growth rate (average annual %)	2010-2015	1.3
Urban population growth rate (average annual %)	2010-2015	1.4
Rural population growth rate (average annual %)	2010-2015	0.5
Urban population (%)	2014	92.1
Population aged 0-14 years (%)	2014	27.9
Population aged 60+ years (females and males, % of total)	2014	16.7/14.0
Sex ratio (males per 100 females)	2014	98.2
Life expectancy at birth (females and males, years)	2010-2015	83.5/79.8
Infant mortality rate (per 1 000 live births)	2010-2015	3.3
Fertility rate, total (live births per woman)	2010-2015	2.9
Contraceptive prevalence (ages 15-49, %)[n]	2007-2013	68.0[o]
International migrant stock (000 and % of total population)[p]	mid-2013	2 046.9/26.5
Refugees and others of concern to UNHCR	mid-2014	52 975[q]
Education: Government expenditure (% of GDP)	2007-2013	5.6
Education: Primary-secondary gross enrolment ratio (f/m per 100)	2007-2013	104.3/103.0
Education: Female third-level students (% of total)	2007-2013	55.8
Intentional homicide rate (per 100,000 population)	2008-2012	1.8
Seats held by women in national parliaments (%)	2015	22.5

Environmental indicators		
Threatened species	2014	151
Forested area (% of land area)	2012	7.1
Proportion of terrestrial and marine areas protected (%)	2014	8.6
Population using improved drinking water sources (%)	2012	100.0
Population using improved sanitation facilities (%)	2012	100.0
CO_2 emission estimates (000 metric tons and metric tons per capita)	2011	69 523/9.2
Energy supply per capita (Gigajoules)	2012	132.0

a Designation and data provided by Israel. The position of the United Nations on Jerusalem is stated in A/RES/181 (II) and subsequent General Assembly and Security Council resolutions. Including East Jerusalem. b Market rate. c Series linked to former series. d ISIC Rev.4 (BC). e ISIC Rev.3. f 2009. g Excluding mining and quarrying. h Break in series. i Excluding nationals residing abroad. j 2012. k ITU estimate. l Population aged 20 and over. m See technical notes. n Age group 18 to 39 years. o 1987-1988. p Including refugees. q Refers to the end of 2013.

Italy

Region	Southern Europe	
Population (est., 000)	61 070	
Capital city	Rome	
Currency	Euro (EUR)	

Surface area (sq km)	301 339	
Pop. density (per sq km)	202.7	
Capital city pop. (000)	3 697	
UN membership date	14 December 1955	

Economic indicators	2005	2010	2013
GDP: Gross domestic product (million current US$)	1 853 466	2 126 620	2 149 485
GDP: Growth rate at constant 2005 prices (annual %)	1.0	1.7	−1.9
GDP per capita (current US$)	31 590.4	35 145.5	35 243.1
GNI: Gross national income per capita (current US$)	31 625.4	35 055.4	35 182.7
Gross fixed capital formation (% of GDP)	21.3	20.1	18.0
Exchange rates (national currency per US$)[a]	0.85	0.75	0.73
Balance of payments, current account (million US$)	−29 744	−70 093	20 879
CPI: Consumer price index (2000=100)	112[b]	123[b]	133
Index of industrial production (2010=100)[c]	112	100	91
Agricultural production index (2004-2006=100)	100	97	90
Food production index (2004-2006=100)	100	97	91
Unemployment (% of labour force)	7.7	8.4	12.2
Employment in industrial sector (% of employed)	30.8[d]	28.8	27.8[e]
Employment in agricultural sector (% of employed)	4.2[d]	3.8	3.7[e]
Labour force participation, adult female pop. (%)	37.7	38.0	39.6
Labour force participation, adult male pop. (%)	61.1	59.3	59.5
Tourist arrivals at national borders (000)[f]	36 513	43 626	47 704
Energy production, primary (Petajoules)[g]	1 170	1 226	1 337[e]
Mobile-cellular subscriptions (per 100 inhabitants)	121.9	154.8	158.9
Individuals using the Internet (%)	35.0	53.7	58.5

Total trade		Major trading partners			2013
	(million US$)[h]	(% of exports)[h]			(% of imports)[h]
Exports	518 103.2	Germany	12.4	Germany	14.8
Imports	479 342.2	France	10.8	France	8.5
Balance	38 761.0	United States	6.9	China	6.4

Social indicators		
Population growth rate (average annual %)	2010-2015	0.2
Urban population growth rate (average annual %)	2010-2015	0.4
Rural population growth rate (average annual %)	2010-2015	−0.2
Urban population (%)	2014	68.8
Population aged 0-14 years (%)	2014	14.1
Population aged 60+ years (females and males, % of total)	2014	29.9/24.7
Sex ratio (males per 100 females)	2014	94.6
Life expectancy at birth (females and males, years)	2010-2015	84.9/79.5
Infant mortality rate (per 1 000 live births)	2010-2015	2.8
Fertility rate, total (live births per woman)	2010-2015	1.5
Contraceptive prevalence (ages 15-49, %)[i]	2007-2013	62.7[j]
International migrant stock (000 and % of total population)	mid-2013	5 721.5/9.4
Refugees and others of concern to UNHCR	mid-2014	98 813[k]
Education: Government expenditure (% of GDP)	2007-2013	4.3
Education: Primary-secondary gross enrolment ratio (f/m per 100)	2007-2013	98.5/99.7
Education: Female third-level students (% of total)	2007-2013	57.5
Intentional homicide rate (per 100,000 population)	2008-2012	0.9
Seats held by women in national parliaments (%)	2015	31.0

Environmental indicators		
Threatened species	2014	276
Forested area (% of land area)	2012	31.6
Proportion of terrestrial and marine areas protected (%)	2014	13.3
Population using improved drinking water sources (%)	2012	100.0
CO$_2$ emission estimates (000 metric tons and metric tons per capita)[h]	2011	397 994/6.6
Energy supply per capita (Gigajoules)[g]	2012	110.0

a Market rate. b Excluding tobacco. c ISIC Rev.4 (BCD). d ISIC Rev.3. e 2012. f Excluding seasonal and border workers. g Including San Marino and the Holy See. h Including San Marino. i Age group 20 to 49 years. j 1995-1996. k Refugee population refers to the end of 2013.

Jamaica

Region	Caribbean	Surface area (sq km)	10 991	
Population (est., 000)	2 799	Pop. density (per sq km)	254.7	
Capital city	Kingston	Capital city pop. (000)	587	
Currency	Jamaican Dollar (JMD)	UN membership date	18 September 1962	

Economic indicators	2005	2010	2013
GDP: Gross domestic product (million current US$)	11 239	13 234	14 270
GDP: Growth rate at constant 2005 prices (annual %)	0.9	−1.5	0.6
GDP per capita (current US$)	4 190.4	4 827.4	5 125.9
GNI: Gross national income per capita (current US$)	3 938.1	4 647.0	5 029.8
Gross fixed capital formation (% of GDP)	26.8	19.9	21.0
Exchange rates (national currency per US$)[a]	64.38	85.60	106.05
Balance of payments, current account (million US$)	−1 071	−934	−1 312
CPI: Consumer price index (2000=100)	166	296	372
Agricultural production index (2004-2006=100)	96	99	106
Food production index (2004-2006=100)	96	99	106
Unemployment (% of labour force)	10.9	12.4	15.0
Employment in industrial sector (% of employed)[b]	17.7[c]	15.9[def]	15.5[deg]
Employment in agricultural sector (% of employed)[b]	18.1[c]	20.2[def]	18.1[deg]
Labour force participation, adult female pop. (%)	57.5	55.7	56.1
Labour force participation, adult male pop. (%)	76.2	71.5	70.9
Tourist arrivals at national borders (000)[hi]	1 479	1 922	2 008
Energy production, primary (Petajoules)	15	6	7[g]
Mobile-cellular subscriptions (per 100 inhabitants)	73.9	116.1	100.4
Individuals using the Internet (%)	12.8[j]	27.7[k]	37.8[j]

Total trade		Major trading partners			2013
	(million US$)	(% of exports)		(% of imports)	
Exports	1 569.1	United States	49.1	United States	34.1
Imports	6 216.2	Canada	14.3	Venezuela	14.9
Balance	−4 647.1	Netherlands	6.9	Trinidad and Tobago	12.3

Social indicators

Population growth rate (average annual %)	2010-2015	0.5
Urban population growth rate (average annual %)	2010-2015	0.9
Rural population growth rate (average annual %)	2010-2015	0.1
Urban population (%)	2014	54.6
Population aged 0-14 years (%)	2014	26.5
Population aged 60+ years (females and males, % of total)	2014	12.0/11.1
Sex ratio (males per 100 females)	2014	97.0
Life expectancy at birth (females and males, years)	2010-2015	76.0/70.9
Infant mortality rate (per 1 000 live births)	2010-2015	20.9
Fertility rate, total (live births per woman)	2010-2015	2.3
Contraceptive prevalence (ages 15-49, %)	2007-2013	72.5
International migrant stock (000 and % of total population)	mid-2013	34.9/1.3
Refugees and others of concern to UNHCR	mid-2014	23
Education: Government expenditure (% of GDP)	2007-2013	6.3
Education: Primary-secondary gross enrolment ratio (f/m per 100)	2007-2013	84.5/85.7
Education: Female third-level students (% of total)	2007-2013	68.7
Intentional homicide rate (per 100,000 population)	2008-2012	39.3
Seats held by women in national parliaments (%)	2015	12.7

Environmental indicators

Threatened species	2014	292
Forested area (% of land area)	2012	31.1
Proportion of terrestrial and marine areas protected (%)	2014	1.4
Population using improved drinking water sources (%)	2012	93.0
Population using improved sanitation facilities (%)	2012	80.0
CO_2 emission estimates (000 metric tons and metric tons per capita)	2011	7 756/2.8
Energy supply per capita (Gigajoules)	2012	37.0

a Market rate. b Population aged 14 and over. c ISIC Rev.2. d ISIC Rev.3. e Average of quarterly estimates. f Break in series. g 2012. h Arrivals of non-resident tourists by air. i Including nationals residing abroad. j ITU estimate. k Population aged 14 and over using the Internet via any device.

Japan

Region	Eastern Asia	Surface area (sq km)	377 930 [a]
Population (est., 000)	127 000	Pop. density (per sq km)	336.1
Capital city	Tokyo	Capital city pop. (000)	37 833 [b]
Currency	Yen (JPY)	UN membership date	18 December 1956

Economic indicators	2005	2010	2013
GDP: Gross domestic product (million current US$)	4 571 867	5 495 387	4 898 532
GDP: Growth rate at constant 2005 prices (annual %)	1.3	4.7	1.5
GDP per capita (current US$)	36 005.0	43 150.9	38 527.6
GNI: Gross national income per capita (current US$)	36 844.5	44 311.5	39 947.4
Gross fixed capital formation (% of GDP)	22.3	20.0	21.7
Exchange rates (national currency per US$) [c]	117.97	81.45	105.30
Balance of payments, current account (million US$)	170 123	217 550	34 068
CPI: Consumer price index (2000=100)	98 [d]	97	97
Index of industrial production (2010=100) [e]	...	100	97
Agricultural production index (2004-2006=100)	101	97	98
Food production index (2004-2006=100)	101	97	98
Unemployment (% of labour force)	4.4	5.0	4.0
Employment in industrial sector (% of employed)	27.9 [fg]	25.3 [fgh]	...
Employment in agricultural sector (% of employed)	4.4 [fg]	3.7 [fgh]	...
Labour force participation, adult female pop. (%)	48.4	49.4	48.8
Labour force participation, adult male pop. (%)	73.3	71.6	70.4
Tourist arrivals at national borders (000) [ij]	6 728	8 611	10 364
Energy production, primary (Petajoules) [k]	4 167	4 127	1 186 [l]
Mobile-cellular subscriptions (per 100 inhabitants)	76.0 [m]	96.8 [n]	115.2 [no]
Individuals using the Internet (%)	66.9 [p]	78.2 [p]	86.3 [q]

Total trade		Major trading partners			2013
	(million US$)	(% of exports)			(% of imports)
Exports	715 097.2	United States	18.8	China	21.7
Imports	833 166.1	China	18.1	United States	8.6
Balance	−118 068.9	Republic of Korea	7.9	Australia	6.1

Social indicators		
Population growth rate (average annual %)	2010-2015	−0.1
Urban population growth rate (average annual %)	2010-2015	0.6
Rural population growth rate (average annual %)	2010-2015	−7.6
Urban population (%)	2014	93.0
Population aged 0-14 years (%)	2014	13.0
Population aged 60+ years (females and males, % of total)	2014	35.5/29.9
Sex ratio (males per 100 females)	2014	94.7
Life expectancy at birth (females and males, years)	2010-2015	86.9/80.0
Infant mortality rate (per 1 000 live births)	2010-2015	2.2
Fertility rate, total (live births per woman)	2010-2015	1.4
Contraceptive prevalence (ages 15-49, %) [r]	2007-2013	54.3 [s]
International migrant stock (000 and % of total population) [t]	mid-2013	2 437.2/1.9
Refugees and others of concern to UNHCR	mid-2014	11 231 [u]
Education: Government expenditure (% of GDP)	2007-2013	3.9
Education: Primary-secondary gross enrolment ratio (f/m per 100)	2007-2013	102.1/102.0
Education: Female third-level students (% of total)	2007-2013	46.2
Intentional homicide rate (per 100,000 population)	2008-2012	0.3
Seats held by women in national parliaments (%)	2015	9.5

Environmental indicators		
Threatened species	2014	362
Forested area (% of land area)	2012	68.6
Proportion of terrestrial and marine areas protected (%)	2014	2.1
Population using improved drinking water sources (%)	2012	100.0
Population using improved sanitation facilities (%)	2012	100.0
CO_2 emission estimates (000 metric tons and metric tons per capita)	2011	1 187 657/9.3
Energy supply per capita (Gigajoules) [k]	2012	148.0

a Data refer to 1 October 2007. b Major metropolitan areas. c Market rate. d Series linked to former series. e ISIC Rev.4 (BCD). f ISIC Rev.3. g Average of monthly estimates. h Break in series. i Arrivals of non-resident visitors at national borders. j Excluding nationals residing abroad. k Including Okinawa. l 2012. m Including Personal Handy-phone System. n Including Personal Handy-phone System and data cards. o December. p Population aged 6 and over. q Population aged 15-74. r Age group 20 to 49 years. s 2005. t Refers to foreign citizens. u UNHCR estimate.

Jordan

Region	Western Asia	Surface area (sq km)	89 328
Population (est., 000)	7 505	Pop. density (per sq km)	84.0
Capital city	Amman	Capital city pop. (000)	1 148 [a]
Currency	Jordanian Dinar (JOD)	UN membership date	14 December 1955

Economic indicators

	2005	2010	2013
GDP: Gross domestic product (million current US$)	12 589	26 425	33 594
GDP: Growth rate at constant 2005 prices (annual %)	8.2	2.3	2.8
GDP per capita (current US$)	2 402.7	4 094.1	4 618.5
GNI: Gross national income per capita (current US$)	2 466.9	4 080.0	4 560.5
Gross fixed capital formation (% of GDP)	30.6	23.5	21.1
Exchange rates (national currency per US$) [b]	0.71	0.71	0.71
Balance of payments, current account (million US$)	−2 271	−1 882	−3 359
CPI: Consumer price index (2000=100)	113	149	172
Index of industrial production (2010=100) [c]	95	100	102
Agricultural production index (2004-2006=100)	98	129	137
Food production index (2004-2006=100)	97	129	137
Unemployment (% of labour force)	14.9	12.5	12.6
Employment in industrial sector (% of employed)	20.7 [d]	18.7	17.5 [e]
Employment in agricultural sector (% of employed)	3.4 [d]	2.0	2.0 [e]
Labour force participation, adult female pop. (%)	12.3	15.6	15.6
Labour force participation, adult male pop. (%)	67.5	67.9	66.6
Tourist arrivals at national borders (000) [f]	2 987	4 207	3 945
Energy production, primary (Petajoules)	10	9	8 [e]
Mobile-cellular subscriptions (per 100 inhabitants)	59.9	102.6	141.8
Individuals using the Internet (%)	12.9	27.2 [g]	44.2 [h]

Total trade		Major trading partners			2013
	(million US$)	(% of exports)			(% of imports)
Exports	7 919.6	Iraq	17.5	Saudi Arabia	18.7
Imports	21 549.0	United States	15.2	China	10.4
Balance	−13 629.4	Saudi Arabia	12.2	United States	6.3

Social indicators

Population growth rate (average annual %)	2010-2015	3.5
Urban population growth rate (average annual %)	2010-2015	3.8
Rural population growth rate (average annual %)	2010-2015	2.1
Urban population (%)	2014	83.5
Population aged 0-14 years (%)	2014	33.7
Population aged 60+ years (females and males, % of total)	2014	5.6/5.2
Sex ratio (males per 100 females)	2014	104.1
Life expectancy at birth (females and males, years)	2010-2015	75.5/72.2
Infant mortality rate (per 1 000 live births)	2010-2015	17.1
Fertility rate, total (live births per woman)	2010-2015	3.3
Contraceptive prevalence (ages 15-49, %)	2007-2013	61.2
International migrant stock (000 and % of total population) [i][j]	mid-2013	2 925.8/40.2
Refugees and others of concern to UNHCR	mid-2014	747 045 [k]
Education: Government expenditure (% of GDP)	2007-2013	5.0 [l]
Education: Primary-secondary gross enrolment ratio (f/m per 100)	2007-2013	93.4/93.1
Education: Female third-level students (% of total)	2007-2013	52.8
Intentional homicide rate (per 100,000 population)	2008-2012	2.0
Seats held by women in national parliaments (%)	2015	12.0

Environmental indicators

Threatened species	2014	103
Forested area (% of land area)	2012	1.1
Proportion of terrestrial and marine areas protected (%)	2014	2.1
Population using improved drinking water sources (%)	2012	96.0
Population using improved sanitation facilities (%)	2012	98.0
CO_2 emission estimates (000 metric tons and metric tons per capita)	2011	22 259/3.3
Energy supply per capita (Gigajoules)	2012	47.0

a Excluding Syrian refugees. **b** Official rate. **c** ISIC Rev.3 (CDE). **d** ISIC Rev.3. **e** 2012. **f** Including nationals residing abroad. **g** Population aged 5 and over. **h** ITU estimate. **i** Refers to foreign citizens. **j** Including refugees. **k** Refugee figure for Iraqis in Jordan is a Government estimate. UNHCR has registered and is assisting 28,800 Iraqis at mid-2014. **l** 1999.

Kazakhstan

Region	Central Asia	Surface area (sq km)		2 724 900
Population (est., 000)	16 607	Pop. density (per sq km)		6.1
Capital city	Astana	Capital city pop. (000)		741
Currency	Tenge (KZT)	UN membership date		2 March 1992

Economic indicators	2005	2010	2013
GDP: Gross domestic product (million current US$)	57 124	148 047	224 415
GDP: Growth rate at constant 2005 prices (annual %)	9.7	7.3	6.0
GDP per capita (current US$)	3 792.0	9 298.8	13 650.1
GNI: Gross national income per capita (current US$)	3 435.8	8 082.1	11 818.7
Gross fixed capital formation (% of GDP)	28.0	24.3	23.4
Exchange rates (national currency per US$) [a]	133.98	147.50	154.06
Balance of payments, current account (million US$)	−1 031	1 411	−118
CPI: Consumer price index (2000=100)	140	198[b]	...
Agricultural production index (2004-2006=100)	100	107	127
Food production index (2004-2006=100)	100	108	126
Unemployment (% of labour force)	8.1	5.8	5.2
Employment in industrial sector (% of employed)	18.0[c]	18.7[d]	19.4[e]
Employment in agricultural sector (% of employed)	32.4[c]	28.3[d]	25.5[e]
Labour force participation, adult female pop. (%)	64.6	66.9	67.7
Labour force participation, adult male pop. (%)	75.2	76.6	77.9
Tourist arrivals at national borders (000)	3 143	3 196	4 926
Energy production, primary (Petajoules)	5 119	6 770	7 029[e]
Mobile-cellular subscriptions (per 100 inhabitants)	35.8	121.9	180.5
Individuals using the Internet (%)	3.0	31.6[f]	54.0[g]

Total trade		Major trading partners			2013
	(million US$)	(% of exports)			(% of imports)
Exports	82 510.0	Italy	18.5	Russian Federation	36.2
Imports	48 871.9	China	17.4	China	16.8
Balance	33 638.1	Netherlands	11.8	Germany	5.7

Social indicators		
Population growth rate (average annual %)	2010-2015	1.0
Urban population growth rate (average annual %)	2010-2015	0.9
Rural population growth rate (average annual %)	2010-2015	1.3
Urban population (%)	2014	53.3
Population aged 0-14 years (%)	2014	26.0
Population aged 60+ years (females and males, % of total)	2014	12.6/8.0
Sex ratio (males per 100 females)	2014	92.8
Life expectancy at birth (females and males, years)	2010-2015	72.3/60.9
Infant mortality rate (per 1 000 live births)	2010-2015	24.6
Fertility rate, total (live births per woman)	2010-2015	2.4
Contraceptive prevalence (ages 15-49, %)	2007-2013	51.0
International migrant stock (000 and % of total population)	mid-2013	3 476.2/21.1
Refugees and others of concern to UNHCR	mid-2014	11 326
Education: Government expenditure (% of GDP)	2007-2013	3.1
Education: Primary-secondary gross enrolment ratio (f/m per 100)	2007-2013	99.5/101.1
Education: Female third-level students (% of total)	2007-2013	58.5
Intentional homicide rate (per 100,000 population)	2008-2012	7.8
Seats held by women in national parliaments (%)	2015	26.2

Environmental indicators		
Threatened species	2014	77
Forested area (% of land area)	2012	1.2
Proportion of terrestrial and marine areas protected (%)	2014	3.3
Population using improved drinking water sources (%)	2012	93.0
Population using improved sanitation facilities (%)	2012	97.0
CO_2 emission estimates (000 metric tons and metric tons per capita)	2011	261 761/16.2
Energy supply per capita (Gigajoules)	2012	202.0

a Official rate. **b** 2008. **c** ISIC Rev.3. **d** Break in series. **e** 2012. **f** Population aged 16-74. **g** ITU estimate.

Kenya

Region	Eastern Africa	Surface area (sq km)	591 958	
Population (est., 000)	45 546	Pop. density (per sq km)	78.5	
Capital city	Nairobi	Capital city pop. (000)	3 768	
Currency	Kenya Shilling (KES)	UN membership date	16 December 1963	

Economic indicators	2005	2010	2013
GDP: Gross domestic product (million current US$)	21 493	39 701	54 443
GDP: Growth rate at constant 2005 prices (annual %)	5.9	7.7	6.0
GDP per capita (current US$)	600.6	970.5	1 227.5
GNI: Gross national income per capita (current US$)	597.1	966.0	1 218.1
Gross fixed capital formation (% of GDP)	19.1	20.5	20.7
Exchange rates (national currency per US$)[a]	72.37	80.75	86.31
Balance of payments, current account (million US$)	−252	−2 369	−4 253[b]
CPI: Consumer price index (2000=100)[c]	100[d]	134[e]	176
Agricultural production index (2004-2006=100)	103	123	123
Food production index (2004-2006=100)	103	124	123
Unemployment (% of labour force)	9.5	9.3	9.2
Employment in industrial sector (% of employed)	6.7[fg]	...	...
Employment in agricultural sector (% of employed)	61.1[fg]	...	...
Labour force participation, adult female pop. (%)	60.2	61.5	62.2
Labour force participation, adult male pop. (%)	70.0	71.7	72.4
Tourist arrivals at national borders (000)	1 399	1 470	1 434
Energy production, primary (Petajoules)	338	374	356[b]
Mobile-cellular subscriptions (per 100 inhabitants)	12.9	61.0	70.6
Individuals using the Internet (%)	3.1	14.0	39.0[h]

Total trade		Major trading partners				2013
	(million US$)	(% of exports)			(% of imports)	
Exports	5 537.0	Uganda	11.9	India		18.3
Imports	16 394.5	United Kingdom	7.9	China		12.9
Balance	−10 857.5	United Rep. Tanzania	7.7	United Arab Emirates		8.3

Social indicators		
Population growth rate (average annual %)	2010-2015	2.7
Urban population growth rate (average annual %)	2010-2015	4.3
Rural population growth rate (average annual %)	2010-2015	2.1
Urban population (%)	2014	25.2
Population aged 0-14 years (%)	2014	42.0
Population aged 60+ years (females and males, % of total)	2014	4.7/4.1
Sex ratio (males per 100 females)	2014	99.6
Life expectancy at birth (females and males, years)	2010-2015	63.5/59.7
Infant mortality rate (per 1 000 live births)	2010-2015	51.6
Fertility rate, total (live births per woman)	2010-2015	4.4
Contraceptive prevalence (ages 15-49, %)	2007-2013	45.5
International migrant stock (000 and % of total population)[i]	mid-2013	955.5/2.2
Refugees and others of concern to UNHCR	mid-2014	589 772
Education: Government expenditure (% of GDP)	2007-2013	6.6
Education: Primary-secondary gross enrolment ratio (f/m per 100)	2007-2013	92.1/94.1
Education: Female third-level students (% of total)	2007-2013	41.2
Intentional homicide rate (per 100,000 population)	2008-2012	6.4
Seats held by women in national parliaments (%)	2015	19.7

Environmental indicators		
Threatened species	2014	428
Forested area (% of land area)	2012	6.1
Proportion of terrestrial and marine areas protected (%)	2014	10.6
Population using improved drinking water sources (%)	2012	62.0
Population using improved sanitation facilities (%)	2012	30.0
CO_2 emission estimates (000 metric tons and metric tons per capita)	2011	13 568/0.3
Energy supply per capita (Gigajoules)	2012	12.0

a Official rate. b 2012. c Index base 2007=100. d 2007. e Series linked to former series. f Household income and expenditure survey. g ISIC Rev.2. h ITU estimate. i Including refugees.

Kiribati

Region	Oceania-Micronesia	Surface area (sq km)	726 [a]
Population (est., 000)	104	Pop. density (per sq km)	143.2
Capital city	Bairiki [b]	Capital city pop. (000)	4 [c]
Currency	Australian Dollar (AUD)	UN membership date	14 September 1999

Economic indicators	2005	2010	2013
GDP: Gross domestic product (million current US$)	112	153	175
GDP: Growth rate at constant 2005 prices (annual %)	5.0	−1.6	2.9
GDP per capita (current US$)	1 239.5	1 567.4	1 705.2
GNI: Gross national income per capita (current US$)	1 406.7	2 290.0	2 552.9
Gross fixed capital formation (% of GDP)	49.5	41.8	44.2
Exchange rates (national currency per US$) [d]	1.36	0.98	1.13
Balance of payments, current account (million US$)	−19 [e]	1	−15 [f]
CPI: Consumer price index (2000=100) [g]	110	125 [h]	...
Agricultural production index (2004-2006=100)	95	118	121
Food production index (2004-2006=100)	95	118	121
Tourist arrivals at national borders (000) [i]	4	5	6
Energy production, primary (Petajoules)	0	0	0 [f]
Mobile-cellular subscriptions (per 100 inhabitants)	0.7	10.8	16.6 [j]
Individuals using the Internet (%)	4.0 [j]	9.1	11.5 [j]

Total trade		Major trading partners			2013
	(million US$)	(% of exports)			(% of imports)
Exports	6.7	Morocco	23.9	Australia	26.8
Imports	97.1	Marshall Islands	13.4	Singapore	21.1
Balance	−90.4	Fiji	11.9	Fiji	14.9

Social indicators		
Population growth rate (average annual %)	2010-2015	1.5
Urban population growth rate (average annual %)	2010-2015	1.8
Rural population growth rate (average annual %)	2010-2015	1.4
Urban population (%)	2014	44.2
Population aged 0-14 years (%)	2014	31.4
Population aged 60+ years (females and males, % of total)	2014	7.5/5.9
Sex ratio (males per 100 females)	2014	99.0
Life expectancy at birth (females and males, years)	2010-2015	71.6/65.9
Infant mortality rate (per 1 000 live births)	2010-2015	34.3
Fertility rate, total (live births per woman)	2010-2015	3.0
Contraceptive prevalence (ages 15-49, %)	2007-2013	22.3
International migrant stock (000 and % of total population)	mid-2013	2.6/2.6
Education: Government expenditure (% of GDP)	2007-2013	12.0 [k]
Education: Primary-secondary gross enrolment ratio (f/m per 100)	2007-2013	106.3/99.4
Intentional homicide rate (per 100,000 population)	2008-2012	8.2
Seats held by women in national parliaments (%)	2015	8.7

Environmental indicators		
Threatened species	2014	100
Forested area (% of land area)	2012	15.0
Proportion of terrestrial and marine areas protected (%)	2014	11.8
Population using improved drinking water sources (%)	2012	67.0
Population using improved sanitation facilities (%)	2012	40.0
CO_2 emission estimates (000 metric tons and metric tons per capita)	2011	62/0.6
Energy supply per capita (Gigajoules)	2012	9.0 [l]

a Land area only. Excluding 84 square km of uninhabited islands. b Refers to the island of Tarawa. c 2010.
d Official rate. e 2006. f 2012. g Tarawa. h 2008. i Air arrivals. Tarawa and Christmas Island. j ITU estimate.
k 2001. l UNSD estimate.

Kuwait

Region	Western Asia	Surface area (sq km)	17 818
Population (est., 000)	3 479	Pop. density (per sq km)	195.3
Capital city	Kuwait City	Capital city pop. (000)	2 680
Currency	Kuwaiti Dinar (KWD)	UN membership date	14 May 1963

Economic indicators	2005	2010	2013
GDP: Gross domestic product (million current US$)	80 798	115 412	175 831
GDP: Growth rate at constant 2005 prices (annual %)	10.6	−6.0	−0.4
GDP per capita (current US$)	35 185.9	38 579.0	52 197.6
GNI: Gross national income per capita (current US$)	39 042.6	41 728.1	55 809.1
Gross fixed capital formation (% of GDP)	14.6	17.9	14.1
Exchange rates (national currency per US$)[a]	0.29	0.28	0.28
Balance of payments, current account (million US$)	30 071	36 727	69 783
CPI: Consumer price index (2000=100)	109	141	153[b]
Index of industrial production (2010=100)[c]	113	100	129
Agricultural production index (2004-2006=100)	97	134	171
Food production index (2004-2006=100)	97	135	172
Unemployment (% of labour force)	2.0	1.8	3.1
Employment in industrial sector (% of employed)	20.6[de]	...	...
Employment in agricultural sector (% of employed)	2.7[de]	...	...
Labour force participation, adult female pop. (%)	44.4	42.8	43.6
Labour force participation, adult male pop. (%)	81.9	82.3	83.1
Tourist arrivals at national borders (000)[f]	3 474	5 208	6 217
Energy production, primary (Petajoules)[g]	6 080	5 557	7 136[h]
Mobile-cellular subscriptions (per 100 inhabitants)	60.2[i]	133.0	190.3[j]
Individuals using the Internet (%)	25.9	61.4[j]	75.5[j]

Total trade		Major trading partners		2013
	(million US$)	(% of exports)		(% of imports)
Exports	114 404.1	...	China	13.5
Imports	29 645.6	...	United States	9.9
Balance	84 758.5	...	United Arab Emirates	8.9

Social indicators		
Population growth rate (average annual %)	2010-2015	3.6
Urban population growth rate (average annual %)	2010-2015	3.6
Rural population growth rate (average annual %)	2010-2015	2.7
Urban population (%)	2014	98.3
Population aged 0-14 years (%)	2014	24.7
Population aged 60+ years (females and males, % of total)	2014	3.9/3.7
Sex ratio (males per 100 females)	2014	148.5
Life expectancy at birth (females and males, years)	2010-2015	75.5/73.4
Infant mortality rate (per 1 000 live births)	2010-2015	8.6
Fertility rate, total (live births per woman)	2010-2015	2.6
Contraceptive prevalence (ages 15-49, %)	2007-2013	52.0[k]
International migrant stock (000 and % of total population)[lm]	mid-2013	2 028.1/60.2
Refugees and others of concern to UNHCR	mid-2014	94 652
Education: Government expenditure (% of GDP)[n]	2007-2013	3.8[o]
Education: Primary-secondary gross enrolment ratio (f/m per 100)	2007-2013	102.9/103.1
Education: Female third-level students (% of total)	2007-2013	63.9
Intentional homicide rate (per 100,000 population)	2008-2012	0.4
Seats held by women in national parliaments (%)	2015	1.5

Environmental indicators		
Threatened species	2014	42
Forested area (% of land area)	2012	<
Proportion of terrestrial and marine areas protected (%)	2014	11.0
Population using improved drinking water sources (%)	2012	99.0
Population using improved sanitation facilities (%)	2012	100.0
CO_2 emission estimates (000 metric tons and metric tons per capita)	2011	91 030/29.1
Energy supply per capita (Gigajoules)[g]	2012	482.0

a Official rate. b Series linked to former series. c ISIC Rev.3 (CDE). d Population census. e ISIC Rev.3. f Arrivals of non-resident visitors at national borders. g Data for crude petroleum production include 50 per cent of the output of the Neutral Zone. h 2012. i Incomplete coverage. j ITU estimate. k 1999. l Refers to foreign citizens. m Including refugees. n UNESCO estimate. o 2006.

Kyrgyzstan

Region	Central Asia	Surface area (sq km)	199 949
Population (est., 000)	5 625	Pop. density (per sq km)	28.1
Capital city	Bishkek	Capital city pop. (000)	858
Currency	Som (KGS)	UN membership date	2 March 1992

Economic indicators	2005	2010	2013
GDP: Gross domestic product (million current US$)	2 460	4 794	7 226
GDP: Growth rate at constant 2005 prices (annual %)	-0.2	-0.5	10.5
GDP per capita (current US$)	487.9	898.8	1 302.6
GNI: Gross national income per capita (current US$)	471.9	834.8	1 269.3
Gross fixed capital formation (% of GDP)	16.2	28.1	30.6
Exchange rates (national currency per US$)[a]	41.30	47.10	49.25
Balance of payments, current account (million US$)	-37	-317	-1 684
CPI: Consumer price index (2000=100)	122	129[b]	...
Index of industrial production (2010=100)[c]	145	100	...
Agricultural production index (2004-2006=100)	98	105	112
Food production index (2004-2006=100)	98	107	114
Unemployment (% of labour force)	8.1	8.6	8.0
Employment in industrial sector (% of employed)	17.6[de]	20.6[def]	...
Employment in agricultural sector (% of employed)	38.5[de]	34.0[def]	...
Labour force participation, adult female pop. (%)	54.1	55.2	56.0
Labour force participation, adult male pop. (%)	75.9	78.2	79.5
Tourist arrivals at national borders (000)[g]	...	855	3 076
Energy production, primary (Petajoules)	60	53	73[h]
Mobile-cellular subscriptions (per 100 inhabitants)	10.7	98.9	121.5
Individuals using the Internet (%)	10.5	18.4[i]	23.4[i]

Total trade		Major trading partners			2013
	(million US$)		(% of exports)		(% of imports)
Exports	1 773.2	Switzerland	28.9	Russian Federation	33.2
Imports	5 983.0	Kazakhstan	21.6	China	23.9
Balance	-4 209.8	United Arab Emirates	12.5	Kazakhstan	9.3

Social indicators		
Population growth rate (average annual %)	2010-2015	1.4
Urban population growth rate (average annual %)	2010-2015	1.6
Rural population growth rate (average annual %)	2010-2015	1.2
Urban population (%)	2014	35.6
Population aged 0-14 years (%)	2014	30.6
Population aged 60+ years (females and males, % of total)	2014	7.6/5.4
Sex ratio (males per 100 females)	2014	97.3
Life expectancy at birth (females and males, years)	2010-2015	71.8/63.4
Infant mortality rate (per 1 000 live births)	2010-2015	33.1
Fertility rate, total (live births per woman)	2010-2015	3.1
Contraceptive prevalence (ages 15-49, %)	2007-2013	36.3
International migrant stock (000 and % of total population)	mid-2013	227.0/4.1
Refugees and others of concern to UNHCR	mid-2014	16 137
Education: Government expenditure (% of GDP)	2007-2013	6.8
Education: Primary-secondary gross enrolment ratio (f/m per 100)[j]	2007-2013	92.1/92.8
Education: Female third-level students (% of total)	2007-2013	61.4
Intentional homicide rate (per 100,000 population)	2008-2012	9.1
Seats held by women in national parliaments (%)	2015	23.3

Environmental indicators		
Threatened species	2014	41
Forested area (% of land area)	2012	5.2
Proportion of terrestrial and marine areas protected (%)	2014	6.9
Population using improved drinking water sources (%)	2012	88.0
Population using improved sanitation facilities (%)	2012	92.0
CO_2 emission estimates (000 metric tons and metric tons per capita)	2011	6 615/1.2
Energy supply per capita (Gigajoules)	2012	32.0

a Official rate. b 2006. c ISIC Rev.3 (CDE). d ISIC Rev.3. e November. f 2008. g Arrivals of non-resident visitors at national borders. h 2012. i ITU estimate. j National estimate.

Lao People's Democratic Republic

Region	South-Eastern Asia	Surface area (sq km)	236 800
Population (est., 000)	6 894	Pop. density (per sq km)	29.1
Capital city	Vientiane	Capital city pop. (000)	946
Currency	Kip (LAK)	UN membership date	14 December 1955

Economic indicators	2005	2010	2013
GDP: Gross domestic product (million current US$)	2 717	6 744	10 760
GDP: Growth rate at constant 2005 prices (annual %)	6.8	8.1	8.0
GDP per capita (current US$)	469.2	1 054.4	1 589.4
GNI: Gross national income per capita (current US$)	457.9	985.7	1 510.7
Gross fixed capital formation (% of GDP)	34.3	29.0	31.7
Exchange rates (national currency per US$)[a]	10 743.00	8 058.78	8 027.76
Balance of payments, current account (million US$)	−174	29	−376
CPI: Consumer price index (2000=100)	163[b]	208	248
Agricultural production index (2004-2006=100)	100	130	156
Food production index (2004-2006=100)	100	128	153
Unemployment (% of labour force)	1.4	1.4	1.4
Labour force participation, adult female pop. (%)	77.5	76.4	76.3
Labour force participation, adult male pop. (%)	79.6	78.7	79.1
Tourist arrivals at national borders (000)	672	1 670	2 510
Energy production, primary (Petajoules)	80	79	82[c]
Mobile-cellular subscriptions (per 100 inhabitants)	11.4	62.6	66.2
Individuals using the Internet (%)	0.9	7.0	12.5[d]

Social indicators		
Population growth rate (average annual %)	2010-2015	1.9
Urban population growth rate (average annual %)	2010-2015	4.9
Rural population growth rate (average annual %)	2010-2015	0.2
Urban population (%)	2014	37.6
Population aged 0-14 years (%)	2014	34.7
Population aged 60+ years (females and males, % of total)	2014	6.5/5.4
Sex ratio (males per 100 females)	2014	99.2
Life expectancy at birth (females and males, years)	2010-2015	69.4/66.7
Infant mortality rate (per 1 000 live births)	2010-2015	36.2
Fertility rate, total (live births per woman)	2010-2015	3.1
Contraceptive prevalence (ages 15-49, %)	2007-2013	49.8
International migrant stock (000 and % of total population)[ef]	mid-2013	21.8/0.3
Refugees and others of concern to UNHCR	mid-2014	0[g]
Education: Government expenditure (% of GDP)	2007-2013	2.8
Education: Primary-secondary gross enrolment ratio (f/m per 100)	2007-2013	75.7/81.7
Education: Female third-level students (% of total)	2007-2013	46.2
Intentional homicide rate (per 100,000 population)	2008-2012	5.9
Seats held by women in national parliaments (%)	2015	25.0

Environmental indicators		
Threatened species	2014	200
Forested area (% of land area)	2012	67.6
Proportion of terrestrial and marine areas protected (%)	2014	16.7
Population using improved drinking water sources (%)	2012	72.0
Population using improved sanitation facilities (%)	2012	65.0
CO_2 emission estimates (000 metric tons and metric tons per capita)	2011	1 203/0.2
Energy supply per capita (Gigajoules)	2012	12.0

a Market rate. b Series linked to former series. c 2012. d ITU estimate. e Refers to foreign citizens. f Including refugees. g Value is zero, not available or not applicable.

Latvia

Region	Northern Europe
Population (est., 000)	2 041
Capital city	Riga
Currency	Lats (LVL)

Surface area (sq km)	64 562
Pop. density (per sq km)	31.6
Capital city pop. (000)	629
UN membership date	17 September 1991

Economic indicators	2005	2010	2013
GDP: Gross domestic product (million current US$)	17 091	23 867	30 886
GDP: Growth rate at constant 2005 prices (annual %)	10.2	−2.9	4.2
GDP per capita (current US$)	7 672.7	11 417.0	15 064.0
GNI: Gross national income per capita (current US$)	7 130.8	11 659.3	15 097.5
Gross fixed capital formation (% of GDP)	31.3	19.1	23.3
Exchange rates (national currency per US$)[a]	0.59	0.54	0.52
Balance of payments, current account (million US$)	−1 992	724	−250
CPI: Consumer price index (2000=100)	122	169	180
Index of industrial production (2010=100)[b]	102	100	115
Agricultural production index (2004-2006=100)	105	109	117
Food production index (2004-2006=100)	105	109	118
Unemployment (% of labour force)	8.9	18.7	11.1
Employment in industrial sector (% of employed)[c]	25.8[de]	24.0	23.5[fg]
Employment in agricultural sector (% of employed)[c]	12.1[de]	8.8	8.4[fg]
Labour force participation, adult female pop. (%)	50.9	53.8	54.9
Labour force participation, adult male pop. (%)	66.3	65.4	67.6
Tourist arrivals at national borders (000)[h]	1 116	1 373	1 536
Energy production, primary (Petajoules)	78	89	98[f]
Mobile-cellular subscriptions (per 100 inhabitants)	84.0	110.3[i]	136.6[i]
Individuals using the Internet (%)	46.0	68.4	75.2

Total trade		Major trading partners			2013
	(million US$)	(% of exports)			(% of imports)
Exports	13 324.7	Lithuania	17.2	Lithuania	20.4
Imports	16 778.9	Estonia	12.7	Germany	11.6
Balance	−3 454.2	Russian Federation	11.6	Poland	9.9

Social indicators		
Population growth rate (average annual %)	2010-2015	−0.6
Urban population growth rate (average annual %)	2010-2015	−0.7
Rural population growth rate (average annual %)	2010-2015	−0.4
Urban population (%)	2014	67.4
Population aged 0-14 years (%)	2014	15.2
Population aged 60+ years (females and males, % of total)	2014	29.5/18.4
Sex ratio (males per 100 females)	2014	84.3
Life expectancy at birth (females and males, years)	2010-2015	77.5/66.6
Infant mortality rate (per 1 000 live births)	2010-2015	7.3
Fertility rate, total (live births per woman)	2010-2015	1.6
Contraceptive prevalence (ages 15-49, %)[j]	2007-2013	67.8[k]
International migrant stock (000 and % of total population)	mid-2013	282.9/13.8
Refugees and others of concern to UNHCR	mid-2014	254 250
Education: Government expenditure (% of GDP)	2007-2013	4.9
Education: Primary-secondary gross enrolment ratio (f/m per 100)	2007-2013	99.1/101.2
Education: Female third-level students (% of total)	2007-2013	59.6
Intentional homicide rate (per 100,000 population)	2008-2012	4.7
Seats held by women in national parliaments (%)	2015	18.0

Environmental indicators		
Threatened species	2014	25
Forested area (% of land area)	2012	54.3
Proportion of terrestrial and marine areas protected (%)	2014	17.8
Population using improved drinking water sources (%)	2012	98.0
CO$_2$ emission estimates (000 metric tons and metric tons per capita)	2011	7 800/3.8
Energy supply per capita (Gigajoules)	2012	90.0

a Official rate. **b** ISIC Rev.4 (BCD). **c** Population aged 15-74. **d** ISIC Rev.3. **e** Excluding conscripts. **f** 2012. **g** Break in series. **h** Non-resident departures. **i** ITU estimate. **j** Age group 18 to 49 years. **k** 1995.

Lebanon

Region	Western Asia	Surface area (sq km)	10 452
Population (est., 000)	4 966	Pop. density (per sq km)	477.5
Capital city	Beirut	Capital city pop. (000)	2 179[a]
Currency	Lebanese Pound (LBP)	UN membership date	24 October 1945

Economic indicators	2005	2010	2013
GDP: Gross domestic product (million current US$)	21 490	38 420	47 221
GDP: Growth rate at constant 2005 prices (annual %)	2.8	8.0	3.0
GDP per capita (current US$)	5 390.2	8 850.3	9 792.8
GNI: Gross national income per capita (current US$)	5 518.9	8 819.3	9 511.9
Gross fixed capital formation (% of GDP)	22.2	25.3	27.2
Exchange rates (national currency per US$)[b]	1 507.50	1 507.50	1 507.50
Balance of payments, current account (million US$)	−2 748	−7 552	−10 983
CPI: Consumer price index (2000=100)	105[c]	105[d]	124[d]
Agricultural production index (2004-2006=100)	97	95	97
Food production index (2004-2006=100)	97	94	97
Unemployment (% of labour force)	8.2	6.2	6.5
Labour force participation, adult female pop. (%)	20.3	22.0	23.3
Labour force participation, adult male pop. (%)	70.6	70.0	70.9
Tourist arrivals at national borders (000)	1 140	2 168	1 274
Energy production, primary (Petajoules)	10	9	9[e]
Mobile-cellular subscriptions (per 100 inhabitants)	24.9[f]	66.0	80.6
Individuals using the Internet (%)	10.1[g]	43.7[fh]	70.5[f]

Total trade		Major trading partners			2013
	(million US$)		(% of exports)		(% of imports)
Exports	3 937.1	Syria	13.3	China	10.8
Imports	21 234.2	South Africa	10.1	Italy	8.4
Balance	−17 297.1	Saudi Arabia	8.8	France	7.2

Social indicators		
Population growth rate (average annual %)	2010-2015	3.0
Urban population growth rate (average annual %)	2010-2015	3.2
Rural population growth rate (average annual %)	2010-2015	2.1
Urban population (%)	2014	87.7
Population aged 0-14 years (%)	2014	20.1
Population aged 60+ years (females and males, % of total)	2014	12.5/12.0
Sex ratio (males per 100 females)	2014	103.1
Life expectancy at birth (females and males, years)	2010-2015	82.1/77.9
Infant mortality rate (per 1 000 live births)	2010-2015	8.4
Fertility rate, total (live births per woman)	2010-2015	1.5
Contraceptive prevalence (ages 15-49, %)	2007-2013	58.0[i]
International migrant stock (000 and % of total population)[j]	mid-2013	849.7/17.6
Refugees and others of concern to UNHCR	mid-2014	1 122 874
Education: Government expenditure (% of GDP)	2007-2013	2.6
Education: Primary-secondary gross enrolment ratio (f/m per 100)	2007-2013	90.0/94.3
Education: Female third-level students (% of total)	2007-2013	54.3
Intentional homicide rate (per 100,000 population)	2008-2012	2.2
Seats held by women in national parliaments (%)	2015	3.1

Environmental indicators		
Threatened species	2014	64
Forested area (% of land area)	2012	13.4
Proportion of terrestrial and marine areas protected (%)	2014	0.9
Population using improved drinking water sources (%)	2012	100.0
CO$_2$ emission estimates (000 metric tons and metric tons per capita)	2011	20 488/4.6
Energy supply per capita (Gigajoules)	2012	63.0

a Excluding Syrian refugees. b Market rate. c Beirut. d Index base 2008=100. e 2012. f ITU estimate. g Population aged 6 and over. h Population aged 15 and over. i 2004. j Including refugees.

Lesotho

Region	Southern Africa	Surface area (sq km)	30 355
Population (est., 000)	2 098	Pop. density (per sq km)	69.1
Capital city	Maseru	Capital city pop. (000)	267
Currency	Loti (LSL)	UN membership date	17 October 1966

Economic indicators	2005	2010	2013
GDP: Gross domestic product (million current US$)	1 368	2 176	2 230
GDP: Growth rate at constant 2005 prices (annual %)	2.7	7.1	5.8
GDP per capita (current US$)	710.5	1 083.0	1 074.9
GNI: Gross national income per capita (current US$)	967.6	1 305.3	1 294.0
Gross fixed capital formation (% of GDP)	21.1	25.7	27.3
Exchange rates (national currency per US$)[a]	6.32	6.63	10.49
Balance of payments, current account (million US$)	−27	−405	−77
CPI: Consumer price index (2000=100)	140	198[b]	231
Agricultural production index (2004-2006=100)	102	110	111
Food production index (2004-2006=100)	102	111	112
Unemployment (% of labour force)	36.4	24.7	24.7
Labour force participation, adult female pop. (%)	61.8	58.7	59.0
Labour force participation, adult male pop. (%)	75.5	73.0	73.5
Tourist arrivals at national borders (000)[c]	304	426	433
Energy production, primary (Petajoules)	20	21	21[d]
Mobile-cellular subscriptions (per 100 inhabitants)	13.0	49.2	86.3
Individuals using the Internet (%)[e]	2.6	3.9	5.0

Social indicators		
Population growth rate (average annual %)	2010-2015	1.1
Urban population growth rate (average annual %)	2010-2015	3.1
Rural population growth rate (average annual %)	2010-2015	0.4
Urban population (%)	2014	26.8
Population aged 0-14 years (%)	2014	36.0
Population aged 60+ years (females and males, % of total)	2014	7.6/5.0
Sex ratio (males per 100 females)	2014	97.7
Life expectancy at birth (females and males, years)	2010-2015	49.6/49.2
Infant mortality rate (per 1 000 live births)	2010-2015	60.1
Fertility rate, total (live births per woman)	2010-2015	3.1
Contraceptive prevalence (ages 15-49, %)	2007-2013	47.0
International migrant stock (000 and % of total population)[fg]	mid-2013	3.1/0.2
Refugees and others of concern to UNHCR	mid-2014	39
Education: Government expenditure (% of GDP)	2007-2013	13.0
Education: Primary-secondary gross enrolment ratio (f/m per 100)	2007-2013	89.6/83.6
Education: Female third-level students (% of total)	2007-2013	59.4
Intentional homicide rate (per 100,000 population)	2008-2012	38.0
Seats held by women in national parliaments (%)	2015	26.7

Environmental indicators		
Threatened species	2014	17
Forested area (% of land area)	2012	1.5
Proportion of terrestrial and marine areas protected (%)	2014	0.5
Population using improved drinking water sources (%)	2012	81.0
Population using improved sanitation facilities (%)	2012	30.0
CO_2 emission estimates (000 metric tons and metric tons per capita)	2011	2 200/1.1
Energy supply per capita (Gigajoules)	2012	23.0[h]

a Principal rate. b Series linked to former series. c Arrivals of non-resident visitors at national borders.
d 2012. e ITU estimate. f Refers to foreign citizens. g Including refugees. h UNSD estimate.

Liberia

Region	Western Africa	Surface area (sq km)	111 369	
Population (est., 000)	4 397	Pop. density (per sq km)	39.5	
Capital city	Monrovia	Capital city pop. (000)	1 224	
Currency	Liberian Dollar (LRD)	UN membership date	2 November 1945	

Economic indicators	2005	2010	2013
GDP: Gross domestic product (million current US$)	608	1 074	1 946
GDP: Growth rate at constant 2005 prices (annual %)	9.5	10.8	8.1
GDP per capita (current US$)	185.9	271.4	453.2
GNI: Gross national income per capita (current US$)	135.3	233.7	406.7
Gross fixed capital formation (% of GDP)	13.3	26.4	25.6
Exchange rates (national currency per US$)[a]	56.50	71.50	82.50
Balance of payments, current account (million US$)	−184	−415	−536
Agricultural production index (2004-2006=100)	105	100	101
Food production index (2004-2006=100)	104	120	121
Unemployment (% of labour force)	5.0	3.7	3.7
Employment in industrial sector (% of employed)	2.5[bcd]	9.2[e]	...
Employment in agricultural sector (% of employed)	47.6[bcd]	48.9[e]	...
Labour force participation, adult female pop. (%)	58.5	58.1	58.2
Labour force participation, adult male pop. (%)	62.9	64.3	64.8
Energy production, primary (Petajoules)	53	64	69[f]
Mobile-cellular subscriptions (per 100 inhabitants)	4.9	39.7	59.5
Individuals using the Internet (%)	0.6[bg]	2.3	4.6[g]

Social indicators		
Population growth rate (average annual %)	2010-2015	2.6
Urban population growth rate (average annual %)	2010-2015	3.4
Rural population growth rate (average annual %)	2010-2015	1.8
Urban population (%)	2014	49.3
Population aged 0-14 years (%)	2014	42.6
Population aged 60+ years (females and males, % of total)	2014	5.2/4.4
Sex ratio (males per 100 females)	2014	101.5
Life expectancy at birth (females and males, years)	2010-2015	61.2/59.3
Infant mortality rate (per 1 000 live births)	2010-2015	61.2
Fertility rate, total (live births per woman)	2010-2015	4.8
Contraceptive prevalence (ages 15-49, %)	2007-2013	20.2
International migrant stock (000 and % of total population)	mid-2013	225.5/5.3
Refugees and others of concern to UNHCR	mid-2014	39 806
Education: Government expenditure (% of GDP)	2007-2013	2.8
Education: Primary-secondary gross enrolment ratio (f/m per 100)	2007-2013	65.1/73.8
Education: Female third-level students (% of total)	2007-2013	38.1
Intentional homicide rate (per 100,000 population)	2008-2012	3.2
Seats held by women in national parliaments (%)	2015	11.0

Environmental indicators		
Threatened species	2014	158
Forested area (% of land area)	2012	44.3
Proportion of terrestrial and marine areas protected (%)	2014	0.8
Population using improved drinking water sources (%)	2012	75.0
Population using improved sanitation facilities (%)	2012	17.0
CO_2 emission estimates (000 metric tons and metric tons per capita)	2011	891/0.2
Energy supply per capita (Gigajoules)	2012	20.0

a Principal rate. b 2007. c Core Welfare Indicators Questionnaire (World Bank). d ISIC Rev.2. e Break in series. f 2012. g ITU estimate.

Libya

Region	Northern Africa	Surface area (sq km)	1 759 540
Population (est., 000)	6 253	Pop. density (per sq km)	3.6
Capital city	Tripoli	Capital city pop. (000)	1 126
Currency	Libyan Dinar (LYD)	UN membership date	14 December 1955

Economic indicators	2005	2010	2013
GDP: Gross domestic product (million current US$)	45 451	80 942	74 597
GDP: Growth rate at constant 2005 prices (annual %)	10.3	4.3	−16.2
GDP per capita (current US$)	8 124.4	13 399.7	12 028.8
GNI: Gross national income per capita (current US$)	8 072.5	13 319.1	11 956.5
Gross fixed capital formation (% of GDP)	27.8	40.2	31.5
Exchange rates (national currency per US$)[a]	1.35	1.25	1.25
Balance of payments, current account (million US$)	14 945	16 801	−108
Agricultural production index (2004-2006=100)	101	110	111
Food production index (2004-2006=100)	101	110	111
Unemployment (% of labour force)	19.8	18.8	19.6
Labour force participation, adult female pop. (%)	29.6	29.8	30.0
Labour force participation, adult male pop. (%)	75.0	76.1	76.4
Tourist arrivals at national borders (000)[b]	81	34[c]	...
Energy production, primary (Petajoules)	4 062	4 295	3 590[d]
Mobile-cellular subscriptions (per 100 inhabitants)	35.8	180.5[e]	165.0[e]
Individuals using the Internet (%)[e]	3.9	14.0	16.5

Total trade		Major trading partners			2013
	(million US$)[f]	(% of exports)[f]		(% of imports)[f]	
Exports	36 440.4	Italy	42.3	Turkey	10.6
Imports	17 674.4	France	15.5	Europe nes	10.0[g]
Balance	18 766.0	China	9.4	China	9.8

Social indicators

Population growth rate (average annual %)	2010-2015	0.9
Urban population growth rate (average annual %)	2010-2015	1.1
Rural population growth rate (average annual %)	2010-2015	0.1
Urban population (%)	2014	78.4
Population aged 0-14 years (%)	2014	29.4
Population aged 60+ years (females and males, % of total)	2014	7.6/7.1
Sex ratio (males per 100 females)	2014	98.9
Life expectancy at birth (females and males, years)	2010-2015	77.2/73.4
Infant mortality rate (per 1 000 live births)	2010-2015	13.8
Fertility rate, total (live births per woman)	2010-2015	2.4
Contraceptive prevalence (ages 15-49, %)	2007-2013	41.9
International migrant stock (000 and % of total population)[h]	mid-2013	756.0/12.2
Refugees and others of concern to UNHCR	mid-2014	108 594[i]
Education: Government expenditure (% of GDP)	2007-2013	2.7[j]
Education: Primary-secondary gross enrolment ratio (f/m per 100)	2007-2013	112.5/106.0[k]
Education: Female third-level students (% of total)[l]	2007-2013	51.4[m]
Intentional homicide rate (per 100,000 population)	2008-2012	1.7
Seats held by women in national parliaments (%)	2015	16.0

Environmental indicators

Threatened species	2014	49
Forested area (% of land area)	2012	<
Proportion of terrestrial and marine areas protected (%)	2014	0.3
Population using improved sanitation facilities (%)	2012	97.0
CO$_2$ emission estimates (000 metric tons and metric tons per capita)	2011	39 021/6.4
Energy supply per capita (Gigajoules)	2012	116.0

a Official rate. **b** Arrivals of non-resident tourists in hotels and similar establishments. **c** 2008. **d** 2012. **e** ITU estimate. **f** 2010. **g** See technical notes. **h** Refers to foreign citizens. **i** Refugee and asylum-seeker population refers to the end of 2013. **j** 1999. **k** 2006. **l** UNESCO estimate. **m** 2003.

Liechtenstein

Region	Western Europe	Surface area (sq km)	160
Population (est., 000)	37	Pop. density (per sq km)	232.5
Capital city	Vaduz	Capital city pop. (000)	5
Currency	Swiss Franc (CHF)	UN membership date	18 September 1990

Economic indicators	2005	2010	2013
GDP: Gross domestic product (million current US$)	3 658	5 082	5 647
GDP: Growth rate at constant 2005 prices (annual %)	4.8	7.4	1.9
GDP per capita (current US$)	105 306.8	140 707.1	152 933.1
GNI: Gross national income per capita (current US$)	89 979.9	118 657.5	119 918.4
Gross fixed capital formation (% of GDP)	24.5	22.8	23.4
Exchange rates (national currency per US$)[a]	1.31[b]	0.95	0.89
Agricultural production index (2004-2006=100)	100	100	100
Food production index (2004-2006=100)	100	100	100
Tourist arrivals at national borders (000)[c]	50	50	52
Energy production, primary (Petajoules)	...	2[d]	3[de]
Mobile-cellular subscriptions (per 100 inhabitants)	79.2	98.3[f]	97.8[f]
Individuals using the Internet (%)	63.4	80.0[f]	93.8[f]

Social indicators		
Population growth rate (average annual %)	2010-2015	0.7
Urban population growth rate (average annual %)	2010-2015	0.5
Rural population growth rate (average annual %)	2010-2015	0.8
Urban population (%)	2014	14.3
Population aged 0-14 years (%)[ghi]	2014	15.8[j]
Population aged 60+ years (females and males, % of total)[ghi]	2014	21.4/19.2[j]
Sex ratio (males per 100 females)[ghi]	2014	97.9[j]
Fertility rate, total (live births per woman)[g]	2010-2015	1.7[j]
International migrant stock (000 and % of total population)[k]	mid-2013	12.2/33.1
Refugees and others of concern to UNHCR	mid-2014	125[l]
Education: Government expenditure (% of GDP)	2007-2013	2.1
Education: Primary-secondary gross enrolment ratio (f/m per 100)[m]	2007-2013	102.9/112.7
Education: Female third-level students (% of total)	2007-2013	34.6
Intentional homicide rate (per 100,000 population)	2008-2012	0.0
Seats held by women in national parliaments (%)	2015	20.0

Environmental indicators		
Threatened species	2014	4
Forested area (% of land area)	2012	43.1
Proportion of terrestrial and marine areas protected (%)	2014	44.3
CO$_2$ emission estimates (000 metric tons and metric tons per capita)	2011	51/1.4
Energy supply per capita (Gigajoules)	2012	129.0

a UN operational exchange rate. **b** December 2005. **c** Arrivals of non-resident tourists in hotels and similar establishments. **d** UNSD estimate. **e** 2012. **f** ITU estimate. **g** Data compiled by the United Nations Demographic Yearbook system. **h** Data refer to the latest available census. **i** De jure estimate. **j** 2011. **k** Refers to foreign citizens. **l** Refugee population refers to the end of 2013. **m** National estimate.

Lithuania

Region	Northern Europe	Surface area (sq km)	65 300
Population (est., 000)	3 008	Pop. density (per sq km)	46.1
Capital city	Vilnius	Capital city pop. (000)	519
Currency	Litas (LTL)	UN membership date	17 September 1991

Economic indicators	2005	2010	2013
GDP: Gross domestic product (million current US$)	26 141	37 095	46 403
GDP: Growth rate at constant 2005 prices (annual %)	7.8	1.6	3.3
GDP per capita (current US$)	7 953.5	12 089.3	15 380.9
GNI: Gross national income per capita (current US$)	7 853.8	11 864.0	14 966.6
Gross fixed capital formation (% of GDP)	23.4	17.0	18.3
Exchange rates (national currency per US$) [a]	2.91	2.61	2.51
Balance of payments, current account (million US$)	−1 831	15	675
CPI: Consumer price index (2000=100)	104[b]	134	146[b]
Index of industrial production (2010=100) [c]	97	100	114
Agricultural production index (2004-2006=100)	106	99	118
Food production index (2004-2006=100)	106	99	118
Unemployment (% of labour force)	8.3	17.8	11.8
Employment in industrial sector (% of employed)	29.1[de]	24.4	24.8[fg]
Employment in agricultural sector (% of employed)	14.0[de]	9.0	8.9[fg]
Labour force participation, adult female pop. (%)	51.0	54.3	55.8
Labour force participation, adult male pop. (%)	63.3	64.2	67.3
Tourist arrivals at national borders (000)	2 000	1 507	2 012
Energy production, primary (Petajoules)	169	63	65[f]
Mobile-cellular subscriptions (per 100 inhabitants)	132.5[h]	159.4	151.3
Individuals using the Internet (%)	36.2[i]	62.1[i]	68.5

Total trade		Major trading partners			2013
	(million US$)	(% of exports)			(% of imports)
Exports	32 599.7	Russian Federation	19.8	Russian Federation	28.1
Imports	34 813.2	Latvia	10.0	Germany	10.5
Balance	−2 213.5	Poland	7.4	Poland	9.5

Social indicators		
Population growth rate (average annual %)	2010-2015	−0.5
Urban population growth rate (average annual %)	2010-2015	−0.5
Rural population growth rate (average annual %)	2010-2015	−0.3
Urban population (%)	2014	66.5
Population aged 0-14 years (%)	2014	15.3
Population aged 60+ years (females and males, % of total)	2014	25.5/15.5
Sex ratio (males per 100 females)	2014	85.3
Life expectancy at birth (females and males, years)	2010-2015	78.1/66.0
Infant mortality rate (per 1 000 live births)	2010-2015	5.4
Fertility rate, total (live births per woman)	2010-2015	1.5
Contraceptive prevalence (ages 15-49, %) [j]	2007-2013	62.9[k]
International migrant stock (000 and % of total population)	mid-2013	147.8/4.9
Refugees and others of concern to UNHCR	mid-2014	4 800
Education: Government expenditure (% of GDP)	2007-2013	5.2
Education: Primary-secondary gross enrolment ratio (f/m per 100)	2007-2013	102.1/105.7
Education: Female third-level students (% of total)	2007-2013	58.4
Intentional homicide rate (per 100,000 population)	2008-2012	6.7
Seats held by women in national parliaments (%)	2015	23.4

Environmental indicators		
Threatened species	2014	23
Forested area (% of land area)	2012	34.7
Proportion of terrestrial and marine areas protected (%)	2014	16.3
Population using improved drinking water sources (%)	2012	96.0
Population using improved sanitation facilities (%)	2012	94.0
CO_2 emission estimates (000 metric tons and metric tons per capita)	2011	13 740/4.5
Energy supply per capita (Gigajoules)	2012	99.0

a Official rate. **b** Series linked to former series. **c** ISIC Rev.4 (BCDE). **d** ISIC Rev.3. **e** Excluding conscripts. **f** 2012. **g** Break in series. **h** Active mobile subscriptions. **i** Population aged 16 to 74 using the Internet in the last 12 months. **j** Age group 18 to 49 years. **k** 2006.

Luxembourg

Region	Western Europe	Surface area (sq km)	2 586	
Population (est., 000)	537	Pop. density (per sq km)	207.6	
Capital city	Luxembourg	Capital city pop. (000)	107	
Currency	Euro (EUR)	UN membership date	24 October 1945	

Economic indicators	2005	2010	2013
GDP: Gross domestic product (million current US$)	37 024	52 144	60 131
GDP: Growth rate at constant 2005 prices (annual %)	4.1	5.1	2.0
GDP per capita (current US$)	80 864.5	102 668.2	113 373.1
GNI: Gross national income per capita (current US$)	71 332.9	67 088.4	72 004.9
Gross fixed capital formation (% of GDP)	20.6	16.1	16.9
Exchange rates (national currency per US$)[a]	0.85	0.75	0.73
Balance of payments, current account (million US$)	4 406	4 090	3 161
CPI: Consumer price index (2000=100)	112[b]	125	135
Index of industrial production (2010=100)[c]	113	100	95
Agricultural production index (2004-2006=100)	99	93	94
Food production index (2004-2006=100)	99	93	94
Unemployment (% of labour force)	4.5	4.4	5.9
Employment in industrial sector (% of employed)	17.2[d]	12.6	12.4[e]
Employment in agricultural sector (% of employed)	1.8[d]	1.0	1.3[e]
Labour force participation, adult female pop. (%)	45.4	48.8	50.7
Labour force participation, adult male pop. (%)	64.7	65.4	64.6
Tourist arrivals at national borders (000)[f]	913	805	945
Energy production, primary (Petajoules)	5	5	5[e]
Mobile-cellular subscriptions (per 100 inhabitants)	111.4	143.1	148.6
Individuals using the Internet (%)	70.0	90.6	93.8

Total trade		Major trading partners			2013
	(million US$)	(% of exports)			(% of imports)
Exports	13 753.5	Germany	27.8	Belgium	24.6
Imports	23 895.9	France	14.7	Germany	23.5
Balance	−10 142.4	Belgium	13.3	France	12.9

Social indicators		
Population growth rate (average annual %)	2010-2015	1.4
Urban population growth rate (average annual %)	2010-2015	1.7
Rural population growth rate (average annual %)	2010-2015	−1.7
Urban population (%)	2014	89.9
Population aged 0-14 years (%)	2014	17.4
Population aged 60+ years (females and males, % of total)	2014	21.2/17.8
Sex ratio (males per 100 females)	2014	99.2
Life expectancy at birth (females and males, years)	2010-2015	83.0/77.9
Infant mortality rate (per 1 000 live births)	2010-2015	2.0
Fertility rate, total (live births per woman)	2010-2015	1.7
International migrant stock (000 and % of total population)	mid-2013	229.4/43.3
Refugees and others of concern to UNHCR	mid-2014	1 960
Education: Government expenditure (% of GDP)	2007-2013	3.8[g]
Education: Primary-secondary gross enrolment ratio (f/m per 100)	2007-2013	99.5/97.4
Education: Female third-level students (% of total)	2007-2013	52.1
Intentional homicide rate (per 100,000 population)	2008-2012	0.8
Seats held by women in national parliaments (%)	2015	28.3

Environmental indicators		
Threatened species	2014	9
Forested area (% of land area)	2012	33.5
Proportion of terrestrial and marine areas protected (%)	2014	34.6
Population using improved drinking water sources (%)	2012	100.0
Population using improved sanitation facilities (%)	2012	100.0
CO_2 emission estimates (000 metric tons and metric tons per capita)	2011	10 832/21.0
Energy supply per capita (Gigajoules)	2012	329.0

a Market rate. b Series linked to former series. c ISIC Rev.4 (BCD). d ISIC Rev.3. e 2012. f Arrivals of non-resident tourists in all types of accommodation establishments. g 2001.

Madagascar

Region	Eastern Africa	Surface area (sq km)	587 295
Population (est., 000)	23 572	Pop. density (per sq km)	40.2
Capital city	Antananarivo	Capital city pop. (000)	2 487
Currency	Malagasy Ariary (MGA)	UN membership date	20 September 1960

Economic indicators	2005	2010	2013
GDP: Gross domestic product (million current US$)	5 039	8 745	10 612
GDP: Growth rate at constant 2005 prices (annual %)	4.6	0.4	2.0
GDP per capita (current US$)	275.5	414.9	462.9
GNI: Gross national income per capita (current US$)	295.1	410.9	448.2
Gross fixed capital formation (% of GDP)	22.2	20.7	15.7
Exchange rates (national currency per US$)[a]	2 159.82	2 146.12	2 236.09
Balance of payments, current account (million US$)	−554	...	...
CPI: Consumer price index (2000=100)	153	263	325
Agricultural production index (2004-2006=100)	103	124	119
Food production index (2004-2006=100)	103	124	119
Unemployment (% of labour force)	2.6	3.6	3.6
Employment in industrial sector (% of employed)	3.7[bc]	...	...
Employment in agricultural sector (% of employed)	80.4[b]	...	...
Labour force participation, adult female pop. (%)	84.1	87.2	86.6
Labour force participation, adult male pop. (%)	89.1	91.0	90.5
Tourist arrivals at national borders (000)[d]	277	196	196
Energy production, primary (Petajoules)	104	124	124[e]
Mobile-cellular subscriptions (per 100 inhabitants)	2.8	36.6	36.1
Individuals using the Internet (%)[f]	0.6	1.7	2.2

Total trade		Major trading partners			2013
	(million US$)		(% of exports)		(% of imports)
Exports	1 838.0	France	25.0	United Arab Emirates	21.4
Imports	3 085.4	United States	7.3	China	14.6
Balance	−1 247.4	China	7.1	France	5.9

Social indicators		
Population growth rate (average annual %)	2010-2015	2.8
Urban population growth rate (average annual %)	2010-2015	4.7
Rural population growth rate (average annual %)	2010-2015	1.8
Urban population (%)	2014	34.5
Population aged 0-14 years (%)	2014	42.0
Population aged 60+ years (females and males, % of total)	2014	4.9/4.3
Sex ratio (males per 100 females)	2014	99.4
Life expectancy at birth (females and males, years)	2010-2015	66.0/63.0
Infant mortality rate (per 1 000 live births)	2010-2015	36.8
Fertility rate, total (live births per woman)	2010-2015	4.5
Contraceptive prevalence (ages 15-49, %)	2007-2013	39.9
International migrant stock (000 and % of total population)[g]	mid-2013	34.3/0.2
Refugees and others of concern to UNHCR	mid-2014	14
Education: Government expenditure (% of GDP)	2007-2013	...
Education: Primary-secondary gross enrolment ratio (f/m per 100)	2007-2013	85.5/87.1
Education: Female third-level students (% of total)	2007-2013	48.0
Intentional homicide rate (per 100,000 population)	2008-2012	11.1
Seats held by women in national parliaments (%)	2015	20.5

Environmental indicators		
Threatened species	2014	929
Forested area (% of land area)	2012	21.4
Proportion of terrestrial and marine areas protected (%)	2014	2.0
Population using improved drinking water sources (%)	2012	50.0
Population using improved sanitation facilities (%)	2012	14.0
CO_2 emission estimates (000 metric tons and metric tons per capita)	2011	2 450/0.1
Energy supply per capita (Gigajoules)	2012	7.0

a Official rate. **b** ISIC Rev.2. **c** Excluding mining and quarrying. **d** Arrivals of non-resident tourists by air. **e** 2012. **f** ITU estimate. **g** Refers to foreign citizens.

Malawi

Region	Eastern Africa	Surface area (sq km)	118 484	
Population (est., 000)	16 829	Pop. density (per sq km)	142.0	
Capital city	Lilongwe	Capital city pop. (000)	867	
Currency	Malawi Kwacha (MWK)	UN membership date	1 December 1964	

Economic indicators	2005	2010	2013
GDP: Gross domestic product (million current US$)	3 656	6 960	5 146
GDP: Growth rate at constant 2005 prices (annual %)	3.3	6.9	5.4
GDP per capita (current US$)	282.9	463.6	314.5
GNI: Gross national income per capita (current US$)	277.2	450.9	307.9
Gross fixed capital formation (% of GDP)	14.3	10.1	16.9
Exchange rates (national currency per US$)[a]	123.78	150.80	434.96
Balance of payments, current account (million US$)	−507	−786	−800[b]
CPI: Consumer price index (2000=100)	199	309	513[c]
Agricultural production index (2004-2006=100)	85	155	187
Food production index (2004-2006=100)	85	157	193
Unemployment (% of labour force)	7.9	7.5	7.6
Labour force participation, adult female pop. (%)	79.2	85.1	84.6
Labour force participation, adult male pop. (%)	86.3	81.2	81.5
Tourist arrivals at national borders (000)[d]	438	746	770[b]
Energy production, primary (Petajoules)	80	85	86[b]
Mobile-cellular subscriptions (per 100 inhabitants)	3.3	20.8	32.3
Individuals using the Internet (%)	0.4	2.3	5.4[e]

Total trade		Major trading partners			2013
	(million US$)	(% of exports)			(% of imports)
Exports	1 208.0	Canada	11.5	South Africa	21.7
Imports	2 844.6	Belgium	8.3	Mozambique	12.1
Balance	−1 636.6	South Africa	7.6	China	9.3

Social indicators		
Population growth rate (average annual %)	2010-2015	2.8
Urban population growth rate (average annual %)	2010-2015	3.8
Rural population growth rate (average annual %)	2010-2015	2.7
Urban population (%)	2014	16.1
Population aged 0-14 years (%)	2014	45.0
Population aged 60+ years (females and males, % of total)	2014	5.4/4.4
Sex ratio (males per 100 females)	2014	100.6
Life expectancy at birth (females and males, years)	2010-2015	55.2/54.9
Infant mortality rate (per 1 000 live births)	2010-2015	86.1
Fertility rate, total (live births per woman)	2010-2015	5.4
Contraceptive prevalence (ages 15-49, %)	2007-2013	46.1
International migrant stock (000 and % of total population)[f]	mid-2013	206.6/1.3
Refugees and others of concern to UNHCR	mid-2014	19 369
Education: Government expenditure (% of GDP)	2007-2013	5.4
Education: Primary-secondary gross enrolment ratio (f/m per 100)	2007-2013	94.2/93.3
Education: Female third-level students (% of total)	2007-2013	39.2
Intentional homicide rate (per 100,000 population)	2008-2012	1.8
Seats held by women in national parliaments (%)	2015	16.7

Environmental indicators		
Threatened species	2014	171
Forested area (% of land area)	2012	33.6
Proportion of terrestrial and marine areas protected (%)	2014	16.8
Population using improved drinking water sources (%)	2012	85.0
Population using improved sanitation facilities (%)	2012	10.0
CO_2 emission estimates (000 metric tons and metric tons per capita)	2011	1 206/0.1
Energy supply per capita (Gigajoules)	2012	6.0

a Official rate. b 2012. c Series linked to former series. d Departures. e ITU estimate. f Including refugees.

Malaysia

Region	South-Eastern Asia	
Population (est., 000)	30 188[a]	
Capital city	Kuala Lumpur[b]	
Currency	Ringgit (MYR)	

Surface area (sq km)	330 290	
Pop. density (per sq km)	91.5[a]	
Capital city pop. (000)	6 629[c]	
UN membership date	17 September 1957	

Economic indicators

	2005	2010	2013
GDP: Gross domestic product (million current US$)	143 534	247 534	312 434
GDP: Growth rate at constant 2005 prices (annual %)	5.3	7.4	4.7
GDP per capita (current US$)	5 554.0	8 754.2	10 513.7
GNI: Gross national income per capita (current US$)	5 309.4	8 465.1	10 137.8
Gross fixed capital formation (% of GDP)	22.3	22.6	26.9
Exchange rates (national currency per US$)[d]	3.78	3.08	3.28
Balance of payments, current account (million US$)	19 980	26 998	11 732
CPI: Consumer price index (2000=100)	109[e]	124	133
Index of industrial production (2010=100)[f]	...	100	110
Agricultural production index (2004-2006=100)	100	111	121
Food production index (2004-2006=100)	100	115	128
Unemployment (% of labour force)	3.5	3.4	3.2
Employment in industrial sector (% of employed)[g]	29.7[h]	27.6[i]	28.4[j]
Employment in agricultural sector (% of employed)[g]	14.6[h]	13.3[i]	12.6[j]
Labour force participation, adult female pop. (%)	44.3	44.1	44.4
Labour force participation, adult male pop. (%)	77.6	75.0	75.5
Tourist arrivals at national borders (000)[k]	16 431	24 577	25 715
Energy production, primary (Petajoules)	3 769	3 449	3 367[j]
Mobile-cellular subscriptions (per 100 inhabitants)	75.6	119.7	144.7
Individuals using the Internet (%)	48.6	56.3[l]	67.0[l]

Total trade

	(million US$)	Major trading partners			2013	
		(% of exports)			(% of imports)	
Exports	228 316.1	Singapore	13.9	China	16.4
Imports	205 813.5	China	13.5	Singapore	12.4
Balance	22 502.6	Japan	11.0	Japan	8.7

Social indicators

Population growth rate (average annual %)[a]	2010-2015	1.6
Urban population growth rate (average annual %)[a]	2010-2015	2.7
Rural population growth rate (average annual %)[a]	2010-2015	−1.2
Urban population (%)[a]	2014	74.0
Population aged 0-14 years (%)[a]	2014	25.7
Population aged 60+ years (females and males, % of total)[a]	2014	8.7/8.9
Sex ratio (males per 100 females)[a]	2014	94.4
Life expectancy at birth (females and males, years)[a]	2010-2015	77.3/72.7
Infant mortality rate (per 1 000 live births)[a]	2010-2015	4.1
Fertility rate, total (live births per woman)[a]	2010-2015	2.0
Contraceptive prevalence (ages 15-49, %)[m]	2007-2013	49.0[n]
International migrant stock (000 and % of total population)[ao]	mid-2013	2 469.2/8.3
Refugees and others of concern to UNHCR	mid-2014	265 559
Education: Government expenditure (% of GDP)	2007-2013	5.9
Education: Primary-secondary gross enrolment ratio (f/m per 100)	2007-2013	83.2/84.7[p]
Education: Female third-level students (% of total)	2007-2013	56.0
Intentional homicide rate (per 100,000 population)	2008-2012	2.4
Seats held by women in national parliaments (%)	2015	10.4

Environmental indicators

Threatened species	2014	1 236
Forested area (% of land area)	2012	61.7
Proportion of terrestrial and marine areas protected (%)	2014	8.0
Population using improved drinking water sources (%)	2012	100.0
Population using improved sanitation facilities (%)	2012	96.0
CO_2 emission estimates (000 metric tons and metric tons per capita)	2011	225 693/7.9
Energy supply per capita (Gigajoules)	2012	107.0

a Including Sabah and Sarawak. b Kuala Lumpur is the capital and Putrajaya is the administrative capital. c Refers to the Greater Kuala Lumpur. d Official rate. e Series linked to former series. f ISIC Rev.4 (BCD). g Population aged 15-64. h ISIC Rev.3. i Break in series. j 2012. k Including Singapore residents crossing the frontier by road through Johore Causeway. l Refers to total population. m Data refer to Peninsular Malaysia. n 2004. o Including refugees. p 2005.

Maldives

Region	Southern Asia	Surface area (sq km)	300	
Population (est., 000)	352	Pop. density (per sq km)	1 179.8	
Capital city	Male	Capital city pop. (000)	156	
Currency	Rufiyaa (MVR)	UN membership date	21 September 1965	

Economic indicators	2005	2010	2013
GDP: Gross domestic product (million current US$)	1 091	2 335	2 836
GDP: Growth rate at constant 2005 prices (annual %)	–9.1	6.9	3.7
GDP per capita (current US$)	3 665.6	7 169.0	8 220.0
GNI: Gross national income per capita (current US$)	3 434.9	6 185.1	6 779.5
Gross fixed capital formation (% of GDP)	34.5	26.2	15.9
Exchange rates (national currency per US$)[a]	12.80	12.80	15.41
Balance of payments, current account (million US$)	–273	–196	–176
CPI: Consumer price index (2000=100)[b]	107[c]	146	191
Agricultural production index (2004-2006=100)	89	72	64
Food production index (2004-2006=100)	89	72	64
Unemployment (% of labour force)	13.4	11.7	11.6
Employment in industrial sector (% of employed)	24.3[defg]	...	...
Employment in agricultural sector (% of employed)	11.5[defg]	...	...
Labour force participation, adult female pop. (%)	50.2	55.1	56.2
Labour force participation, adult male pop. (%)	74.6	76.4	77.5
Tourist arrivals at national borders (000)[h]	395	792	1 125
Energy production, primary (Petajoules)	0	0	0[i]
Mobile-cellular subscriptions (per 100 inhabitants)	68.4	151.8	181.2
Individuals using the Internet (%)	6.9[jk]	26.5[l]	44.1[m]

Total trade		Major trading partners			2013
	(million US$)	(% of exports)		(% of imports)	
Exports	166.5	Thailand	37.1	United Arab Emirates	28.4
Imports	1 733.3	France	13.5	Singapore	16.2
Balance	–1 566.8	Iran	6.5	India	8.9

Social indicators		
Population growth rate (average annual %)	2010-2015	1.9
Urban population growth rate (average annual %)	2010-2015	4.5
Rural population growth rate (average annual %)	2010-2015	–0.1
Urban population (%)	2014	44.5
Population aged 0-14 years (%)	2014	28.4
Population aged 60+ years (females and males, % of total)	2014	6.6/7.0
Sex ratio (males per 100 females)	2014	101.3
Life expectancy at birth (females and males, years)	2010-2015	78.8/76.7
Infant mortality rate (per 1 000 live births)	2010-2015	10.4
Fertility rate, total (live births per woman)	2010-2015	2.3
Contraceptive prevalence (ages 15-49, %)	2007-2013	34.7
International migrant stock (000 and % of total population)[n]	mid-2013	84.2/24.4
Education: Government expenditure (% of GDP)	2007-2013	6.2
Education: Primary-secondary gross enrolment ratio (f/m per 100)[o]	2007-2013	102.4/100.7[p]
Education: Female third-level students (% of total)	2007-2013	52.5
Intentional homicide rate (per 100,000 population)	2008-2012	3.9
Seats held by women in national parliaments (%)	2015	5.9

Environmental indicators		
Threatened species	2014	69
Forested area (% of land area)	2012	3.0
Proportion of terrestrial and marine areas protected (%)	2014	0.1
Population using improved drinking water sources (%)	2012	99.0
Population using improved sanitation facilities (%)	2012	99.0
CO_2 emission estimates (000 metric tons and metric tons per capita)	2011	1 104/3.3
Energy supply per capita (Gigajoules)	2012	56.0

a Market rate. b Male. c Series linked to former series. d 2006. e Population census. f ISIC Rev.3. g Excluding conscripts. h Arrivals by air. i 2012. j Country estimate. k Excluding mobile Internet users. l Population aged 15 and over. m ITU estimate. n Refers to foreign citizens. o UNESCO estimate. p 2004.

Mali

Region	Western Africa	Surface area (sq km)	1 240 192
Population (est., 000)	15 768	Pop. density (per sq km)	12.7
Capital city	Bamako	Capital city pop. (000)	2 386
Currency	CFA Franc (XOF)	UN membership date	28 September 1960

Economic indicators	2005	2010	2013
GDP: Gross domestic product (million current US$)	5 486	9 400	10 943
GDP: Growth rate at constant 2005 prices (annual %)	6.1	5.8	1.7
GDP per capita (current US$)	459.4	672.1	715.1
GNI: Gross national income per capita (current US$)	441.6	642.2	671.4
Gross fixed capital formation (% of GDP)	15.4	21.2	21.6
Exchange rates (national currency per US$)[a]	556.04	490.91	475.64
Balance of payments, current account (million US$)	−438	−1 190	−656[b]
CPI: Consumer price index (2000=100)[c]	112	131[d]	141
Index of industrial production (2010=100)[e]	135	100	116
Agricultural production index (2004-2006=100)	103	142	141
Food production index (2004-2006=100)	103	154	150
Unemployment (% of labour force)	8.5	8.1	8.2
Employment in industrial sector (% of employed)	5.6[fg]	...	...
Employment in agricultural sector (% of employed)	66.0[fg]	...	...
Labour force participation, adult female pop. (%)	38.1	50.2	50.8
Labour force participation, adult male pop. (%)	70.0	81.4	81.4
Tourist arrivals at national borders (000)	...	169	142
Energy production, primary (Petajoules)	49	52	53[h]
Mobile-cellular subscriptions (per 100 inhabitants)	6.4	53.2	129.1
Individuals using the Internet (%)	0.5	1.9[i]	2.3[i]

Total trade		Major trading partners			2013
	(million US$)[h]	(% of exports)[h]			(% of imports)[h]
Exports	2 610.4	South Africa	51.8	Senegal	25.1
Imports	3 462.7	Switzerland	11.6	France	10.8
Balance	−852.3	China	7.8	China	10.6

Social indicators		
Population growth rate (average annual %)	2010-2015	3.0
Urban population growth rate (average annual %)	2010-2015	5.1
Rural population growth rate (average annual %)	2010-2015	1.8
Urban population (%)	2014	39.1
Population aged 0-14 years (%)	2014	47.5
Population aged 60+ years (females and males, % of total)	2014	4.7/3.7
Sex ratio (males per 100 females)	2014	101.6
Life expectancy at birth (females and males, years)	2010-2015	54.7/54.9
Infant mortality rate (per 1 000 live births)	2010-2015	86.7
Fertility rate, total (live births per woman)	2010-2015	6.9
Contraceptive prevalence (ages 15-49, %)	2007-2013	10.3
International migrant stock (000 and % of total population)[j]	mid-2013	195.6/1.3
Refugees and others of concern to UNHCR	mid-2014	287 166
Education: Government expenditure (% of GDP)	2007-2013	4.8
Education: Primary-secondary gross enrolment ratio (f/m per 100)	2007-2013	64.1/77.0
Education: Female third-level students (% of total)	2007-2013	28.9
Intentional homicide rate (per 100,000 population)	2008-2012	7.5
Seats held by women in national parliaments (%)	2015	9.5

Environmental indicators		
Threatened species	2014	39
Forested area (% of land area)	2012	10.1
Proportion of terrestrial and marine areas protected (%)	2014	8.4
Population using improved drinking water sources (%)	2012	67.0
Population using improved sanitation facilities (%)	2012	22.0
CO_2 emission estimates (000 metric tons and metric tons per capita)	2011	1 250/0.1
Energy supply per capita (Gigajoules)	2012	5.0

a Official rate. b 2011. c Bamako. d Series linked to former series. e ISIC Rev.3 (CDE). f 2006. g ISIC Rev. 3. h 2012. i ITU estimate. j Including refugees.

Malta

Region	Southern Europe	Surface area (sq km)	316
Population (est., 000)	430	Pop. density (per sq km)	1 361.2
Capital city	Valletta	Capital city pop. (000)	197
Currency	Euro (EUR)	UN membership date	1 December 1964

Economic indicators	2005	2010	2013
GDP: Gross domestic product (million current US$)	6 393	8 741	9 971
GDP: Growth rate at constant 2005 prices (annual %)	3.8	3.5	2.5
GDP per capita (current US$)	15 414.5	20 578.7	23 243.3
GNI: Gross national income per capita (current US$)	14 866.2	19 711.2	22 191.0
Gross fixed capital formation (% of GDP)	22.2	21.1	17.7
Exchange rates (national currency per US$)	0.36[ab]	0.75[cd]	0.73[cd]
Balance of payments, current account (million US$)	−524	−574	85
CPI: Consumer price index (2000=100)	113	127[e]	135
Index of industrial production (2010=100)[f]	98	100	100
Agricultural production index (2004-2006=100)	97	99	92
Food production index (2004-2006=100)	97	99	92
Unemployment (% of labour force)	7.3	6.9	6.5
Employment in industrial sector (% of employed)	29.5[g]	25.2	22.1[h]
Employment in agricultural sector (% of employed)	1.7[g]	1.3	1.0[h]
Labour force participation, adult female pop. (%)	30.3	34.6	37.9
Labour force participation, adult male pop. (%)	68.6	67.2	66.3
Tourist arrivals at national borders (000)[i]	1 171	1 339	1 582
Energy production, primary (Petajoules)	0	0	0[h]
Mobile-cellular subscriptions (per 100 inhabitants)	78.1	107.3	129.8
Individuals using the Internet (%)	41.2	63.0	68.9

Total trade		Major trading partners			2013
	(million US$)	(% of exports)			(% of imports)
Exports	5 206.2	Bunkers	13.8[j]	Italy	24.7
Imports	7 525.4	Germany	8.9	Germany	5.6
Balance	−2 319.2	Singapore	6.9	United Kingdom	5.4

Social indicators		
Population growth rate (average annual %)	2010-2015	0.3
Urban population growth rate (average annual %)	2010-2015	0.5
Rural population growth rate (average annual %)	2010-2015	−2.7
Urban population (%)	2014	95.3
Population aged 0-14 years (%)	2014	14.4
Population aged 60+ years (females and males, % of total)	2014	25.8/22.4
Sex ratio (males per 100 females)	2014	99.9
Life expectancy at birth (females and males, years)	2010-2015	82.0/77.4
Infant mortality rate (per 1 000 live births)	2010-2015	4.8
Fertility rate, total (live births per woman)	2010-2015	1.4
Contraceptive prevalence (ages 15-49, %)[k]	2007-2013	85.8[l]
International migrant stock (000 and % of total population)	mid-2013	34.5/8.0
Refugees and others of concern to UNHCR	mid-2014	10 921[m]
Education: Government expenditure (% of GDP)	2007-2013	8.0
Education: Primary-secondary gross enrolment ratio (f/m per 100)	2007-2013	91.2/89.1
Education: Female third-level students (% of total)	2007-2013	56.1
Intentional homicide rate (per 100,000 population)	2008-2012	2.8
Seats held by women in national parliaments (%)	2015	12.9

Environmental indicators		
Threatened species	2014	31
Forested area (% of land area)	2012	0.9
Proportion of terrestrial and marine areas protected (%)	2014	0.5
Population using improved drinking water sources (%)	2012	100.0
Population using improved sanitation facilities (%)	2012	100.0
CO_2 emission estimates (000 metric tons and metric tons per capita)	2011	2 512/5.9
Energy supply per capita (Gigajoules)	2012	66.0

a Official rate. **b** Maltese Liri (MTL). **c** Market rate. **d** Euro. **e** Series linked to former series. **f** ISIC Rev.4 (BCDE). **g** ISIC Rev.3. **h** 2012. **i** Departures by air and sea. **j** See technical notes. **k** Age group 20 to 45 years. **l** 1993. **m** Refugee population refers to the end of 2013.

Marshall Islands

Region	Oceania-Micronesia	Surface area (sq km)	181
Population (est., 000)	53	Pop. density (per sq km)	291.6
Capital city	Majuro	Capital city pop. (000)	31
Currency	U.S. Dollar (USD)	UN membership date	17 September 1991

Economic indicators	2005	2010	2013
GDP: Gross domestic product (million current US$)	139	177	189
GDP: Growth rate at constant 2005 prices (annual %)	2.0	5.9	0.8
GDP per capita (current US$)	2 676.7	3 379.1	3 585.8
GNI: Gross national income per capita (current US$)	3 468.9	4 117.6	4 466.9
Gross fixed capital formation (% of GDP)	56.8	56.8	56.8
Balance of payments, current account (million US$)	−3	−47	−14[a]
CPI: Consumer price index (2000=100)[b]	107	135[c]	...
Agricultural production index (2004-2006=100)	97	175	103
Food production index (2004-2006=100)	97	175	103
Tourist arrivals at national borders (000)	9[d]	5[e]	5[ae]
Mobile-cellular subscriptions (per 100 inhabitants)	1.3	...	...
Individuals using the Internet (%)	3.9	7.0[f]	11.7[f]

Social indicators		
Population growth rate (average annual %)	2010-2015	0.2
Urban population growth rate (average annual %)	2010-2015	0.6
Rural population growth rate (average annual %)	2010-2015	−0.7
Urban population (%)	2014	72.4
Population aged 0-14 years (%)[gh]	2014	40.2
Population aged 60+ years (females and males, % of total)[hij]	2014	4.6/4.4[k]
Sex ratio (males per 100 females)[gh]	2014	105.3
Life expectancy at birth (females and males, years)[g]	2010-2015	72.6/67.3[l]
Infant mortality rate (per 1 000 live births)[g]	2010-2015	26.3[l]
Fertility rate, total (live births per woman)[g]	2010-2015	4.1[l]
Contraceptive prevalence (ages 15-49, %)	2007-2013	44.6
International migrant stock (000 and % of total population)	mid-2013	1.7/3.2
Education: Government expenditure (% of GDP)	2007-2013	12.2[m]
Education: Primary-secondary gross enrolment ratio (f/m per 100)	2007-2013	106.5/105.1
Education: Female third-level students (% of total)	2007-2013	48.9
Intentional homicide rate (per 100,000 population)	2008-2012	4.7
Seats held by women in national parliaments (%)	2015	3.0

Environmental indicators		
Threatened species	2014	95
Forested area (% of land area)	2012	70.2
Proportion of terrestrial and marine areas protected (%)	2014	0.2
Population using improved drinking water sources (%)	2012	95.0
Population using improved sanitation facilities (%)	2012	76.0
CO$_2$ emission estimates (000 metric tons and metric tons per capita)	2011	103/2.0
Energy supply per capita (Gigajoules)	2012	28.0[n]

a 2012. b Majuro. c 2008. d Arrivals by air and sea. e Arrivals by air. f ITU estimate. g Data compiled by the Secretariat of the Pacific Community Demography Programme. h De facto estimate. i Data compiled by the United Nations Demographic Yearbook system. j Data refer to the latest available census. k 2010. l 2011. m 2003. n UNSD estimate.

Martinique

Region	Caribbean	Surface area (sq km)	1 128
Population (est., 000)	405	Pop. density (per sq km)	367.3
Capital city	Fort-de-France	Capital city pop. (000)	86
Currency	Euro (EUR)		

Economic indicators	2005	2010	2013
Exchange rates (national currency per US$) [a]	0.84	0.76	0.72
CPI: Consumer price index (2000=100)	111	121	128
Agricultural production index (2004-2006=100)	99	81	101
Food production index (2004-2006=100)	99	81	101
Unemployment (% of labour force)	18.7	21.0	21.3
Employment in industrial sector (% of employed)	...	11.9[bc]	11.8[bcd]
Employment in agricultural sector (% of employed)	...	4.1[bc]	3.9[bcd]
Labour force participation, adult female pop. (%)	46.2	48.9	49.7
Labour force participation, adult male pop. (%)	53.1	55.5	55.5
Tourist arrivals at national borders (000)	484	478	490
Energy production, primary (Petajoules) [e]	0	1	1[d]

Social indicators		
Population growth rate (average annual %)	2010-2015	0.2
Urban population growth rate (average annual %)	2010-2015	0.2
Rural population growth rate (average annual %)	2010-2015	0.5
Urban population (%)	2014	88.9
Population aged 0-14 years (%)	2014	18.2
Population aged 60+ years (females and males, % of total)	2014	23.7/21.5
Sex ratio (males per 100 females)	2014	85.1
Life expectancy at birth (females and males, years)	2010-2015	84.4/77.9
Infant mortality rate (per 1 000 live births)	2010-2015	6.2
Fertility rate, total (live births per woman)	2010-2015	1.8
Contraceptive prevalence (ages 15-49, %)	2007-2013	35.5[f]
International migrant stock (000 and % of total population)	mid-2013	60.7/15.0
Intentional homicide rate (per 100,000 population)	2008-2012	2.7

Environmental indicators		
Threatened species	2014	39
Forested area (% of land area)	2012	45.8
Proportion of terrestrial and marine areas protected (%)	2014	11.6
CO_2 emission estimates (000 metric tons and metric tons per capita)	2011	2 450/6.1
Energy supply per capita (Gigajoules)	2012	84.0

a UN operational exchange rate. b March to June. c Excluding institutional population. d 2012. e UNSD estimate. f 1976.

Mauritania

Region	Western Africa	Surface area (sq km)	1 030 700
Population (est., 000)	3 984	Pop. density (per sq km)	3.9
Capital city	Nouakchott	Capital city pop. (000)	945
Currency	Ouguiya (MRO)	UN membership date	27 October 1961

Economic indicators	2005	2010	2013
GDP: Gross domestic product (million current US$)	2 184	4 338	5 516
GDP: Growth rate at constant 2005 prices (annual %)	9.0	3.5	6.7
GDP per capita (current US$)	694.3	1 201.8	1 418.2
GNI: Gross national income per capita (current US$)	714.9	1 173.8	1 326.1
Gross fixed capital formation (% of GDP)	59.0	36.6	40.8
Exchange rates (national currency per US$)[a]	270.61	282.00	299.00
Balance of payments, current account (million US$)	...	−1 226[b]	−1 262
CPI: Consumer price index (2000=100)	139	185	214
Index of industrial production (2010=100)[c]	...	100	115
Agricultural production index (2004-2006=100)	100	113	120
Food production index (2004-2006=100)	100	113	120
Unemployment (% of labour force)	32.1	31.1	31.0
Labour force participation, adult female pop. (%)	25.9	28.3	28.7
Labour force participation, adult male pop. (%)	78.5	78.9	79.1
Energy production, primary (Petajoules)	15	34	31[b]
Mobile-cellular subscriptions (per 100 inhabitants)	23.7	76.9	102.5
Individuals using the Internet (%)	0.7	4.0[d]	6.2[d]

Total trade		Major trading partners			2013
	(million US$)		(% of exports)		(% of imports)
Exports	2 462.5	China	50.5	Hungary	20.4
Imports	3 978.5	Switzerland	13.5	United Arab Emirates	18.9
Balance	−1 516.0	Italy	6.4	France	9.8

Social indicators		
Population growth rate (average annual %)	2010-2015	2.5
Urban population growth rate (average annual %)	2010-2015	3.5
Rural population growth rate (average annual %)	2010-2015	0.9
Urban population (%)	2014	59.3
Population aged 0-14 years (%)	2014	39.9
Population aged 60+ years (females and males, % of total)	2014	5.6/4.4
Sex ratio (males per 100 females)	2014	101.5
Life expectancy at birth (females and males, years)	2010-2015	63.0/59.9
Infant mortality rate (per 1 000 live births)	2010-2015	71.7
Fertility rate, total (live births per woman)	2010-2015	4.7
Contraceptive prevalence (ages 15-49, %)	2007-2013	9.3
International migrant stock (000 and % of total population)[ef]	mid-2013	90.2/2.3
Refugees and others of concern to UNHCR	mid-2014	80 559
Education: Government expenditure (% of GDP)	2007-2013	3.8
Education: Primary-secondary gross enrolment ratio (f/m per 100)	2007-2013	64.2/62.7
Education: Female third-level students (% of total)	2007-2013	30.0
Intentional homicide rate (per 100,000 population)	2008-2012	5.0
Seats held by women in national parliaments (%)	2015	25.2

Environmental indicators		
Threatened species	2014	69
Forested area (% of land area)	2012	<
Proportion of terrestrial and marine areas protected (%)	2014	1.4
Population using improved drinking water sources (%)	2012	50.0
Population using improved sanitation facilities (%)	2012	27.0
CO_2 emission estimates (000 metric tons and metric tons per capita)	2011	2 310/0.6
Energy supply per capita (Gigajoules)	2012	13.0

a Market rate. b 2012. c ISIC Rev.4 (BCDE). d ITU estimate. e Refers to foreign citizens. f Including refugees.

Mauritius

Region	Eastern Africa	Surface area (sq km)	1 969[a]
Population (est., 000)	1 249[b]	Pop. density (per sq km)	612.3[b]
Capital city	Port Louis	Capital city pop. (000)	136
Currency	Mauritius Rupee (MUR)	UN membership date	24 April 1968

Economic indicators	2005	2010	2013
GDP: Gross domestic product (million current US$)	6 489	9 718	11 938
GDP: Growth rate at constant 2005 prices (annual %)	1.8	4.1	3.3
GDP per capita (current US$)	5 350.4	7 896.8	9 593.3
GNI: Gross national income per capita (current US$)	5 310.8	7 991.9	9 604.5
Gross fixed capital formation (% of GDP)	21.5	24.9	21.2
Exchange rates (national currency per US$)[c]	30.67	30.39	30.08
Balance of payments, current account (million US$)	−324	−1 006	−1 179
CPI: Consumer price index (2000=100)	128	176	201[d]
Index of industrial production (2010=100)[e]	...	100	108
Agricultural production index (2004-2006=100)	98	99	94
Food production index (2004-2006=100)	98	99	94
Unemployment (% of labour force)	9.6	7.7	8.3
Employment in industrial sector (% of employed)	32.4[f]	28.2[fghi]	27.6[ghij]
Employment in agricultural sector (% of employed)	10.0[f]	8.7[fghi]	7.8[ghij]
Labour force participation, adult female pop. (%)	41.1	43.3	43.6
Labour force participation, adult male pop. (%)	76.8	74.6	74.2
Tourist arrivals at national borders (000)	761	935	993
Energy production, primary (Petajoules)	12	11	10[j]
Mobile-cellular subscriptions (per 100 inhabitants)	54.2	96.8	123.2
Individuals using the Internet (%)	15.2[k]	28.3[l]	39.0

Total trade		Major trading partners			2013
	(million US$)	(% of exports)			(% of imports)
Exports	2 344.6	United Kingdom	16.6	India	24.2
Imports	5 397.6	France	14.7	China	14.7
Balance	−3 053.0	United States	10.1	France	8.2

Social indicators		
Population growth rate (average annual %)[b]	2010-2015	0.4
Urban population growth rate (average annual %)[b]	2010-2015	−0.1
Rural population growth rate (average annual %)[b]	2010-2015	0.7
Urban population (%)[b]	2014	39.8
Population aged 0-14 years (%)[b]	2014	19.4
Population aged 60+ years (females and males, % of total)[b]	2014	15.6/12.7
Sex ratio (males per 100 females)[b]	2014	97.3
Life expectancy at birth (females and males, years)[b]	2010-2015	77.0/70.2
Infant mortality rate (per 1 000 live births)[b]	2010-2015	11.5
Fertility rate, total (live births per woman)[b]	2010-2015	1.5
Contraceptive prevalence (ages 15-49, %)	2007-2013	75.8[m]
International migrant stock (000 and % of total population)[b]	mid-2013	45.0/3.6
Refugees and others of concern to UNHCR	mid-2014	0[n]
Education: Government expenditure (% of GDP)	2007-2013	3.7
Education: Primary-secondary gross enrolment ratio (f/m per 100)	2007-2013	102.1/100.5
Education: Female third-level students (% of total)	2007-2013	54.7
Intentional homicide rate (per 100,000 population)	2008-2012	2.8
Seats held by women in national parliaments (%)	2015	11.6

Environmental indicators		
Threatened species	2014	250
Forested area (% of land area)	2012	17.3
Proportion of terrestrial and marine areas protected (%)	2014	0.0
Population using improved drinking water sources (%)	2012	100.0
Population using improved sanitation facilities (%)	2012	91.0
CO_2 emission estimates (000 metric tons and metric tons per capita)	2011	3 916/3.2
Energy supply per capita (Gigajoules)	2012	51.0

a Excluding the islands of St. Brandon and Agalega. **b** Including Agalega, Rodrigues and Saint Brandon. **c** Market rate. **d** Series linked to former series. **e** ISIC Rev.4 (BCDE). **f** ISIC Rev.3. **g** Population aged 16 and over. **h** Average of quarterly estimates. **i** Break in series. **j** 2012. **k** ITU estimate. **l** Population aged 5 and over. **m** 2002. **n** Value is zero, not available or not applicable.

Mexico

Region	Central America
Population (est., 000)	123 799
Capital city	Mexico City
Currency	Mexican Peso (MXN)

Surface area (sq km)	1 964 375
Pop. density (per sq km)	63.2
Capital city pop. (000)	20 843 [a]
UN membership date	7 November 1945

Economic indicators	2005	2010	2013
GDP: Gross domestic product (million current US$)	864 810	1 049 925	1 259 201
GDP: Growth rate at constant 2005 prices (annual %)	3.1	5.2	1.4
GDP per capita (current US$)	7 810.0	8 906.2	10 293.3
GNI: Gross national income per capita (current US$)	7 672.0	8 809.5	10 084.7
Gross fixed capital formation (% of GDP)	21.3	21.2	21.1
Exchange rates (national currency per US$) [b]	10.78	12.36	13.08
Balance of payments, current account (million US$)	−8 956	−4 067	−26 284
CPI: Consumer price index (2000=100)	127	158	177
Index of industrial production (2010=100) [c]	99	100	107
Agricultural production index (2004-2006=100)	98	108	115
Food production index (2004-2006=100)	98	108	115
Unemployment (% of labour force)	3.5	5.2	4.9
Employment in industrial sector (% of employed) [d]	25.5 [ef]	25.5 [eg]	24.1 [fgh]
Employment in agricultural sector (% of employed) [d]	14.9 [ef]	13.1 [eg]	13.4 [fgh]
Labour force participation, adult female pop. (%)	41.1	43.8	45.1
Labour force participation, adult male pop. (%)	80.8	80.5	79.9
Tourist arrivals at national borders (000) [i]	21 915	23 290	24 151
Energy production, primary (Petajoules)	10 305	8 952	8 861 [j]
Mobile-cellular subscriptions (per 100 inhabitants)	42.6	77.5	85.8 [k]
Individuals using the Internet (%)	17.2 [lm]	31.1 [l]	43.5

Total trade		Major trading partners			2013
	(million US$)	(% of exports)			(% of imports)
Exports	379 960.8	United States	78.9	United States	49.3
Imports	381 210.1	Canada	2.7	China	16.1
Balance	−1 249.3	Spain	1.9	Japan	4.5

Social indicators

Population growth rate (average annual %)	2010-2015	1.2
Urban population growth rate (average annual %)	2010-2015	1.6
Rural population growth rate (average annual %)	2010-2015	−0.1
Urban population (%)	2014	79.0
Population aged 0-14 years (%)	2014	28.0
Population aged 60+ years (females and males, % of total)	2014	10.6/9.0
Sex ratio (males per 100 females)	2014	94.0
Life expectancy at birth (females and males, years)	2010-2015	79.7/74.9
Infant mortality rate (per 1 000 live births)	2010-2015	14.2
Fertility rate, total (live births per woman)	2010-2015	2.2
Contraceptive prevalence (ages 15-49, %)	2007-2013	72.5
International migrant stock (000 and % of total population) [n]	mid-2013	1 103.5/0.9
Refugees and others of concern to UNHCR	mid-2014	4 036
Education: Government expenditure (% of GDP)	2007-2013	5.2
Education: Primary-secondary gross enrolment ratio (f/m per 100)	2007-2013	97.1/93.7
Education: Female third-level students (% of total)	2007-2013	49.6
Intentional homicide rate (per 100,000 population)	2008-2012	21.5
Seats held by women in national parliaments (%)	2015	38.0

Environmental indicators

Threatened species	2014	1 091
Forested area (% of land area)	2012	33.2
Proportion of terrestrial and marine areas protected (%)	2014	6.0
Population using improved drinking water sources (%)	2012	95.0
Population using improved sanitation facilities (%)	2012	85.0
CO_2 emission estimates (000 metric tons and metric tons per capita)	2011	466 549/3.9
Energy supply per capita (Gigajoules)	2012	64.0

a Refers to the total population in seventy-six municipalities of the Metropolitan Area of Mexico City. **b** Principal rate. **c** ISIC Rev.4 (BCDE). **d** ISIC Rev.2. **e** Population aged 14 and over. **f** Second quarter. **g** Break in series. **h** 2011. **i** Including nationals residing abroad. **j** 2012. **k** Preliminary. **l** Refers to total population. **m** ITU estimate. **n** Including refugees.

Micronesia (Federated States of)

Region	Oceania-Micronesia	Surface area (sq km)	702	
Population (est., 000)	104	Pop. density (per sq km)	148.0	
Capital city	Palikir	Capital city pop. (000)	7	
Currency	U.S. Dollar (USD)	UN membership date	17 September 1991	

Economic indicators

	2005	2010	2013
GDP: Gross domestic product (million current US$)	250	294	333
GDP: Growth rate at constant 2005 prices (annual %)	2.2	3.2	0.7
GDP per capita (current US$)	2 353.8	2 841.0	3 215.9
GNI: Gross national income per capita (current US$)	2 436.2	2 946.8	3 302.4
Gross fixed capital formation (% of GDP)	31.1	31.0	31.2
Balance of payments, current account (million US$)	...	−44	−32
Agricultural production index (2004-2006=100)	101	98	102
Food production index (2004-2006=100)	101	98	102
Tourist arrivals at national borders (000)[ab]	19	45	42
Energy production, primary (Petajoules)	0	0	0[c]
Mobile-cellular subscriptions (per 100 inhabitants)	13.3	26.6	30.3
Individuals using the Internet (%)	11.9	20.0[d]	27.8[d]

Total trade

	(million US$)	Major trading partners (% of exports)		2013 (% of imports)
Exports	27.6	... United States		37.0
Imports	187.7	... Guam		22.1
Balance	−160.1	... Areas nes		6.9[e]

Social indicators

Population growth rate (average annual %)	2010-2015	0.2
Urban population growth rate (average annual %)	2010-2015	0.3
Rural population growth rate (average annual %)	2010-2015	0.1
Urban population (%)	2014	22.4
Population aged 0-14 years (%)	2014	34.6
Population aged 60+ years (females and males, % of total)	2014	7.8/6.8
Sex ratio (males per 100 females)	2014	104.9
Life expectancy at birth (females and males, years)	2010-2015	69.9/68.0
Infant mortality rate (per 1 000 live births)	2010-2015	32.7
Fertility rate, total (live births per woman)	2010-2015	3.3
International migrant stock (000 and % of total population)	mid-2013	2.6/2.5
Refugees and others of concern to UNHCR	mid-2014	0[f]
Education: Government expenditure (% of GDP)[g]	2007-2013	6.7[h]
Education: Primary-secondary gross enrolment ratio (f/m per 100)	2007-2013	98.6/96.5[i]
Intentional homicide rate (per 100,000 population)	2008-2012	4.6
Seats held by women in national parliaments (%)	2015	0.0

Environmental indicators

Threatened species	2014	163
Forested area (% of land area)	2012	91.7
Population using improved drinking water sources (%)	2012	89.0
Population using improved sanitation facilities (%)	2012	57.0
CO_2 emission estimates (000 metric tons and metric tons per capita)	2011	128/1.3
Energy supply per capita (Gigajoules)	2012	20.0[j]

a Arrivals in the States of Kosrae, Chuuk, Pohnpei and Yap. b Excluding citizens of the Federated States of Micronesia. c 2012. d ITU estimate. e See technical notes. f Value is zero, not available or not applicable. g UNESCO estimate. h 2000. i 2005. j UNSD estimate.

Monaco

		Surface area (sq km)	2
Region	Western Europe		
Population (est., 000)	38	Pop. density (per sq km)	25 547.7
Capital city	Monaco	Capital city pop. (000)	38
Currency	Euro (EUR)	UN membership date	28 May 1993

Economic indicators	2005	2010	2013
GDP: Gross domestic product (million current US$)	4 203	5 362	6 559
GDP: Growth rate at constant 2005 prices (annual %)	1.6	2.2	9.3
GDP per capita (current US$)	124 319.0	145 541.4	173 377.4
GNI: Gross national income per capita (current US$)	124 319.0	145 541.4	173 377.4
Gross fixed capital formation (% of GDP)	21.8	22.1	22.1
Exchange rates (national currency per US$) [a]	0.84	0.76	0.72
Tourist arrivals at national borders (000) [b]	286	279	328
Mobile-cellular subscriptions (per 100 inhabitants)	50.9	63.6	93.7
Individuals using the Internet (%)	55.5	75.0	90.7[c]

Social indicators		
Population growth rate (average annual %)	2010-2015	0.8
Urban population growth rate (average annual %)	2010-2015	0.8
Urban population (%)	2014	100.0
Population aged 0-14 years (%) [def]	2014	12.8[g]
Population aged 60+ years (females and males, % of total) [def]	2014	33.3/29.3[g]
Sex ratio (males per 100 females) [def]	2014	94.7[g]
International migrant stock (000 and % of total population)	mid-2013	24.3/64.2
Refugees and others of concern to UNHCR	mid-2014	34[h]
Education: Government expenditure (% of GDP)	2007-2013	1.6
Intentional homicide rate (per 100,000 population)	2008-2012	0.0
Seats held by women in national parliaments (%)	2015	20.8

Environmental indicators		
Threatened species	2014	15
Proportion of terrestrial and marine areas protected (%)	2014	99.7
Population using improved drinking water sources (%)	2012	100.0
Population using improved sanitation facilities (%)	2012	100.0

a UN operational exchange rate. b Arrivals of non-resident tourists in hotels and similar establishments. c ITU estimate. d Data compiled by the United Nations Demographic Yearbook system. e Data refer to the latest available census. f Census, de jure, complete tabulation. g 2008. h Refugee population refers to the end of 2013.

Mongolia

Region	Eastern Asia	Surface area (sq km)	1 564 116	
Population (est., 000)	2 881	Pop. density (per sq km)	1.8	
Capital city	Ulaanbaatar	Capital city pop. (000)	1 334	
Currency	Togrog (MNT)	UN membership date	27 October 1961	

Economic indicators	2005	2010	2013
GDP: Gross domestic product (million current US$)	2 523	6 201	11 516
GDP: Growth rate at constant 2005 prices (annual %)	7.3	6.4	11.7
GDP per capita (current US$)	998.8	2 285.7	4 056.4
GNI: Gross national income per capita (current US$)	978.6	2 079.2	3 787.0
Gross fixed capital formation (% of GDP)	28.0	32.5	44.2
Exchange rates (national currency per US$)[a]	1 221.00	1 256.47	1 654.10
Balance of payments, current account (million US$)	84	−886	−3 192
CPI: Consumer price index (2000=100)[b]	110[c]	166	181[d]
Index of industrial production (2010=100)[e]	88	100	96
Agricultural production index (2004-2006=100)	97	115	145
Food production index (2004-2006=100)	97	115	147
Unemployment (% of labour force)	6.9	6.5	4.9
Employment in industrial sector (% of employed)	16.8[fgh]	16.2[i]	17.3[d]
Employment in agricultural sector (% of employed)	39.9[fgh]	33.0[i]	32.6[d]
Labour force participation, adult female pop. (%)	55.4	55.1	56.6
Labour force participation, adult male pop. (%)	65.2	67.6	69.3
Tourist arrivals at national borders (000)[j]	338	456	418
Energy production, primary (Petajoules)	129	605	732[k]
Mobile-cellular subscriptions (per 100 inhabitants)	22.1	92.5	124.2
Individuals using the Internet (%)	9.0[cl]	10.2[m]	17.7[l]

Total trade		Major trading partners			2013
	(million US$)		(% of exports)		(% of imports)
Exports	4 269.1	China	86.7	China	28.1
Imports	6 357.8	United Kingdom	4.7	Russian Federation	24.6
Balance	−2 088.7	Canada	3.2	United States	8.1

Social indicators		
Population growth rate (average annual %)	2010-2015	1.5
Urban population growth rate (average annual %)	2010-2015	2.8
Rural population growth rate (average annual %)	2010-2015	−1.5
Urban population (%)	2014	71.2
Population aged 0-14 years (%)	2014	27.4
Population aged 60+ years (females and males, % of total)	2014	6.8/5.3
Sex ratio (males per 100 females)	2014	98.1
Life expectancy at birth (females and males, years)	2010-2015	71.5/63.6
Infant mortality rate (per 1 000 live births)	2010-2015	25.8
Fertility rate, total (live births per woman)	2010-2015	2.4
Contraceptive prevalence (ages 15-49, %)	2007-2013	54.9
International migrant stock (000 and % of total population)[n]	mid-2013	17.2/0.6
Refugees and others of concern to UNHCR	mid-2014	26
Education: Government expenditure (% of GDP)	2007-2013	5.5
Education: Primary-secondary gross enrolment ratio (f/m per 100)	2007-2013	107.2/104.6
Education: Female third-level students (% of total)	2007-2013	58.3
Intentional homicide rate (per 100,000 population)	2008-2012	9.7
Seats held by women in national parliaments (%)	2015	14.9

Environmental indicators		
Threatened species	2014	36
Forested area (% of land area)	2012	6.9
Proportion of terrestrial and marine areas protected (%)	2014	17.2
Population using improved drinking water sources (%)	2012	85.0
Population using improved sanitation facilities (%)	2012	56.0
CO_2 emission estimates (000 metric tons and metric tons per capita)	2011	19 079/6.9
Energy supply per capita (Gigajoules)	2012	99.0

a Market rate. b Index base 2006=100. c 2007. d 2011. e ISIC Rev.3 (CDE). f ISIC Rev.3. g Population aged 16 and over. h December. i Break in series. j Excluding diplomats and foreign residents in Mongolia. k 2012. l ITU estimate. m Refers to total population. n Refers to foreign citizens.

Montenegro

Region	Southern Europe	
Population (est., 000)	622	
Capital city	Podgorica	
Currency	Euro (EUR)	

Surface area (sq km)	13 812
Pop. density (per sq km)	45.0
Capital city pop. (000)	165
UN membership date	28 June 2006

Economic indicators	2005	2010	2013
GDP: Gross domestic product (million current US$)	2 257	4 111	4 418
GDP: Growth rate at constant 2005 prices (annual %)	4.2	2.5	3.5
GDP per capita (current US$)	3 665.2	6 629.5	7 109.1
GNI: Gross national income per capita (current US$)	3 700.6	6 583.1	7 248.8
Gross fixed capital formation (% of GDP)	18.0	21.1	19.2
Exchange rates (national currency per US$) [a]	0.85	0.75	0.73
Balance of payments, current account (million US$)	−1 464[b]	−952	−649
CPI: Consumer price index (2000=100)	100[c]	122[c]	...
Index of industrial production (2010=100) [d]	127	100	92
Agricultural production index (2004-2006=100)	...	91	98
Food production index (2004-2006=100)	...	91	98
Unemployment (% of labour force)	19.4	19.7	19.8
Employment in industrial sector (% of employed)	19.2[efg]	20.0[eh]	18.1[i]
Employment in agricultural sector (% of employed)	8.6[efg]	6.2[eh]	5.7[i]
Labour force participation, adult female pop. (%)	42.9	43.0	43.0
Labour force participation, adult male pop. (%)	59.7	58.9	57.3
Tourist arrivals at national borders (000) [j]	272	1 088	1 324
Energy production, primary (Petajoules)	27	37	29[i]
Mobile-cellular subscriptions (per 100 inhabitants)	88.2	188.7[k]	160.0[k]
Individuals using the Internet (%) [k]	27.1	37.5	56.8

Total trade		Major trading partners			2013
	(million US$)	(% of exports)			(% of imports)
Exports	494.4	Serbia	35.8	Serbia	28.6
Imports	2 348.9	Croatia	16.0	Greece	8.5
Balance	−1 854.5	Slovenia	9.7	China	8.1

Social indicators		
Population growth rate (average annual %)	2010-2015	0.1
Urban population growth rate (average annual %)	2010-2015	0.3
Rural population growth rate (average annual %)	2010-2015	−0.5
Urban population (%)	2014	63.8
Population aged 0-14 years (%)	2014	18.5
Population aged 60+ years (females and males, % of total)	2014	21.5/17.4
Sex ratio (males per 100 females)	2014	97.6
Life expectancy at birth (females and males, years)	2010-2015	77.1/72.4
Infant mortality rate (per 1 000 live births)	2010-2015	9.6
Fertility rate, total (live births per woman)	2010-2015	1.7
Contraceptive prevalence (ages 15-49, %)	2007-2013	39.4[l]
International migrant stock (000 and % of total population)	mid-2013	50.7/8.2
Refugees and others of concern to UNHCR	mid-2014	19 910
Education: Primary-secondary gross enrolment ratio (f/m per 100)	2007-2013	94.8/94.1
Education: Female third-level students (% of total)	2007-2013	54.3
Intentional homicide rate (per 100,000 population)	2008-2012	2.7
Seats held by women in national parliaments (%)	2015	17.3

Environmental indicators		
Threatened species	2014	83
Forested area (% of land area)	2012	40.4
Proportion of terrestrial and marine areas protected (%)	2014	2.7
Population using improved drinking water sources (%)	2012	98.0
Population using improved sanitation facilities (%)	2012	90.0
CO_2 emission estimates (000 metric tons and metric tons per capita)	2011	2 571/4.1
Energy supply per capita (Gigajoules)	2012	68.0

a Market rate. **b** 2007. **c** Index base 2005=100. **d** ISIC Rev.3 (CDE). **e** ISIC Rev.3. **f** Population aged 15-64. **g** October. **h** Break in series. **i** 2012. **j** Arrivals of non-resident tourists in all types of accommodation establishments. **k** ITU estimate. **l** 2005-2006.

Montserrat

Region	Caribbean	Surface area (sq km)	103
Population (est., 000)	5	Pop. density (per sq km)	50.3
Capital city	Brades Estate	Capital city pop. (000)	.5
Currency	E.C. Dollar (XCD)		

Economic indicators	2005	2010	2013
GDP: Gross domestic product (million current US$)	50	58	59
GDP: Growth rate at constant 2005 prices (annual %)	3.1	−2.8	2.0
GDP per capita (current US$)	10 382.3	11 651.0	11 565.4
GNI: Gross national income per capita (current US$)	9 793.1	10 882.3	10 898.8
Gross fixed capital formation (% of GDP)	31.8	25.7	37.5
Exchange rates (national currency per US$)[a]	2.70	2.70	2.70
Balance of payments, current account (million US$)	−16	−19	−27
Agricultural production index (2004-2006=100)	98	99	101
Food production index (2004-2006=100)	98	99	101
Tourist arrivals at national borders (000)	10	6	7
Mobile-cellular subscriptions (per 100 inhabitants)	89.2[b]	84.8	88.4[c]
Individuals using the Internet (%)	25.9[b]	35.0	54.6[c]

Total trade		Major trading partners			2013
	(million US$)	(% of exports)		(% of imports)	
Exports	6.0	Dominica	55.0	United States	70.3
Imports	42.1	United States	20.0	Trinidad and Tobago	7.1
Balance	−36.1	Saint Kitts and Nevis	5.0	United Kingdom	3.8

Social indicators		
Population growth rate (average annual %)	2010-2015	0.9
Urban population growth rate (average annual %)	2010-2015	0.7
Rural population growth rate (average annual %)	2010-2015	0.9
Urban population (%)	2014	9.0
Population aged 0-14 years (%)[def]	2014	19.7[g]
Population aged 60+ years (females and males, % of total)[def]	2014	19.1/20.1[g]
Sex ratio (males per 100 females)[def]	2014	107.2[g]
Contraceptive prevalence (ages 15-49, %)[h]	2007-2013	52.6[i]
International migrant stock (000 and % of total population)	mid-2013	1.3/26.0
Refugees and others of concern to UNHCR	mid-2014	0[j]
Education: Government expenditure (% of GDP)	2007-2013	5.1
Education: Primary-secondary gross enrolment ratio (f/m per 100)[k]	2007-2013	108.9/101.2
Education: Female third-level students (% of total)	2007-2013	85.3
Intentional homicide rate (per 100,000 population)	2008-2012	20.4

Environmental indicators		
Threatened species	2014	45
Forested area (% of land area)	2012	25.0
Proportion of terrestrial and marine areas protected (%)	2014	2.5
CO_2 emission estimates (000 metric tons and metric tons per capita)	2011	81/16.0
Energy supply per capita (Gigajoules)	2012	224.0[l]

a Official rate. **b** 2006. **c** ITU estimate. **d** Data compiled by the United Nations Demographic Yearbook system. **e** Data refer to the latest available census. **f** Census, de jure, complete tabulation. **g** 2011. **h** Age group 15 to 44 years. **i** 1984. **j** Value is zero, not available or not applicable. **k** National estimate. **l** UNSD estimate.

Morocco

Region	Northern Africa	Surface area (sq km)	446 550	
Population (est., 000)	33 493	Pop. density (per sq km)	75.0	
Capital city	Rabat	Capital city pop. (000)	1 932[a]	
Currency	Morocco Dirham (MAD)	UN membership date	12 November 1956	

Economic indicators	2005	2010	2013
GDP: Gross domestic product (million current US$)	59 524	90 771	103 836
GDP: Growth rate at constant 2005 prices (annual %)	3.0	3.6	4.4
GDP per capita (current US$)	1 975.9	2 868.6	3 145.8
GNI: Gross national income per capita (current US$)	1 950.5	2 790.7	3 058.8
Gross fixed capital formation (% of GDP)	27.5	30.7	30.2
Exchange rates (national currency per US$)[b]	9.25	8.36	8.15
Balance of payments, current account (million US$)	1 041	−3 925	−7 844
CPI: Consumer price index (2000=100)	107	108[cd]	113[d]
Agricultural production index (2004-2006=100)	93	126	134
Food production index (2004-2006=100)	93	127	135
Unemployment (% of labour force)	11.0	9.1	9.2
Employment in industrial sector (% of employed)[e]	19.5	22.1[f]	21.4[g]
Employment in agricultural sector (% of employed)[e]	45.4	40.2[f]	39.2[g]
Labour force participation, adult female pop. (%)	27.9	25.9	26.5
Labour force participation, adult male pop. (%)	78.2	75.7	75.8
Tourist arrivals at national borders (000)[h]	5 843	9 288	10 046
Energy production, primary (Petajoules)	72	81	77[g]
Mobile-cellular subscriptions (per 100 inhabitants)	41.1	101.1	128.5
Individuals using the Internet (%)	15.1[i]	52.0[j]	56.0

Total trade		Major trading partners			2013
	(million US$)		(% of exports)		(% of imports)
Exports	21 965.4	France	21.5	Spain	13.5
Imports	45 186.4	Spain	18.9	France	12.9
Balance	−23 221.0	Brazil	6.0	United States	7.5

Social indicators

Population growth rate (average annual %)	2010-2015	1.4
Urban population growth rate (average annual %)	2010-2015	2.3
Rural population growth rate (average annual %)	2010-2015	0.2
Urban population (%)	2014	59.7
Population aged 0-14 years (%)	2014	27.9
Population aged 60+ years (females and males, % of total)	2014	8.9/7.3
Sex ratio (males per 100 females)	2014	97.8
Life expectancy at birth (females and males, years)	2010-2015	72.6/69.0
Infant mortality rate (per 1 000 live births)	2010-2015	26.3
Fertility rate, total (live births per woman)	2010-2015	2.8
Contraceptive prevalence (ages 15-49, %)	2007-2013	67.4
International migrant stock (000 and % of total population)[k]	mid-2013	50.8/0.2
Refugees and others of concern to UNHCR	mid-2014	4 161
Education: Government expenditure (% of GDP)	2007-2013	6.6
Education: Primary-secondary gross enrolment ratio (f/m per 100)	2007-2013	87.4/95.7
Education: Female third-level students (% of total)	2007-2013	47.2
Intentional homicide rate (per 100,000 population)	2008-2012	2.2
Seats held by women in national parliaments (%)	2015	17.0

Environmental indicators

Threatened species	2014	169
Forested area (% of land area)	2012	11.5
Proportion of terrestrial and marine areas protected (%)	2014	20.1
Population using improved drinking water sources (%)	2012	84.0
Population using improved sanitation facilities (%)	2012	75.0
CO_2 emission estimates (000 metric tons and metric tons per capita)	2011	56 538/1.8
Energy supply per capita (Gigajoules)	2012	25.0

a Including Salé and Temara. b Official rate. c Series replacing former series. d Index base 2006=100. e ISIC Rev.3. f Break in series. g 2012. h Including nationals residing abroad. i Population aged 12 to 65 using the Internet at least once during the last month. j Estimate for population aged 6 to 74 in electrified areas. k Refers to foreign citizens.

Mozambique

Region	Eastern Africa	Surface area (sq km)	801 590	
Population (est., 000)	26 473	Pop. density (per sq km)	33.0	
Capital city	Maputo	Capital city pop. (000)	1 174	
Currency	Metical (MZN)	UN membership date	16 September 1975	

Economic indicators	2005	2010	2013
GDP: Gross domestic product (million current US$)	7 595	10 165	15 628
GDP: Growth rate at constant 2005 prices (annual %)	8.7	7.1	7.4
GDP per capita (current US$)	361.5	424.1	605.0
GNI: Gross national income per capita (current US$)	342.4	421.4	604.7
Gross fixed capital formation (% of GDP)	13.8	15.4	15.7
Exchange rates (national currency per US$)[a]	24.18	32.58	30.08
Balance of payments, current account (million US$)	−761	−1 450	−5 892
CPI: Consumer price index (2000=100)	173	287	341
Agricultural production index (2004-2006=100)	96	148	157
Food production index (2004-2006=100)	95	153	161
Unemployment (% of labour force)	8.3	8.3	8.3
Labour force participation, adult female pop. (%)	87.4	86.2	85.5
Labour force participation, adult male pop. (%)	83.3	83.0	82.8
Tourist arrivals at national borders (000)	578	1 718[b]	1 886
Energy production, primary (Petajoules)	430	516	666[c]
Mobile-cellular subscriptions (per 100 inhabitants)	7.2	30.1	48.0
Individuals using the Internet (%)	0.9[d]	4.2	5.4[d]

Total trade		Major trading partners			2013
	(million US$)	(% of exports)			(% of imports)
Exports	4 023.7	Netherlands	28.6	South Africa	32.7
Imports	10 099.1	South Africa	22.4	United Arab Emirates	8.5
Balance	−6 075.4	India	16.9	China	6.4

Social indicators		
Population growth rate (average annual %)	2010-2015	2.5
Urban population growth rate (average annual %)	2010-2015	3.3
Rural population growth rate (average annual %)	2010-2015	2.1
Urban population (%)	2014	31.9
Population aged 0-14 years (%)	2014	45.3
Population aged 60+ years (females and males, % of total)	2014	5.6/4.5
Sex ratio (males per 100 females)	2014	95.9
Life expectancy at birth (females and males, years)	2010-2015	51.1/49.2
Infant mortality rate (per 1 000 live births)	2010-2015	74.3
Fertility rate, total (live births per woman)	2010-2015	5.2
Contraceptive prevalence (ages 15-49, %)	2007-2013	11.6
International migrant stock (000 and % of total population)[ef]	mid-2013	218.8/0.9
Refugees and others of concern to UNHCR	mid-2014	16 571
Education: Government expenditure (% of GDP)	2007-2013	5.0[g]
Education: Primary-secondary gross enrolment ratio (f/m per 100)	2007-2013	73.3/80.7
Education: Female third-level students (% of total)	2007-2013	41.0
Intentional homicide rate (per 100,000 population)	2008-2012	12.4
Seats held by women in national parliaments (%)	2015	39.6

Environmental indicators		
Threatened species	2014	261
Forested area (% of land area)	2012	49.1
Proportion of terrestrial and marine areas protected (%)	2014	10.9
Population using improved drinking water sources (%)	2012	49.0
Population using improved sanitation facilities (%)	2012	21.0
CO_2 emission estimates (000 metric tons and metric tons per capita)	2011	3 282/0.2
Energy supply per capita (Gigajoules)	2012	18.0

a Principal rate. b Methodology revised. c 2012. d ITU estimate. e Refers to foreign citizens. f Including refugees. g 2006.

Myanmar

Region	South-Eastern Asia	
Population (est., 000)	53 719	
Capital city	Nay Pyi Taw	
Currency	Kyat (MMK)	
Surface area (sq km)	676 577	
Pop. density (per sq km)	79.4	
Capital city pop. (000)	1 016	
UN membership date	19 April 1948	

Economic indicators	2005	2010	2013
GDP: Gross domestic product (million current US$)	11 931	41 518	63 031
GDP: Growth rate at constant 2005 prices (annual %)	13.6	10.2	7.5
GDP per capita (current US$)	237.8	799.5	1 183.5
GNI: Gross national income per capita (current US$)	237.8	799.5	1 183.1
Gross fixed capital formation (% of GDP)	12.7	22.9	35.7
Exchange rates (national currency per US$)[a]	5.99	5.58	988.00
Balance of payments, current account (million US$)	582	1 574	−1 128
CPI: Consumer price index (2000=100)	297	156[b]	166[bc]
Agricultural production index (2004-2006=100)	99	135	132
Food production index (2004-2006=100)	99	135	131
Unemployment (% of labour force)	3.4	3.5	3.4
Labour force participation, adult female pop. (%)	74.5	75.1	75.2
Labour force participation, adult male pop. (%)	81.2	82.1	82.3
Tourist arrivals at national borders (000)	660	792	2 044
Energy production, primary (Petajoules)	927	959	990[c]
Mobile-cellular subscriptions (per 100 inhabitants)	0.3	1.1[d]	12.8
Individuals using the Internet (%)	0.1	0.3	1.2[d]

Total trade		Major trading partners			2013
	(million US$)[e]	(% of exports)[e]			(% of imports)[e]
Exports	7 625.2	Thailand	41.7	China	27.1
Imports	4 164.3	China, Hong Kong SAR	21.1	Singapore	27.0
Balance	3 460.9	India	12.6	Thailand	11.4

Social indicators		
Population growth rate (average annual %)	2010-2015	0.8
Urban population growth rate (average annual %)	2010-2015	2.5
Rural population growth rate (average annual %)	2010-2015	<
Urban population (%)	2014	33.6
Population aged 0-14 years (%)	2014	24.5
Population aged 60+ years (females and males, % of total)	2014	9.5/7.9
Sex ratio (males per 100 females)	2014	94.4
Life expectancy at birth (females and males, years)	2010-2015	67.1/63.0
Infant mortality rate (per 1 000 live births)	2010-2015	48.9
Fertility rate, total (live births per woman)	2010-2015	2.0
Contraceptive prevalence (ages 15-49, %)	2007-2013	46.0
International migrant stock (000 and % of total population)[f]	mid-2013	103.1/0.2
Refugees and others of concern to UNHCR	mid-2014	1 184 001[g]
Education: Government expenditure (% of GDP)	2007-2013	0.8
Education: Primary-secondary gross enrolment ratio (f/m per 100)	2007-2013	78.8/78.0
Education: Female third-level students (% of total)	2007-2013	55.3
Intentional homicide rate (per 100,000 population)	2008-2012	15.2
Seats held by women in national parliaments (%)	2015	6.2

Environmental indicators		
Threatened species	2014	285
Forested area (% of land area)	2012	47.7
Proportion of terrestrial and marine areas protected (%)	2014	4.1
Population using improved drinking water sources (%)	2012	86.0
Population using improved sanitation facilities (%)	2012	77.0
CO_2 emission estimates (000 metric tons and metric tons per capita)	2011	10 440/0.2
Energy supply per capita (Gigajoules)	2012	13.0

a Official rate. **b** Index base 2006=100. **c** 2012. **d** ITU estimate. **e** 2010. **f** Refers to foreign citizens. **g** Stateless persons population refers to persons without citizenship in Rakhine State only.

Namibia

Region	Southern Africa	Surface area (sq km)	824 268
Population (est., 000)	2 348	Pop. density (per sq km)	2.9
Capital city	Windhoek	Capital city pop. (000)	356
Currency	Namibia Dollar (NAD)	UN membership date	23 April 1990

Economic indicators	2005	2010	2013
GDP: Gross domestic product (million current US$)	7 261	11 141	12 580
GDP: Growth rate at constant 2005 prices (annual %)	1.8	6.6	4.4
GDP per capita (current US$)	3 582.3	5 113.2	5 461.6
GNI: Gross national income per capita (current US$)	3 526.8	4 876.7	5 408.0
Gross fixed capital formation (% of GDP)	18.6	23.3	24.7
Exchange rates (national currency per US$)[a]	6.32	6.63	10.49
Balance of payments, current account (million US$)	333	−390	−540
CPI: Consumer price index (2000=100)[b]	114	160	189[c]
Index of industrial production (2010=100)[d]	86	100	110
Agricultural production index (2004-2006=100)	103	90	90
Food production index (2004-2006=100)	104	91	90
Unemployment (% of labour force)	20.2	22.1	16.9
Employment in industrial sector (% of employed)	14.8[efg]	17.7[fhij]	13.8[jkl]
Employment in agricultural sector (% of employed)	29.9[efg]	16.3[fhij]	27.4[jkl]
Labour force participation, adult female pop. (%)	55.5	56.5	54.7
Labour force participation, adult male pop. (%)	67.7	66.3	63.7
Tourist arrivals at national borders (000)	778	984	1 176
Energy production, primary (Petajoules)	13	13	14[k]
Mobile-cellular subscriptions (per 100 inhabitants)	22.1	89.5	110.2
Individuals using the Internet (%)	4.0[m]	11.6	13.9[m]

Total trade		Major trading partners			2013
	(million US$)	(% of exports)		(% of imports)	
Exports	6 337.2	South Africa	26.7	South Africa	61.8
Imports	7 574.5	Botswana	13.7	Switzerland	5.8
Balance	−1 237.3	Switzerland	8.8	Marshall Islands	4.1

Social indicators		
Population growth rate (average annual %)	2010-2015	1.9
Urban population growth rate (average annual %)	2010-2015	4.2
Rural population growth rate (average annual %)	2010-2015	0.1
Urban population (%)	2014	45.7
Population aged 0-14 years (%)	2014	35.5
Population aged 60+ years (females and males, % of total)	2014	6.3/4.7
Sex ratio (males per 100 females)	2014	94.5
Life expectancy at birth (females and males, years)	2010-2015	67.0/61.6
Infant mortality rate (per 1 000 live births)	2010-2015	33.5
Fertility rate, total (live births per woman)	2010-2015	3.1
Contraceptive prevalence (ages 15-49, %)	2007-2013	55.1
International migrant stock (000 and % of total population)	mid-2013	51.5/2.2
Refugees and others of concern to UNHCR	mid-2014	4 382
Education: Government expenditure (% of GDP)	2007-2013	8.5
Education: Primary-secondary gross enrolment ratio (f/m per 100)	2007-2013	93.3/90.6
Education: Female third-level students (% of total)	2007-2013	56.8
Intentional homicide rate (per 100,000 population)	2008-2012	17.2
Seats held by women in national parliaments (%)	2015	41.3

Environmental indicators		
Threatened species	2014	105
Forested area (% of land area)	2012	8.7
Proportion of terrestrial and marine areas protected (%)	2014	23.2
Population using improved drinking water sources (%)	2012	92.0
Population using improved sanitation facilities (%)	2012	32.0
CO_2 emission estimates (000 metric tons and metric tons per capita)	2011	2 776/1.3
Energy supply per capita (Gigajoules)	2012	29.0

a Official rate. b Index base 2002=100. c Series linked to former series. d ISIC Rev.3 (CDE). e 2004. f ISIC Rev.3. g Population aged 15-69. h 2008. i Excluding regular military living in barracks. j Break in series. k 2012. l October. m ITU estimate.

Nauru

Region	Oceania-Micronesia	Surface area (sq km)	21
Population (est., 000)	10	Pop. density (per sq km)	480.1
Capital city	Nauru	Capital city pop. (000)	10
Currency	Australian Dollar (AUD)	UN membership date	14 September 1999

Economic indicators	2005	2010	2013
GDP: Gross domestic product (million current US$)	26	62	153
GDP: Growth rate at constant 2005 prices (annual %)	−12.1	20.1	26.4
GDP per capita (current US$)	2 599.4	6 233.9	15 211.1
GNI: Gross national income per capita (current US$)	3 030.4	6 492.0	15 737.4
Gross fixed capital formation (% of GDP)	42.8	43.7	43.0
Exchange rates (national currency per US$)[a]	1.37	0.99	1.12
Agricultural production index (2004-2006=100)	101	104	106
Food production index (2004-2006=100)	101	104	106
Mobile-cellular subscriptions (per 100 inhabitants)	0.0	61.9	67.8[b]

Social indicators		
Population growth rate (average annual %)	2010-2015	0.2
Urban population growth rate (average annual %)	2010-2015	0.2
Urban population (%)	2014	100.0
Population aged 0-14 years (%)[cd]	2014	38.9
Sex ratio (males per 100 females)[cd]	2014	101.9
Life expectancy at birth (females and males, years)[c]	2010-2015	63.2/57.5[e]
Infant mortality rate (per 1 000 live births)[c]	2010-2015	33.0[f]
Fertility rate, total (live births per woman)[c]	2010-2015	4.3[f]
Contraceptive prevalence (ages 15-49, %)	2007-2013	35.6
International migrant stock (000 and % of total population)[g]	mid-2013	2.1/20.6
Refugees and others of concern to UNHCR	mid-2014	534[h]
Education: Primary-secondary gross enrolment ratio (f/m per 100)[i]	2007-2013	83.7/82.6
Intentional homicide rate (per 100,000 population)	2008-2012	1.3
Seats held by women in national parliaments (%)	2015	5.3

Environmental indicators		
Threatened species	2014	80
Population using improved drinking water sources (%)	2012	96.0
Population using improved sanitation facilities (%)	2012	66.0
CO_2 emission estimates (000 metric tons and metric tons per capita)	2011	51/5.2
Energy supply per capita (Gigajoules)	2012	72.0[j]

a UN operational exchange rate. b 2012. c Data compiled by the Secretariat of the Pacific Community Demography Programme. d De facto estimate. e 2007-2011. f 2009-2011. g Refers to foreign citizens. h Refers to the end of 2013. i National estimate. j UNSD estimate.

Nepal

Region	Southern Asia	Surface area (sq km)	147 181
Population (est., 000)	28 121	Pop. density (per sq km)	191.1
Capital city	Kathmandu	Capital city pop. (000)	1 142[a]
Currency	Nepalese Rupee (NPR)	UN membership date	14 December 1955

Economic indicators	2005	2010	2013
GDP: Gross domestic product (million current US$)	8 259	16 305	18 179
GDP: Growth rate at constant 2005 prices (annual %)	3.1	4.8	3.7
GDP per capita (current US$)	326.5	607.3	654.0
GNI: Gross national income per capita (current US$)	327.4	612.0	657.0
Gross fixed capital formation (% of GDP)	19.9	22.2	21.2
Exchange rates (national currency per US$)[b]	74.05	71.95	98.97
Balance of payments, current account (million US$)	153	−128	1 151
CPI: Consumer price index (2000=100)	123	193[c]	251
Agricultural production index (2004-2006=100)	100	114	132
Food production index (2004-2006=100)	100	114	132
Unemployment (% of labour force)	2.5	2.7	2.7
Labour force participation, adult female pop. (%)	80.5	79.9	79.9
Labour force participation, adult male pop. (%)	89.0	87.6	87.1
Tourist arrivals at national borders (000)[d]	375	603	798
Energy production, primary (Petajoules)	167	170	168[e]
Mobile-cellular subscriptions (per 100 inhabitants)	0.9	34.3	71.5
Individuals using the Internet (%)	0.8	7.9[f]	13.3[g]

Total trade		Major trading partners			2013
(million US$)		(% of exports)			(% of imports)
Exports	863.3	India	67.0	India	63.6
Imports	6 451.7	United States	7.9	China	9.4
Balance	−5 588.4	Germany	3.9	United Arab Emirates	6.1

Social indicators		
Population growth rate (average annual %)	2010-2015	1.2
Urban population growth rate (average annual %)	2010-2015	3.2
Rural population growth rate (average annual %)	2010-2015	0.7
Urban population (%)	2014	18.2
Population aged 0-14 years (%)	2014	33.8
Population aged 60+ years (females and males, % of total)	2014	7.9/8.0
Sex ratio (males per 100 females)	2014	93.5
Life expectancy at birth (females and males, years)	2010-2015	69.3/67.1
Infant mortality rate (per 1 000 live births)	2010-2015	35.5
Fertility rate, total (live births per woman)	2010-2015	2.3
Contraceptive prevalence (ages 15-49, %)	2007-2013	49.7
International migrant stock (000 and % of total population)[h]	mid-2013	971.3/3.5
Refugees and others of concern to UNHCR	mid-2014	42 025
Education: Government expenditure (% of GDP)	2007-2013	4.7
Education: Primary-secondary gross enrolment ratio (f/m per 100)	2007-2013	97.6/91.0
Education: Female third-level students (% of total)	2007-2013	41.7
Intentional homicide rate (per 100,000 population)	2008-2012	2.9
Seats held by women in national parliaments (%)	2015	29.5

Environmental indicators		
Threatened species	2014	100
Forested area (% of land area)	2012	25.4
Proportion of terrestrial and marine areas protected (%)	2014	22.9
Population using improved drinking water sources (%)	2012	88.0
Population using improved sanitation facilities (%)	2012	37.0
CO_2 emission estimates (000 metric tons and metric tons per capita)	2011	4 334/0.2
Energy supply per capita (Gigajoules)	2012	9.0

a Refers to the municipality. b Official rate. c Series linked to former series. d Including arrivals from India. e 2012. f December. g ITU estimate. h Including refugees.

Netherlands

Region	Western Europe	Surface area (sq km)	37 354	
Population (est., 000)	16 802	Pop. density (per sq km)	404.6	
Capital city	Amsterdam[a]	Capital city pop. (000)	1 084	
Currency	Euro (EUR)	UN membership date	10 December 1945	

Economic indicators	2005	2010	2013
GDP: Gross domestic product (million current US$)	672 357	836 390	853 539
GDP: Growth rate at constant 2005 prices (annual %)	2.3	1.1	−0.7
GDP per capita (current US$)	41 243.2	50 338.7	50 929.5
GNI: Gross national income per capita (current US$)	41 273.3	50 656.9	51 038.8
Gross fixed capital formation (% of GDP)	20.5	19.8	18.3
Exchange rates (national currency per US$)[b]	0.85	0.75	0.73
Balance of payments, current account (million US$)	46 618	57 760	87 089
CPI: Consumer price index (2000=100)	113	122	131
Index of industrial production (2010=100)[c]	94	100	100
Agricultural production index (2004-2006=100)	100	111	113
Food production index (2004-2006=100)	100	112	113
Unemployment (% of labour force)	4.7	4.5	6.7
Employment in industrial sector (% of employed)	19.6[d]	15.9[e]	15.3[f]
Employment in agricultural sector (% of employed)	3.2[d]	2.8[e]	2.5[f]
Labour force participation, adult female pop. (%)	56.8	58.2	58.5
Labour force participation, adult male pop. (%)	72.5	71.3	70.6
Tourist arrivals at national borders (000)[g]	10 012	10 883	12 783
Energy production, primary (Petajoules)[h]	2 604	2 924	2 711[i]
Mobile-cellular subscriptions (per 100 inhabitants)	97.1	115.4[j]	113.7[k]
Individuals using the Internet (%)	81.0[l]	90.7[l]	94.0

Total trade		Major trading partners			2013
	(million US$)	(% of exports)			(% of imports)
Exports	571 246.9	Germany	24.7	Germany	16.6
Imports	506 162.3	Belgium	11.1	Belgium	9.8
Balance	65 084.6	United Kingdom	8.5	China	8.3

Social indicators		
Population growth rate (average annual %)	2010-2015	0.3
Urban population growth rate (average annual %)	2010-2015	1.1
Rural population growth rate (average annual %)	2010-2015	−5.9
Urban population (%)	2014	89.9
Population aged 0-14 years (%)	2014	17.0
Population aged 60+ years (females and males, % of total)	2014	25.4/22.3
Sex ratio (males per 100 females)	2014	98.4
Life expectancy at birth (females and males, years)	2010-2015	82.8/78.9
Infant mortality rate (per 1 000 live births)	2010-2015	3.6
Fertility rate, total (live births per woman)	2010-2015	1.8
Contraceptive prevalence (ages 15-49, %)[m]	2007-2013	69.0
International migrant stock (000 and % of total population)	mid-2013	1 964.9/11.7
Refugees and others of concern to UNHCR	mid-2014	76 658[no]
Education: Government expenditure (% of GDP)	2007-2013	5.9
Education: Primary-secondary gross enrolment ratio (f/m per 100)	2007-2013	116.9/118.6
Education: Female third-level students (% of total)	2007-2013	51.4
Intentional homicide rate (per 100,000 population)	2008-2012	0.9
Seats held by women in national parliaments (%)	2015	37.3

Environmental indicators		
Threatened species	2014	30
Forested area (% of land area)	2012	10.8
Proportion of terrestrial and marine areas protected (%)	2014	18.1
Population using improved drinking water sources (%)	2012	100.0
Population using improved sanitation facilities (%)	2012	100.0
CO₂ emission estimates (000 metric tons and metric tons per capita)	2011	168 007/10.1
Energy supply per capita (Gigajoules)[h]	2012	194.0

a Amsterdam is the capital and The Hague is the seat of government. b Market rate. c ISIC Rev.4 (BCDE). d ISIC Rev.3. e Break in series. f 2011. g Arrivals of non-resident tourists in all types of accommodation establishments. h Excluding Suriname and the Netherlands Antilles. i 2012. j July. k Third quarter. l Population aged 16 to 74 using the Internet in the last 12 months. m Age group 18 to 45 years. n Refugee population refers to the end of 2013. o The number of pending asylum-seekers is not available.

New Caledonia

Region	Oceania-Melanesia	Surface area (sq km)		18 575
Population (est., 000)	260	Pop. density (per sq km)		14.0
Capital city	Nouméa	Capital city pop. (000)		181
Currency	CFP Franc (XPF)			

Economic indicators	2005	2010	2013
GDP: Gross domestic product (million current US$)	6 236	9 064	9 712
GDP: Growth rate at constant 2005 prices (annual %)	3.6	3.9	2.4
GDP per capita (current US$)	27 266.1	36 789.2	37 862.3
GNI: Gross national income per capita (current US$)	27 266.1	36 789.2	37 862.3
Gross fixed capital formation (% of GDP)	28.5	43.1	40.9
Exchange rates (national currency per US$)[a]	100.84	90.81	86.46
Balance of payments, current account (million US$)	−112	−1 360	−1 889[b]
CPI: Consumer price index (2000=100)[c]	108	119	126
Agricultural production index (2004-2006=100)	100	98	103
Food production index (2004-2006=100)	100	98	103
Employment in industrial sector (% of employed)	21.3[def]	22.4[defg]	...
Employment in agricultural sector (% of employed)	3.1[def]	2.7[defg]	...
Labour force participation, adult female pop. (%)	47.7	45.8	45.8
Labour force participation, adult male pop. (%)	69.9	67.3	67.3
Tourist arrivals at national borders (000)[h]	101	99	108
Energy production, primary (Petajoules)	1	1	2[b]
Mobile-cellular subscriptions (per 100 inhabitants)	58.7	89.6	93.8[i]
Individuals using the Internet (%)	32.4	42.0[i]	66.0[i]

Total trade		Major trading partners				2013
	(million US$)		(% of exports)			(% of imports)
Exports	1 237.4	France	15.7	France		23.4
Imports	3 237.0	Japan	14.5	Singapore		19.5
Balance	−1 999.6	Australia	13.1	Australia		8.9

Social indicators		
Population growth rate (average annual %)	2010-2015	1.3
Urban population growth rate (average annual %)	2010-2015	2.2
Rural population growth rate (average annual %)	2010-2015	−0.6
Urban population (%)	2014	69.7
Population aged 0-14 years (%)	2014	22.4
Population aged 60+ years (females and males, % of total)	2014	14.7/13.8
Sex ratio (males per 100 females)	2014	102.1
Life expectancy at birth (females and males, years)	2010-2015	79.3/73.6
Infant mortality rate (per 1 000 live births)	2010-2015	13.1
Fertility rate, total (live births per woman)	2010-2015	2.1
International migrant stock (000 and % of total population)	mid-2013	63.0/24.6
Intentional homicide rate (per 100,000 population)	2008-2012	3.3

Environmental indicators		
Threatened species	2014	493
Forested area (% of land area)	2012	45.9
Proportion of terrestrial and marine areas protected (%)	2014	91.0
CO_2 emission estimates (000 metric tons and metric tons per capita)	2011	3 854/15.4
Energy supply per capita (Gigajoules)	2012	180.0

a UN operational exchange rate. **b** 2012. **c** Nouméa. **d** Population census. **e** ISIC Rev.3. **f** Population aged 14 and over. **g** 2008. **h** Including nationals residing abroad. **i** ITU estimate.

New Zealand

Region	Oceania	Surface area (sq km)	275 042
Population (est., 000)	4 551	Pop. density (per sq km)	16.8
Capital city	Wellington	Capital city pop. (000)	380
Currency	New Zealand Dollar (NZD)	UN membership date	24 October 1945

Economic indicators	2005	2010	2013
GDP: Gross domestic product (million current US$)	115 064	145 284	189 025
GDP: Growth rate at constant 2005 prices (annual %)	3.4	1.3	2.8
GDP per capita (current US$)	27 832.7	33 260.0	41 951.8
GNI: Gross national income per capita (current US$)	26 039.7	31 591.1	40 317.9
Gross fixed capital formation (% of GDP)	24.7	19.9	22.1
Exchange rates (national currency per US$) [a]	1.47	1.30	1.22
Balance of payments, current account (million US$)	−8 025	−3 433	−5 932
CPI: Consumer price index (2000=100)	113	130	138
Index of industrial production (2010=100) [bc]	104	100	100
Agricultural production index (2004-2006=100)	99	104	108
Food production index (2004-2006=100)	99	105	110
Unemployment (% of labour force)	3.8	6.5	6.2
Employment in industrial sector (% of employed)	22.0 [def]	20.9 [egh]	...
Employment in agricultural sector (% of employed)	7.1 [def]	6.6 [egh]	...
Labour force participation, adult female pop. (%)	60.3	61.5	62.0
Labour force participation, adult male pop. (%)	74.8	74.2	73.8
Tourist arrivals at national borders (000)	2 353	2 435	2 629
Energy production, primary (Petajoules)	573	771	740 [i]
Mobile-cellular subscriptions (per 100 inhabitants)	85.4	107.8 [j]	105.8 [j]
Individuals using the Internet (%) [k]	62.7	80.5	82.8

Total trade		Major trading partners			2013
	(million US$)	(% of exports)		(% of imports)	
Exports	39 443.6	China	20.7	China	17.1
Imports	39 619.2	Australia	19.0	Australia	13.3
Balance	−175.6	United States	8.5	United States	9.4

Social indicators		
Population growth rate (average annual %)	2010-2015	1.0
Urban population growth rate (average annual %)	2010-2015	1.1
Rural population growth rate (average annual %)	2010-2015	0.9
Urban population (%)	2014	86.3
Population aged 0-14 years (%)	2014	20.1
Population aged 60+ years (females and males, % of total)	2014	20.5/18.7
Sex ratio (males per 100 females)	2014	96.5
Life expectancy at birth (females and males, years)	2010-2015	82.9/79.1
Infant mortality rate (per 1 000 live births)	2010-2015	4.3
Fertility rate, total (live births per woman)	2010-2015	2.1
Contraceptive prevalence (ages 15-49, %) [l]	2007-2013	75.0 [m]
International migrant stock (000 and % of total population)	mid-2013	1 132.8/25.1
Refugees and others of concern to UNHCR	mid-2014	1 678 [n]
Education: Government expenditure (% of GDP)	2007-2013	7.4
Education: Primary-secondary gross enrolment ratio (f/m per 100)	2007-2013	111.7/108.4
Education: Female third-level students (% of total)	2007-2013	58.2
Intentional homicide rate (per 100,000 population)	2008-2012	0.9
Seats held by women in national parliaments (%)	2015	31.4

Environmental indicators		
Threatened species	2014	197
Forested area (% of land area)	2012	31.3
Proportion of terrestrial and marine areas protected (%)	2014	29.8
Population using improved drinking water sources (%)	2012	100.0
CO_2 emission estimates (000 metric tons and metric tons per capita)	2011	31 232/7.1
Energy supply per capita (Gigajoules)	2012	193.0

a Market rate. b ISIC Rev.4 (BCDE). c Twelve months ending 31 March of the year stated. d ISIC Rev.3. e Average of quarterly estimates. f Excluding Chathams, Antarctic Territory and other minor offshore islands. g 2009. h Break in series. i 2012. j Including subscriptions active in the last 90 days only. k ITU estimate. l Age group 20 to 49 years. m 1995. n Refugee population refers to the end of 2013.

Nicaragua

Region	Central America	Surface area (sq km)	130 373
Population (est., 000)	6 169	Pop. density (per sq km)	47.5
Capital city	Managua	Capital city pop. (000)	951
Currency	Córdoba (NIO)	UN membership date	24 October 1945

Economic indicators	2005	2010	2013
GDP: Gross domestic product (million current US$)	6 321	8 938	11 256
GDP: Growth rate at constant 2005 prices (annual %)	4.3	3.3	4.6
GDP per capita (current US$)	1 158.8	1 535.2	1 851.1
GNI: Gross national income per capita (current US$)	1 126.9	1 494.2	1 799.6
Gross fixed capital formation (% of GDP)	23.0	18.4	22.9
Exchange rates (national currency per US$)[a]	17.15	21.88	25.33
Balance of payments, current account (million US$)	−784	−857	−1 280
CPI: Consumer price index (2000=100)[b]	147	234[c]	291
Agricultural production index (2004-2006=100)	104	118	138
Food production index (2004-2006=100)	102	119	140
Unemployment (% of labour force)	5.6	8.0	7.2
Employment in industrial sector (% of employed)	19.7[def]	16.5[de]	...
Employment in agricultural sector (% of employed)	28.9[def]	32.2[de]	...
Labour force participation, adult female pop. (%)	43.5	46.2	47.4
Labour force participation, adult male pop. (%)	80.5	80.0	80.3
Tourist arrivals at national borders (000)[g]	712	1 011	1 229
Energy production, primary (Petajoules)	82	73	75[h]
Mobile-cellular subscriptions (per 100 inhabitants)	20.5	68.1	112.0
Individuals using the Internet (%)	2.6	10.0[i]	15.5[i]

Total trade		Major trading partners			2013
	(million US$)	(% of exports)		(% of imports)	
Exports	4 594.1	United States	45.3	United States	16.5
Imports	5 498.8	Mexico	13.2	Curaçao	14.7
Balance	−904.7	Venezuela	8.4	China	11.5

Social indicators

Population growth rate (average annual %)	2010-2015	1.4
Urban population growth rate (average annual %)	2010-2015	2.0
Rural population growth rate (average annual %)	2010-2015	0.7
Urban population (%)	2014	58.5
Population aged 0-14 years (%)	2014	32.3
Population aged 60+ years (females and males, % of total)	2014	7.5/6.6
Sex ratio (males per 100 females)	2014	97.8
Life expectancy at birth (females and males, years)	2010-2015	77.7/71.6
Infant mortality rate (per 1 000 live births)	2010-2015	16.6
Fertility rate, total (live births per woman)	2010-2015	2.5
Contraceptive prevalence (ages 15-49, %)	2007-2013	80.4
International migrant stock (000 and % of total population)[j]	mid-2013	41.5/0.7
Refugees and others of concern to UNHCR	mid-2014	265
Education: Government expenditure (% of GDP)	2007-2013	4.4
Education: Primary-secondary gross enrolment ratio (f/m per 100)	2007-2013	95.5/94.0
Education: Female third-level students (% of total)	2007-2013	52.2[k]
Intentional homicide rate (per 100,000 population)	2008-2012	11.3
Seats held by women in national parliaments (%)	2015	39.1

Environmental indicators

Threatened species	2014	134
Forested area (% of land area)	2012	24.7
Proportion of terrestrial and marine areas protected (%)	2014	22.0
Population using improved drinking water sources (%)	2012	85.0
Population using improved sanitation facilities (%)	2012	52.0
CO_2 emission estimates (000 metric tons and metric tons per capita)	2011	4 899/0.8
Energy supply per capita (Gigajoules)	2012	23.0

a Principal rate. b Index base 1999=100. c Series linked to former series. d ISIC Rev.2. e Population aged 10 and over. f November. g Including nationals residing abroad. h 2012. i ITU estimate. j Including refugees. k 2002.

Niger

Region	Western Africa	
Population (est., 000)	18 535	
Capital city	Niamey	
Currency	CFA Franc (XOF)	

Surface area (sq km)	1 267 000
Pop. density (per sq km)	14.6
Capital city pop. (000)	1 058
UN membership date	20 September 1960

Economic indicators	2005	2010	2013
GDP: Gross domestic product (million current US$)	3 369	5 719	7 407
GDP: Growth rate at constant 2005 prices (annual %)	7.4	8.4	4.1
GDP per capita (current US$)	255.5	359.8	415.4
GNI: Gross national income per capita (current US$)	254.8	357.0	409.4
Gross fixed capital formation (% of GDP)	21.6	38.9	34.4
Exchange rates (national currency per US$)[a]	556.04	490.91	475.64
Balance of payments, current account (million US$)	−312	−1 136	−1 098[b]
CPI: Consumer price index (2000=100)[cd]	114	128[e]	136
Agricultural production index (2004-2006=100)	102	145	132
Food production index (2004-2006=100)	102	145	132
Unemployment (% of labour force)	5.1	5.1	5.1
Employment in industrial sector (% of employed)	11.1[fgh]	...	...
Employment in agricultural sector (% of employed)	56.9[fgh]	...	...
Labour force participation, adult female pop. (%)	39.2	39.8	40.0
Labour force participation, adult male pop. (%)	90.7	90.1	89.7
Tourist arrivals at national borders (000)	58	74	123
Energy production, primary (Petajoules)	71[i]	61	89[b]
Mobile-cellular subscriptions (per 100 inhabitants)	2.5	23.1	39.3[j]
Individuals using the Internet (%)[j]	0.2	0.8	1.7

Total trade		Major trading partners			2013
	(million US$)		(% of exports)		(% of imports)
Exports	1 337.2	France	39.6	China	23.7
Imports	1 714.1	Burkina Faso	16.3	France	10.1
Balance	−376.9	Nigeria	15.4	Togo	6.3

Social indicators

Population growth rate (average annual %)	2010-2015	3.9
Urban population growth rate (average annual %)	2010-2015	5.1
Rural population growth rate (average annual %)	2010-2015	3.6
Urban population (%)	2014	18.5
Population aged 0-14 years (%)	2014	50.1
Population aged 60+ years (females and males, % of total)	2014	4.3/4.1
Sex ratio (males per 100 females)	2014	101.7
Life expectancy at birth (females and males, years)	2010-2015	58.4/58.0
Infant mortality rate (per 1 000 live births)	2010-2015	53.6
Fertility rate, total (live births per woman)	2010-2015	7.6
Contraceptive prevalence (ages 15-49, %)	2007-2013	13.9
International migrant stock (000 and % of total population)[k]	mid-2013	132.3/0.7
Refugees and others of concern to UNHCR	mid-2014	96 264
Education: Government expenditure (% of GDP)	2007-2013	4.4
Education: Primary-secondary gross enrolment ratio (f/m per 100)	2007-2013	40.7/50.8
Education: Female third-level students (% of total)	2007-2013	27.8
Intentional homicide rate (per 100,000 population)	2008-2012	4.7
Seats held by women in national parliaments (%)	2015	13.3

Environmental indicators

Threatened species	2014	31
Forested area (% of land area)	2012	0.9
Proportion of terrestrial and marine areas protected (%)	2014	17.6
Population using improved drinking water sources (%)	2012	52.0
Population using improved sanitation facilities (%)	2012	9.0
CO_2 emission estimates (000 metric tons and metric tons per capita)	2011	1 423/0.1
Energy supply per capita (Gigajoules)	2012	5.0

a Official rate. b 2012. c Niamey. d African population. e Series linked to former series. f Core Welfare Indicators Questionnaire (World Bank). g ISIC Rev.2. h April to July. i UNSD estimate. j ITU estimate. k Including refugees.

Nigeria

Region	Western Africa	Surface area (sq km)	923 768
Population (est., 000)	178 517	Pop. density (per sq km)	193.3
Capital city	Abuja	Capital city pop. (000)	2 301
Currency	Naira (NGN)	UN membership date	7 October 1960

Economic indicators	2005	2010	2013
GDP: Gross domestic product (million current US$)	180 502	369 062	514 965
GDP: Growth rate at constant 2005 prices (annual %)	6.5	7.8	5.4
GDP per capita (current US$)	1 293.1	2 310.9	2 966.1
GNI: Gross national income per capita (current US$)	1 242.4	2 074.3	2 663.5
Gross fixed capital formation (% of GDP)	8.0	17.0	14.5
Exchange rates (national currency per US$)[a]	129.00	150.66	155.20
Balance of payments, current account (million US$)	36 529	14 459	20 353[b]
CPI: Consumer price index (2000=100)[c]	207	338[d]	456
Agricultural production index (2004-2006=100)	100	104	110
Food production index (2004-2006=100)	100	104	111
Unemployment (% of labour force)	7.6	7.6	7.5
Employment in industrial sector (% of employed)	11.5[efgh]	...	...
Employment in agricultural sector (% of employed)	44.6[efgh]	...	...
Labour force participation, adult female pop. (%)	47.6	47.9	48.2
Labour force participation, adult male pop. (%)	62.1	63.2	63.7
Tourist arrivals at national borders (000)	1 010	1 555	600
Energy production, primary (Petajoules)	9 723	10 737	11 347[b]
Mobile-cellular subscriptions (per 100 inhabitants)	13.3	54.7	73.3
Individuals using the Internet (%)	3.6	24.0[i]	38.0

Total trade		Major trading partners			2013
	(million US$)		(% of exports)		(% of imports)
Exports	90 554.5	India	12.6	China	21.7
Imports	44 598.2	Netherlands	10.5	United States	8.7
Balance	45 956.3	Brazil	9.5	Areas nes	5.5[j]

Social indicators		
Population growth rate (average annual %)	2010-2015	2.8
Urban population growth rate (average annual %)	2010-2015	4.7
Rural population growth rate (average annual %)	2010-2015	1.2
Urban population (%)	2014	46.9
Population aged 0-14 years (%)	2014	44.4
Population aged 60+ years (females and males, % of total)	2014	4.7/4.2
Sex ratio (males per 100 females)	2014	103.7
Life expectancy at birth (females and males, years)	2010-2015	52.6/52.0
Infant mortality rate (per 1 000 live births)	2010-2015	76.3
Fertility rate, total (live births per woman)	2010-2015	6.0
Contraceptive prevalence (ages 15-49, %)	2007-2013	15.1
International migrant stock (000 and % of total population)[kl]	mid-2013	1 233.6/0.7
Refugees and others of concern to UNHCR	mid-2014	2 526
Education: Primary-secondary gross enrolment ratio (f/m per 100)[m] 2007-2013		63.2/69.6
Education: Female third-level students (% of total)	2007-2013	40.7[n]
Intentional homicide rate (per 100,000 population)	2008-2012	20.0
Seats held by women in national parliaments (%)	2015	6.7

Environmental indicators		
Threatened species	2014	332
Forested area (% of land area)	2012	9.0
Proportion of terrestrial and marine areas protected (%)	2014	11.8
Population using improved drinking water sources (%)	2012	64.0
Population using improved sanitation facilities (%)	2012	28.0
CO_2 emission estimates (000 metric tons and metric tons per capita)	2011	88 026/0.6
Energy supply per capita (Gigajoules)	2012	33.0

a Principal rate. b 2012. c Rural and urban areas. d Series linked to former series. e 2004. f Living standards survey. g ISIC Rev.2. h September of the preceding year to August of the current year. i ITU estimate. j See technical notes. k Refers to foreign citizens. l Including refugees. m UNESCO estimate. n 2005.

Niue

Region	Oceania-Polynesia	Surface area (sq km)	260
Population (est., 000)	1	Pop. density (per sq km)	5.0
Capital city	Alofi	Capital city pop. (000)	1
Currency	New Zealand Dollar (NZD)		

Economic indicators	2005	2010	2013
Exchange rates (national currency per US$)[a]	1.46	1.31	1.22
CPI: Consumer price index (2000=100)	119	158[b]	...
Agricultural production index (2004-2006=100)	101	93	92
Food production index (2004-2006=100)	101	93	92
Tourist arrivals at national borders (000)[c]	3	6	7
Energy production, primary (Petajoules)	0	0	0[d]
Mobile-cellular subscriptions (per 100 inhabitants)	37.6[e]	...	...
Individuals using the Internet (%)	51.7	77.0[f]	86.9[f]

Social indicators		
Population growth rate (average annual %)	2010-2015	−2.9
Urban population growth rate (average annual %)	2010-2015	−0.9
Rural population growth rate (average annual %)	2010-2015	−4.2
Urban population (%)	2014	41.8
Population aged 0-14 years (%)[gh]	2014	24.7
Population aged 60+ years (females and males, % of total)[ijk]	2014	18.0/15.8[l]
Sex ratio (males per 100 females)[gh]	2014	100.0
Life expectancy at birth (females and males, years)[g]	2010-2015	72.8/66.1[m]
Infant mortality rate (per 1 000 live births)[g]	2010-2015	10.2[m]
Fertility rate, total (live births per woman)[g]	2010-2015	2.2[m]
International migrant stock (000 and % of total population)	mid-2013	0.6/41.1
Education: Primary-secondary gross enrolment ratio (f/m per 100)[n]	2007-2013	124.3/96.1[o]
Intentional homicide rate (per 100,000 population)	2008-2012	3.6

Environmental indicators		
Threatened species	2014	50
Forested area (% of land area)	2012	70.8
Proportion of terrestrial and marine areas protected (%)	2014	0.0
Population using improved drinking water sources (%)	2012	99.0
Population using improved sanitation facilities (%)	2012	100.0
CO_2 emission estimates (000 metric tons and metric tons per capita)	2011	11/6.5
Energy supply per capita (Gigajoules)	2012	76.0[p]

a UN operational exchange rate. b 2009. c Including Niueans residing usually in New Zealand. d 2012. e 2004. f ITU estimate. g Data compiled by the Secretariat of the Pacific Community Demography Programme. h De facto estimate. i Data compiled by the United Nations Demographic Yearbook system. j Data refer to the latest available census. k De jure estimate. l 2010. m 2006-2011. n National estimate. o 2005. p UNSD estimate.

Northern Mariana Islands

Region	Oceania-Micronesia	Surface area (sq km)	457
Population (est., 000)	55	Pop. density (per sq km)	117.5
Capital city	Garapan[a]	Capital city pop. (000)	4[b]
Currency	U.S. Dollar (USD)		

Economic indicators	2005	2010	2013
CPI: Consumer price index (2000=100)[c]	100	122[d]	...
Tourist arrivals at national borders (000)[e]	498	375	...
Mobile-cellular subscriptions (per 100 inhabitants)	31.0[f]	...	...

Social indicators		
Population growth rate (average annual %)	2010-2015	0.4
Urban population growth rate (average annual %)	2010-2015	0.4
Rural population growth rate (average annual %)	2010-2015	0.9
Urban population (%)	2014	89.3
Population aged 0-14 years (%)[gh]	2014	24.9
Population aged 60+ years (females and males, % of total)[hij]	2014	6.5/7.0[k]
Sex ratio (males per 100 females)[gh]	2014	106.3
Life expectancy at birth (females and males, years)[g]	2010-2015	77.6/75.0[l]
Infant mortality rate (per 1 000 live births)[g]	2010-2015	4.9[m]
Fertility rate, total (live births per woman)[i]	2010-2015	2.2[b]
Contraceptive prevalence (ages 15-49, %)	2007-2013	20.5[n]
International migrant stock (000 and % of total population)	mid-2013	24.2/44.9

Environmental indicators		
Threatened species	2014	99
Forested area (% of land area)	2012	65.2
Proportion of terrestrial and marine areas protected (%)	2014	26.3

a Refers to the island of Saipan. **b** 2010. **c** Saipan. **d** 2009. **e** Arrivals by air. **f** 2004. **g** Data compiled by the Secretariat of the Pacific Community Demography Programme. **h** De facto estimate. **i** Data compiled by the United Nations Demographic Yearbook system. **j** Data refer to the latest available census. **k** 2003. **l** 2008-2012. **m** 2006-2008. **n** 1970.

Norway

Region	Northern Europe	Surface area (sq km)	323 787 [a]
Population (est., 000)	5 092 [b]	Pop. density (per sq km)	13.2 [b]
Capital city	Oslo	Capital city pop. (000)	970
Currency	Norwegian Krone (NOK)	UN membership date	27 November 1945

Economic indicators	2005	2010	2013
GDP: Gross domestic product (million current US$)	308 722	428 527	522 349
GDP: Growth rate at constant 2005 prices (annual %)	2.6	0.6	0.7
GDP per capita (current US$)	66 759.6	87 610.9	103 585.8
GNI: Gross national income per capita (current US$)	67 501.5	88 642.5	105 265.6
Gross fixed capital formation (% of GDP)	20.3	20.6	23.7
Exchange rates (national currency per US$) [c]	6.77	5.86	6.08
Balance of payments, current account (million US$)	49 967	50 258	57 392
CPI: Consumer price index (2000=100)	109	122	127
Index of industrial production (2010=100) [d]	114	100	94
Agricultural production index (2004-2006=100)	99	102	102
Food production index (2004-2006=100)	99	102	102
Unemployment (% of labour force)	4.6	3.6	3.5
Employment in industrial sector (% of employed)	20.8 [e]	19.7 [f]	20.2 [fg]
Employment in agricultural sector (% of employed)	3.3 [e]	2.5 [f]	2.2 [fg]
Labour force participation, adult female pop. (%)	60.3	61.4	61.2
Labour force participation, adult male pop. (%)	70.5	70.0	68.7
Tourist arrivals at national borders (000) [h]	3 824	4 767	...
Energy production, primary (Petajoules)	9 372	8 606	8 411 [g]
Mobile-cellular subscriptions (per 100 inhabitants)	102.8	114.5	116.5 [i]
Individuals using the Internet (%)	82.0	93.4	95.1

Total trade		Major trading partners			2013
	(million US$) [b]	(% of exports) [b]			(% of imports) [b]
Exports	154 391.1	United Kingdom	24.1	Sweden	13.3
Imports	89 815.6	Germany	17.3	Germany	12.4
Balance	64 575.5	Netherlands	10.8	China	9.2

Social indicators		
Population growth rate (average annual %) [b]	2010-2015	1.0
Urban population growth rate (average annual %) [b]	2010-2015	1.4
Rural population growth rate (average annual %) [b]	2010-2015	−0.4
Urban population (%) [b]	2014	80.2
Population aged 0-14 years (%) [b]	2014	18.6
Population aged 60+ years (females and males, % of total) [b]	2014	23.4/20.2
Sex ratio (males per 100 females) [b]	2014	100.3
Life expectancy at birth (females and males, years) [b]	2010-2015	83.5/79.3
Infant mortality rate (per 1 000 live births) [b]	2010-2015	2.6
Fertility rate, total (live births per woman) [b]	2010-2015	1.9
Contraceptive prevalence (ages 15-49, %) [j]	2007-2013	88.4 [k]
International migrant stock (000 and % of total population) [b]	mid-2013	694.5/13.8
Refugees and others of concern to UNHCR	mid-2014	54 517 [l]
Education: Government expenditure (% of GDP)	2007-2013	6.6
Education: Primary-secondary gross enrolment ratio (f/m per 100)	2007-2013	104.7/105.3
Education: Female third-level students (% of total)	2007-2013	60.1
Intentional homicide rate (per 100,000 population)	2008-2012	2.2
Seats held by women in national parliaments (%)	2015	39.6

Environmental indicators		
Threatened species	2014	43
Forested area (% of land area)	2012	28.0
Proportion of terrestrial and marine areas protected (%)	2014	9.1
Population using improved drinking water sources (%)	2012	100.0
Population using improved sanitation facilities (%)	2012	100.0
CO_2 emission estimates (000 metric tons and metric tons per capita)	2011	45 533/9.2
Energy supply per capita (Gigajoules)	2012	247.0

a Excluding Svalbard and Jan Mayen Islands. b Including Svalbard and Jan Mayen Islands. c Official rate. d ISIC Rev.4 (BCD). e ISIC Rev.3. f Population aged 15-74. g 2012. h Arrivals of non-resident tourists at national borders. i Second quarter. j Age group 20 to 44 years. k 2005. l Refugee population refers to the end of 2013.

Oman

Region	Western Asia	Surface area (sq km)	309 500
Population (est., 000)	3 926	Pop. density (per sq km)	12.7
Capital city	Masqat	Capital city pop. (000)	812[a]
Currency	Oman Rial (OMR)	UN membership date	7 October 1971

Economic indicators	2005	2010	2013
GDP: Gross domestic product (million current US$)	31 082	58 641	79 656
GDP: Growth rate at constant 2005 prices (annual %)	2.5	4.8	4.8
GDP per capita (current US$)	12 322.8	20 922.6	21 929.0
GNI: Gross national income per capita (current US$)	11 917.5	19 644.9	20 662.5
Gross fixed capital formation (% of GDP)	22.0	27.0	28.0
Exchange rates (national currency per US$)[b]	0.38	0.38	0.38
Balance of payments, current account (million US$)	5 178	5 039	5 117
CPI: Consumer price index (2000=100)	102	134	145
Index of industrial production (2010=100)[c]	60	100	108
Agricultural production index (2004-2006=100)	112	122	124
Food production index (2004-2006=100)	112	122	125
Unemployment (% of labour force)	8.4	8.2	7.9
Employment in industrial sector (% of employed)	...	36.9[def]	...
Employment in agricultural sector (% of employed)	...	5.2[def]	...
Labour force participation, adult female pop. (%)	25.5	27.8	29.0
Labour force participation, adult male pop. (%)	76.5	79.8	82.6
Tourist arrivals at national borders (000)[g]	896	1 442	1 551
Energy production, primary (Petajoules)	2 351	2 869	3 098[h]
Mobile-cellular subscriptions (per 100 inhabitants)	52.9	164.3	154.7
Individuals using the Internet (%)	6.7	35.8[i]	66.5[ij]

Total trade		Major trading partners		2013
	(million US$)	(% of exports)		(% of imports)
Exports	55 497.1	...	United Arab Emirates	29.6
Imports	34 331.2	...	Japan	9.7
Balance	21 165.9	...	India	9.1

Social indicators		
Population growth rate (average annual %)	2010-2015	7.9
Urban population growth rate (average annual %)	2010-2015	8.5
Rural population growth rate (average annual %)	2010-2015	5.8
Urban population (%)	2014	77.2
Population aged 0-14 years (%)	2014	22.6
Population aged 60+ years (females and males, % of total)	2014	5.2/3.4
Sex ratio (males per 100 females)	2014	183.1
Life expectancy at birth (females and males, years)	2010-2015	78.9/74.7
Infant mortality rate (per 1 000 live births)	2010-2015	7.3
Fertility rate, total (live births per woman)	2010-2015	2.9
Contraceptive prevalence (ages 15-49, %)	2007-2013	24.4
International migrant stock (000 and % of total population)[k]	mid-2013	1 112.0/30.6
Refugees and others of concern to UNHCR	mid-2014	270
Education: Government expenditure (% of GDP)	2007-2013	4.2
Education: Primary-secondary gross enrolment ratio (f/m per 100)	2007-2013	100.9/103.3
Education: Female third-level students (% of total)	2007-2013	52.8
Intentional homicide rate (per 100,000 population)	2008-2012	1.1
Seats held by women in national parliaments (%)	2015	1.2

Environmental indicators		
Threatened species	2014	91
Forested area (% of land area)	2012	<
Proportion of terrestrial and marine areas protected (%)	2014	4.0
Population using improved drinking water sources (%)	2012	93.0
Population using improved sanitation facilities (%)	2012	97.0
CO_2 emission estimates (000 metric tons and metric tons per capita)	2011	64 855/21.5
Energy supply per capita (Gigajoules)	2012	364.0

a Refers to Muscat governorate. **b** Official rate. **c** ISIC Rev.3 (CDE). **d** Population census. **e** ISIC Rev.3. **f** December. **g** Inbound Tourism Survey. **h** 2012. **i** Population aged 5 and over. **j** Excluding population living in workers' camps. **k** Refers to foreign citizens.

Pakistan

Region	Southern Asia	
Population (est., 000)	185 133	
Capital city	Islamabad	
Currency	Pakistani Rupee (PKR)	

Surface area (sq km)	796 095
Pop. density (per sq km)	232.6
Capital city pop. (000)	1 297
UN membership date	30 September 1947

Economic indicators	2005	2010	2013
GDP: Gross domestic product (million current US$)	117 708	174 508	225 419
GDP: Growth rate at constant 2005 prices (annual %)	7.7	1.6	6.1
GDP per capita (current US$)	745.1	1 007.9	1 237.6
GNI: Gross national income per capita (current US$)	759.5	1 046.2	1 297.1
Gross fixed capital formation (% of GDP)	15.1	14.2	12.6
Exchange rates (national currency per US$)[a]	59.83	85.71	105.68
Balance of payments, current account (million US$)	−3 606	−1 354	−4 328
CPI: Consumer price index (2000=100)	129	234	295
Agricultural production index (2004-2006=100)	100	110	95
Food production index (2004-2006=100)	101	113	94
Unemployment (% of labour force)	7.1	5.0	5.1
Employment in industrial sector (% of employed)	20.3[bcd]	20.1[bcef]	...
Employment in agricultural sector (% of employed)	43.0[bcd]	44.7[bcef]	...
Labour force participation, adult female pop. (%)	19.3	23.9	24.6
Labour force participation, adult male pop. (%)	84.1	82.8	82.9
Tourist arrivals at national borders (000)	798	907	966[g]
Energy production, primary (Petajoules)	2 020	2 113	2 220[gh]
Mobile-cellular subscriptions (per 100 inhabitants)	8.1	57.3	70.1
Individuals using the Internet (%)	6.3	8.0[i]	10.9[i]

Total trade		Major trading partners			2013
	(million US$)	(% of exports)			(% of imports)
Exports	25 120.9	United States	14.9	United Arab Emirates	17.7
Imports	43 775.2	China	10.6	China	15.1
Balance	−18 654.3	Afghanistan	8.0	Kuwait	9.0

Social indicators		
Population growth rate (average annual %)	2010-2015	1.7
Urban population growth rate (average annual %)	2010-2015	2.8
Rural population growth rate (average annual %)	2010-2015	1.0
Urban population (%)	2014	38.3
Population aged 0-14 years (%)	2014	33.3
Population aged 60+ years (females and males, % of total)	2014	6.6/6.5
Sex ratio (males per 100 females)	2014	105.7
Life expectancy at birth (females and males, years)	2010-2015	67.4/65.6
Infant mortality rate (per 1 000 live births)	2010-2015	65.1
Fertility rate, total (live births per woman)	2010-2015	3.2
Contraceptive prevalence (ages 15-49, %)	2007-2013	35.4
International migrant stock (000 and % of total population)[j]	mid-2013	4 080.8/2.2
Refugees and others of concern to UNHCR	mid-2014	2 844 283
Education: Government expenditure (% of GDP)	2007-2013	2.5
Education: Primary-secondary gross enrolment ratio (f/m per 100)	2007-2013	54.1/66.4
Education: Female third-level students (% of total)	2007-2013	48.1
Intentional homicide rate (per 100,000 population)	2008-2012	7.7
Seats held by women in national parliaments (%)	2015	20.7

Environmental indicators		
Threatened species	2014	123
Forested area (% of land area)	2012	2.1
Proportion of terrestrial and marine areas protected (%)	2014	8.6
Population using improved drinking water sources (%)	2012	91.0
Population using improved sanitation facilities (%)	2012	48.0
CO_2 emission estimates (000 metric tons and metric tons per capita)	2011	163 453/0.9
Energy supply per capita (Gigajoules)	2012	17.0[h]

a Market rate. b ISIC Rev.2. c Population aged 10 and over. d July. e 2008. f January. g 2012. h UNSD estimate. i ITU estimate. j Including refugees.

Palau

Region	Oceania-Micronesia	Surface area (sq km)	459
Population (est., 000)	21	Pop. density (per sq km)	46.0
Capital city	Melekeok	Capital city pop. (000)	12[a]
Currency	U.S. Dollar (USD)	UN membership date	15 December 1994

Economic indicators		2005	2010	2013
GDP: Gross domestic product (million current US$)		188	205	240
GDP: Growth rate at constant 2005 prices (annual %)		6.2	−3.4	−0.3
GDP per capita (current US$)		9 446.3	10 028.3	11 479.8
GNI: Gross national income per capita (current US$)		8 180.0	8 584.7	10 014.5
Gross fixed capital formation (% of GDP)		35.7	22.2	24.8
Tourist arrivals at national borders (000)[b]		81	86	105
Energy production, primary (Petajoules)[c]		0	0	0[d]
Mobile-cellular subscriptions (per 100 inhabitants)		30.4	70.9	90.4[e]

Total trade		Major trading partners		2013
	(million US$)	(% of exports)		(% of imports)
Imports	168.6	... United States		27.9
		... Singapore		23.8
		... Japan		20.9

Social indicators		
Population growth rate (average annual %)	2010-2015	0.8
Urban population growth rate (average annual %)	2010-2015	1.7
Rural population growth rate (average annual %)	2010-2015	−4.3
Urban population (%)	2014	86.5
Population aged 0-14 years (%)[fg]	2014	19.9
Population aged 60+ years (females and males, % of total)[hij]	2014	10.1/6.7[k]
Sex ratio (males per 100 females)[fg]	2014	111.9
Life expectancy at birth (females and males, years)[h]	2010-2015	72.1/66.3[k]
Infant mortality rate (per 1 000 live births)[f]	2010-2015	12.2[l]
Fertility rate, total (live births per woman)[f]	2010-2015	1.7[l]
Contraceptive prevalence (ages 15-49, %)[m]	2007-2013	32.8[n]
International migrant stock (000 and % of total population)	mid-2013	5.6/26.7
Refugees and others of concern to UNHCR	mid-2014	1
Education: Government expenditure (% of GDP)[o]	2007-2013	7.3[p]
Education: Primary-secondary gross enrolment ratio (f/m per 100)[q]	2007-2013	93.6/97.4
Education: Female third-level students (% of total)	2007-2013	58.2
Intentional homicide rate (per 100,000 population)	2008-2012	3.1
Seats held by women in national parliaments (%)	2015	0.0

Environmental indicators		
Threatened species	2014	177
Forested area (% of land area)	2012	87.6
Proportion of terrestrial and marine areas protected (%)	2014	0.2
Population using improved drinking water sources (%)	2012	95.0[l]
Population using improved sanitation facilities (%)	2012	100.0
CO_2 emission estimates (000 metric tons and metric tons per capita)	2011	224/10.9
Energy supply per capita (Gigajoules)	2012	153.0[c]

a Refers to Koror. b Air arrivals (Palau International Airport). c UNSD estimate. d 2012. e ITU estimate.
f Data compiled by the Secretariat of the Pacific Community Demography Programme. g De facto estimate.
h Data compiled by the United Nations Demographic Yearbook system. i Data refer to the latest available
census. j Census, de jure, complete tabulation. k 2005. l 2010. m Age group 15 to 44 years. n 2003. o
UNESCO estimate. p 2002. q National estimate.

Panama

Region	Central America	Surface area (sq km)	75 320	
Population (est., 000)	3 926	Pop. density (per sq km)	52.0	
Capital city	Panama City	Capital city pop. (000)	1 638[a]	
Currency	Balboa (PAB)	UN membership date	13 November 1945	

Economic indicators	2005	2010	2013
GDP: Gross domestic product (million current US$)	15 465	27 053	40 467
GDP: Growth rate at constant 2005 prices (annual %)	7.2	7.5	8.4
GDP per capita (current US$)	4 594.5	7 355.1	10 472.3
GNI: Gross national income per capita (current US$)	4 167.7	6 749.7	10 266.6
Gross fixed capital formation (% of GDP)	16.8	24.5	29.4
Balance of payments, current account (million US$)	−1 022	−3 076	−4 920
CPI: Consumer price index (2000=100)[bc]	103	127	148
Agricultural production index (2004-2006=100)	99	107	116
Food production index (2004-2006=100)	99	107	117
Unemployment (% of labour force)	9.8	6.5	4.1
Employment in industrial sector (% of employed)[d]	17.0[e]	18.7[f]	18.2[gh]
Employment in agricultural sector (% of employed)[d]	19.3[e]	17.4[f]	16.7[gh]
Labour force participation, adult female pop. (%)	47.9	48.8	49.0
Labour force participation, adult male pop. (%)	81.2	82.0	81.8
Tourist arrivals at national borders (000)	702	1 324	1 658
Energy production, primary (Petajoules)	32	32	35[g]
Mobile-cellular subscriptions (per 100 inhabitants)	52.0	180.7	163.0[i]
Individuals using the Internet (%)	11.5	40.1	42.9[j]

Total trade		Major trading partners				2013
	(million US$)	(% of exports)			(% of imports)	
Exports	843.9	United States	18.8	United States		24.3
Imports	13 024.0	Canada	7.8	Panama		17.7[k]
Balance	−12 180.1	China	6.1	Free zones		9.8[l]

Social indicators		
Population growth rate (average annual %)	2010-2015	1.6
Urban population growth rate (average annual %)	2010-2015	2.1
Rural population growth rate (average annual %)	2010-2015	0.8
Urban population (%)	2014	66.3
Population aged 0-14 years (%)	2014	28.0
Population aged 60+ years (females and males, % of total)	2014	11.2/10.0
Sex ratio (males per 100 females)	2014	102.0
Life expectancy at birth (females and males, years)	2010-2015	80.4/74.7
Infant mortality rate (per 1 000 live births)	2010-2015	14.6
Fertility rate, total (live births per woman)	2010-2015	2.5
Contraceptive prevalence (ages 15-49, %)	2007-2013	52.2
International migrant stock (000 and % of total population)	mid-2013	158.4/4.1
Refugees and others of concern to UNHCR	mid-2014	18 386
Education: Government expenditure (% of GDP)	2007-2013	3.3
Education: Primary-secondary gross enrolment ratio (f/m per 100)	2007-2013	86.9/85.8
Education: Female third-level students (% of total)	2007-2013	60.0
Intentional homicide rate (per 100,000 population)	2008-2012	17.2
Seats held by women in national parliaments (%)	2015	19.3

Environmental indicators		
Threatened species	2014	363
Forested area (% of land area)	2012	43.4
Proportion of terrestrial and marine areas protected (%)	2014	5.2
Population using improved drinking water sources (%)	2012	94.0
Population using improved sanitation facilities (%)	2012	73.0
CO_2 emission estimates (000 metric tons and metric tons per capita)	2011	9 666/2.6
Energy supply per capita (Gigajoules)	2012	41.0

a Refers to the metropolitan area of Panama City. **b** Urban areas. **c** Index base 2003=100. **d** August. **e** ISIC Rev.2. **f** ISIC Rev.3. **g** 2012. **h** Break in series. **i** Estimate. **j** ITU estimate. **k** Data refer to returned goods or goods resulting from outward processing, i.e. minor processing or, in general, operations which do not change the country of origin. When these goods come back they are recorded as re-imports and the country of origin is the country itself. **l** See technical notes.

Papua New Guinea

Region	Oceania-Melanesia	Surface area (sq km)	462 840
Population (est., 000)	7 476	Pop. density (per sq km)	16.2
Capital city	Port Moresby	Capital city pop. (000)	338
Currency	Kina (PGK)	UN membership date	10 October 1975

Economic indicators	2005	2010	2013
GDP: Gross domestic product (million current US$)	4 866	9 707	15 420
GDP: Growth rate at constant 2005 prices (annual %)	3.9	7.6	5.1
GDP per capita (current US$)	798.3	1 415.2	2 106.2
GNI: Gross national income per capita (current US$)	710.0	1 291.7	1 913.1
Gross fixed capital formation (% of GDP)	16.5	21.2	21.5
Exchange rates (national currency per US$)[a]	3.10	2.64	2.42
Balance of payments, current account (million US$)	539	−633	−2 300[b]
CPI: Consumer price index (2000=100)	146	189	...
Agricultural production index (2004-2006=100)	100	112	118
Food production index (2004-2006=100)	99	112	118
Unemployment (% of labour force)	2.6	2.4	2.1
Labour force participation, adult female pop. (%)	71.3	70.6	70.5
Labour force participation, adult male pop. (%)	74.4	74.1	74.0
Tourist arrivals at national borders (000)	69	140	174
Energy production, primary (Petajoules)	170	80	66[b]
Mobile-cellular subscriptions (per 100 inhabitants)	1.2	27.8	41.0[c]
Individuals using the Internet (%)	1.7	1.3[d]	6.5[c]

Total trade		Major trading partners			2013
	(million US$)[b]	(% of exports)[b]			(% of imports)[b]
Exports	4 517.7	Australia	35.9	Australia	34.4
Imports	8 340.7	Japan	11.7	Singapore	14.3
Balance	−3 823.0	Germany	7.0	China	6.9

Social indicators		
Population growth rate (average annual %)	2010-2015	2.1
Urban population growth rate (average annual %)	2010-2015	2.1
Rural population growth rate (average annual %)	2010-2015	2.1
Urban population (%)	2014	13.0
Population aged 0-14 years (%)	2014	37.6
Population aged 60+ years (females and males, % of total)	2014	5.6/4.3
Sex ratio (males per 100 females)	2014	104.1
Life expectancy at birth (females and males, years)	2010-2015	64.5/60.3
Infant mortality rate (per 1 000 live births)	2010-2015	47.6
Fertility rate, total (live births per woman)	2010-2015	3.8
Contraceptive prevalence (ages 15-49, %)	2007-2013	32.4
International migrant stock (000 and % of total population)[ef]	mid-2013	25.4/0.4
Refugees and others of concern to UNHCR	mid-2014	9 782[g]
Education: Primary-secondary gross enrolment ratio (f/m per 100)	2007-2013	76.7/87.7
Education: Female third-level students (% of total)[h]	2007-2013	35.2[i]
Seats held by women in national parliaments (%)	2015	2.7

Environmental indicators		
Threatened species	2014	471
Forested area (% of land area)	2012	62.8
Proportion of terrestrial and marine areas protected (%)	2014	0.7
Population using improved drinking water sources (%)	2012	40.0
Population using improved sanitation facilities (%)	2012	19.0
CO_2 emission estimates (000 metric tons and metric tons per capita)	2011	5 229/0.7
Energy supply per capita (Gigajoules)	2012	19.0

a Official rate. **b** 2012. **c** ITU estimate. **d** Population aged 10 and over. **e** Refers to foreign citizens. **f** Including refugees. **g** Refers to the end of 2013. **h** UNESCO estimate. **i** 1999.

Paraguay

Region	South America	Surface area (sq km)	406 752
Population (est., 000)	6 918	Pop. density (per sq km)	17.0
Capital city	Asunción	Capital city pop. (000)	2 307 [a]
Currency	Guaraní (PYG)	UN membership date	24 October 1945

Economic indicators	2005	2010	2013
GDP: Gross domestic product (million current US$)	8 735	20 048	29 208
GDP: Growth rate at constant 2005 prices (annual %)	2.1	13.1	13.0
GDP per capita (current US$)	1 479.4	3 103.5	4 293.8
GNI: Gross national income per capita (current US$)	1 250.4	2 895.8	4 065.8
Gross fixed capital formation (% of GDP)	16.6	15.9	15.8
Exchange rates (national currency per US$) [b]	6 120.00	4 573.75	4 524.00
Balance of payments, current account (million US$)	−68	−57	621
CPI: Consumer price index (2000=100) [c]	150	212	244
Index of industrial production (2010=100) [d]	91	100	113
Agricultural production index (2004-2006=100)	97	137	157
Food production index (2004-2006=100)	98	142	163
Unemployment (% of labour force)	5.8	5.7	5.2
Employment in industrial sector (% of employed) [ef]	15.7 [g]	18.8	16.1 [hij]
Employment in agricultural sector (% of employed) [ef]	32.4 [g]	26.8	27.2 [hij]
Labour force participation, adult female pop. (%)	54.6	54.8	55.7
Labour force participation, adult male pop. (%)	85.7	84.7	84.8
Tourist arrivals at national borders (000) [k]	341	465	610
Energy production, primary (Petajoules)	288	325	341 [h]
Mobile-cellular subscriptions (per 100 inhabitants)	32.0	91.7	103.7
Individuals using the Internet (%) [l]	7.9	19.8	36.9

Total trade		Major trading partners			2013
	(million US$)	(% of exports)			(% of imports)
Exports	9 432.3	Brazil	30.0	China	28.3
Imports	12 142.0	Russian Federation	10.0	Brazil	26.4
Balance	−2 709.7	Argentina	7.6	Argentina	14.2

Social indicators		
Population growth rate (average annual %)	2010-2015	1.7
Urban population growth rate (average annual %)	2010-2015	2.1
Rural population growth rate (average annual %)	2010-2015	1.1
Urban population (%)	2014	59.4
Population aged 0-14 years (%)	2014	32.1
Population aged 60+ years (females and males, % of total)	2014	8.7/8.1
Sex ratio (males per 100 females)	2014	101.5
Life expectancy at birth (females and males, years)	2010-2015	74.5/70.0
Infant mortality rate (per 1 000 live births)	2010-2015	30.4
Fertility rate, total (live births per woman)	2010-2015	2.9
Contraceptive prevalence (ages 15-49, %) [m]	2007-2013	79.4
International migrant stock (000 and % of total population)	mid-2013	185.8/2.7
Refugees and others of concern to UNHCR	mid-2014	137
Education: Government expenditure (% of GDP)	2007-2013	5.0
Education: Primary-secondary gross enrolment ratio (f/m per 100)	2007-2013	82.4/82.6
Education: Female third-level students (% of total)	2007-2013	57.8
Intentional homicide rate (per 100,000 population)	2008-2012	9.7
Seats held by women in national parliaments (%)	2015	15.0

Environmental indicators		
Threatened species	2014	58
Forested area (% of land area)	2012	43.4
Proportion of terrestrial and marine areas protected (%)	2014	6.5
Population using improved drinking water sources (%)	2012	94.0
Population using improved sanitation facilities (%)	2012	80.0
CO$_2$ emission estimates (000 metric tons and metric tons per capita)	2011	5 299/0.8
Energy supply per capita (Gigajoules)	2012	36.0

a Refers to the metropolitan area of Asunción. b Market rate. c Asunción. d ISIC Rev.3 (CDE). e Population aged 10 and over. f ISIC Rev.2. g October to December. h 2012. i Excluding the departments of Boquerón and Alto Paraguay. j Break in series. k Excluding nationals residing abroad and crew members. l Population aged 10 and over using the Internet in the last 3 months. m Age group 15 to 44 years.

Peru

Region	South America	Surface area (sq km)	1 285 216
Population (est., 000)	30 769	Pop. density (per sq km)	23.9
Capital city	Lima	Capital city pop. (000)	9 722 [a]
Currency	Nuevo Sol (PEN)	UN membership date	31 October 1945

Economic indicators	2005	2010	2013
GDP: Gross domestic product (million current US$)	76 080	147 070	200 269
GDP: Growth rate at constant 2005 prices (annual %)	6.3	8.5	5.6
GDP per capita (current US$)	2 744.3	5 025.8	6 593.1
GNI: Gross national income per capita (current US$)	2 580.9	4 655.6	6 362.9
Gross fixed capital formation (% of GDP)	17.1	23.2	25.4
Exchange rates (national currency per US$) [b]	3.43	2.81	2.80
Balance of payments, current account (million US$)	1 148	−3 782	−9 126
CPI: Consumer price index (2000=100) [cd]	110	126 [e]	139
Index of industrial production (2010=100) [f]	...	100	113
Agricultural production index (2004-2006=100)	99	128	144
Food production index (2004-2006=100)	100	130	147
Unemployment (% of labour force)	5.2	4.0	3.9
Employment in industrial sector (% of employed) [g]	14.6 [h]	17.7	17.4 [i]
Employment in agricultural sector (% of employed) [g]	32.9 [h]	25.7	25.8 [i]
Labour force participation, adult female pop. (%)	57.6	67.6	68.2
Labour force participation, adult male pop. (%)	79.2	84.4	84.4
Tourist arrivals at national borders (000) [jk]	1 571	2 299	3 164 [l]
Energy production, primary (Petajoules)	455	810	977 [m]
Mobile-cellular subscriptions (per 100 inhabitants)	20.1	99.5	98.1
Individuals using the Internet (%)	17.1 [n]	34.8 [o]	39.2 [o]

Total trade		Major trading partners			2013
	(million US$)	(% of exports)		(% of imports)	
Exports	41 871.7	United States	17.8	United States	20.3
Imports	43 357.3	China	17.5	China	19.4
Balance	−1 485.6	Switzerland	7.2	Brazil	5.4

Social indicators		
Population growth rate (average annual %)	2010-2015	1.3
Urban population growth rate (average annual %)	2010-2015	1.7
Rural population growth rate (average annual %)	2010-2015	−0.3
Urban population (%)	2014	78.3
Population aged 0-14 years (%)	2014	28.4
Population aged 60+ years (females and males, % of total)	2014	10.2/8.9
Sex ratio (males per 100 females)	2014	100.5
Life expectancy at birth (females and males, years)	2010-2015	77.4/72.0
Infant mortality rate (per 1 000 live births)	2010-2015	16.7
Fertility rate, total (live births per woman)	2010-2015	2.4
Contraceptive prevalence (ages 15-49, %)	2007-2013	75.5
International migrant stock (000 and % of total population)	mid-2013	104.9/0.4
Refugees and others of concern to UNHCR	mid-2014	1 787
Education: Government expenditure (% of GDP)	2007-2013	3.3
Education: Primary-secondary gross enrolment ratio (f/m per 100)	2007-2013	97.4/98.9
Education: Female third-level students (% of total)	2007-2013	51.6
Intentional homicide rate (per 100,000 population)	2008-2012	9.6
Seats held by women in national parliaments (%)	2015	22.3

Environmental indicators		
Threatened species	2014	642
Forested area (% of land area)	2012	52.9
Proportion of terrestrial and marine areas protected (%)	2014	19.4
Population using improved drinking water sources (%)	2012	87.0
Population using improved sanitation facilities (%)	2012	73.0
CO_2 emission estimates (000 metric tons and metric tons per capita)	2011	53 069/1.8
Energy supply per capita (Gigajoules)	2012	30.0

a Refers to Gran Lima. b Market rate. c Lima. d Metropolitan areas. e Series linked to former series. f ISIC Rev.4 (BCDE). g ISIC Rev.2. h Third quarter. i 2011. j Estimated series including tourists with identity document other than a passport. k Including nationals residing abroad. l Preliminary. m 2012. n ITU estimate. o Population aged 6 and over.

Philippines

Region	South-Eastern Asia	Surface area (sq km) 300 000
Population (est., 000)	100 097	Pop. density (per sq km) 333.7
Capital city	Manila	Capital city pop. (000) 12 764[a]
Currency	Philippine Peso (PHP)	UN membership date 24 October 1945

Economic indicators	2005	2010	2013
GDP: Gross domestic product (million current US$)	103 096	199 637	272 067
GDP: Growth rate at constant 2005 prices (annual %)	4.8	7.6	7.2
GDP per capita (current US$)	1 201.3	2 136.4	2 765.1
GNI: Gross national income per capita (current US$)	1 515.2	2 579.2	3 316.4
Gross fixed capital formation (% of GDP)	20.1	20.7	20.5
Exchange rates (national currency per US$)[b]	53.07	43.88	44.41
Balance of payments, current account (million US$)	1 990	7 179	10 393
CPI: Consumer price index (2000=100)	130	166	185
Agricultural production index (2004-2006=100)	100	112	120
Food production index (2004-2006=100)	100	113	120
Unemployment (% of labour force)	7.7	7.3	7.1
Employment in industrial sector (% of employed)	15.6[cde]	15.0[cf]	15.4[fgh]
Employment in agricultural sector (% of employed)	36.0[cde]	33.2[cf]	32.2[fgh]
Labour force participation, adult female pop. (%)	49.8	50.3	51.1
Labour force participation, adult male pop. (%)	80.0	79.3	79.7
Tourist arrivals at national borders (000)[i]	2 623	3 520	4 681
Energy production, primary (Petajoules)	762	865	897[g]
Mobile-cellular subscriptions (per 100 inhabitants)	40.5	89.0	104.5
Individuals using the Internet (%)	5.4[j]	25.0	37.0[j]

Total trade		Major trading partners			2013
	(million US$)	(% of exports)		(% of imports)	
Exports	56 697.8	Japan	21.3	China	13.1
Imports	65 705.4	United States	14.7	United States	11.3
Balance	–9 007.6	China	12.4	Japan	8.5

Social indicators		
Population growth rate (average annual %)	2010-2015	1.7
Urban population growth rate (average annual %)	2010-2015	1.3
Rural population growth rate (average annual %)	2010-2015	2.0
Urban population (%)	2014	44.5
Population aged 0-14 years (%)	2014	33.8
Population aged 60+ years (females and males, % of total)	2014	7.4/5.8
Sex ratio (males per 100 females)	2014	100.3
Life expectancy at birth (females and males, years)	2010-2015	72.2/65.3
Infant mortality rate (per 1 000 live births)	2010-2015	21.0
Fertility rate, total (live births per woman)	2010-2015	3.1
Contraceptive prevalence (ages 15-49, %)	2007-2013	48.9
International migrant stock (000 and % of total population)[kl]	mid-2013	213.2/0.2
Refugees and others of concern to UNHCR	mid-2014	580 039
Education: Government expenditure (% of GDP)	2007-2013	2.7
Education: Primary-secondary gross enrolment ratio (f/m per 100)	2007-2013	98.3/97.1
Education: Female third-level students (% of total)	2007-2013	54.3
Intentional homicide rate (per 100,000 population)	2008-2012	8.8
Seats held by women in national parliaments (%)	2015	27.2

Environmental indicators		
Threatened species	2014	761
Forested area (% of land area)	2012	26.1
Proportion of terrestrial and marine areas protected (%)	2014	2.4
Population using improved drinking water sources (%)	2012	92.0
Population using improved sanitation facilities (%)	2012	74.0
CO_2 emission estimates (000 metric tons and metric tons per capita)	2011	82 012/0.9
Energy supply per capita (Gigajoules)	2012	18.0

a Refers to the National Capital Region. b Market rate. c ISIC Rev.3. d October. e Excluding regular military living in barracks. f Break in series. g 2012. h Average of quarterly estimates. i Including nationals residing abroad. j ITU estimate. k Refers to foreign citizens. l Including refugees.

Poland

Region	Eastern Europe	Surface area (sq km)	311 888	
Population (est., 000)	38 221	Pop. density (per sq km)	118.2	
Capital city	Warsaw	Capital city pop. (000)	1 718	
Currency	Zloty (PLN)	UN membership date	24 October 1945	

Economic indicators	2005	2010	2013
GDP: Gross domestic product (million current US$)	304 412	476 688	525 863
GDP: Growth rate at constant 2005 prices (annual %)	3.6	3.7	1.7
GDP per capita (current US$)	7 967.6	12 479.2	13 760.1
GNI: Gross national income per capita (current US$)	7 920.0	12 012.5	13 258.9
Gross fixed capital formation (% of GDP)	18.7	19.8	18.8
Exchange rates (national currency per US$)[a]	3.26	2.96	3.01
Balance of payments, current account (million US$)	−7 242	−24 030	−7 105
CPI: Consumer price index (2000=100)	115	131	143
Index of industrial production (2010=100)[b]	74	100	111
Agricultural production index (2004-2006=100)	99	101	106
Food production index (2004-2006=100)	99	101	106
Unemployment (% of labour force)	17.7	9.6	10.4
Employment in industrial sector (% of employed)	29.2[cd]	30.2	30.4[ef]
Employment in agricultural sector (% of employed)	17.4[cd]	12.8	12.6[ef]
Labour force participation, adult female pop. (%)	47.5	48.3	48.9
Labour force participation, adult male pop. (%)	62.5	64.3	64.9
Tourist arrivals at national borders (000)	15 200	12 470	15 800
Energy production, primary (Petajoules)	3 293	2 815	2 990[e]
Mobile-cellular subscriptions (per 100 inhabitants)	76.3	122.9	150.0[g]
Individuals using the Internet (%)	38.8	62.3	62.9

Total trade		Major trading partners			2013
	(million US$)		(% of exports)		(% of imports)
Exports	203 847.9	Germany	25.0	Germany	21.5
Imports	205 613.8	United Kingdom	6.5	Russian Federation	12.3
Balance	−1 765.9	Czech Republic	6.1	China	9.4

Social indicators		
Population growth rate (average annual %)	2010-2015	<
Urban population growth rate (average annual %)	2010-2015	−0.1
Rural population growth rate (average annual %)	2010-2015	0.2
Urban population (%)	2014	60.6
Population aged 0-14 years (%)	2014	15.0
Population aged 60+ years (females and males, % of total)	2014	24.8/18.5
Sex ratio (males per 100 females)	2014	93.3
Life expectancy at birth (females and males, years)	2010-2015	80.5/72.2
Infant mortality rate (per 1 000 live births)	2010-2015	5.5
Fertility rate, total (live births per woman)	2010-2015	1.4
Contraceptive prevalence (ages 15-49, %)[h]	2007-2013	72.7[i]
International migrant stock (000 and % of total population)	mid-2013	663.8/1.7
Refugees and others of concern to UNHCR	mid-2014	30 151[j]
Education: Government expenditure (% of GDP)	2007-2013	4.9
Education: Primary-secondary gross enrolment ratio (f/m per 100)	2007-2013	98.9/99.6
Education: Female third-level students (% of total)	2007-2013	59.9
Intentional homicide rate (per 100,000 population)	2008-2012	1.2
Seats held by women in national parliaments (%)	2015	24.1

Environmental indicators		
Threatened species	2014	53
Forested area (% of land area)	2012	30.7
Proportion of terrestrial and marine areas protected (%)	2014	29.3
CO2 emission estimates (000 metric tons and metric tons per capita)	2011	317 287/8.3
Energy supply per capita (Gigajoules)	2012	108.0

a Official rate. **b** ISIC Rev.4 (BCDE). **c** ISIC Rev.3. **d** Excluding conscripts and regular military living in barracks. **e** 2012. **f** Break in series. **g** ITU estimate. **h** Age group 20 to 49 years. **i** 1991. **j** Refugee population refers to the end of 2013.

Portugal

Region	Southern Europe	Surface area (sq km)	92 212
Population (est., 000)	10 610	Pop. density (per sq km)	115.4
Capital city	Lisbon	Capital city pop. (000)	2 869[a]
Currency	Euro (EUR)	UN membership date	14 December 1955

Economic indicators	2005	2010	2013
GDP: Gross domestic product (million current US$)	197 300	238 303	227 324
GDP: Growth rate at constant 2005 prices (annual %)	0.8	1.9	−1.4
GDP per capita (current US$)	18 770.8	22 503.1	21 429.2
GNI: Gross national income per capita (current US$)	18 481.8	21 722.7	20 958.6
Gross fixed capital formation (% of GDP)	23.2	20.6	15.2
Exchange rates (national currency per US$)[b]	0.85	0.75	0.73
Balance of payments, current account (million US$)	−19 821	−24 215	1 160
CPI: Consumer price index (2000=100)[c]	117	127	136[d]
Index of industrial production (2010=100)[e]	109	100	94
Agricultural production index (2004-2006=100)	97	104	104
Food production index (2004-2006=100)	97	105	104
Unemployment (% of labour force)	7.6	10.8	16.5
Employment in industrial sector (% of employed)	30.6[f]	27.7	25.6[gh]
Employment in agricultural sector (% of employed)	11.8[f]	10.9	10.5[gh]
Labour force participation, adult female pop. (%)	55.4	56.3	54.9
Labour force participation, adult male pop. (%)	69.3	67.9	66.2
Tourist arrivals at national borders (000)[i]	5 769	6 756	8 097
Energy production, primary (Petajoules)[j]	151	233	192[g]
Mobile-cellular subscriptions (per 100 inhabitants)	108.9	115.3[k]	113.0
Individuals using the Internet (%)	35.0	53.3	62.1

Total trade		Major trading partners			2013
	(million US$)		(% of exports)		(% of imports)
Exports	62 745.8	Spain	23.6	Spain	26.9
Imports	75 572.1	Germany	11.6	Germany	10.4
Balance	−12 826.3	France	11.6	France	6.2

Social indicators		
Population growth rate (average annual %)	2010-2015	<
Urban population growth rate (average annual %)	2010-2015	1.0
Rural population growth rate (average annual %)	2010-2015	−1.5
Urban population (%)	2014	62.9
Population aged 0-14 years (%)	2014	14.6
Population aged 60+ years (females and males, % of total)	2014	27.6/22.4
Sex ratio (males per 100 females)	2014	94.0
Life expectancy at birth (females and males, years)	2010-2015	82.8/76.8
Infant mortality rate (per 1 000 live births)	2010-2015	2.8
Fertility rate, total (live births per woman)	2010-2015	1.3
Contraceptive prevalence (ages 15-49, %)	2007-2013	86.8[l]
International migrant stock (000 and % of total population)	mid-2013	893.9/8.4
Refugees and others of concern to UNHCR	mid-2014	1 434[m]
Education: Government expenditure (% of GDP)	2007-2013	5.3
Education: Primary-secondary gross enrolment ratio (f/m per 100)	2007-2013	109.2/109.8
Education: Female third-level students (% of total)	2007-2013	53.5
Intentional homicide rate (per 100,000 population)	2008-2012	1.2
Seats held by women in national parliaments (%)	2015	31.3

Environmental indicators		
Threatened species	2014	254
Forested area (% of land area)	2012	37.8
Proportion of terrestrial and marine areas protected (%)	2014	1.9
Population using improved drinking water sources (%)	2012	100.0
Population using improved sanitation facilities (%)	2012	100.0
CO_2 emission estimates (000 metric tons and metric tons per capita)	2011	49 725/4.7
Energy supply per capita (Gigajoules)[j]	2012	84.0

a Refers to Grande Lisboa, the Peninsula of Setúbal, and the municipality Azambuja. b Market rate. c Excluding rent. d Series linked to former series. e ISIC Rev.4 (BCDE). f ISIC Rev.3. g 2012. h Break in series. i Arrivals of non-resident tourists in all types of accommodation establishments. j Including the Azores and Madeira. k Including machine to machine (M2M) subscriptions. l 2005-2006. m Refugee population refers to the end of 2013.

Puerto Rico

Region	Caribbean	Surface area (sq km)	8 870
Population (est., 000)	3 684	Pop. density (per sq km)	415.1
Capital city	San Juan	Capital city pop. (000)	2 466 [a]
Currency	U.S. Dollar (USD)		

Economic indicators	2005	2010	2013
GDP: Gross domestic product (million current US$)	87 276	100 352	105 149
GDP: Growth rate at constant 2005 prices (annual %)	−1.4	−0.3	−0.9
GDP per capita (current US$)	23 204.7	27 051.4	28 508.7
GNI: Gross national income per capita (current US$)	15 382.1	17 716.1	19 009.6
Gross fixed capital formation (% of GDP)	13.6	9.6	9.8
CPI: Consumer price index (2000=100)	111	131	138
Agricultural production index (2004-2006=100)	97	105	111
Food production index (2004-2006=100)	97	107	112
Unemployment (% of labour force)	11.5	16.2	14.2
Employment in industrial sector (% of employed) [bc]	19.0	13.7 [d]	14.0 [e]
Employment in agricultural sector (% of employed) [bc]	2.1	1.6 [d]	1.6 [e]
Labour force participation, adult female pop. (%)	38.1	35.1	34.4
Labour force participation, adult male pop. (%)	61.0	53.7	51.9
Tourist arrivals at national borders (000) [f]	3 686	3 186	3 200
Energy production, primary (Petajoules)	0	1	1 [e]
Mobile-cellular subscriptions (per 100 inhabitants)	53.0	79.1	83.7
Individuals using the Internet (%)	23.4 [g]	45.3	73.9 [g]

Social indicators		
Population growth rate (average annual %)	2010-2015	−0.2
Urban population growth rate (average annual %)	2010-2015	−0.2
Rural population growth rate (average annual %)	2010-2015	0.6
Urban population (%)	2014	93.6
Population aged 0-14 years (%)	2014	19.2
Population aged 60+ years (females and males, % of total)	2014	21.2/17.3
Sex ratio (males per 100 females)	2014	92.7
Life expectancy at birth (females and males, years)	2010-2015	82.5/75.0
Infant mortality rate (per 1 000 live births)	2010-2015	6.3
Fertility rate, total (live births per woman)	2010-2015	1.6
Contraceptive prevalence (ages 15-49, %) [h]	2007-2013	84.1 [i]
International migrant stock (000 and % of total population)	mid-2013	319.4/8.7
Education: Primary-secondary gross enrolment ratio (f/m per 100)	2007-2013	86.7/83.3
Education: Female third-level students (% of total)	2007-2013	58.6
Intentional homicide rate (per 100,000 population)	2008-2012	26.5

Environmental indicators		
Threatened species	2014	119
Forested area (% of land area)	2012	64.2
Proportion of terrestrial and marine areas protected (%)	2014	0.6
Energy supply per capita (Gigajoules)	2012	7.0 [j]

a Refers to the Metropolitan Statistical Area. b ISIC Rev.2. c Population aged 16 and over. d Break in series. e 2012. f Arrivals of non-resident tourists by air. g ITU estimate. h Age group 18 to 44 years. i 2002. j UNSD estimate.

Qatar

Region	Western Asia	Surface area (sq km)	11 607
Population (est., 000)	2 268	Pop. density (per sq km)	206.2
Capital city	Doha	Capital city pop. (000)	699
Currency	Qatari Rial (QAR)	UN membership date	21 September 1971

Economic indicators	2005	2010	2013
GDP: Gross domestic product (million current US$)	44 531	125 122	202 450
GDP: Growth rate at constant 2005 prices (annual %)	7.5	16.7	6.5
GDP per capita (current US$)	54 228.8	71 510.2	93 352.0
GNI: Gross national income per capita (current US$)	47 268.4	64 112.6	87 390.4
Gross fixed capital formation (% of GDP)	32.0	31.4	29.4
Exchange rates (national currency per US$) [a]	3.64	3.64	3.64
Balance of payments, current account (million US$)	...	51 978[b]	62 587
CPI: Consumer price index (2000=100) [c]	119	162	173
Index of industrial production (2010=100) [d]	53	100	119
Agricultural production index (2004-2006=100)	95	120	134
Food production index (2004-2006=100)	95	120	134
Unemployment (% of labour force)	1.1	0.4	0.5
Employment in industrial sector (% of employed) [e]	41.6[fg]	58.4[gh]	51.9[i]
Employment in agricultural sector (% of employed) [e]	3.0[fg]	1.6[gh]	1.4[i]
Labour force participation, adult female pop. (%)	44.7	50.5	50.8
Labour force participation, adult male pop. (%)	94.1	95.6	95.5
Tourist arrivals at national borders (000)	...	1 700	2 611
Energy production, primary (Petajoules)	3 896	7 428	9 184[i]
Mobile-cellular subscriptions (per 100 inhabitants)	87.3[j]	125.0[k]	152.6
Individuals using the Internet (%)	24.7	69.0[l]	85.3[lm]

Total trade		Major trading partners			2013
	(million US$)		(% of exports)		(% of imports)
Exports	136 855.1	Japan	29.2	United States	11.9
Imports	27 034.1	Republic of Korea	17.9	China	9.8
Balance	109 821.0	India	10.5	United Arab Emirates	7.3

Social indicators		
Population growth rate (average annual %)	2010-2015	5.9
Urban population growth rate (average annual %)	2010-2015	6.0
Rural population growth rate (average annual %)	2010-2015	−5.6
Urban population (%)	2014	99.2
Population aged 0-14 years (%)	2014	13.7
Population aged 60+ years (females and males, % of total)	2014	2.9/1.5
Sex ratio (males per 100 females)	2014	325.6
Life expectancy at birth (females and males, years)	2010-2015	79.4/77.7
Infant mortality rate (per 1 000 live births)	2010-2015	6.5
Fertility rate, total (live births per woman)	2010-2015	2.1
Contraceptive prevalence (ages 15-49, %)	2007-2013	38.0
International migrant stock (000 and % of total population) [n]	mid-2013	1 601.0/73.8
Refugees and others of concern to UNHCR	mid-2014	1 381
Education: Government expenditure (% of GDP)	2007-2013	2.5
Education: Primary-secondary gross enrolment ratio (f/m per 100)	2007-2013	102.5/111.2[o]
Education: Female third-level students (% of total)	2007-2013	63.7
Intentional homicide rate (per 100,000 population)	2008-2012	1.1
Seats held by women in national parliaments (%)	2015	0.0

Environmental indicators		
Threatened species	2014	35
Proportion of terrestrial and marine areas protected (%)	2014	1.2
Population using improved drinking water sources (%)	2012	100.0
Population using improved sanitation facilities (%)	2012	100.0
CO_2 emission estimates (000 metric tons and metric tons per capita)	2011	83 875/43.9
Energy supply per capita (Gigajoules)	2012	770.0

a Official rate. b 2011. c Index base 2002=100. d ISIC Rev.3 (CDE). e Paid employment only. f 2006. g ISIC Rev.3. h 2009. i 2012. j Active and inactive subscriptions. k Active subscriptions. l Refers to overall population. m Preliminary. n Refers to foreign citizens. o 2005.

Republic of Korea

Region	Eastern Asia	Surface area (sq km)	100 188
Population (est., 000)	49 512	Pop. density (per sq km)	497.4
Capital city	Seoul	Capital city pop. (000)	9 775[a]
Currency	South Korean Won (KRW)	UN membership date	17 September 1991

Economic indicators	2005	2010	2013
GDP: Gross domestic product (million current US$)	898 137	1 094 499	1 304 554
GDP: Growth rate at constant 2005 prices (annual %)	3.9	6.5	3.0
GDP per capita (current US$)	19 095.9	22 588.5	26 481.6
GNI: Gross national income per capita (current US$)	18 946.6	22 611.2	26 718.3
Gross fixed capital formation (% of GDP)	30.9	30.5	29.7
Exchange rates (national currency per US$)[b]	1 011.60	1 134.80	1 055.40
Balance of payments, current account (million US$)	12 655	28 850	79 884
CPI: Consumer price index (2000=100)[c]	100[d]	116	125
Index of industrial production (2010=100)[e]	72	100	108
Agricultural production index (2004-2006=100)	100	102	104
Food production index (2004-2006=100)	100	102	104
Unemployment (% of labour force)	3.7	3.7	3.1
Employment in industrial sector (% of employed)	26.8[f]	17.0[fg]	...
Employment in agricultural sector (% of employed)	7.9[f]	6.6[fg]	...
Labour force participation, adult female pop. (%)	50.0	49.3	50.1
Labour force participation, adult male pop. (%)	73.4	71.7	72.1
Tourist arrivals at national borders (000)[hi]	6 023	8 798	12 176
Energy production, primary (Petajoules)	1 776	1 855	1 908[j]
Mobile-cellular subscriptions (per 100 inhabitants)	81.5	104.8	111.0
Individuals using the Internet (%)[k]	73.5	83.7	84.8

Total trade		Major trading partners			2013
	(million US$)	(% of exports)			(% of imports)
Exports	559 618.6	China	26.1	China	16.1
Imports	515 573.0	United States	11.1	Japan	11.6
Balance	44 045.6	Japan	6.2	United States	8.1

Social indicators		
Population growth rate (average annual %)	2010-2015	0.5
Urban population growth rate (average annual %)	2010-2015	0.7
Rural population growth rate (average annual %)	2010-2015	−0.1
Urban population (%)	2014	82.4
Population aged 0-14 years (%)	2014	14.5
Population aged 60+ years (females and males, % of total)	2014	19.9/15.5
Sex ratio (males per 100 females)	2014	98.9
Life expectancy at birth (females and males, years)	2010-2015	84.6/77.9
Infant mortality rate (per 1 000 live births)	2010-2015	3.4
Fertility rate, total (live births per woman)	2010-2015	1.3
Contraceptive prevalence (ages 15-49, %)[l]	2007-2013	80.0
International migrant stock (000 and % of total population)[m]	mid-2013	1 232.2/2.5
Refugees and others of concern to UNHCR	mid-2014	3 635
Education: Government expenditure (% of GDP)	2007-2013	4.9
Education: Primary-secondary gross enrolment ratio (f/m per 100)	2007-2013	98.9/100.1
Education: Female third-level students (% of total)	2007-2013	39.8
Intentional homicide rate (per 100,000 population)	2008-2012	0.9
Seats held by women in national parliaments (%)	2015	16.3

Environmental indicators		
Threatened species	2014	75
Forested area (% of land area)	2012	63.8
Proportion of terrestrial and marine areas protected (%)	2014	2.6
Population using improved drinking water sources (%)	2012	98.0
Population using improved sanitation facilities (%)	2012	100.0
CO_2 emission estimates (000 metric tons and metric tons per capita)	2011	589 426/12.1
Energy supply per capita (Gigajoules)	2012	224.0

a Refers to Seoul Special City. b Market rate. c Index base 2005=100. d Series replacing former series.
e ISIC Rev.4 (BCD). f ISIC Rev.3. g Break in series. h Arrivals of non-resident visitors at national borders.
i Including nationals residing abroad and crew members. j 2012. k Population aged 3 and over. l Age
group 15 to 44 years. m Refers to foreign citizens.

Republic of Moldova

Region	Eastern Europe	Surface area (sq km)	33 846
Population (est., 000)	3 461[a]	Pop. density (per sq km)	102.3[a]
Capital city	Chisinau	Capital city pop. (000)	721
Currency	Moldovan Leu (MDL)	UN membership date	2 March 1992

Economic indicators	2005	2010	2013
GDP: Gross domestic product (million current US$)	2 988	5 812	7 970
GDP: Growth rate at constant 2005 prices (annual %)	7.5	7.1	8.9
GDP per capita (current US$)	793.3	1 626.5	2 285.4
GNI: Gross national income per capita (current US$)	900.5	1 762.3	2 483.8
Gross fixed capital formation (% of GDP)	24.6	22.6	22.9
Exchange rates (national currency per US$)[b]	12.83	12.15	13.06
Balance of payments, current account (million US$)	−226	−437	−399
CPI: Consumer price index (2000=100)[c]	99[d]	152	180
Agricultural production index (2004-2006=100)	100	93	101
Food production index (2004-2006=100)	100	93	101
Unemployment (% of labour force)	7.3	7.4	5.1
Employment in industrial sector (% of employed)[e]	16.0	18.7[f]	19.3[g]
Employment in agricultural sector (% of employed)[e]	40.7	27.5[f]	26.4[g]
Labour force participation, adult female pop. (%)	46.9	37.6	37.6
Labour force participation, adult male pop. (%)	50.6	44.9	44.2
Tourist arrivals at national borders (000)[h]	23	8	12
Energy production, primary (Petajoules)	4	4	5[g]
Mobile-cellular subscriptions (per 100 inhabitants)	28.9	71.4[i]	106.0[i]
Individuals using the Internet (%)	14.6	32.3[i]	48.8[i]

Total trade		Major trading partners			2013
	(million US$)	(% of exports)		(% of imports)	
Exports	2 428.3	Russian Federation	26.0	Russian Federation	14.3
Imports	5 492.4	Romania	16.9	Romania	13.1
Balance	−3 064.1	Italy	7.6	Ukraine	12.0

Social indicators		
Population growth rate (average annual %)[a]	2010-2015	−0.8
Urban population growth rate (average annual %)[a]	2010-2015	−0.7
Rural population growth rate (average annual %)[a]	2010-2015	−0.8
Urban population (%)[a]	2014	44.9
Population aged 0-14 years (%)[a]	2014	16.6
Population aged 60+ years (females and males, % of total)[a]	2014	20.2/15.0
Sex ratio (males per 100 females)[a]	2014	90.0
Life expectancy at birth (females and males, years)[a]	2010-2015	72.8/64.9
Infant mortality rate (per 1 000 live births)[a]	2010-2015	14.0
Fertility rate, total (live births per woman)[a]	2010-2015	1.5
Contraceptive prevalence (ages 15-49, %)	2007-2013	67.8[j]
International migrant stock (000 and % of total population)[a]	mid-2013	391.5/11.2
Refugees and others of concern to UNHCR	mid-2014	2 370
Education: Government expenditure (% of GDP)	2007-2013	8.4
Education: Primary-secondary gross enrolment ratio (f/m per 100)[k]	2007-2013	90.5/89.8
Education: Female third-level students (% of total)	2007-2013	55.5
Intentional homicide rate (per 100,000 population)	2008-2012	6.5
Seats held by women in national parliaments (%)	2015	20.8

Environmental indicators		
Threatened species	2014	29
Forested area (% of land area)	2012	12.0
Proportion of terrestrial and marine areas protected (%)	2014	3.8
Population using improved drinking water sources (%)	2012	97.0
Population using improved sanitation facilities (%)	2012	87.0
CO_2 emission estimates (000 metric tons and metric tons per capita)	2011	4 980/1.4
Energy supply per capita (Gigajoules)	2012	24.0

a Including Transnistria. **b** Official rate. **c** Index base 2005=100. **d** Series replacing former series. **e** Excluding the Transnistria region and Bender. **f** Break in series. **g** 2012. **h** Excluding the left side of the river Nistru and the municipality of Bender. **i** ITU estimate. **j** 2005. **k** National estimate.

Réunion

Region	Eastern Africa	Surface area (sq km)	2 513
Population (est., 000)	885	Pop. density (per sq km)	352.7
Capital city	Saint-Denis	Capital city pop. (000)	144
Currency	Euro (EUR)		

Economic indicators	2005	2010	2013
Exchange rates (national currency per US$)[a]	0.84	0.76	0.72
CPI: Consumer price index (2000=100)	110	121	126
Agricultural production index (2004-2006=100)	99	104	107
Food production index (2004-2006=100)	99	104	107
Unemployment (% of labour force)	30.1	28.9	29.0
Employment in industrial sector (% of employed)	...	14.1[bc]	13.1[bcd]
Employment in agricultural sector (% of employed)	...	4.2[bc]	3.9[bcd]
Labour force participation, adult female pop. (%)	51.1	51.9	51.7
Labour force participation, adult male pop. (%)	64.9	64.4	64.0
Tourist arrivals at national borders (000)	409	420	416
Energy production, primary (Petajoules)	6	8	8[d]

Social indicators		
Population growth rate (average annual %)	2010-2015	1.2
Urban population growth rate (average annual %)	2010-2015	1.4
Rural population growth rate (average annual %)	2010-2015	−2.5
Urban population (%)	2014	94.8
Population aged 0-14 years (%)	2014	24.9
Population aged 60+ years (females and males, % of total)	2014	14.1/11.8
Sex ratio (males per 100 females)	2014	96.2
Life expectancy at birth (females and males, years)	2010-2015	82.9/76.0
Infant mortality rate (per 1 000 live births)	2010-2015	4.2
Fertility rate, total (live births per woman)	2010-2015	2.2
Contraceptive prevalence (ages 15-49, %)[e]	2007-2013	66.6[f]
International migrant stock (000 and % of total population)	mid-2013	136.5/15.6
Intentional homicide rate (per 100,000 population)	2008-2012	1.8

Environmental indicators		
Threatened species	2014	126
Forested area (% of land area)	2012	35.7
Proportion of terrestrial and marine areas protected (%)	2014	23.5
CO_2 emission estimates (000 metric tons and metric tons per capita)	2011	4 510/5.3
Energy supply per capita (Gigajoules)	2012	70.0

a UN operational exchange rate. b March to June. c Excluding institutional population. d 2012. e Age group 20 to 44 years. f 1997.

Romania

Region	Eastern Europe	Surface area (sq km)	238 391	
Population (est., 000)	21 640	Pop. density (per sq km)	90.8	
Capital city	Bucharest	Capital city pop. (000)	1 872	
Currency	Romanian Leu (RON)	UN membership date	14 December 1955	

Economic indicators	2005	2010	2013
GDP: Gross domestic product (million current US$)	99 699	167 998	192 094
GDP: Growth rate at constant 2005 prices (annual %)	4.2	−0.8	3.5
GDP per capita (current US$)	4 508.6	7 684.7	8 852.8
GNI: Gross national income per capita (current US$)	4 376.1	7 590.5	8 632.6
Gross fixed capital formation (% of GDP)	24.3	26.0	24.7
Exchange rates (national currency per US$)[a]	3.11	3.20	3.26
Balance of payments, current account (million US$)	−8 504	−7 258	−1 780
CPI: Consumer price index (2000=100)[b]	232	313	355
Index of industrial production (2010=100)[c]	81	100	119
Agricultural production index (2004-2006=100)	95	91	97
Food production index (2004-2006=100)	95	91	97
Unemployment (% of labour force)	7.2	7.3	7.3
Employment in industrial sector (% of employed)	30.3[d]	28.7	28.6[e]
Employment in agricultural sector (% of employed)	32.1[d]	30.1	29.0[e]
Labour force participation, adult female pop. (%)	48.0	48.2	48.7
Labour force participation, adult male pop. (%)	62.5	64.5	64.9
Tourist arrivals at national borders (000)[f]	5 839	7 498	8 019
Energy production, primary (Petajoules)	1 173	1 155	1 142[e]
Mobile-cellular subscriptions (per 100 inhabitants)	60.4	111.4	105.6
Individuals using the Internet (%)	21.5[g]	39.9	49.8

Total trade		Major trading partners			2013
	(million US$)		(% of exports)		(% of imports)
Exports	65 881.4	Germany	18.5	Germany	18.6
Imports	73 452.2	Italy	11.5	Italy	11.0
Balance	−7 570.8	France	6.8	Hungary	8.2

Social indicators		
Population growth rate (average annual %)	2010-2015	−0.3
Urban population growth rate (average annual %)	2010-2015	<
Rural population growth rate (average annual %)	2010-2015	−0.6
Urban population (%)	2014	54.4
Population aged 0-14 years (%)	2014	15.1
Population aged 60+ years (females and males, % of total)	2014	24.2/18.4
Sex ratio (males per 100 females)	2014	94.9
Life expectancy at birth (females and males, years)	2010-2015	77.4/70.2
Infant mortality rate (per 1 000 live births)	2010-2015	10.5
Fertility rate, total (live births per woman)	2010-2015	1.4
Contraceptive prevalence (ages 15-49, %)[h]	2007-2013	69.8[i]
International migrant stock (000 and % of total population)	mid-2013	198.8/0.9
Refugees and others of concern to UNHCR	mid-2014	2 716
Education: Government expenditure (% of GDP)	2007-2013	3.1
Education: Primary-secondary gross enrolment ratio (f/m per 100)	2007-2013	94.0/95.5
Education: Female third-level students (% of total)	2007-2013	56.0
Intentional homicide rate (per 100,000 population)	2008-2012	1.7
Seats held by women in national parliaments (%)	2015	13.7

Environmental indicators		
Threatened species	2014	87
Forested area (% of land area)	2012	28.9
Proportion of terrestrial and marine areas protected (%)	2014	22.1
CO_2 emission estimates (000 metric tons and metric tons per capita)	2011	84 832/3.9
Energy supply per capita (Gigajoules)	2012	68.0

a Principal rate. **b** Annual average is the weighted mean of monthly data. **c** ISIC Rev.4 (BCD). **d** ISIC Rev. 3. **e** 2012. **f** Arrivals of non-resident visitors at national borders. **g** ITU estimate. **h** Age group 18 to 49 years. **i** 2005.

Russian Federation

Region	Eastern Europe	Surface area (sq km)	17 098 246
Population (est., 000)	142 468	Pop. density (per sq km)	8.3
Capital city	Moscow	Capital city pop. (000)	12 063
Currency	Russian Rouble (RUB)	UN membership date	24 October 1945

Economic indicators	2005	2010	2013
GDP: Gross domestic product (million current US$)	764 016	1 524 917	2 096 774
GDP: Growth rate at constant 2005 prices (annual %)	6.4	4.5	1.3
GDP per capita (current US$)	5 308.1	10 617.9	14 679.8
GNI: Gross national income per capita (current US$)	5 157.2	10 279.0	14 118.8
Gross fixed capital formation (% of GDP)	18.0	21.6	21.5
Exchange rates (national currency per US$)[a]	28.78	30.48	32.73
Balance of payments, current account (million US$)	84 389	67 452	34 141
CPI: Consumer price index (2000=100)	200	325	396
Index of industrial production (2010=100)[b]	91	100	109
Agricultural production index (2004-2006=100)	100	94	117
Food production index (2004-2006=100)	100	94	117
Unemployment (% of labour force)	7.1	7.3	5.6
Employment in industrial sector (% of employed)	29.8[cd]	27.9[cdef]	...
Employment in agricultural sector (% of employed)	10.2[cd]	9.7[cdef]	...
Labour force participation, adult female pop. (%)	56.2	56.4	57.1
Labour force participation, adult male pop. (%)	68.7	70.8	71.7
Tourist arrivals at national borders (000)[g]	22 201	22 281	30 792
Energy production, primary (Petajoules)	50 506	54 277	55 898[h]
Mobile-cellular subscriptions (per 100 inhabitants)	83.4	165.5	152.8
Individuals using the Internet (%)	15.2	43.0	61.4[d]

Total trade		Major trading partners			2013
	(million US$)	(% of exports)			(% of imports)
Exports	527 265.9	Netherlands	13.1	China	16.9
Imports	314 945.1	Areas nes	12.8[i]	Germany	12.0
Balance	212 320.8	China	6.8	United States	5.3

Social indicators		
Population growth rate (average annual %)	2010-2015	−0.2
Urban population growth rate (average annual %)	2010-2015	−0.1
Rural population growth rate (average annual %)	2010-2015	−0.5
Urban population (%)	2014	73.9
Population aged 0-14 years (%)	2014	16.1
Population aged 60+ years (females and males, % of total)	2014	23.5/14.6
Sex ratio (males per 100 females)	2014	85.6
Life expectancy at birth (females and males, years)	2010-2015	74.3/61.7
Infant mortality rate (per 1 000 live births)	2010-2015	9.7
Fertility rate, total (live births per woman)	2010-2015	1.5
Contraceptive prevalence (ages 15-49, %)[j]	2007-2013	68.0
International migrant stock (000 and % of total population)	mid-2013	11 048.1/7.7
Refugees and others of concern to UNHCR	mid-2014	204 082
Education: Government expenditure (% of GDP)	2007-2013	4.1
Education: Primary-secondary gross enrolment ratio (f/m per 100)	2007-2013	96.6/97.8
Education: Female third-level students (% of total)	2007-2013	55.0
Intentional homicide rate (per 100,000 population)	2008-2012	9.2
Seats held by women in national parliaments (%)	2015	13.6

Environmental indicators		
Threatened species	2014	217
Forested area (% of land area)	2012	49.4
Proportion of terrestrial and marine areas protected (%)	2014	8.8
Population using improved drinking water sources (%)	2012	97.0
Population using improved sanitation facilities (%)	2012	70.0
CO_2 emission estimates (000 metric tons and metric tons per capita)	2011	1 808 073/12.6
Energy supply per capita (Gigajoules)	2012	222.0

a Official rate. b ISIC Rev.3 (CDE). c ISIC Rev.3. d Population aged 15-72. e 2009. f Break in series. g Arrivals of non-resident visitors at national borders. h 2012. i See technical notes. j Age group 15 to 44 years.

Rwanda

Region	Eastern Africa		Surface area (sq km)	26 338
Population (est., 000)	12 100		Pop. density (per sq km)	459.4
Capital city	Kigali		Capital city pop. (000)	1 223
Currency	Rwanda Franc (RWF)		UN membership date	18 September 1962

Economic indicators	2005	2010	2013
GDP: Gross domestic product (million current US$)	2 581	5 699	7 601
GDP: Growth rate at constant 2005 prices (annual %)	9.4	6.3	4.7
GDP per capita (current US$)	273.7	525.9	645.4
GNI: Gross national income per capita (current US$)	270.9	514.8	635.5
Gross fixed capital formation (% of GDP)	17.0	22.2	25.3
Exchange rates (national currency per US$)[a]	553.72	594.45	670.08
Balance of payments, current account (million US$)	−65	−414	−562
CPI: Consumer price index (2000=100)[b]	138	214	240[c]
Agricultural production index (2004-2006=100)	100	145	170
Food production index (2004-2006=100)	101	146	172
Unemployment (% of labour force)	0.6	0.6	0.6
Employment in industrial sector (% of employed)	3.8[d]	...	...
Employment in agricultural sector (% of employed)	78.8[d]	...	...
Labour force participation, adult female pop. (%)	85.7	86.7	86.4
Labour force participation, adult male pop. (%)	83.9	85.6	85.3
Tourist arrivals at national borders (000)	494[e]	504	864
Energy production, primary (Petajoules)	63	76	81[cf]
Mobile-cellular subscriptions (per 100 inhabitants)	2.4	32.8	56.8
Individuals using the Internet (%)[g]	0.6	8.0	8.7

Total trade		Major trading partners			2013
	(million US$)	(% of exports)			(% of imports)
Exports	620.5	United Rep. Tanzania	41.2	China	15.7
Imports	1 701.4	Dem. Rep. of Congo	21.7	Uganda	11.7
Balance	−1 080.9	Uganda	14.0	Japan	10.5

Social indicators		
Population growth rate (average annual %)	2010-2015	2.7
Urban population growth rate (average annual %)	2010-2015	6.4
Rural population growth rate (average annual %)	2010-2015	1.4
Urban population (%)	2014	27.8
Population aged 0-14 years (%)	2014	42.1
Population aged 60+ years (females and males, % of total)	2014	4.5/3.8
Sex ratio (males per 100 females)	2014	95.5
Life expectancy at birth (females and males, years)	2010-2015	65.3/61.9
Infant mortality rate (per 1 000 live births)	2010-2015	49.8
Fertility rate, total (live births per woman)	2010-2015	4.6
Contraceptive prevalence (ages 15-49, %)	2007-2013	51.6
International migrant stock (000 and % of total population)[h]	mid-2013	452.4/3.8
Refugees and others of concern to UNHCR	mid-2014	76 191
Education: Government expenditure (% of GDP)	2007-2013	5.1
Education: Primary-secondary gross enrolment ratio (f/m per 100)	2007-2013	84.5/82.1
Education: Female third-level students (% of total)	2007-2013	44.9
Intentional homicide rate (per 100,000 population)	2008-2012	23.1
Seats held by women in national parliaments (%)	2015	63.8

Environmental indicators		
Threatened species	2014	61
Forested area (% of land area)	2012	18.4
Proportion of terrestrial and marine areas protected (%)	2014	9.4
Population using improved drinking water sources (%)	2012	71.0
Population using improved sanitation facilities (%)	2012	64.0
CO_2 emission estimates (000 metric tons and metric tons per capita)	2011	664/0.1
Energy supply per capita (Gigajoules)	2012	8.0[f]

a Official rate. b Kigali. c 2012. d ISIC Rev.3. e 2006. f UNSD estimate. g ITU estimate. h Including refugees.

Saint Helena

Region	Western Africa	Surface area (sq km)	122	
Population (est., 000)	4 [a]	Pop. density (per sq km)	33.8 [a]	
Capital city	Jamestown	Capital city pop. (000)	1	
Currency	St.Helena Pound (SHP)			

Economic indicators	2005	2010	2013
Exchange rates (national currency per US$) [b]	0.58	0.65	0.60
CPI: Consumer price index (2000=100)	116	155 [c]	176
Employment in industrial sector (% of employed)	...	20.0 [defgh]	...
Employment in agricultural sector (% of employed)	...	7.3 [defgh]	...
Energy production, primary (Petajoules)	0	0	0 [i]
Individuals using the Internet (%)	15.9	24.9	37.6 [ij]

Social indicators		
Population growth rate (average annual %) [a]	2010-2015	−0.6
Urban population growth rate (average annual %) [a]	2010-2015	−0.6
Rural population growth rate (average annual %) [a]	2010-2015	−0.6
Urban population (%) [a]	2014	39.4
International migrant stock (000 and % of total population) [a]	mid-2013	0.6/14.3

Environmental indicators		
Threatened species [a]	2014	80
Forested area (% of land area) [a]	2012	5.1
CO$_2$ emission estimates (000 metric tons and metric tons per capita)	2011	11/2.9
Energy supply per capita (Gigajoules)	2012	42.0

a Including Ascension and Tristan da Cunha. b UN operational exchange rate. c Series linked to former series. d 2008. e Population census. f ISIC Rev.3. g Population aged 15-69. h March. i 2012. j ITU estimate.

Saint Kitts and Nevis

Region	Caribbean	Surface area (sq km)	261
Population (est., 000)	55	Pop. density (per sq km)	209.9
Capital city	Basseterre	Capital city pop. (000)	14
Currency	E.C. Dollar (XCD)	UN membership date	23 September 1983

Economic indicators	2005	2010	2013
GDP: Gross domestic product (million current US$)	546	717	743
GDP: Growth rate at constant 2005 prices (annual %)	9.9	−2.4	2.0
GDP per capita (current US$)	11 108.7	13 695.5	13 710.1
GNI: Gross national income per capita (current US$)	10 393.6	13 138.0	13 361.5
Gross fixed capital formation (% of GDP)	42.0	33.0	29.1
Exchange rates (national currency per US$)[a]	2.70	2.70	2.70
Balance of payments, current account (million US$)	−65	−139	−63
CPI: Consumer price index (2000=100)[b]	111	136	148
Agricultural production index (2004-2006=100)	91	34	42
Food production index (2004-2006=100)	91	34	42
Tourist arrivals at national borders (000)[c]	141	98	107
Energy production, primary (Petajoules)	1	...	...
Mobile-cellular subscriptions (per 100 inhabitants)	103.8[d]	152.8	142.1[e]
Individuals using the Internet (%)[e]	34.0	76.0	80.0

Total trade		Major trading partners			2013
	(million US$)[f]	(% of exports)[f]		(% of imports)[f]	
Exports	44.9	United States	81.7	United States	67.3
Imports	246.7	Antigua and Barbuda	3.1	Trinidad and Tobago	6.3
Balance	−201.8	Trinidad and Tobago	2.7	United Kingdom	4.1

Social indicators		
Population growth rate (average annual %)	2010-2015	1.1
Urban population growth rate (average annual %)	2010-2015	1.3
Rural population growth rate (average annual %)	2010-2015	1.1
Urban population (%)	2014	32.0
Life expectancy at birth (females and males, years)[g]	2010-2015	70.7/68.2[h]
Contraceptive prevalence (ages 15-49, %)[i]	2007-2013	40.6[j]
International migrant stock (000 and % of total population)	mid-2013	5.7/10.5
Refugees and others of concern to UNHCR	mid-2014	2
Education: Government expenditure (% of GDP)	2007-2013	4.2
Education: Primary-secondary gross enrolment ratio (f/m per 100)	2007-2013	95.9/87.3
Education: Female third-level students (% of total)	2007-2013	67.3
Intentional homicide rate (per 100,000 population)	2008-2012	33.6
Seats held by women in national parliaments (%)	2015	6.7

Environmental indicators		
Threatened species	2014	44
Forested area (% of land area)	2012	42.3
Proportion of terrestrial and marine areas protected (%)	2014	0.3
Population using improved drinking water sources (%)	2012	98.0
CO_2 emission estimates (000 metric tons and metric tons per capita)	2011	268/5.1
Energy supply per capita (Gigajoules)	2012	73.0[k]

a Official rate. **b** Index base 2001=100. **c** Arrivals of non-resident tourists by air. **d** December. **e** ITU estimate. **f** 2011. **g** Data compiled by the United Nations Demographic Yearbook system. **h** 1998. **i** Age group 15 to 44 years. **j** 1984. **k** UNSD estimate.

Saint Lucia

Region	Caribbean	Surface area (sq km)	539 [a]
Population (est., 000)	184	Pop. density (per sq km)	340.6
Capital city	Castries	Capital city pop. (000)	22
Currency	E.C. Dollar (XCD)	UN membership date	18 September 1979

Economic indicators	2005	2010	2013
GDP: Gross domestic product (million current US$)	937	1 252	1 336
GDP: Growth rate at constant 2005 prices (annual %)	−1.3	0.2	−3.3
GDP per capita (current US$)	5 661.9	7 059.6	7 328.4
GNI: Gross national income per capita (current US$)	5 030.0	6 538.8	6 600.0
Gross fixed capital formation (% of GDP)	28.8	27.8	23.3
Exchange rates (national currency per US$) [b]	2.70	2.70	2.70
Balance of payments, current account (million US$)	−129	−203	−100
CPI: Consumer price index (2000=100)	112	128	139
Agricultural production index (2004-2006=100)	89	91	94
Food production index (2004-2006=100)	89	91	94
Employment in industrial sector (% of employed)	16.1 [cde]	...	...
Employment in agricultural sector (% of employed)	14.8 [cd]	...	...
Labour force participation, adult female pop. (%)	63.1	62.4	62.7
Labour force participation, adult male pop. (%)	77.6	75.9	76.2
Tourist arrivals at national borders (000) [f]	318	306	319
Energy production, primary (Petajoules)	0	0	0 [g]
Mobile-cellular subscriptions (per 100 inhabitants)	63.9	111.7	116.3
Individuals using the Internet (%)	21.6	43.3	35.2 [h]

Social indicators		
Population growth rate (average annual %)	2010-2015	0.8
Urban population growth rate (average annual %)	2010-2015	0.9
Rural population growth rate (average annual %)	2010-2015	0.8
Urban population (%)	2014	18.5
Population aged 0-14 years (%)	2014	23.6
Population aged 60+ years (females and males, % of total)	2014	13.0/11.6
Sex ratio (males per 100 females)	2014	96.4
Life expectancy at birth (females and males, years)	2010-2015	77.4/72.1
Infant mortality rate (per 1 000 live births)	2010-2015	10.5
Fertility rate, total (live births per woman)	2010-2015	1.9
Contraceptive prevalence (ages 15-49, %) [i]	2007-2013	47.3 [j]
International migrant stock (000 and % of total population)	mid-2013	12.2/6.7
Refugees and others of concern to UNHCR	mid-2014	5
Education: Government expenditure (% of GDP)	2007-2013	4.7
Education: Primary-secondary gross enrolment ratio (f/m per 100)	2007-2013	95.5/94.3
Education: Female third-level students (% of total)	2007-2013	66.4
Intentional homicide rate (per 100,000 population)	2008-2012	21.6
Seats held by women in national parliaments (%)	2015	16.7

Environmental indicators		
Threatened species	2014	52
Forested area (% of land area)	2012	77.1
Proportion of terrestrial and marine areas protected (%)	2014	0.7
Population using improved drinking water sources (%)	2012	94.0
Population using improved sanitation facilities (%)	2012	65.0 [k]
CO$_2$ emission estimates (000 metric tons and metric tons per capita)	2011	407/2.3
Energy supply per capita (Gigajoules)	2012	33.0

a Refers to habitable area. Excluding St. Lucia's Forest Reserve. **b** Official rate. **c** 2004. **d** ISIC Rev.3. **e** Excluding mining and quarrying. **f** Excluding nationals residing abroad. **g** 2012. **h** ITU estimate. **i** Age group 15 to 44 years. **j** 1988. **k** 2010.

Saint Pierre and Miquelon

Region	Northern America	Surface area (sq km)	242
Population (est., 000)	6	Pop. density (per sq km)	25.0
Capital city	Saint-Pierre	Capital city pop. (000)	5

Economic indicators	2005	2010	2013
CPI: Consumer price index (2000=100)	114	...	...
Agricultural production index (2004-2006=100)	92	109	110
Food production index (2004-2006=100)	92	109	110
Energy production, primary (Petajoules)	0[a]	0	0[b]

Social indicators		
Population growth rate (average annual %)	2010-2015	<
Urban population growth rate (average annual %)	2010-2015	0.1
Rural population growth rate (average annual %)	2010-2015	−0.9
Urban population (%)	2014	90.3
Population aged 0-14 years (%)[cde]	2014	19.1[f]
Population aged 60+ years (females and males, % of total)[cde]	2014	20.7/14.8[f]
Sex ratio (males per 100 females)[cde]	2014	98.2[f]
International migrant stock (000 and % of total population)	mid-2013	1.0/16.1
Intentional homicide rate (per 100,000 population)	2008-2012	16.5

Environmental indicators		
Threatened species	2014	7
Forested area (% of land area)	2012	12.4
CO$_2$ emission estimates (000 metric tons and metric tons per capita)	2011	70/11.7
Energy supply per capita (Gigajoules)	2012	164.0[a]

a UNSD estimate. b 2012. c Data compiled by the United Nations Demographic Yearbook system. d Data refer to the latest available census. e Census, de facto, complete tabulation. f 2006.

Saint Vincent and the Grenadines

Region	Caribbean	Surface area (sq km)	389
Population (est., 000)	109	Pop. density (per sq km)	281.9
Capital city	Kingstown	Capital city pop. (000)	27
Currency	E.C. Dollar (XCD)	UN membership date	16 September 1980

Economic indicators	2005	2010	2013
GDP: Gross domestic product (million current US$)	551	681	709
GDP: Growth rate at constant 2005 prices (annual %)	2.5	−3.4	1.6
GDP per capita (current US$)	5 064.2	6 233.7	6 484.2
GNI: Gross national income per capita (current US$)	4 792.0	6 119.4	6 450.2
Gross fixed capital formation (% of GDP)	25.1	25.2	25.2
Exchange rates (national currency per US$)[a]	2.70	2.70	2.70
Balance of payments, current account (million US$)	−102	−208	−210
CPI: Consumer price index (2000=100)[b]	109	135	155
Agricultural production index (2004-2006=100)	104	120	119
Food production index (2004-2006=100)	104	120	119
Labour force participation, adult female pop. (%)	53.3	55.5	55.7
Labour force participation, adult male pop. (%)	79.1	78.5	78.0
Tourist arrivals at national borders (000)[c]	96	72	72
Energy production, primary (Petajoules)	0	0[d]	0[de]
Mobile-cellular subscriptions (per 100 inhabitants)	64.9	120.6	114.6
Individuals using the Internet (%)	9.2	38.5[f]	52.0[f]

Total trade		Major trading partners			2013
	(million US$)[e]	(% of exports)[e]		(% of imports)[e]	
Exports	43.0	Saint Lucia	25.6	United States	35.6
Imports	403.2	Trinidad and Tobago	15.8	Trinidad and Tobago	26.8
Balance	−360.2	Barbados	14.4	Venezuela	5.6

Social indicators		
Population growth rate (average annual %)	2010-2015	<
Urban population growth rate (average annual %)	2010-2015	0.7
Rural population growth rate (average annual %)	2010-2015	−0.7
Urban population (%)	2014	50.2
Population aged 0-14 years (%)	2014	24.9
Population aged 60+ years (females and males, % of total)	2014	11.3/9.8
Sex ratio (males per 100 females)	2014	101.9
Life expectancy at birth (females and males, years)	2010-2015	74.7/70.3
Infant mortality rate (per 1 000 live births)	2010-2015	17.0
Fertility rate, total (live births per woman)	2010-2015	2.0
Contraceptive prevalence (ages 15-49, %)[g]	2007-2013	58.3[h]
International migrant stock (000 and % of total population)	mid-2013	10.3/9.4
Refugees and others of concern to UNHCR	mid-2014	0[i]
Education: Government expenditure (% of GDP)	2007-2013	5.1
Education: Primary-secondary gross enrolment ratio (f/m per 100)	2007-2013	101.6/106.8
Intentional homicide rate (per 100,000 population)	2008-2012	25.6
Seats held by women in national parliaments (%)	2015	13.0

Environmental indicators		
Threatened species	2014	48
Forested area (% of land area)	2012	68.9
Proportion of terrestrial and marine areas protected (%)	2014	0.5
Population using improved drinking water sources (%)	2012	95.0
CO_2 emission estimates (000 metric tons and metric tons per capita)	2011	238/2.2
Energy supply per capita (Gigajoules)	2012	33.0[d]

a Official rate. b St. Vincent. c Arrivals of non-resident tourists by air. d UNSD estimate. e 2012. f ITU estimate. g Age group 15 to 44 years. h 1988. i Value is zero, not available or not applicable.

Samoa

Region	Oceania-Polynesia	Surface area (sq km)	2 842	
Population (est., 000)	192	Pop. density (per sq km)	67.8	
Capital city	Apia	Capital city pop. (000)	37	
Currency	Tala (WST)	UN membership date	15 December 1976	

Economic indicators	2005	2010	2013
GDP: Gross domestic product (million current US$)	434	597	691
GDP: Growth rate at constant 2005 prices (annual %)	5.1	2.1	1.0
GDP per capita (current US$)	2 413.5	3 211.2	3 632.1
GNI: Gross national income per capita (current US$)	2 272.9	3 122.0	3 478.7
Gross fixed capital formation (% of GDP)	10.4	9.0	9.0
Exchange rates (national currency per US$) [a]	2.76	2.34	2.34
Balance of payments, current account (million US$)	−47	−43	−46
CPI: Consumer price index (2000=100) [b]	133	174	189
Agricultural production index (2004-2006=100)	102	106	110
Food production index (2004-2006=100)	102	106	110
Labour force participation, adult female pop. (%)	28.3	24.1	23.5
Labour force participation, adult male pop. (%)	69.2	60.5	58.4
Tourist arrivals at national borders (000)	102	122	116
Energy production, primary (Petajoules)	1	1	1[c]
Mobile-cellular subscriptions (per 100 inhabitants)	13.3	...	...
Individuals using the Internet (%)	3.4	7.0[d]	15.3[d]

Total trade		Major trading partners			2013
	(million US$)		(% of exports)		(% of imports)
Exports	62.1	Australia	45.4	New Zealand	29.9
Imports	366.6	Areas nes	24.0[e]	Singapore	22.8
Balance	−304.5	American Samoa	9.0	United States	12.4

Social indicators		
Population growth rate (average annual %)	2010-2015	0.8
Urban population growth rate (average annual %)	2010-2015	−0.2
Rural population growth rate (average annual %)	2010-2015	1.0
Urban population (%)	2014	19.3
Population aged 0-14 years (%)	2014	37.5
Population aged 60+ years (females and males, % of total)	2014	8.7/6.8
Sex ratio (males per 100 females)	2014	106.5
Life expectancy at birth (females and males, years)	2010-2015	76.4/70.0
Infant mortality rate (per 1 000 live births)	2010-2015	19.7
Fertility rate, total (live births per woman)	2010-2015	4.2
Contraceptive prevalence (ages 15-49, %)	2007-2013	28.7
International migrant stock (000 and % of total population)	mid-2013	5.6/3.0
Education: Government expenditure (% of GDP)	2007-2013	5.8
Education: Primary-secondary gross enrolment ratio (f/m per 100)	2007-2013	97.6/93.0
Education: Female third-level students (% of total)	2007-2013	44.3[f]
Intentional homicide rate (per 100,000 population)	2008-2012	3.6
Seats held by women in national parliaments (%)	2015	6.1

Environmental indicators		
Threatened species	2014	90
Forested area (% of land area)	2012	60.4
Proportion of terrestrial and marine areas protected (%)	2014	0.2
Population using improved drinking water sources (%)	2012	99.0
Population using improved sanitation facilities (%)	2012	92.0
CO$_2$ emission estimates (000 metric tons and metric tons per capita)	2011	235/1.3
Energy supply per capita (Gigajoules)	2012	23.0[g]

a Official rate. **b** Excluding rent. **c** 2012. **d** ITU estimate. **e** See technical notes. **f** 2000. **g** UNSD estimate.

San Marino

Region	Southern Europe	Surface area (sq km)	61
Population (est., 000)	32	Pop. density (per sq km)	518.6
Capital city	San Marino	Capital city pop. (000)	4
Currency	Euro (EUR)	UN membership date	2 March 1992

Economic indicators	2005	2010	2013
GDP: Gross domestic product (million current US$)	2 027	2 139	1 802
GDP: Growth rate at constant 2005 prices (annual %)	2.3	−4.7	−4.5
GDP per capita (current US$)	68 091.7	69 321.9	57 292.8
GNI: Gross national income per capita (current US$)	59 718.7	60 629.5	48 987.3
Gross fixed capital formation (% of GDP)	33.1	23.8	22.6
Exchange rates (national currency per US$)[a]	0.85	0.75	0.73
CPI: Consumer price index (2000=100)[b]	103	118	127
Employment in industrial sector (% of employed)	39.3[cde]	36.9[cdef]	...
Employment in agricultural sector (% of employed)	0.5[cd]	0.3[cdf]	...
Tourist arrivals at national borders (000)[gh]	50	120	70
Mobile-cellular subscriptions (per 100 inhabitants)	57.6	99.1	117.0
Individuals using the Internet (%)	50.3	49.6[i]	50.8[j]

Social indicators		
Population growth rate (average annual %)	2010-2015	0.6
Urban population growth rate (average annual %)	2010-2015	0.6
Rural population growth rate (average annual %)	2010-2015	0.3
Urban population (%)	2014	94.2
Population aged 0-14 years (%)[klm]	2014	15.2[n]
Population aged 60+ years (females and males, % of total)[klm]	2014	23.2/19.7[n]
Sex ratio (males per 100 females)[klm]	2014	96.2[n]
Life expectancy at birth (females and males, years)[k]	2010-2015	84.6/78.0[o]
International migrant stock (000 and % of total population)[p]	mid-2013	4.9/15.4
Education: Primary-secondary gross enrolment ratio (f/m per 100)[q]	2007-2013	93.9/93.6
Education: Female third-level students (% of total)	2007-2013	56.4
Intentional homicide rate (per 100,000 population)	2008-2012	0.7
Seats held by women in national parliaments (%)	2015	16.7

Environmental indicators		
Threatened species	2014	1

a Market rate. **b** Index base 2003=100. **c** ISIC Rev.3. **d** December. **e** Refers to manufacturing and construction only. **f** 2008. **g** Arrivals of non-resident tourists in hotels and similar establishments. **h** Including Italian tourists. **i** 2011. **j** ITU estimate. **k** Data compiled by the United Nations Demographic Yearbook system. **l** Data refer to the latest available census. **m** De facto estimate. **n** 2004. **o** 2000. **p** Refers to foreign citizens. **q** National estimate.

Sao Tome and Principe

Region	Middle Africa	Surface area (sq km)	964
Population (est., 000)	198	Pop. density (per sq km)	205.3
Capital city	São Tomé	Capital city pop. (000)	71
Currency	Dobra (STD)	UN membership date	16 September 1975

Economic indicators

	2005	2010	2013
GDP: Gross domestic product (million current US$)	125	217	342
GDP: Growth rate at constant 2005 prices (annual %)	1.6	4.6	4.3
GDP per capita (current US$)	807.0	1 216.3	1 769.6
GNI: Gross national income per capita (current US$)	792.9	1 214.1	1 764.6
Gross fixed capital formation (% of GDP)	26.5	21.8	31.6
Exchange rates (national currency per US$)[a]	11 929.70	18 335.60	17 765.20
Balance of payments, current account (million US$)	−36	−88	−80
CPI: Consumer price index (2000=100)[b]	561	1 432	1 958
Agricultural production index (2004-2006=100)	100	102	111
Food production index (2004-2006=100)	100	102	111
Labour force participation, adult female pop. (%)	41.2	44.0	45.3
Labour force participation, adult male pop. (%)	74.9	76.7	77.8
Tourist arrivals at national borders (000)	16	8	...
Energy production, primary (Petajoules)	1	1	1[c]
Mobile-cellular subscriptions (per 100 inhabitants)	7.7	57.6	64.9
Individuals using the Internet (%)	13.8[d]	18.8	23.0[d]

Total trade

		Major trading partners			2013
	(million US$)		(% of exports)		(% of imports)
Exports	6.9	Netherlands	29.0	Portugal	59.2
Imports	152.1	Belgium	20.3	Angola	24.9
Balance	−145.2	France	11.6	United States	2.1

Social indicators

Population growth rate (average annual %)	2010-2015	2.6
Urban population growth rate (average annual %)	2010-2015	3.6
Rural population growth rate (average annual %)	2010-2015	0.8
Urban population (%)	2014	64.5
Population aged 0-14 years (%)	2014	41.5
Population aged 60+ years (females and males, % of total)	2014	5.2/4.2
Sex ratio (males per 100 females)	2014	97.6
Life expectancy at birth (females and males, years)	2010-2015	68.2/64.2
Infant mortality rate (per 1 000 live births)	2010-2015	43.5
Fertility rate, total (live births per woman)	2010-2015	4.1
Contraceptive prevalence (ages 15-49, %)	2007-2013	38.4
International migrant stock (000 and % of total population)[e]	mid-2013	6.3/3.3
Refugees and others of concern to UNHCR	mid-2014	0[f]
Education: Government expenditure (% of GDP)	2007-2013	9.5
Education: Primary-secondary gross enrolment ratio (f/m per 100)	2007-2013	102.9/101.2
Education: Female third-level students (% of total)	2007-2013	45.7
Intentional homicide rate (per 100,000 population)	2008-2012	3.3
Seats held by women in national parliaments (%)	2015	18.2

Environmental indicators

Threatened species	2014	81
Forested area (% of land area)	2012	28.1
Population using improved drinking water sources (%)	2012	97.0
Population using improved sanitation facilities (%)	2012	34.0
CO$_2$ emission estimates (000 metric tons and metric tons per capita)	2011	103/0.6
Energy supply per capita (Gigajoules)	2012	14.0[g]

a Official rate. b Index base 1996=100. c 2012. d ITU estimate. e Refers to foreign citizens. f Value is zero, not available or not applicable. g UNSD estimate.

Saudi Arabia

Region	Western Asia	Surface area (sq km)	2 206 714
Population (est., 000)	29 369	Pop. density (per sq km)	13.7
Capital city	Riyadh	Capital city pop. (000)	6 195
Currency	Saudi Riyal (SAR)	UN membership date	24 October 1945

Economic indicators	2005	2010	2013
GDP: Gross domestic product (million current US$)	328 461	526 811	748 450
GDP: Growth rate at constant 2005 prices (annual %)	7.3	7.4	4.0
GDP per capita (current US$)	13 303.4	19 326.6	25 961.8
GNI: Gross national income per capita (current US$)	13 413.3	19 585.0	25 961.8
Gross fixed capital formation (% of GDP)	19.3	24.5	23.2
Exchange rates (national currency per US$)[a]	3.74	3.75	3.75
Balance of payments, current account (million US$)	90 060	66 751	132 640
CPI: Consumer price index (2000=100)	100[b]	130[b]	135[cd]
Index of industrial production (2010=100)[e]	89	100	119
Agricultural production index (2004-2006=100)	100	108	107
Food production index (2004-2006=100)	100	108	108
Unemployment (% of labour force)	5.9	5.4	5.7
Employment in industrial sector (% of employed)[f]	20.3[g]	20.4[h]	24.7[i]
Employment in agricultural sector (% of employed)[f]	4.0[g]	4.1[h]	4.7[i]
Labour force participation, adult female pop. (%)	17.6	17.7	20.2
Labour force participation, adult male pop. (%)	74.1	75.1	78.3
Tourist arrivals at national borders (000)[j]	8 037	10 850	13 380
Energy production, primary (Petajoules)[j]	24 162	22 115	26 010[i]
Mobile-cellular subscriptions (per 100 inhabitants)	57.4	189.2	176.5
Individuals using the Internet (%)	12.7	41.0	60.5[k]

Total trade		Major trading partners			2013
	(million US$)	(% of exports)[l]			(% of imports)
Exports	375 396.6	Asia nes	53.3	United States	13.2
Imports	163 712.8	N & C Ame nes	14.4	China	12.8
Balance	211 683.8	Europe nes	10.1	Germany	7.2

Social indicators		
Population growth rate (average annual %)	2010-2015	1.9
Urban population growth rate (average annual %)	2010-2015	2.1
Rural population growth rate (average annual %)	2010-2015	0.7
Urban population (%)	2014	82.9
Population aged 0-14 years (%)	2014	28.6
Population aged 60+ years (females and males, % of total)	2014	5.8/4.7
Sex ratio (males per 100 females)	2014	137.3
Life expectancy at birth (females and males, years)	2010-2015	77.5/73.8
Infant mortality rate (per 1 000 live births)	2010-2015	11.2
Fertility rate, total (live births per woman)	2010-2015	2.7
Contraceptive prevalence (ages 15-49, %)	2007-2013	23.8
International migrant stock (000 and % of total population)[mn]	mid-2013	9 060.4/31.4
Refugees and others of concern to UNHCR	mid-2014	70 664
Education: Government expenditure (% of GDP)	2007-2013	5.1
Education: Primary-secondary gross enrolment ratio (f/m per 100)[o]	2007-2013	111.9/109.9
Education: Female third-level students (% of total)	2007-2013	47.9
Intentional homicide rate (per 100,000 population)	2008-2012	0.8
Seats held by women in national parliaments (%)	2015	19.9

Environmental indicators		
Threatened species	2014	116
Forested area (% of land area)	2012	<
Proportion of terrestrial and marine areas protected (%)	2014	28.2
Population using improved drinking water sources (%)	2012	97.0
Population using improved sanitation facilities (%)	2012	100.0
CO_2 emission estimates (000 metric tons and metric tons per capita)	2011	520 278/18.7
Energy supply per capita (Gigajoules)[j]	2012	294.0

a Official rate. b All cities. c Series linked to former series. d All cities. e ISIC Rev.3 (CDE). f ISIC Rev.3. g 2006. h 2009. i 2012. j Data for crude petroleum production include 50 per cent of the output of the Neutral Zone. k ITU estimate. l See technical notes. m Refers to foreign citizens. n Including refugees. o UNESCO estimate.

Senegal

Region	Western Africa	
Population (est., 000)	14 548	
Capital city	Dakar	
Currency	CFA Franc (XOF)	

Surface area (sq km)	196 712 [a]
Pop. density (per sq km)	74.0
Capital city pop. (000)	3 393
UN membership date	28 September 1960

Economic indicators	2005	2010	2013
GDP: Gross domestic product (million current US$)	8 708	12 926	15 152
GDP: Growth rate at constant 2005 prices (annual %)	5.6	4.2	2.4
GDP per capita (current US$)	772.6	998.1	1 072.1
GNI: Gross national income per capita (current US$)	767.8	988.4	988.5
Gross fixed capital formation (% of GDP)	23.3	22.2	24.8
Exchange rates (national currency per US$) [b]	556.04	490.91	475.64
Balance of payments, current account (million US$)	−676	−589	−1 147 [c]
CPI: Consumer price index (2000=100) [d]	108	122 [e]	129
Index of industrial production (2010=100) [f]	97	100	101
Agricultural production index (2004-2006=100)	110	151	126
Food production index (2004-2006=100)	110	152	126
Unemployment (% of labour force)	10.1	10.2	10.3
Employment in industrial sector (% of employed)	14.8 [gh]	...	...
Employment in agricultural sector (% of employed)	33.7 [gh]	...	...
Labour force participation, adult female pop. (%)	64.7	65.7	66.0
Labour force participation, adult male pop. (%)	87.9	87.9	88.0
Tourist arrivals at national borders (000)	769	900	1 063
Energy production, primary (Petajoules)	47	49	52 [i]
Mobile-cellular subscriptions (per 100 inhabitants)	15.4	64.4	92.9
Individuals using the Internet (%)	4.8	16.0 [j]	20.9 [k]

Total trade		Major trading partners			2013
	(million US$)		(% of exports)		(% of imports)
Exports	2 665.9	Mali	15.9	France	15.4
Imports	6 659.4	Bunkers	9.9 [l]	Nigeria	10.6
Balance	−3 993.5	Switzerland	8.8	Netherlands	8.4

Social indicators		
Population growth rate (average annual %)	2010-2015	2.9
Urban population growth rate (average annual %)	2010-2015	3.6
Rural population growth rate (average annual %)	2010-2015	2.4
Urban population (%)	2014	43.4
Population aged 0-14 years (%)	2014	43.4
Population aged 60+ years (females and males, % of total)	2014	5.0/4.0
Sex ratio (males per 100 females)	2014	96.4
Life expectancy at birth (females and males, years)	2010-2015	64.7/61.8
Infant mortality rate (per 1 000 live births)	2010-2015	49.3
Fertility rate, total (live births per woman)	2010-2015	5.0
Contraceptive prevalence (ages 15-49, %)	2007-2013	17.8
International migrant stock (000 and % of total population) [m]	mid-2013	209.4/1.5
Refugees and others of concern to UNHCR	mid-2014	17 085
Education: Government expenditure (% of GDP)	2007-2013	5.6
Education: Primary-secondary gross enrolment ratio (f/m per 100) [n]	2007-2013	62.8/62.1
Education: Female third-level students (% of total) [o]	2007-2013	37.3
Intentional homicide rate (per 100,000 population)	2008-2012	2.8
Seats held by women in national parliaments (%)	2015	42.7

Environmental indicators		
Threatened species	2014	107
Forested area (% of land area)	2012	43.6
Proportion of terrestrial and marine areas protected (%)	2014	14.5
Population using improved drinking water sources (%)	2012	74.0
Population using improved sanitation facilities (%)	2012	52.0
CO_2 emission estimates (000 metric tons and metric tons per capita)	2011	7 858/0.6
Energy supply per capita (Gigajoules)	2012	10.0

a Surface area is based on the 2002 population and housing census. **b** Official rate. **c** 2011. **d** Dakar. **e** Series linked to former series. **f** ISIC Rev.3 (CDE). **g** 2006. **h** ISIC Rev.3. **i** 2012. **j** Population aged 12 and over. **k** ITU estimate. **l** See technical notes. **m** Including refugees. **n** National estimate. **o** UNESCO estimate.

Serbia

Region	Southern Europe	Surface area (sq km)	88 361
Population (est., 000)	9 468[a]	Pop. density (per sq km)	107.2[a]
Capital city	Belgrade	Capital city pop. (000)	1 181[b]
Currency	Serbian Dinar (RSD)	UN membership date	1 November 2000

Economic indicators	2005	2010	2013
GDP: Gross domestic product (million current US$)	26 252	39 460	45 520
GDP: Growth rate at constant 2005 prices (annual %)	5.5	0.6	2.6
GDP per capita (current US$)	3 528.1	5 411.9	6 313.1
GNI: Gross national income per capita (current US$)	3 489.9	5 291.5	6 134.1
Gross fixed capital formation (% of GDP)	20.1	18.6	17.2
Exchange rates (national currency per US$)[c]	72.22	79.28	83.13
Balance of payments, current account (million US$)	−6 890[d]	−2 550	−2 790
CPI: Consumer price index (2000=100)	330	137[e]	153[ef]
Index of industrial production (2010=100)[g]	103	100	106
Agricultural production index (2004-2006=100)	...	103	105
Food production index (2004-2006=100)	...	103	105
Unemployment (% of labour force)	20.8	19.2	22.2
Employment in industrial sector (% of employed)	27.6[hi]	26.0[jk]	26.5[il]
Employment in agricultural sector (% of employed)	23.3[hi]	22.2[jk]	21.0[il]
Labour force participation, adult female pop. (%)	45.7	43.9	44.5
Labour force participation, adult male pop. (%)	64.2	60.4	60.9
Tourist arrivals at national borders (000)[m]	453	683	922
Energy production, primary (Petajoules)	431	441	450[l]
Mobile-cellular subscriptions (per 100 inhabitants)	67.0[n]	125.3[n]	119.4
Individuals using the Internet (%)	26.3[o]	40.9	51.5[o]

Total trade		Major trading partners			2013
	(million US$)	(% of exports)		(% of imports)	
Exports	14 610.8	Italy	16.3	Italy	11.5
Imports	20 551.0	Germany	11.9	Germany	11.0
Balance	−5 940.2	Bosnia-Herzegovina	8.2	Russian Federation	9.3

Social indicators		
Population growth rate (average annual %)[a]	2010-2015	−0.5
Urban population growth rate (average annual %)[a]	2010-2015	−0.3
Rural population growth rate (average annual %)[a]	2010-2015	−0.6
Urban population (%)[a]	2014	55.5
Population aged 0-14 years (%)[a]	2014	16.0
Population aged 60+ years (females and males, % of total)[a]	2014	23.8/19.3
Sex ratio (males per 100 females)[a]	2014	95.6
Life expectancy at birth (females and males, years)[a]	2010-2015	76.8/71.2
Infant mortality rate (per 1 000 live births)[a]	2010-2015	10.9
Fertility rate, total (live births per woman)[a]	2010-2015	1.4
Contraceptive prevalence (ages 15-49, %)	2007-2013	60.8
International migrant stock (000 and % of total population)[a]	mid-2013	532.5/5.6
Refugees and others of concern to UNHCR	mid-2014	269 836[p]
Education: Government expenditure (% of GDP)	2007-2013	4.8
Education: Primary-secondary gross enrolment ratio (f/m per 100)[q]	2007-2013	97.4/95.7
Education: Female third-level students (% of total)	2007-2013	55.8
Intentional homicide rate (per 100,000 population)	2008-2012	1.2
Seats held by women in national parliaments (%)	2015	34.0

Environmental indicators		
Threatened species	2014	57
Forested area (% of land area)	2012	32.1
Proportion of terrestrial and marine areas protected (%)	2014	6.8
Population using improved drinking water sources (%)	2012	99.0
Population using improved sanitation facilities (%)	2012	97.0
CO_2 emission estimates (000 metric tons and metric tons per capita)	2011	49 185/5.1
Energy supply per capita (Gigajoules)[r]	2012	63.0

a Including Kosovo. b Refers to Belgrade settlement. c Official rate. d 2007. e Index base 2006=100. f 2011. g ISIC Rev.4 (BCD). h ISIC Rev.3. i October. j Average of semi-annual estimates. k Break in series. l 2012. m Arrivals of non-resident tourists in all types of accommodation establishments. n Including inactive prepaid subscriptions. o ITU estimate. p Refugee population refers to the end of 2013. q National estimate. r Excluding Kosovo.

Seychelles

Region	Eastern Africa	Surface area (sq km)	457
Population (est., 000)	93	Pop. density (per sq km)	205.1
Capital city	Victoria	Capital city pop. (000)	26
Currency	Seychelles Rupee (SCR)	UN membership date	21 September 1976

Economic indicators

	2005	2010	2013
GDP: Gross domestic product (million current US$)	919	970	1 445
GDP: Growth rate at constant 2005 prices (annual %)	9.0	6.0	5.6
GDP per capita (current US$)	10 553.1	10 634.7	15 565.4
GNI: Gross national income per capita (current US$)	10 093.0	9 664.0	14 019.4
Gross fixed capital formation (% of GDP)	35.1	35.4	38.3
Exchange rates (national currency per US$)[a]	5.50	12.15	12.08
Balance of payments, current account (million US$)	−174	−214	−228
CPI: Consumer price index (2000=100)	115	215	247
Agricultural production index (2004-2006=100)	98	91	110
Food production index (2004-2006=100)	98	94	114
Tourist arrivals at national borders (000)	129	175	230
Energy production, primary (Petajoules)	0	0	0[b]
Mobile-cellular subscriptions (per 100 inhabitants)	67.5	128.9[c]	147.3
Individuals using the Internet (%)	25.4	41.0[d]	50.4[d]

Social indicators

Population growth rate (average annual %)	2010-2015	0.6
Urban population growth rate (average annual %)	2010-2015	1.1
Rural population growth rate (average annual %)	2010-2015	−0.1
Urban population (%)	2014	53.6
Population aged 0-14 years (%)	2014	22.2
Population aged 60+ years (females and males, % of total)	2014	12.7/9.4
Sex ratio (males per 100 females)	2014	103.2
Life expectancy at birth (females and males, years)	2010-2015	78.0/68.9
Infant mortality rate (per 1 000 live births)	2010-2015	8.2
Fertility rate, total (live births per woman)	2010-2015	2.2
International migrant stock (000 and % of total population)	mid-2013	12.1/13.0
Education: Government expenditure (% of GDP)	2007-2013	3.6
Education: Primary-secondary gross enrolment ratio (f/m per 100)	2007-2013	93.4/91.2
Education: Female third-level students (% of total)	2007-2013	75.0
Intentional homicide rate (per 100,000 population)	2008-2012	9.5
Seats held by women in national parliaments (%)	2015	43.8

Environmental indicators

Threatened species	2014	435
Forested area (% of land area)	2012	88.5
Proportion of terrestrial and marine areas protected (%)	2014	0.1
Population using improved drinking water sources (%)	2012	96.0
Population using improved sanitation facilities (%)	2012	97.0
CO_2 emission estimates (000 metric tons and metric tons per capita)	2011	598/6.5
Energy supply per capita (Gigajoules)	2012	116.0

a Official rate. b 2012. c January 2011. d ITU estimate.

Sierra Leone

Region	Western Africa	
Population (est., 000)	6 205	
Capital city	Freetown	
Currency	Leone (SLL)	

Surface area (sq km)	72 300	
Pop. density (per sq km)	86.5	
Capital city pop. (000)	986	
UN membership date	27 September 1961	

Economic indicators	2005	2010	2013
GDP: Gross domestic product (million current US$)	1 651	2 578	4 929
GDP: Growth rate at constant 2005 prices (annual %)	4.5	5.4	20.1
GDP per capita (current US$)	322.4	448.2	809.1
GNI: Gross national income per capita (current US$)	324.6	453.2	735.9
Gross fixed capital formation (% of GDP)	10.9	30.7	13.9
Exchange rates (national currency per US$)[a]	2 932.52	4 198.01	4 356.37
Balance of payments, current account (million US$)	−105	−585	−383
CPI: Consumer price index (2000=100)[b]	132	239[c]	345
Agricultural production index (2004-2006=100)	93	149	169
Food production index (2004-2006=100)	93	149	169
Unemployment (% of labour force)	3.4	3.4	3.2
Employment in industrial sector (% of employed)	6.5[defgh]	...	...
Employment in agricultural sector (% of employed)	68.5[defgh]	...	...
Labour force participation, adult female pop. (%)	65.5	65.7	65.7
Labour force participation, adult male pop. (%)	67.0	68.6	69.0
Tourist arrivals at national borders (000)[i]	40	39	81
Energy production, primary (Petajoules)	50	52	52[j]
Mobile-cellular subscriptions (per 100 inhabitants)	14.3[kl]	34.8[mn]	44.1[l]
Individuals using the Internet (%)	0.2	0.6[l]	1.7[l]

Social indicators		
Population growth rate (average annual %)	2010-2015	1.9
Urban population growth rate (average annual %)	2010-2015	2.8
Rural population growth rate (average annual %)	2010-2015	1.3
Urban population (%)	2014	39.6
Population aged 0-14 years (%)	2014	41.2
Population aged 60+ years (females and males, % of total)	2014	4.5/4.2
Sex ratio (males per 100 females)	2014	98.7
Life expectancy at birth (females and males, years)	2010-2015	45.6/45.1
Infant mortality rate (per 1 000 live births)	2010-2015	116.7
Fertility rate, total (live births per woman)	2010-2015	4.8
Contraceptive prevalence (ages 15-49, %)	2007-2013	16.6
International migrant stock (000 and % of total population)[o]	mid-2013	96.4/1.6
Refugees and others of concern to UNHCR	mid-2014	2 429
Education: Government expenditure (% of GDP)	2007-2013	2.9
Education: Primary-secondary gross enrolment ratio (f/m per 100)	2007-2013	88.8/91.6
Education: Female third-level students (% of total)[p]	2007-2013	28.8[q]
Intentional homicide rate (per 100,000 population)	2008-2012	1.9
Seats held by women in national parliaments (%)	2015	12.4

Environmental indicators		
Threatened species	2014	156
Forested area (% of land area)	2012	37.2
Proportion of terrestrial and marine areas protected (%)	2014	3.8
Population using improved drinking water sources (%)	2012	60.0
Population using improved sanitation facilities (%)	2012	13.0
CO_2 emission estimates (000 metric tons and metric tons per capita)	2011	898/0.2
Energy supply per capita (Gigajoules)	2012	11.0

a Market rate. **b** Index base 2003=100. **c** Series linked to former series. **d** 2004. **e** Population census. **f** ISIC Rev.3. **g** Population aged 10 and over. **h** December. **i** Arrivals by air. **j** 2012. **k** 2007. **l** ITU estimate. **m** February 2011. **n** Including multiple subscriptions by single individuals. **o** Including refugees. **p** UNESCO estimate. **q** 2002.

Singapore

Region	South-Eastern Asia	Surface area (sq km)	716[a]
Population (est., 000)	5 517	Pop. density (per sq km)	8 077.8
Capital city	Singapore	Capital city pop. (000)	5 517
Currency	Singapore Dollar (SGD)	UN membership date	21 September 1965

Economic indicators	2005	2010	2013
GDP: Gross domestic product (million current US$)	125 429	233 292	295 744
GDP: Growth rate at constant 2005 prices (annual %)	7.4	15.1	4.1
GDP per capita (current US$)	27 900.8	45 933.0	54 648.6
GNI: Gross national income per capita (current US$)	26 027.9	45 668.5	53 363.0
Gross fixed capital formation (% of GDP)	21.1	23.5	23.1
Exchange rates (national currency per US$)[b]	1.66	1.29	1.27
Balance of payments, current account (million US$)	27 868	55 943	54 555
CPI: Consumer price index (2000=100)	103	117	132
Agricultural production index (2004-2006=100)	90	92	112
Food production index (2004-2006=100)	90	92	112
Unemployment (% of labour force)	4.1	3.1	2.8
Employment in industrial sector (% of employed)	21.7[cdef]	21.8[cdefgh]	...
Employment in agricultural sector (% of employed)	1.1[cdei]	1.1[cdeghi]	...
Labour force participation, adult female pop. (%)	53.5	57.3	58.8
Labour force participation, adult male pop. (%)	76.7	77.5	77.2
Tourist arrivals at national borders (000)	7 079	9 161	11 899
Mobile-cellular subscriptions (per 100 inhabitants)	97.5	145.4	155.6[j]
Individuals using the Internet (%)	61.0[k]	71.0[lm]	73.0[lm]

Total trade		Major trading partners				2013
	(million US$)	(% of exports)			(% of imports)	
Exports	410 249.7	Malaysia	12.2	China	11.7	
Imports	373 015.7	China	11.8	Malaysia	10.9	
Balance	37 234.0	China, Hong Kong SAR	11.2	United States	10.4	

Social indicators

Population growth rate (average annual %)	2010-2015	2.0
Urban population growth rate (average annual %)	2010-2015	2.0
Urban population (%)	2014	100.0
Population aged 0-14 years (%)	2014	15.7
Population aged 60+ years (females and males, % of total)	2014	17.3/15.5
Sex ratio (males per 100 females)	2014	97.5
Life expectancy at birth (females and males, years)	2010-2015	84.6/79.7
Infant mortality rate (per 1 000 live births)	2010-2015	1.8
Fertility rate, total (live births per woman)	2010-2015	1.3
Contraceptive prevalence (ages 15-49, %)[n]	2007-2013	62.0[o]
International migrant stock (000 and % of total population)	mid-2013	2 323.3/42.9
Refugees and others of concern to UNHCR	mid-2014	3
Education: Government expenditure (% of GDP)	2007-2013	2.9
Education: Female third-level students (% of total)	2007-2013	49.9
Intentional homicide rate (per 100,000 population)	2008-2012	0.2
Seats held by women in national parliaments (%)	2015	25.3

Environmental indicators

Threatened species	2014	287
Forested area (% of land area)	2012	3.3
Proportion of terrestrial and marine areas protected (%)	2014	3.4
Population using improved drinking water sources (%)	2012	100.0
Population using improved sanitation facilities (%)	2012	100.0
CO_2 emission estimates (000 metric tons and metric tons per capita)	2011	22 394/4.3
Energy supply per capita (Gigajoules)	2012	229.0

a The land area of Singapore comprises the mainland and other islands. b Market rate. c ISIC Rev.3. d June. e Data refer to permanent residents. f Refers to manufacturing and construction only. g 2009. h Break in series. i Including mining and quarrying, electricity, gas and water supply and not classifiable by economic activity. j December. k Population aged 15 and over. l Estimate. m Population aged 7 and over. n Age group 15 to 44 years. o 1997.

Slovakia

Region	Eastern Europe	Surface area (sq km)	49 036[a]
Population (est., 000)	5 454	Pop. density (per sq km)	111.2
Capital city	Bratislava	Capital city pop. (000)	403
Currency	Euro (EUR)	UN membership date	19 January 1993

Economic indicators	2005	2010	2013
GDP: Gross domestic product (million current US$)	48 948	89 007	97 713
GDP: Growth rate at constant 2005 prices (annual %)	6.5	4.8	1.4
GDP per capita (current US$)	9 078.8	16 381.3	17 928.2
GNI: Gross national income per capita (current US$)	8 840.6	15 998.3	17 572.4
Gross fixed capital formation (% of GDP)	27.4	22.2	20.5
Exchange rates (national currency per US$)	31.95[bc]	0.75[de]	0.73[de]
Balance of payments, current account (million US$)	−4 005	−3 240	2 026
CPI: Consumer price index (2000=100)	133	153	167
Index of industrial production (2010=100)[fg]	79	100	120
Agricultural production index (2004-2006=100)	102	82	89
Food production index (2004-2006=100)	102	82	89
Unemployment (% of labour force)	16.2	14.4	14.2
Employment in industrial sector (% of employed)	38.8[hi]	37.1	37.5[jk]
Employment in agricultural sector (% of employed)	4.7[hi]	3.2	3.2[jk]
Labour force participation, adult female pop. (%)	51.2	50.8	51.1
Labour force participation, adult male pop. (%)	68.4	67.9	68.6
Tourist arrivals at national borders (000)[lm]	1 515	1 327	1 670
Energy production, primary (Petajoules)	265	250	261[i]
Mobile-cellular subscriptions (per 100 inhabitants)	84.2[n]	109.1	113.9
Individuals using the Internet (%)	55.2	75.7[o]	77.9

Total trade		Major trading partners			2013
	(million US$)	(% of exports)		(% of imports)	
Exports	85 184.2	Germany	20.9	Germany	16.0
Imports	81 295.1	Czech Republic	13.5	Czech Republic	11.0
Balance	3 889.1	Poland	8.3	Russian Federation	10.0

Social indicators		
Population growth rate (average annual %)	2010-2015	0.1
Urban population growth rate (average annual %)	2010-2015	−0.3
Rural population growth rate (average annual %)	2010-2015	0.6
Urban population (%)	2014	53.8
Population aged 0-14 years (%)	2014	15.1
Population aged 60+ years (females and males, % of total)	2014	22.8/16.6
Sex ratio (males per 100 females)	2014	94.7
Life expectancy at birth (females and males, years)	2010-2015	79.2/71.5
Infant mortality rate (per 1 000 live births)	2010-2015	5.4
Fertility rate, total (live births per woman)	2010-2015	1.4
Contraceptive prevalence (ages 15-49, %)[p]	2007-2013	79.8[q]
International migrant stock (000 and % of total population)[r]	mid-2013	149.6/2.8
Refugees and others of concern to UNHCR	mid-2014	2 506[s]
Education: Government expenditure (% of GDP)	2007-2013	4.1
Education: Primary-secondary gross enrolment ratio (f/m per 100)	2007-2013	96.1/95.9
Education: Female third-level students (% of total)	2007-2013	59.6
Intentional homicide rate (per 100,000 population)	2008-2012	1.4
Seats held by women in national parliaments (%)	2015	18.7

Environmental indicators		
Threatened species	2014	46
Forested area (% of land area)	2012	40.2
Proportion of terrestrial and marine areas protected (%)	2014	36.6
Population using improved drinking water sources (%)	2012	100.0
Population using improved sanitation facilities (%)	2012	100.0
CO_2 emission estimates (000 metric tons and metric tons per capita)	2011	34 374/6.3
Energy supply per capita (Gigajoules)	2012	126.0

a Excluding inland water. b Official rate. c Slovak Koruna (SKK). d Market rate. e Euro. f ISIC Rev.4 (BCD). g Break in series from 2008. h ISIC Rev.3. i Excluding conscripts. j 2012. k Break in series. l Arrivals of non-resident tourists in all types of accommodation establishments. m Non-resident tourists staying in commercial accommodation only. n No distinction made between active or inactive subscribers. o Population aged 16 to 74 using the Internet in the last 3 months. p Age group 15 to 44 years. q 1997. r Including refugees. s Refugee population refers to the end of 2013.

Slovenia

Region	Southern Europe	Surface area (sq km)	20 273	
Population (est., 000)	2 076	Pop. density (per sq km)	102.5	
Capital city	Ljubljana	Capital city pop. (000)	279	
Currency	Euro (EUR)	UN membership date	22 May 1992	

Economic indicators	2005	2010	2013
GDP: Gross domestic product (million current US$)	36 345	47 970	47 990
GDP: Growth rate at constant 2005 prices (annual %)	4.0	1.2	−1.0
GDP per capita (current US$)	18 169.3	23 351.9	23 161.2
GNI: Gross national income per capita (current US$)	18 082.8	23 125.0	22 990.6
Gross fixed capital formation (% of GDP)	26.7	21.3	19.7
Exchange rates (national currency per US$)	202.43[ab]	0.75[cd]	0.73[cd]
Balance of payments, current account (million US$)	−681	−59	2 947
CPI: Consumer price index (2000=100)	131	150	160
Index of industrial production (2010=100)[e]	97	100	99
Agricultural production index (2004-2006=100)	99	92	81
Food production index (2004-2006=100)	99	92	81
Unemployment (% of labour force)	6.5	7.2	10.2
Employment in industrial sector (% of employed)	37.2[fgh]	32.5	30.8[i]
Employment in agricultural sector (% of employed)	8.8[fgh]	8.8	8.3[i]
Labour force participation, adult female pop. (%)	52.8	53.1	52.3
Labour force participation, adult male pop. (%)	66.0	65.6	63.2
Tourist arrivals at national borders (000)[j]	1 555	1 869	2 259
Energy production, primary (Petajoules)	146	153	148[i]
Mobile-cellular subscriptions (per 100 inhabitants)	88.0[k]	103.3	110.2
Individuals using the Internet (%)	46.8[l]	70.0	72.7

Total trade		Major trading partners			2013
	(million US$)	(% of exports)			(% of imports)
Exports	28 628.7	Germany	20.4	Germany	17.1
Imports	29 375.4	Italy	11.6	Italy	15.3
Balance	−746.7	Austria	8.7	Austria	8.7

Social indicators		
Population growth rate (average annual %)	2010-2015	0.2
Urban population growth rate (average annual %)	2010-2015	0.1
Rural population growth rate (average annual %)	2010-2015	0.4
Urban population (%)	2014	49.7
Population aged 0-14 years (%)	2014	14.4
Population aged 60+ years (females and males, % of total)	2014	27.4/21.4
Sex ratio (males per 100 females)	2014	98.8
Life expectancy at birth (females and males, years)	2010-2015	82.7/76.2
Infant mortality rate (per 1 000 live births)	2010-2015	2.8
Fertility rate, total (live births per woman)	2010-2015	1.5
Contraceptive prevalence (ages 15-49, %)[m]	2007-2013	78.9[n]
International migrant stock (000 and % of total population)	mid-2013	233.3/11.3
Refugees and others of concern to UNHCR	mid-2014	278
Education: Government expenditure (% of GDP)	2007-2013	5.7
Education: Primary-secondary gross enrolment ratio (f/m per 100)	2007-2013	98.0/98.3
Education: Female third-level students (% of total)	2007-2013	57.7
Intentional homicide rate (per 100,000 population)	2008-2012	0.7
Seats held by women in national parliaments (%)	2015	36.7

Environmental indicators		
Threatened species	2014	123
Forested area (% of land area)	2012	62.4
Proportion of terrestrial and marine areas protected (%)	2014	54.0
Population using improved drinking water sources (%)	2012	100.0
Population using improved sanitation facilities (%)	2012	100.0
CO_2 emission estimates (000 metric tons and metric tons per capita)	2011	15 405/7.5
Energy supply per capita (Gigajoules)	2012	142.0

a Official rate. b Slovenian tolar (SIT). c Market rate. d Euro. e ISIC Rev.4 (BCD). f ISIC Rev.3. g Second quarter. h Excluding conscripts and regular military living in barracks. i 2012. j Arrivals of non-resident tourists in all types of accommodation establishments. k Methodology revised. l Using the Internet within the last 3 months. m Age group 15 to 44 years. n 1994-1995.

Solomon Islands

Region	Oceania-Melanesia	Surface area (sq km)		28 896
Population (est., 000)	573	Pop. density (per sq km)		19.8
Capital city	Honiara	Capital city pop. (000)		73
Currency	Solomon Is. Dollar (SBD)	UN membership date		19 September 1978

Economic indicators	2005	2010	2013
GDP: Gross domestic product (million current US$)	429	720	1 073
GDP: Growth rate at constant 2005 prices (annual %)	12.9	10.6	3.0
GDP per capita (current US$)	915.1	1 366.9	1 911.5
GNI: Gross national income per capita (current US$)	918.7	1 019.4	1 674.6
Gross fixed capital formation (% of GDP)	16.0	20.3	20.9
Exchange rates (national currency per US$)[a]	7.58	8.06	7.36
Balance of payments, current account (million US$)	−90	−224	−49
CPI: Consumer price index (2000=100)[b]	149	226	271
Agricultural production index (2004-2006=100)	103	110	118
Food production index (2004-2006=100)	103	110	118
Unemployment (% of labour force)	3.6	3.7	3.8
Labour force participation, adult female pop. (%)	53.7	53.4	53.4
Labour force participation, adult male pop. (%)	79.1	79.3	79.0
Tourist arrivals at national borders (000)	9[c]	21	24
Energy production, primary (Petajoules)[d]	3	3	3[e]
Mobile-cellular subscriptions (per 100 inhabitants)	1.3	21.9	57.6
Individuals using the Internet (%)	0.8	5.0[f]	8.0[f]

Total trade		Major trading partners			2013
	(million US$)		(% of exports)		(% of imports)
Exports	489.2	China	44.8	Singapore	31.1
Imports	580.2	Australia	22.6	Australia	27.4
Balance	−91.0	Italy	6.3	China	8.3

Social indicators		
Population growth rate (average annual %)	2010-2015	2.1
Urban population growth rate (average annual %)	2010-2015	4.3
Rural population growth rate (average annual %)	2010-2015	1.5
Urban population (%)	2014	21.9
Population aged 0-14 years (%)	2014	39.9
Population aged 60+ years (females and males, % of total)	2014	5.2/5.1
Sex ratio (males per 100 females)	2014	103.1
Life expectancy at birth (females and males, years)	2010-2015	69.0/66.2
Infant mortality rate (per 1 000 live births)	2010-2015	38.0
Fertility rate, total (live births per woman)	2010-2015	4.1
Contraceptive prevalence (ages 15-49, %)	2007-2013	34.6
International migrant stock (000 and % of total population)	mid-2013	7.9/1.4
Refugees and others of concern to UNHCR	mid-2014	3
Education: Government expenditure (% of GDP)	2007-2013	9.9
Education: Primary-secondary gross enrolment ratio (f/m per 100)	2007-2013	93.5/95.9
Intentional homicide rate (per 100,000 population)	2008-2012	4.3
Seats held by women in national parliaments (%)	2015	2.0

Environmental indicators		
Threatened species	2014	238
Forested area (% of land area)	2012	78.7
Proportion of terrestrial and marine areas protected (%)	2014	0.2
Population using improved drinking water sources (%)	2012	81.0
Population using improved sanitation facilities (%)	2012	29.0
CO_2 emission estimates (000 metric tons and metric tons per capita)	2011	198/0.4
Energy supply per capita (Gigajoules)	2012	11.0[d]

a Official rate. b Honiara. c Excluding first quarter. d UNSD estimate. e 2012. f ITU estimate.

Somalia

Region	Eastern Africa	Surface area (sq km)	637 657
Population (est., 000)	10 806	Pop. density (per sq km)	17.0
Capital city	Mogadishu	Capital city pop. (000)	2 014
Currency	Somalia Shilling (SOS)	UN membership date	20 September 1960

Economic indicators	2005	2010	2013
GDP: Gross domestic product (million current US$)	2 316	1 071	1 399
GDP: Growth rate at constant 2005 prices (annual %)	3.0	2.6	2.6
GDP per capita (current US$)	273.5	111.2	133.3
GNI: Gross national income per capita (current US$)	262.5	106.7	127.9
Gross fixed capital formation (% of GDP)	20.3	19.9	19.9
Exchange rates (national currency per US$)[a]	15 141.00	31 900.00[b]	24 300.00[c]
Agricultural production index (2004-2006=100)	100	104	117
Food production index (2004-2006=100)	100	104	117
Unemployment (% of labour force)	6.9	6.9	6.9
Labour force participation, adult female pop. (%)	36.6	37.0	37.2
Labour force participation, adult male pop. (%)	76.5	75.8	75.5
Energy production, primary (Petajoules)	103	124	128[d]
Mobile-cellular subscriptions (per 100 inhabitants)	5.9	6.7[e]	49.4
Individuals using the Internet (%)[e]	1.1	1.3[f]	1.5

Social indicators		
Population growth rate (average annual %)	2010-2015	2.9
Urban population growth rate (average annual %)	2010-2015	4.1
Rural population growth rate (average annual %)	2010-2015	2.1
Urban population (%)	2014	39.1
Population aged 0-14 years (%)	2014	46.9
Population aged 60+ years (females and males, % of total)	2014	4.8/4.1
Sex ratio (males per 100 females)	2014	99.0
Life expectancy at birth (females and males, years)	2010-2015	56.5/53.3
Infant mortality rate (per 1 000 live births)	2010-2015	79.5
Fertility rate, total (live births per woman)	2010-2015	6.6
Contraceptive prevalence (ages 15-49, %)	2007-2013	14.6[g]
International migrant stock (000 and % of total population)[hi]	mid-2013	24.6/0.2
Refugees and others of concern to UNHCR	mid-2014	1 165 505
Education: Primary-secondary gross enrolment ratio (f/m per 100)	2007-2013	13.8/25.8
Intentional homicide rate (per 100,000 population)	2008-2012	8.0
Seats held by women in national parliaments (%)	2015	13.8

Environmental indicators		
Threatened species	2014	166
Forested area (% of land area)	2012	10.5
Proportion of terrestrial and marine areas protected (%)	2014	0.3
CO_2 emission estimates (000 metric tons and metric tons per capita)	2011	576/0.1
Energy supply per capita (Gigajoules)	2012	13.0

a UN operational exchange rate. b September 2009. c April 2012. d 2012. e ITU estimate. f 2011. g 2006.
h Estimate. i Including refugees.

South Africa

Region	Southern Africa	Surface area (sq km)	1 221 037
Population (est., 000)	53 140	Pop. density (per sq km)	43.5
Capital city	Pretoria[a]	Capital city pop. (000)	1 991
Currency	Rand (ZAR)	UN membership date	7 November 1945

Economic indicators	2005	2010	2013
GDP: Gross domestic product (million current US$)	257 772	375 348	366 060
GDP: Growth rate at constant 2005 prices (annual %)	5.3	3.0	2.2
GDP per capita (current US$)	5 344.0	7 295.1	6 936.1
GNI: Gross national income per capita (current US$)	5 241.6	7 139.5	6 754.0
Gross fixed capital formation (% of GDP)	17.3	19.3	20.0
Exchange rates (national currency per US$)[b]	6.32	6.63	10.49
Balance of payments, current account (million US$)	−8 518	−7 023	−20 507
CPI: Consumer price index (2000=100)	128	142	166[c]
Agricultural production index (2004-2006=100)	102	118	122
Food production index (2004-2006=100)	102	118	123
Unemployment (% of labour force)	23.8	24.7	24.9
Employment in industrial sector (% of employed)[d]	25.6[e]	24.5[fgh]	24.3[fgi]
Employment in agricultural sector (% of employed)[d]	7.5[e]	4.9[fgh]	4.6[fgi]
Labour force participation, adult female pop. (%)	46.5	43.5	44.5
Labour force participation, adult male pop. (%)	62.2	59.9	60.5
Tourist arrivals at national borders (000)	7 369[j]	8 074[k]	9 537
Energy production, primary (Petajoules)	6 652	6 911	7 009[l]
Mobile-cellular subscriptions (per 100 inhabitants)	70.4	97.9	147.5
Individuals using the Internet (%)	7.5	24.0[m]	48.9[m]

Total trade		Major trading partners			2013
	(million US$)	(% of exports)			(% of imports)
Exports	95 224.8	China	12.7	China	15.5
Imports	103 461.3	Areas nes	7.5[n]	Germany	10.3
Balance	−8 236.5	United States	7.2	Saudi Arabia	7.8

Social indicators		
Population growth rate (average annual %)	2010-2015	0.8
Urban population growth rate (average annual %)	2010-2015	1.6
Rural population growth rate (average annual %)	2010-2015	−0.6
Urban population (%)	2014	64.3
Population aged 0-14 years (%)	2014	29.4
Population aged 60+ years (females and males, % of total)	2014	10.5/6.8
Sex ratio (males per 100 females)	2014	94.4
Life expectancy at birth (females and males, years)	2010-2015	59.1/54.9
Infant mortality rate (per 1 000 live births)	2010-2015	38.3
Fertility rate, total (live births per woman)	2010-2015	2.4
Contraceptive prevalence (ages 15-49, %)	2007-2013	59.9[o]
International migrant stock (000 and % of total population)[p]	mid-2013	2 399.2/4.6
Refugees and others of concern to UNHCR	mid-2014	309 616[q]
Education: Government expenditure (% of GDP)	2007-2013	6.2
Education: Primary-secondary gross enrolment ratio (f/m per 100)	2007-2013	104.7/104.9
Education: Female third-level students (% of total)	2007-2013	58.0
Intentional homicide rate (per 100,000 population)	2008-2012	31.0
Seats held by women in national parliaments (%)[r]	2015	41.5

Environmental indicators		
Threatened species	2014	528
Forested area (% of land area)	2012	7.6
Proportion of terrestrial and marine areas protected (%)	2014	10.2
Population using improved drinking water sources (%)	2012	95.0
Population using improved sanitation facilities (%)	2012	74.0
CO_2 emission estimates (000 metric tons and metric tons per capita)	2011	477 242/9.2
Energy supply per capita (Gigajoules)	2012	120.0

a Pretoria is the administrative capital, Cape Town is the legislative capital and Bloemfontein is the judiciary capital. b Principal rate. c Series linked to former series. d Population aged 15-64. e ISIC Rev.3. f ISIC Rev.2. g Average of quarterly estimates. h Break in series. i 2011. j Excluding arrivals for work and contract workers. k Methodology revised. l 2012. m ITU estimate. n See technical notes. o 2003-2004. p Including refugees. q Asylum-seekers (pending cases) refers to the end of 2013. r The figures on the distribution of seats do not include the 36 special rotating delegates appointed on an ad hoc basis, and all percentages given are therefore calculated on the basis of the 54 permanent seats.

South Sudan

Region	Eastern Africa	Surface area (sq km)	...
Population (est., 000)	11 739	Pop. density (per sq km)	18.2
Capital city	Juba	Capital city pop. (000)	307
Currency	S. Sudanese Pound (SSP)	UN membership date	14 July 2011

Economic indicators	2005	2010	2013
GDP: Gross domestic product (million current US$)	...	15 720	11 804
GDP: Growth rate at constant 2005 prices (annual %)	...	5.5	13.1
GDP per capita (current US$)	...	1 581.3	1 045.0
GNI: Gross national income per capita (current US$)	...	1 110.0	474.8
Gross fixed capital formation (% of GDP)	...	10.3	11.9
Exchange rates (national currency per US$)[a]	...	...	2.95
Mobile-cellular subscriptions (per 100 inhabitants)	...	...	25.3

Social indicators		
Population growth rate (average annual %)	2010-2015	4.0
Urban population growth rate (average annual %)	2010-2015	5.1
Rural population growth rate (average annual %)	2010-2015	3.8
Urban population (%)	2014	18.6
Population aged 0-14 years (%)	2014	41.8
Population aged 60+ years (females and males, % of total)	2014	5.5/4.9
Sex ratio (males per 100 females)	2014	100.2
Life expectancy at birth (females and males, years)	2010-2015	56.0/53.9
Infant mortality rate (per 1 000 live births)	2010-2015	78.0
Fertility rate, total (live births per woman)	2010-2015	5.0
Contraceptive prevalence (ages 15-49, %)	2007-2013	4.0
International migrant stock (000 and % of total population)[b]	mid-2013	629.6/5.6
Refugees and others of concern to UNHCR	mid-2014	1 556 351[c]
Education: Government expenditure (% of GDP)	2007-2013	0.7
Intentional homicide rate (per 100,000 population)	2008-2012	13.9
Seats held by women in national parliaments (%)	2015	26.5

Environmental indicators		
Threatened species	2014	42
Proportion of terrestrial and marine areas protected (%)	2014	20.8
Population using improved drinking water sources (%)	2012	57.0
Population using improved sanitation facilities (%)	2012	9.0

a Official rate. b Including refugees. c Including 155,200 people who are in an internally displaced person-like situation.

Spain

Region	Southern Europe	Surface area (sq km)	505 992
Population (est., 000)	47 066 [a]	Pop. density (per sq km)	93.0 [a]
Capital city	Madrid	Capital city pop. (000)	6 133
Currency	Euro (EUR)	UN membership date	14 December 1955

Economic indicators	2005	2010	2013
GDP: Gross domestic product (million current US$)	1 157 248	1 431 588	1 393 040
GDP: Growth rate at constant 2005 prices (annual %)	3.7	0.0	−1.2
GDP per capita (current US$)	26 672.4	30 998.8	29 685.3
GNI: Gross national income per capita (current US$)	26 286.7	30 564.2	29 480.4
Gross fixed capital formation (% of GDP)	29.9	23.0	18.5
Exchange rates (national currency per US$) [b]	0.85	0.75	0.73
Balance of payments, current account (million US$)	−83 388	−62 498	10 668
CPI: Consumer price index (2000=100) [c]	114	128	137
Index of industrial production (2010=100) [d]	120	100	90
Agricultural production index (2004-2006=100)	95	103	109
Food production index (2004-2006=100)	94	104	110
Unemployment (% of labour force)	9.3	20.2	26.6
Employment in industrial sector (% of employed) [e]	29.7 [f]	23.1	20.7 [g]
Employment in agricultural sector (% of employed) [e]	5.3 [f]	4.3	4.4 [g]
Labour force participation, adult female pop. (%)	45.8	51.4	52.5
Labour force participation, adult male pop. (%)	68.0	67.3	65.8
Tourist arrivals at national borders (000)	55 914	52 677	60 661
Energy production, primary (Petajoules) [h]	1 256	1 413	1 459 [g]
Mobile-cellular subscriptions (per 100 inhabitants)	98.4	111.3	106.9
Individuals using the Internet (%)	47.9 [i]	65.8	71.6

Total trade		Major trading partners			2013
	(million US$)	(% of exports)			(% of imports)
Exports	310 963.6	France	16.1	Germany	11.1
Imports	332 266.8	Germany	10.1	France	10.9
Balance	−21 303.2	Portugal	7.5	China	6.9

Social indicators		
Population growth rate (average annual %) [a]	2010-2015	0.4
Urban population growth rate (average annual %) [a]	2010-2015	0.7
Rural population growth rate (average annual %) [a]	2010-2015	−0.7
Urban population (%) [a]	2014	79.4
Population aged 0-14 years (%) [a]	2014	15.5
Population aged 60+ years (females and males, % of total) [a]	2014	25.9/20.8
Sex ratio (males per 100 females) [a]	2014	97.7
Life expectancy at birth (females and males, years) [a]	2010-2015	85.2/78.8
Infant mortality rate (per 1 000 live births) [a]	2010-2015	3.1
Fertility rate, total (live births per woman) [a]	2010-2015	1.5
Contraceptive prevalence (ages 15-49, %)	2007-2013	65.7 [j]
International migrant stock (000 and % of total population) [a]	mid-2013	6 466.6/13.8
Refugees and others of concern to UNHCR	mid-2014	11 304 [k]
Education: Government expenditure (% of GDP)	2007-2013	5.0
Education: Primary-secondary gross enrolment ratio (f/m per 100)	2007-2013	116.4/116.2
Education: Female third-level students (% of total)	2007-2013	53.6
Intentional homicide rate (per 100,000 population)	2008-2012	0.8
Seats held by women in national parliaments (%)	2015	41.1

Environmental indicators		
Threatened species	2014	552
Forested area (% of land area)	2012	37.1
Proportion of terrestrial and marine areas protected (%)	2014	10.2
Population using improved drinking water sources (%)	2012	100.0
Population using improved sanitation facilities (%)	2012	100.0
CO_2 emission estimates (000 metric tons and metric tons per capita)	2011	270 676/5.8
Energy supply per capita (Gigajoules) [h]	2012	113.0

a Including Canary Islands, Ceuta and Melilla. b Market rate. c Index base 2001=100. d ISIC Rev.4 (BCD). e Population aged 16 and over. f ISIC Rev.3. g 2012. h Including the Canary Islands. i Population aged 16 to 74 using the Internet within the last 12 months. j 2006. k Refugee population refers to the end of 2013.

Sri Lanka

Region	Southern Asia	Surface area (sq km)	65 610
Population (est., 000)	21 446	Pop. density (per sq km)	326.9
Capital city	Colombo[a]	Capital city pop. (000)	704
Currency	Sri Lanka Rupee (LKR)	UN membership date	14 December 1955

Economic indicators	2005	2010	2013
GDP: Gross domestic product (million current US$)	24 406	49 566	67 203
GDP: Growth rate at constant 2005 prices (annual %)	6.2	8.0	7.2
GDP per capita (current US$)	1 223.3	2 387.7	3 159.1
GNI: Gross national income per capita (current US$)	1 208.3	2 358.0	3 074.7
Gross fixed capital formation (% of GDP)	23.4	25.9	29.2
Exchange rates (national currency per US$)[b]	102.12	110.95	130.75
Balance of payments, current account (million US$)	−650	−1 075	−2 627
CPI: Consumer price index (2000=100)[c]	160	219[d]	269[d]
Agricultural production index (2004-2006=100)	102	124	136
Food production index (2004-2006=100)	102	125	141
Unemployment (% of labour force)	7.7	4.9	4.2
Employment in industrial sector (% of employed)[ef]	25.6	24.2[gh]	17.7[ij]
Employment in agricultural sector (% of employed)[ef]	30.7	32.7[gh]	39.4[ij]
Labour force participation, adult female pop. (%)	34.4	34.8	35.1
Labour force participation, adult male pop. (%)	76.2	76.5	76.3
Tourist arrivals at national borders (000)[k]	549	654	1 275
Energy production, primary (Petajoules)	163	184	173[i]
Mobile-cellular subscriptions (per 100 inhabitants)	16.9	83.6	95.5
Individuals using the Internet (%)	1.8[l]	12.0	21.9[l]

Total trade		Major trading partners			2013
	(million US$)	(% of exports)			(% of imports)
Exports	10 004.9	United States	24.9	India	17.4
Imports	17 930.8	United Kingdom	10.8	China	16.5
Balance	−7 925.9	India	5.4	Singapore	10.0

Social indicators		
Population growth rate (average annual %)	2010-2015	0.8
Urban population growth rate (average annual %)	2010-2015	0.8
Rural population growth rate (average annual %)	2010-2015	0.8
Urban population (%)	2014	18.3
Population aged 0-14 years (%)	2014	25.2
Population aged 60+ years (females and males, % of total)	2014	14.0/12.0
Sex ratio (males per 100 females)	2014	95.4
Life expectancy at birth (females and males, years)	2010-2015	77.4/71.1
Infant mortality rate (per 1 000 live births)	2010-2015	9.0
Fertility rate, total (live births per woman)	2010-2015	2.4
Contraceptive prevalence (ages 15-49, %)[m]	2007-2013	68.4
International migrant stock (000 and % of total population)[no]	mid-2013	325.0/1.5
Refugees and others of concern to UNHCR	mid-2014	44 297[p]
Education: Government expenditure (% of GDP)	2007-2013	1.7
Education: Primary-secondary gross enrolment ratio (f/m per 100)	2007-2013	100.7/97.3
Education: Female third-level students (% of total)	2007-2013	62.2
Intentional homicide rate (per 100,000 population)	2008-2012	3.4
Seats held by women in national parliaments (%)	2015	5.8

Environmental indicators		
Threatened species	2014	576
Forested area (% of land area)	2012	29.2
Proportion of terrestrial and marine areas protected (%)	2014	2.6
Population using improved drinking water sources (%)	2012	94.0
Population using improved sanitation facilities (%)	2012	92.0
CO_2 emission estimates (000 metric tons and metric tons per capita)	2011	15 233/0.7
Energy supply per capita (Gigajoules)	2012	18.0

a Colombo is the capital and Sri Jayewardenepura Kotte is the legislative capital. b Market rate. c Colombo. d Index base 2002=100. e ISIC Rev.3. f Population aged 10 and over. g Excluding the Northern province. h Break in series. i 2012. j Average of quarterly estimates. k Excluding nationals residing abroad. l ITU estimate. m Excluding the Northern Province. n Refers to foreign citizens. o Including refugees. p Provisional.

State of Palestine

Region	Western Asia	Surface area (sq km)	6 020
Population (est., 000)	4 436[a]	Pop. density (per sq km)	736.9[a]

Economic indicators	2005	2010	2013
GDP: Gross domestic product (million current US$)	4 832	8 913	12 579
GDP: Growth rate at constant 2005 prices (annual %)	10.8	8.1	1.9
GDP per capita (current US$)	1 357.3	2 221.1	2 907.6
GNI: Gross national income per capita (current US$)	1 455.3	2 370.4	3 133.6
Gross fixed capital formation (% of GDP)	25.3	20.5	24.3
Balance of payments, current account (million US$)[b]	−1 152	−691	−1 412
CPI: Consumer price index (2000=100)[b]	119	148	160
Index of industrial production (2010=100)[c]	112	100	...
Agricultural production index (2004-2006=100)	107	81	93
Food production index (2004-2006=100)	107	81	93
Unemployment (% of labour force)	26.0	23.7	23.4
Employment in industrial sector (% of employed)	26.3[d]	24.6[ef]	26.3[eg]
Employment in agricultural sector (% of employed)	14.6[d]	11.8[ef]	11.5[eg]
Labour force participation, adult female pop. (%)	14.2	14.7	15.4
Labour force participation, adult male pop. (%)	67.2	66.2	66.4
Tourist arrivals at national borders (000)[h]	88	522	545
Energy production, primary (Petajoules)	8	9	8[g]
Mobile-cellular subscriptions (per 100 inhabitants)	15.9	64.9	73.7
Individuals using the Internet (%)[i]	16.0[j]	37.4[k]	46.6

Total trade		Major trading partners			2013
	(million US$)	(% of exports)			(% of imports)
Exports	900.6	Israel	87.3	Israel	71.6
Imports	5 163.9	Jordan	6.2	Turkey	5.6
Balance	−4 263.3	United States	1.1	China	4.6

Social indicators		
Population growth rate (average annual %)[a]	2010-2015	2.5
Urban population growth rate (average annual %)[a]	2010-2015	2.8
Rural population growth rate (average annual %)[a]	2010-2015	1.6
Urban population (%)[a]	2014	75.0
Population aged 0-14 years (%)[a]	2014	39.5
Population aged 60+ years (females and males, % of total)[a]	2014	4.9/4.4
Sex ratio (males per 100 females)[a]	2014	103.0
Life expectancy at birth (females and males, years)[a]	2010-2015	74.9/71.4
Infant mortality rate (per 1 000 live births)[a]	2010-2015	19.2
Fertility rate, total (live births per woman)[a]	2010-2015	4.1
Contraceptive prevalence (ages 15-49, %)	2007-2013	52.5
International migrant stock (000 and % of total population)[al]	mid-2013	256.5/5.9
Refugees and others of concern to UNHCR	mid-2014	0[m]
Education: Primary-secondary gross enrolment ratio (f/m per 100)	2007-2013	89.5/84.2
Education: Female third-level students (% of total)	2007-2013	59.1
Intentional homicide rate (per 100,000 population)	2008-2012	7.4

Environmental indicators		
Threatened species	2014	22
Forested area (% of land area)	2012	1.5
CO_2 emission estimates (000 metric tons and metric tons per capita)	2011	2 248/0.6
Energy supply per capita (Gigajoules)	2012	14.0

a Including East Jerusalem. b Refers to West Bank and the Gaza Strip. c ISIC Rev.4 (BCD). d ISIC Rev.3.
e ISIC Rev.2. f Break in series. g 2012. h Arrivals of non-resident tourists in hotels and similar establishments. i ITU estimate. j Population aged 10 and over. k Refers to total population. l Refugees are not part of the foreign-born migrant stock in the State of Palestine. m Value is zero, not available or not applicable.

Sudan

Region	Northern Africa	Surface area (sq km)	...
Population (est., 000)	38 764	Pop. density (per sq km)	20.8
Capital city	Khartoum	Capital city pop. (000)	5 000
Currency	Sudanese Pound (SDG)	UN membership date	12 November 1956

Economic indicators	2005	2010	2013
GDP: Gross domestic product (million current US$)	35 183[a]	53 945	54 595
GDP: Growth rate at constant 2005 prices (annual %)	9.0[a]	6.9	3.4
GDP per capita (current US$)	887.9[a]	1 513.1	1 438.1
GNI: Gross national income per capita (current US$)	853.9[a]	1 576.2	1 498.0
Gross fixed capital formation (% of GDP)	20.7[a]	22.5	24.4
Exchange rates (national currency per US$)[b]	2.31	2.48	5.70
Balance of payments, current account (million US$)	−2 473	−1 725	−4 481
Agricultural production index (2004-2006=100)[a]	101	99	113
Food production index (2004-2006=100)	101	100	115
Unemployment (% of labour force)	14.8	14.8	15.2
Labour force participation, adult female pop. (%)	30.2	30.9	31.3
Labour force participation, adult male pop. (%)	75.7	76.0	76.0
Tourist arrivals at national borders (000)[c]	246	495	591
Energy production, primary (Petajoules)[d]	1 145	1 473	734[e]
Mobile-cellular subscriptions (per 100 inhabitants)	4.8[f]	41.5	72.9
Individuals using the Internet (%)	1.3	16.7[g]	22.7[g]

Total trade		Major trading partners			2013
	(million US$)[h]	(% of exports)[h]		(% of imports)[h]	
Exports	8 981.7	China	70.4	China	21.7
Imports	9 546.3	United Arab Emirates	10.5	United Arab Emirates	8.6
Balance	−564.6	Japan	3.5	Saudi Arabia	8.1

Social indicators		
Population growth rate (average annual %)	2010-2015	2.1
Urban population growth rate (average annual %)	2010-2015	2.5
Rural population growth rate (average annual %)	2010-2015	1.9
Urban population (%)	2014	33.6
Population aged 0-14 years (%)	2014	40.9
Population aged 60+ years (females and males, % of total)	2014	5.4/4.8
Sex ratio (males per 100 females)	2014	100.7
Life expectancy at birth (females and males, years)	2010-2015	63.8/60.2
Infant mortality rate (per 1 000 live births)	2010-2015	55.1
Fertility rate, total (live births per woman)	2010-2015	4.5
Contraceptive prevalence (ages 15-49, %)[i]	2007-2013	9.0
International migrant stock (000 and % of total population)[j]	mid-2013	446.7/1.2
Refugees and others of concern to UNHCR	mid-2014	2 479 885[k]
Education: Government expenditure (% of GDP)	2007-2013	2.2
Education: Primary-secondary gross enrolment ratio (f/m per 100)	2007-2013	54.7/60.9
Education: Female third-level students (% of total)	2007-2013	52.2
Intentional homicide rate (per 100,000 population)	2008-2012	11.2
Seats held by women in national parliaments (%)	2015	24.3

Environmental indicators		
Threatened species	2014	122
Proportion of terrestrial and marine areas protected (%)	2014	1.7
Population using improved drinking water sources (%)	2012	55.0
Population using improved sanitation facilities (%)	2012	24.0
CO_2 emission estimates (000 metric tons and metric tons per capita)	2011	16 579/0.4
Energy supply per capita (Gigajoules)	2012	15.0

a Former Sudan. b Principal rate. c Including nationals residing abroad. d Including South Sudan until 2011. e 2012. f ITU estimate excluding Canar, which is counted as a fixed line. g ITU estimate. h 2011. i Data refer to pre-secession Sudan, including data for South Sudan. j Including refugees. k Including 77,300 people who are in an internally displaced person-like situation.

Suriname

Region	South America	Surface area (sq km)	163 820
Population (est., 000)	544	Pop. density (per sq km)	3.3
Capital city	Paramaribo	Capital city pop. (000)	234 [a]
Currency	Surinamese Dollar (SRD)	UN membership date	4 December 1975

Economic indicators	2005	2010	2013
GDP: Gross domestic product (million current US$)	2 193	4 368	5 299
GDP: Growth rate at constant 2005 prices (annual %)	3.9	5.2	2.9
GDP per capita (current US$)	4 390.3	8 321.3	9 825.9
GNI: Gross national income per capita (current US$)	4 313.5	8 122.8	9 597.2
Gross fixed capital formation (% of GDP)	45.6	37.5	41.2
Exchange rates (national currency per US$) [b]	2.74	2.74	3.30
Balance of payments, current account (million US$)	−144	651	−198
CPI: Consumer price index (2000=100) [cd]	171	249	313
Agricultural production index (2004-2006=100)	99	137	146
Food production index (2004-2006=100)	99	137	146
Unemployment (% of labour force)	8.2	7.6	7.8
Employment in industrial sector (% of employed)	23.0 [efgh]	...	...
Employment in agricultural sector (% of employed)	8.0 [efgh]	...	...
Labour force participation, adult female pop. (%)	37.8	40.1	40.5
Labour force participation, adult male pop. (%)	67.3	68.7	68.8
Tourist arrivals at national borders (000)	161	205	249
Energy production, primary (Petajoules)	31	38	40 [i]
Mobile-cellular subscriptions (per 100 inhabitants)	46.6	99.3	127.3
Individuals using the Internet (%)	6.4	31.6	37.4 [j]

Total trade		Major trading partners			2013
	(million US$) [k]	(% of exports) [k]		(% of imports) [k]	
Exports	2 466.9	United Arab Emirates	26.1	United States	26.7
Imports	1 637.8	Canada	18.6	Trinidad and Tobago	25.4
Balance	829.1	United States	11.2	Netherlands	16.0

Social indicators		
Population growth rate (average annual %)	2010-2015	0.9
Urban population growth rate (average annual %)	2010-2015	0.8
Rural population growth rate (average annual %)	2010-2015	1.1
Urban population (%)	2014	66.1
Population aged 0-14 years (%)	2014	26.9
Population aged 60+ years (females and males, % of total)	2014	11.1/8.7
Sex ratio (males per 100 females)	2014	100.4
Life expectancy at birth (females and males, years)	2010-2015	74.2/67.8
Infant mortality rate (per 1 000 live births)	2010-2015	17.4
Fertility rate, total (live births per woman)	2010-2015	2.3
Contraceptive prevalence (ages 15-49, %)	2007-2013	47.6
International migrant stock (000 and % of total population) [l]	mid-2013	41.7/7.7
Refugees and others of concern to UNHCR	mid-2014	1
Education: Primary-secondary gross enrolment ratio (f/m per 100)	2007-2013	97.4/89.6
Education: Female third-level students (% of total)	2007-2013	62.0 [m]
Intentional homicide rate (per 100,000 population)	2008-2012	6.1
Seats held by women in national parliaments (%)	2015	11.8

Environmental indicators		
Threatened species	2014	75
Forested area (% of land area)	2012	94.6
Proportion of terrestrial and marine areas protected (%)	2014	8.6
Population using improved drinking water sources (%)	2012	95.0
Population using improved sanitation facilities (%)	2012	80.0
CO_2 emission estimates (000 metric tons and metric tons per capita)	2011	1 911/3.6
Energy supply per capita (Gigajoules)	2012	69.0

a Refers to the total population of the District of Paramaribo. b Market rate. c Paramaribo. d Index base 2001=100. e 2004. f Population census. g ISIC Rev.3. h August. i 2012. j ITU estimate. k 2011. l Refers to foreign citizens. m 2002.

Swaziland

Region	Southern Africa	Surface area (sq km)	17 363
Population (est., 000)	1 268	Pop. density (per sq km)	73.0
Capital city	Mbabane[a]	Capital city pop. (000)	66
Currency	Lilangeni (SZL)	UN membership date	24 September 1968

Economic indicators	2005	2010	2013
GDP: Gross domestic product (million current US$)	2 584	3 892	3 523
GDP: Growth rate at constant 2005 prices (annual %)	2.5	1.9	2.8
GDP per capita (current US$)	2 339.3	3 261.6	2 819.2
GNI: Gross national income per capita (current US$)	2 500.7	3 303.0	2 930.0
Gross fixed capital formation (% of GDP)	15.0	9.7	10.8
Exchange rates (national currency per US$)[b]	6.32	6.63	10.49
Balance of payments, current account (million US$)	−103	−388	239
CPI: Consumer price index (2000=100)	140	121[cd]	...
Agricultural production index (2004-2006=100)	103	104	112
Food production index (2004-2006=100)	103	104	113
Unemployment (% of labour force)	22.9	22.8	22.5
Labour force participation, adult female pop. (%)	42.9	43.5	43.9
Labour force participation, adult male pop. (%)	70.8	70.7	71.6
Tourist arrivals at national borders (000)	837	868	968
Energy production, primary (Petajoules)	36	39	37[e]
Mobile-cellular subscriptions (per 100 inhabitants)	18.1	60.8	71.5[f]
Individuals using the Internet (%)	3.7[f]	11.0	24.7[f]

Social indicators		
Population growth rate (average annual %)	2010-2015	1.5
Urban population growth rate (average annual %)	2010-2015	1.3
Rural population growth rate (average annual %)	2010-2015	1.5
Urban population (%)	2014	21.3
Population aged 0-14 years (%)	2014	37.5
Population aged 60+ years (females and males, % of total)	2014	6.2/4.8
Sex ratio (males per 100 females)	2014	97.6
Life expectancy at birth (females and males, years)	2010-2015	48.5/49.7
Infant mortality rate (per 1 000 live births)	2010-2015	64.6
Fertility rate, total (live births per woman)	2010-2015	3.4
Contraceptive prevalence (ages 15-49, %)	2007-2013	65.2
International migrant stock (000 and % of total population)[g]	mid-2013	25.5/2.0
Refugees and others of concern to UNHCR	mid-2014	1 133
Education: Government expenditure (% of GDP)	2007-2013	7.8
Education: Primary-secondary gross enrolment ratio (f/m per 100)	2007-2013	88.9/95.0
Education: Female third-level students (% of total)	2007-2013	50.9
Intentional homicide rate (per 100,000 population)	2008-2012	33.8
Seats held by women in national parliaments (%)	2015	6.2

Environmental indicators		
Threatened species	2014	34
Forested area (% of land area)	2012	33.2
Proportion of terrestrial and marine areas protected (%)	2014	4.0
Population using improved drinking water sources (%)	2012	74.0
Population using improved sanitation facilities (%)	2012	57.0
CO_2 emission estimates (000 metric tons and metric tons per capita)	2011	1 049/0.9
Energy supply per capita (Gigajoules)	2012	38.0

a Mbabane is the administrative capital and Lobamba is the legislative capital. b Official rate. c 2009.
d Index base 2007=100. e 2012. f ITU estimate. g Including refugees.

Sweden

Region	Northern Europe	Surface area (sq km)	450 295	
Population (est., 000)	9 631	Pop. density (per sq km)	21.4	
Capital city	Stockholm	Capital city pop. (000)	1 464[a]	
Currency	Swedish Krona (SEK)	UN membership date	19 November 1946	

Economic indicators	2005	2010	2013
GDP: Gross domestic product (million current US$)	389 043	488 378	579 680
GDP: Growth rate at constant 2005 prices (annual %)	2.8	6.0	1.5
GDP per capita (current US$)	43 082.6	52 053.1	60 565.6
GNI: Gross national income per capita (current US$)	43 664.8	53 487.2	62 619.0
Gross fixed capital formation (% of GDP)	22.2	22.3	22.2
Exchange rates (national currency per US$)[b]	7.96	6.71	6.42
Balance of payments, current account (million US$)	26 423	29 402	34 541
CPI: Consumer price index (2000=100)	108	116	120
Index of industrial production (2010=100)[c]	107	100	96
Agricultural production index (2004-2006=100)	100	94	96
Food production index (2004-2006=100)	100	94	96
Unemployment (% of labour force)	7.8	8.7	8.1
Employment in industrial sector (% of employed)	22.0[def]	19.9[gh]	19.5[gi]
Employment in agricultural sector (% of employed)	2.0[def]	2.1[gh]	2.0[gi]
Labour force participation, adult female pop. (%)	59.3	59.0	60.3
Labour force participation, adult male pop. (%)	68.1	68.1	67.9
Tourist arrivals at national borders (000)[j]	4 883	5 183	5 229
Energy production, primary (Petajoules)	1 430	1 364	1 493[i]
Mobile-cellular subscriptions (per 100 inhabitants)	100.8	117.2	124.4[k]
Individuals using the Internet (%)	84.8	90.0[l]	94.8

Total trade		Major trading partners			2013
	(million US$)	(% of exports)			(% of imports)
Exports	167 679.9	Norway	10.5	Germany	17.4
Imports	159 687.6	Germany	9.7	Norway	8.9
Balance	7 992.3	Finland	7.0	Denmark	8.1

Social indicators		
Population growth rate (average annual %)	2010-2015	0.7
Urban population growth rate (average annual %)	2010-2015	0.8
Rural population growth rate (average annual %)	2010-2015	−0.4
Urban population (%)	2014	85.7
Population aged 0-14 years (%)	2014	17.1
Population aged 60+ years (females and males, % of total)	2014	27.2/23.9
Sex ratio (males per 100 females)	2014	99.4
Life expectancy at birth (females and males, years)	2010-2015	83.8/79.7
Infant mortality rate (per 1 000 live births)	2010-2015	2.3
Fertility rate, total (live births per woman)	2010-2015	1.9
Contraceptive prevalence (ages 15-49, %)[m]	2007-2013	75.2[n]
International migrant stock (000 and % of total population)	mid-2013	1 519.5/15.9
Refugees and others of concern to UNHCR	mid-2014	166 902[o]
Education: Government expenditure (% of GDP)	2007-2013	6.8
Education: Primary-secondary gross enrolment ratio (f/m per 100)	2007-2013	99.3/100.3
Education: Female third-level students (% of total)	2007-2013	59.7
Intentional homicide rate (per 100,000 population)	2008-2012	0.7
Seats held by women in national parliaments (%)	2015	43.6

Environmental indicators		
Threatened species	2014	36
Forested area (% of land area)	2012	69.2
Proportion of terrestrial and marine areas protected (%)	2014	13.0
Population using improved drinking water sources (%)	2012	100.0
Population using improved sanitation facilities (%)	2012	100.0
CO_2 emission estimates (000 metric tons and metric tons per capita)	2011	52 145/5.5
Energy supply per capita (Gigajoules)	2012	218.0

a Refers to 'tätort' (according to the administrative divisions of 2005). b Official rate. c ISIC Rev.4 (BCD). d ISIC Rev.3. e Population aged 16-64. f Excluding conscripts. g Population aged 15-74. h Break in series. i 2012. j Arrivals of non-resident tourists in all types of accommodation establishments. k ITU estimate. l Population aged 16-75. m Age group 18 to 44 years. n 1996. o Refugee population refers to the end of 2013.

Switzerland

Region	Western Europe	Surface area (sq km)	41 285	
Population (est., 000)	8 158	Pop. density (per sq km)	197.6	
Capital city	Bern	Capital city pop. (000)	358	
Currency	Swiss Franc (CHF)	UN membership date	10 September 2002	

Economic indicators

	2005	2010	2013
GDP: Gross domestic product (million current US$)	407 543	581 209	685 434
GDP: Growth rate at constant 2005 prices (annual %)	3.0	3.0	1.9
GDP per capita (current US$)	55 009.4	74 223.4	84 853.7
GNI: Gross national income per capita (current US$)	59 708.9	78 715.1	88 815.5
Gross fixed capital formation (% of GDP)	24.8	23.8	21.2
Exchange rates (national currency per US$) [a]	1.31	0.94	0.89
Balance of payments, current account (million US$)	53 149	75 894	97 574
CPI: Consumer price index (2000=100)	104	109	108
Index of industrial production (2010=100) [b]	81	100	106
Agricultural production index (2004-2006=100)	99	103	101
Food production index (2004-2006=100)	99	103	101
Unemployment (% of labour force)	4.4	4.5	4.4
Employment in industrial sector (% of employed)	23.7[c]	21.1[d]	20.3[e]
Employment in agricultural sector (% of employed)	3.8[c]	3.3[d]	3.5[e]
Labour force participation, adult female pop. (%)	59.5	60.8	61.8
Labour force participation, adult male pop. (%)	75.0	75.3	74.9
Tourist arrivals at national borders (000) [f,g]	7 229	8 628	8 967
Energy production, primary (Petajoules) [h]	458	526	530[e]
Mobile-cellular subscriptions (per 100 inhabitants)	92.3	123.2	133.8[i]
Individuals using the Internet (%) [j]	70.1	83.9	86.7

Total trade

	(million US$)[k]	Major trading partners (% of exports)[k]			2013 (% of imports)[k]
Exports	229 156.6	Germany	18.5	Germany	28.1
Imports	200 933.9	United States	11.7	Italy	10.1
Balance	28 222.7	Italy	7.1	France	8.3

Social indicators

Population growth rate (average annual %)	2010-2015	1.0
Urban population growth rate (average annual %)	2010-2015	1.1
Rural population growth rate (average annual %)	2010-2015	0.8
Urban population (%)	2014	73.8
Population aged 0-14 years (%)	2014	14.7
Population aged 60+ years (females and males, % of total)	2014	25.5/21.6
Sex ratio (males per 100 females)	2014	97.3
Life expectancy at birth (females and males, years)	2010-2015	84.9/80.1
Infant mortality rate (per 1 000 live births)	2010-2015	3.7
Fertility rate, total (live births per woman)	2010-2015	1.5
Contraceptive prevalence (ages 15-49, %) [l]	2007-2013	82.0[m]
International migrant stock (000 and % of total population)	mid-2013	2 335.1/28.9
Refugees and others of concern to UNHCR	mid-2014	77 967
Education: Government expenditure (% of GDP)	2007-2013	5.3
Education: Primary-secondary gross enrolment ratio (f/m per 100)	2007-2013	98.2/99.9
Education: Female third-level students (% of total)	2007-2013	49.3
Intentional homicide rate (per 100,000 population)	2008-2012	0.6
Seats held by women in national parliaments (%)	2015	30.5

Environmental indicators

Threatened species	2014	62
Forested area (% of land area)	2012	31.6
Proportion of terrestrial and marine areas protected (%)	2014	9.9
Population using improved drinking water sources (%)	2012	100.0
Population using improved sanitation facilities (%)	2012	100.0
CO_2 emission estimates (000 metric tons and metric tons per capita)	2011	36 597/4.6
Energy supply per capita (Gigajoules) [h]	2012	133.0

a Official rate. b ISIC Rev.4 (BCD). c ISIC Rev.3. d Break in series. e 2012. f Arrivals of non-resident tourists in hotels and similar establishments. g Including health establishments. h Including Liechtenstein for oil statistics. i Estimate. j Population aged 14 and over using the Internet in the last 6 months. k Including Liechtenstein. l Age group 20 to 49 years. m 1994-1995.

Syrian Arab Republic

Region	Western Asia	Surface area (sq km)	185 180
Population (est., 000)	21 987	Pop. density (per sq km)	118.7
Capital city	Damascus	Capital city pop. (000)	2 574[a]
Currency	Syrian Pound (SYP)	UN membership date	24 October 1945

Economic indicators	2005	2010	2013
GDP: Gross domestic product (million current US$)	28 397	60 465	35 164
GDP: Growth rate at constant 2005 prices (annual %)	6.2	3.4	−20.6
GDP per capita (current US$)	1 563.1	2 808.1	1 605.8
GNI: Gross national income per capita (current US$)	1 493.4	2 744.9	1 572.7
Gross fixed capital formation (% of GDP)	23.0	20.8	19.4
Exchange rates (national currency per US$)[b]	52.00	46.58	143.57
Balance of payments, current account (million US$)	299	−367	...
CPI: Consumer price index (2000=100)	122	173	473
Index of industrial production (2010=100)[c]	102	100	...
Agricultural production index (2004-2006=100)	100	89	79
Food production index (2004-2006=100)	99	92	82
Unemployment (% of labour force)	9.2	8.4	10.8
Employment in industrial sector (% of employed)[d]	28.3[e]	32.7	32.7[f]
Employment in agricultural sector (% of employed)[d]	19.6[e]	14.3	14.3[f]
Labour force participation, adult female pop. (%)	16.3	13.2	13.5
Labour force participation, adult male pop. (%)	76.1	72.7	72.7
Tourist arrivals at national borders (000)[g]	3 571[h]	8 546[hi]	...
Energy production, primary (Petajoules)	1 171	1 165	567[j]
Mobile-cellular subscriptions (per 100 inhabitants)	16.2	54.3	56.0
Individuals using the Internet (%)	5.7[k]	20.7	26.2[k]

Total trade		Major trading partners			2013
	(million US$)[l]	(% of exports)[l]			(% of imports)[l]
Exports	11 352.9	Iraq	20.2	Turkey	9.5
Imports	17 561.6	Italy	13.4	China	8.8
Balance	−6 208.7	Germany	13.0	Italy	7.4

Social indicators		
Population growth rate (average annual %)	2010-2015	0.7
Urban population growth rate (average annual %)	2010-2015	1.4
Rural population growth rate (average annual %)	2010-2015	−0.2
Urban population (%)	2014	57.3
Population aged 0-14 years (%)	2014	34.8
Population aged 60+ years (females and males, % of total)	2014	6.8/6.3
Sex ratio (males per 100 females)	2014	103.8
Life expectancy at birth (females and males, years)	2010-2015	77.6/71.6
Infant mortality rate (per 1 000 live births)	2010-2015	17.7
Fertility rate, total (live births per woman)	2010-2015	3.0
Contraceptive prevalence (ages 15-49, %)	2007-2013	53.9
International migrant stock (000 and % of total population)[mn]	mid-2013	1 394.2/6.4
Refugees and others of concern to UNHCR	mid-2014	6 832 691[o]
Education: Government expenditure (% of GDP)	2007-2013	4.9
Education: Primary-secondary gross enrolment ratio (f/m per 100)	2007-2013	56.6/57.3
Education: Female third-level students (% of total)	2007-2013	48.9
Intentional homicide rate (per 100,000 population)	2008-2012	2.2
Seats held by women in national parliaments (%)	2015	12.4

Environmental indicators		
Threatened species	2014	107
Forested area (% of land area)	2012	2.7
Proportion of terrestrial and marine areas protected (%)	2014	0.7
Population using improved drinking water sources (%)	2012	90.0
Population using improved sanitation facilities (%)	2012	96.0
CO_2 emission estimates (000 metric tons and metric tons per capita)	2011	57 671/2.6
Energy supply per capita (Gigajoules)	2012	29.0

a Excluding refugees or internally displaced persons (if applicable). b UN operational exchange rate. c ISIC Rev.3 (CDE). d ISIC Rev.2. e 2006. f 2011. g Arrivals of non-resident tourists in all types of accommodation establishments. h Including nationals residing abroad. i Including Iraqi nationals. j 2012. k ITU estimate. l 2010. m Refers to foreign citizens. n Including refugees. o Refugee figure for Iraqis in the Syrian Arab Republic is a Government estimate. UNHCR has registered and is assisting 27,200 Iraqis at mid-2014.

Tajikistan

Region	Central Asia	Surface area (sq km)	142 600	
Population (est., 000)	8 409	Pop. density (per sq km)	58.8	
Capital city	Dushanbe	Capital city pop. (000)	801	
Currency	Somoni (TJS)	UN membership date	2 March 1992	

Economic indicators	2005	2010	2013
GDP: Gross domestic product (million current US$)	2 312	5 642	8 506
GDP: Growth rate at constant 2005 prices (annual %)	6.7	6.5	7.4
GDP per capita (current US$)	339.8	739.7	1 036.3
GNI: Gross national income per capita (current US$)	434.4	935.6	1 306.6
Gross fixed capital formation (% of GDP)	11.1	24.5	18.4
Exchange rates (national currency per US$)[a]	3.20	4.40	4.77
Balance of payments, current account (million US$)	−19	−370	−248[b]
Index of industrial production (2010=100)[c]	88	100	122
Agricultural production index (2004-2006=100)	99	123	154
Food production index (2004-2006=100)	99	137	170
Unemployment (% of labour force)	11.7	11.6	10.7
Employment in industrial sector (% of employed)	17.9[de]	...	...
Employment in agricultural sector (% of employed)	55.5[de]	...	...
Labour force participation, adult female pop. (%)	57.7	58.3	58.9
Labour force participation, adult male pop. (%)	74.7	76.3	77.1
Tourist arrivals at national borders (000)[f]	...	160	208
Energy production, primary (Petajoules)	65	64	70[b]
Mobile-cellular subscriptions (per 100 inhabitants)	3.9	77.9	91.8[g]
Individuals using the Internet (%)	0.3	11.6[g]	16.0[g]

Social indicators		
Population growth rate (average annual %)	2010-2015	2.4
Urban population growth rate (average annual %)	2010-2015	2.6
Rural population growth rate (average annual %)	2010-2015	2.4
Urban population (%)	2014	26.7
Population aged 0-14 years (%)	2014	36.0
Population aged 60+ years (females and males, % of total)	2014	5.3/4.6
Sex ratio (males per 100 females)	2014	100.6
Life expectancy at birth (females and males, years)	2010-2015	70.7/64.0
Infant mortality rate (per 1 000 live births)	2010-2015	56.8
Fertility rate, total (live births per woman)	2010-2015	3.9
Contraceptive prevalence (ages 15-49, %)	2007-2013	27.9
International migrant stock (000 and % of total population)	mid-2013	275.7/3.4
Refugees and others of concern to UNHCR	mid-2014	5 616
Education: Government expenditure (% of GDP)	2007-2013	4.0
Education: Primary-secondary gross enrolment ratio (f/m per 100)	2007-2013	87.9/94.9
Education: Female third-level students (% of total)	2007-2013	33.9
Intentional homicide rate (per 100,000 population)	2008-2012	1.6
Seats held by women in national parliaments (%)	2015	16.9

Environmental indicators		
Threatened species	2014	42
Forested area (% of land area)	2012	2.9
Proportion of terrestrial and marine areas protected (%)	2014	21.9
Population using improved drinking water sources (%)	2012	72.0
Population using improved sanitation facilities (%)	2012	94.0
CO_2 emission estimates (000 metric tons and metric tons per capita)	2011	2 783/0.4
Energy supply per capita (Gigajoules)	2012	13.0

a Official rate. b 2012. c ISIC Rev.3 (CDE). d 2004. e ISIC Rev.3. f Arrivals of non-resident visitors at national borders. g ITU estimate.

Thailand

Region	South-Eastern Asia	Surface area (sq km)	513 120
Population (est., 000)	67 223	Pop. density (per sq km)	131.0
Capital city	Bangkok	Capital city pop. (000)	9 098
Currency	Baht (THB)	UN membership date	16 December 1946

Economic indicators	2005	2010	2013
GDP: Gross domestic product (million current US$)	188 847	338 778	420 167
GDP: Growth rate at constant 2005 prices (annual %)	4.2	7.4	2.9
GDP per capita (current US$)	2 880.6	5 101.9	6 270.2
GNI: Gross national income per capita (current US$)	2 751.1	4 875.5	5 848.7
Gross fixed capital formation (% of GDP)	27.8	24.2	25.2
Exchange rates (national currency per US$)[a]	41.03	30.15	32.81
Balance of payments, current account (million US$)	−7 647	9 946	−2 678
CPI: Consumer price index (2000=100)	112	129	141
Agricultural production index (2004-2006=100)	98	113	129
Food production index (2004-2006=100)	98	115	129
Unemployment (% of labour force)	1.3	1.0	0.7
Employment in industrial sector (% of employed)	20.2[bc]	20.6[bde]	20.9[def]
Employment in agricultural sector (% of employed)	42.6[bc]	38.2[bde]	39.6[def]
Labour force participation, adult female pop. (%)	66.1	64.4	64.3
Labour force participation, adult male pop. (%)	81.2	80.9	80.7
Tourist arrivals at national borders (000)	11 567[g]	15 936	26 547
Energy production, primary (Petajoules)	2 088	2 929	3 176[fh]
Mobile-cellular subscriptions (per 100 inhabitants)	46.5[i]	108.0	138.0
Individuals using the Internet (%)	15.0	22.4	28.9[j]

Total trade		Major trading partners			2013
	(million US$)	(% of exports)		(% of imports)	
Exports	228 527.4	China	11.9	Japan	16.4
Imports	250 708.2	United States	10.1	China	15.0
Balance	−22 180.8	Japan	9.7	United Arab Emirates	6.9

Social indicators

Population growth rate (average annual %)	2010-2015	0.3
Urban population growth rate (average annual %)	2010-2015	3.0
Rural population growth rate (average annual %)	2010-2015	−2.1
Urban population (%)	2014	49.2
Population aged 0-14 years (%)	2014	17.8
Population aged 60+ years (females and males, % of total)	2014	16.2/14.1
Sex ratio (males per 100 females)	2014	95.9
Life expectancy at birth (females and males, years)	2010-2015	77.7/71.0
Infant mortality rate (per 1 000 live births)	2010-2015	9.9
Fertility rate, total (live births per woman)	2010-2015	1.4
Contraceptive prevalence (ages 15-49, %)	2007-2013	79.3
International migrant stock (000 and % of total population)[k]	mid-2013	3 721.7/5.6
Refugees and others of concern to UNHCR	mid-2014	647 780[l]
Education: Government expenditure (% of GDP)	2007-2013	7.6
Education: Primary-secondary gross enrolment ratio (f/m per 100)	2007-2013	91.7/90.5
Education: Female third-level students (% of total)	2007-2013	57.1
Intentional homicide rate (per 100,000 population)	2008-2012	5.0
Seats held by women in national parliaments (%)	2015	6.1

Environmental indicators

Threatened species	2014	577
Forested area (% of land area)	2012	37.2
Proportion of terrestrial and marine areas protected (%)	2014	12.5
Population using improved drinking water sources (%)	2012	96.0
Population using improved sanitation facilities (%)	2012	93.0
CO_2 emission estimates (000 metric tons and metric tons per capita)	2011	303 371/4.6
Energy supply per capita (Gigajoules)	2012	81.0

a Official rate. b ISIC Rev.3. c Third quarter. d Average of quarterly estimates. e Break in series. f 2012. g Including arrivals of nationals residing abroad. h UNSD estimate. i ITU estimate. j Population aged 6 and over. k Including refugees. l Stateless persons population refers to 2011.

The former Yugoslav Republic of Macedonia

Region	Southern Europe	Surface area (sq km)	25 713
Population (est., 000)	2 108	Pop. density (per sq km)	82.0
Capital city	Skopje	Capital city pop. (000)	501
Currency	Denar (MKD)	UN membership date	8 April 1993

Economic indicators	2005	2010	2013
GDP: Gross domestic product (million current US$)	6 259	9 407	10 767
GDP: Growth rate at constant 2005 prices (annual %)	4.7	3.4	2.7
GDP per capita (current US$)	2 994.5	4 474.9	5 109.9
GNI: Gross national income per capita (current US$)	2 942.2	4 415.7	5 039.2
Gross fixed capital formation (% of GDP)	19.2	23.1	23.6
Exchange rates (national currency per US$)[a]	51.86	46.31	44.63
Balance of payments, current account (million US$)	−159	−198	−195
CPI: Consumer price index (2000=100)	109[b]	125[c]	...
Index of industrial production (2010=100)[d]	100	100	107
Agricultural production index (2004-2006=100)	100	116	115
Food production index (2004-2006=100)	99	116	115
Unemployment (% of labour force)	37.3	32.0	29.0
Employment in industrial sector (% of employed)	32.3[e]	30.0[f]	29.9[g]
Employment in agricultural sector (% of employed)	19.5[e]	18.7[f]	17.3[g]
Labour force participation, adult female pop. (%)	42.2	42.8	43.1
Labour force participation, adult male pop. (%)	63.8	68.6	67.5
Tourist arrivals at national borders (000)[h]	197	262	400
Energy production, primary (Petajoules)	108	66	62[g]
Mobile-cellular subscriptions (per 100 inhabitants)	54.1	102.4	106.2[i]
Individuals using the Internet (%)	26.5[j]	51.9[k]	61.2[i]

Total trade		Major trading partners			2013
	(million US$)		(% of exports)		(% of imports)
Exports	4 266.9	Germany	35.9	United Kingdom	11.0
Imports	6 599.8	Serbia	12.8	Greece	10.6
Balance	−2 332.9	Bulgaria	7.6	Germany	10.5

Social indicators		
Population growth rate (average annual %)	2010-2015	0.1
Urban population growth rate (average annual %)	2010-2015	0.1
Rural population growth rate (average annual %)	2010-2015	<
Urban population (%)	2014	57.0
Population aged 0-14 years (%)	2014	16.6
Population aged 60+ years (females and males, % of total)	2014	20.1/16.8
Sex ratio (males per 100 females)	2014	100.3
Life expectancy at birth (females and males, years)	2010-2015	77.5/72.9
Infant mortality rate (per 1 000 live births)	2010-2015	10.1
Fertility rate, total (live births per woman)	2010-2015	1.4
Contraceptive prevalence (ages 15-49, %)	2007-2013	40.2
International migrant stock (000 and % of total population)[l]	mid-2013	139.8/6.6
Refugees and others of concern to UNHCR	mid-2014	3 120
Education: Government expenditure (% of GDP)	2007-2013	3.5[m]
Education: Primary-secondary gross enrolment ratio (f/m per 100)	2007-2013	84.8/85.3
Education: Female third-level students (% of total)	2007-2013	53.3
Intentional homicide rate (per 100,000 population)	2008-2012	1.4
Seats held by women in national parliaments (%)	2015	33.3

Environmental indicators		
Threatened species	2014	100
Forested area (% of land area)	2012	39.9
Proportion of terrestrial and marine areas protected (%)	2014	9.7
Population using improved drinking water sources (%)	2012	99.0
Population using improved sanitation facilities (%)	2012	91.0
CO_2 emission estimates (000 metric tons and metric tons per capita)	2011	9 336/4.4
Energy supply per capita (Gigajoules)	2012	58.0

a Market rate. b Annual average is the weighted mean of monthly data. c Series linked to former series. d ISIC Rev.4 (BCD). e ISIC Rev.3. f 2011. g 2012. h Arrivals of non-resident tourists in all types of accommodation establishments. i Fourth quarter. j ITU estimate. k Population aged 15-74. l Including refugees. m 2002.

Timor-Leste

Region	South-Eastern Asia	Surface area (sq km)	14 919
Population (est., 000)	1 152	Pop. density (per sq km)	77.5
Capital city	Dili	Capital city pop. (000)	228
Currency	U.S. Dollar (USD)	UN membership date	27 September 2002

Economic indicators	2005	2010	2013
GDP: Gross domestic product (million current US$)	1 813	4 215	4 941
GDP: Growth rate at constant 2005 prices (annual %)	52.7	−1.4	5.4
GDP per capita (current US$)	1 821.0	3 905.2	4 361.6
GNI: Gross national income per capita (current US$)	836.4	3 052.6	3 847.0
Gross fixed capital formation (% of GDP)	5.1	13.0	13.9
Balance of payments, current account (million US$)	541[a]	1 671	2 396
Agricultural production index (2004-2006=100)	98	121	113
Food production index (2004-2006=100)	98	126	119
Unemployment (% of labour force)	7.2	3.9	4.4
Employment in industrial sector (% of employed)	...	9.2	...
Employment in agricultural sector (% of employed)	...	50.6	...
Labour force participation, adult female pop. (%)	32.0	25.0	24.6
Labour force participation, adult male pop. (%)	65.9	51.8	50.8
Tourist arrivals at national borders (000)[b]	14[a]	40	58[c]
Energy production, primary (Petajoules)	201	186	169[c]
Mobile-cellular subscriptions (per 100 inhabitants)	3.3	43.8[d]	57.4[d]
Individuals using the Internet (%)	0.1	0.2[d]	1.1[d]

Total trade		Major trading partners			2013
	(million US$)	(% of exports)			(% of imports)
Exports	53.1	Indonesia	34.8	Indonesia	34.3
Imports	513.7	Germany	14.5	Malaysia	15.4
Balance	−460.6	United States	13.7	Singapore	12.8

Social indicators		
Population growth rate (average annual %)	2010-2015	1.7
Urban population growth rate (average annual %)	2010-2015	3.8
Rural population growth rate (average annual %)	2010-2015	0.7
Urban population (%)	2014	32.1
Population aged 0-14 years (%)	2014	45.2
Population aged 60+ years (females and males, % of total)	2014	5.7/5.0
Sex ratio (males per 100 females)	2014	103.4
Life expectancy at birth (females and males, years)	2010-2015	68.9/65.8
Infant mortality rate (per 1 000 live births)	2010-2015	39.3
Fertility rate, total (live births per woman)	2010-2015	5.9
Contraceptive prevalence (ages 15-49, %)	2007-2013	22.3
International migrant stock (000 and % of total population)	mid-2013	11.6/1.0
Refugees and others of concern to UNHCR	mid-2014	2
Education: Government expenditure (% of GDP)	2007-2013	9.4
Education: Primary-secondary gross enrolment ratio (f/m per 100)	2007-2013	89.8/92.3
Education: Female third-level students (% of total)	2007-2013	41.3
Intentional homicide rate (per 100,000 population)	2008-2012	3.6
Seats held by women in national parliaments (%)	2015	38.5

Environmental indicators		
Threatened species	2014	21
Forested area (% of land area)	2012	48.4
Proportion of terrestrial and marine areas protected (%)	2014	2.1
Population using improved drinking water sources (%)	2012	70.0
Population using improved sanitation facilities (%)	2012	39.0
CO_2 emission estimates (000 metric tons and metric tons per capita)	2011	183/0.2
Energy supply per capita (Gigajoules)	2012	3.0[e]

a 2006. b Arrivals by air at Dili Airport. c 2012. d ITU estimate. e UNSD estimate.

Togo

Region	Western Africa	Surface area (sq km)	56 785	
Population (est., 000)	6 993	Pop. density (per sq km)	123.2	
Capital city	Lomé	Capital city pop. (000)	930	
Currency	CFA Franc (XOF)	UN membership date	20 September 1960	

Economic indicators	2005	2010	2013
GDP: Gross domestic product (million current US$)	2 110	3 173	4 158
GDP: Growth rate at constant 2005 prices (annual %)	1.2	4.0	5.1
GDP per capita (current US$)	380.9	503.1	610.0
GNI: Gross national income per capita (current US$)	374.1	499.5	519.7
Gross fixed capital formation (% of GDP)	16.5	18.0	23.3
Exchange rates (national currency per US$)[a]	556.04	490.91	475.64
Balance of payments, current account (million US$)	−204	−200	...
CPI: Consumer price index (2000=100)[b]	114	134[c]	145
Index of industrial production (2010=100)[d]	81	100	101
Agricultural production index (2004-2006=100)	96	123	121
Food production index (2004-2006=100)	99	129	125
Unemployment (% of labour force)	7.1	7.0	6.9
Employment in industrial sector (% of employed)	6.8[efg]	...	...
Employment in agricultural sector (% of employed)	54.1[efg]	...	...
Labour force participation, adult female pop. (%)	79.8	80.7	80.6
Labour force participation, adult male pop. (%)	80.4	81.0	81.3
Tourist arrivals at national borders (000)[h]	81	202	327
Energy production, primary (Petajoules)	84	99	105[i]
Mobile-cellular subscriptions (per 100 inhabitants)	7.8	41.3	62.5
Individuals using the Internet (%)[j]	1.8	3.0	4.5

Total trade		Major trading partners			2013
	(million US$)		(% of exports)		(% of imports)
Exports	1 002.3	Burkina Faso	19.0	China	15.7
Imports	2 002.2	Benin	12.0	France	7.7
Balance	−999.9	Ghana	11.4	Netherlands	7.4

Social indicators		
Population growth rate (average annual %)	2010-2015	2.6
Urban population growth rate (average annual %)	2010-2015	3.8
Rural population growth rate (average annual %)	2010-2015	1.8
Urban population (%)	2014	39.5
Population aged 0-14 years (%)	2014	41.7
Population aged 60+ years (females and males, % of total)	2014	4.8/4.1
Sex ratio (males per 100 females)	2014	97.4
Life expectancy at birth (females and males, years)	2010-2015	57.3/55.5
Infant mortality rate (per 1 000 live births)	2010-2015	66.4
Fertility rate, total (live births per woman)	2010-2015	4.7
Contraceptive prevalence (ages 15-49, %)	2007-2013	15.2
International migrant stock (000 and % of total population)[k]	mid-2013	202.5/3.0
Refugees and others of concern to UNHCR	mid-2014	22 982
Education: Government expenditure (% of GDP)	2007-2013	4.0
Education: Primary-secondary gross enrolment ratio (f/m per 100)[l]	2007-2013	66.8/88.5
Education: Female third-level students (% of total)	2007-2013	28.2
Intentional homicide rate (per 100,000 population)	2008-2012	10.3
Seats held by women in national parliaments (%)	2015	17.6

Environmental indicators		
Threatened species	2014	65
Forested area (% of land area)	2012	4.9
Proportion of terrestrial and marine areas protected (%)	2014	19.8
Population using improved drinking water sources (%)	2012	61.0
Population using improved sanitation facilities (%)	2012	11.0
CO_2 emission estimates (000 metric tons and metric tons per capita)	2011	2 098/0.3
Energy supply per capita (Gigajoules)	2012	20.0

a Official rate. b Lomé. c Series linked to former series. d ISIC Rev.4 (BCDE). e 2006. f Core Welfare Indicators Questionnaire (World Bank). g ISIC Rev.2. h Arrivals of non-resident tourists in hotels and similar establishments. i 2012. j ITU estimate. k Including refugees. l UNESCO estimate.

Tokelau

Region	Oceania-Polynesia	Surface area (sq km)	12
Population (est., 000)	1	Pop. density (per sq km)	101.8
Capital city	Tokelau[a]	Capital city pop. (000)	...
Currency	New Zealand Dollar (NZD)		

Economic indicators	2005	2010	2013
Exchange rates (national currency per US$)[b]	1.46	1.31	1.22
Agricultural production index (2004-2006=100)	102	120	125
Food production index (2004-2006=100)	102	120	125

Social indicators		
Population growth rate (average annual %)	2010-2015	1.9
Rural population growth rate (average annual %)	2010-2015	1.9
Population aged 0-14 years (%)[cde]	2014	33.2[f]
Population aged 60+ years (females and males, % of total)[cde]	2014	12.6/9.8[f]
Sex ratio (males per 100 females)[cde]	2014	99.2[f]
Life expectancy at birth (females and males, years)[g]	2010-2015	70.4/67.8[h]
Infant mortality rate (per 1 000 live births)[g]	2010-2015	31.3[i]
Fertility rate, total (live births per woman)[g]	2010-2015	2.1[j]
International migrant stock (000 and % of total population)	mid-2013	0.3/24.9
Education: Primary-secondary gross enrolment ratio (f/m per 100)[k]	2007-2013	115.2/105.5[i]

Environmental indicators		
Threatened species	2014	46

a The "capital" rotates yearly between the three atolls of Atafu, Fakaofo and Nukunomu, each with fewer than 500 inhabitants in 2011. **b** UN operational exchange rate. **c** Data compiled by the United Nations Demographic Yearbook system. **d** Data refer to the latest available census. **e** Census, de facto, complete tabulation. **f** 2011. **g** Data compiled by the Secretariat of the Pacific Community Demography Programme. **h** 1990. **i** 2000-2003. **j** 2006-2011. **k** National estimate. **l** 2003.

Tonga

		Surface area (sq km)	747
Region	Oceania-Polynesia	Surface area (sq km)	747
Population (est., 000)	106	Pop. density (per sq km)	162.7
Capital city	Nuku'alofa	Capital city pop. (000)	25
Currency	Pa'anga (TOP)	UN membership date	14 September 1999

Economic indicators

	2005	2010	2013
GDP: Gross domestic product (million current US$)	264	374	440
GDP: Growth rate at constant 2005 prices (annual %)	1.6	3.5	−3.0
GDP per capita (current US$)	2 613.1	3 593.1	4 173.2
GNI: Gross national income per capita (current US$)	2 612.0	3 647.0	4 217.6
Gross fixed capital formation (% of GDP)	21.9	29.6	22.6
Exchange rates (national currency per US$)[a]	2.06	1.81	1.82
Balance of payments, current account (million US$)	−21	−79	−45[b]
CPI: Consumer price index (2000=100)[c]	160	210	227
Agricultural production index (2004-2006=100)	97	136	131
Food production index (2004-2006=100)	97	136	131
Labour force participation, adult female pop. (%)	53.3	53.6	53.5
Labour force participation, adult male pop. (%)	75.2	75.2	74.6
Tourist arrivals at national borders (000)[d]	42	47	45
Energy production, primary (Petajoules)	0	0	0[b]
Mobile-cellular subscriptions (per 100 inhabitants)[e]	29.6	52.2	54.6
Individuals using the Internet (%)[e]	4.9	16.0	35.0

Total trade

Major trading partners					2013

	(million US$)[b]		(% of exports)[b]		(% of imports)[b]
Exports	15.6	New Zealand	26.3	New Zealand	30.0
Imports	199.2	United States	13.5	Singapore	22.9
Balance	−183.6	Japan	12.8	United States	13.0

Social indicators

Population growth rate (average annual %)	2010-2015	0.4
Urban population growth rate (average annual %)	2010-2015	0.7
Rural population growth rate (average annual %)	2010-2015	0.4
Urban population (%)	2014	23.6
Population aged 0-14 years (%)	2014	37.0
Population aged 60+ years (females and males, % of total)	2014	9.3/6.8
Sex ratio (males per 100 females)	2014	100.5
Life expectancy at birth (females and males, years)	2010-2015	75.6/69.7
Infant mortality rate (per 1 000 live births)	2010-2015	20.5
Fertility rate, total (live births per woman)	2010-2015	3.8
International migrant stock (000 and % of total population)	mid-2013	5.4/5.2
Refugees and others of concern to UNHCR	mid-2014	0[f]
Education: Government expenditure (% of GDP)	2007-2013	3.9[g]
Education: Primary-secondary gross enrolment ratio (f/m per 100)	2007-2013	101.1/99.6
Education: Female third-level students (% of total)	2007-2013	60.5[h]
Intentional homicide rate (per 100,000 population)	2008-2012	1.0
Seats held by women in national parliaments (%)	2015	0.0

Environmental indicators

Threatened species	2014	74
Forested area (% of land area)	2012	12.5
Proportion of terrestrial and marine areas protected (%)	2014	1.5
Population using improved drinking water sources (%)	2012	99.0
Population using improved sanitation facilities (%)	2012	91.0
CO$_2$ emission estimates (000 metric tons and metric tons per capita)	2011	103/1.0
Energy supply per capita (Gigajoules)	2012	15.0

a Official rate. b 2012. c Excluding rent. d Arrivals by air. e ITU estimate. f Value is zero, not available or not applicable. g 2004. h 2003.

Trinidad and Tobago

Region	Caribbean	Surface area (sq km)	5 130
Population (est., 000)	1 344	Pop. density (per sq km)	262.0
Capital city	Port of Spain	Capital city pop. (000)	34
Currency	TT Dollar (TTD)	UN membership date	18 September 1962

Economic indicators	2005	2010	2013
GDP: Gross domestic product (million current US$)	15 982	20 578	24 463
GDP: Growth rate at constant 2005 prices (annual %)	6.2	−2.5	2.8
GDP per capita (current US$)	12 323.2	15 494.7	18 239.9
GNI: Gross national income per capita (current US$)	11 741.0	13 816.7	14 780.4
Gross fixed capital formation (% of GDP)	28.7	14.0	14.0
Exchange rates (national currency per US$) [a]	6.31	6.42	6.47
Balance of payments, current account (million US$)	3 881	4 172	2 899[b]
CPI: Consumer price index (2000=100)	126	196	237
Index of industrial production (2010=100) [c]	63	100	95
Agricultural production index (2004-2006=100)	99	96	96
Food production index (2004-2006=100)	99	96	96
Unemployment (% of labour force)	8.0	5.9	5.8
Employment in industrial sector (% of employed)	31.0[d]	32.2[de]	...
Employment in agricultural sector (% of employed)	4.3[d]	3.8[de]	...
Labour force participation, adult female pop. (%)	53.5	52.5	53.0
Labour force participation, adult male pop. (%)	76.2	75.4	75.5
Tourist arrivals at national borders (000)	463	388	434
Energy production, primary (Petajoules)	1 318	1 785	1 669[f]
Mobile-cellular subscriptions (per 100 inhabitants)	71.3	142.6	144.9
Individuals using the Internet (%)	29.0[g]	48.5[h]	63.8[g]

Total trade		Major trading partners			2013
	(million US$)[i]	(% of exports)[i]		(% of imports)[i]	
Exports	10 981.7	United States	48.1	United States	28.0
Imports	6 479.6	Jamaica	6.5	Gabon	12.9
Balance	4 502.1	Barbados	3.4	Colombia	9.5

Social indicators		
Population growth rate (average annual %)	2010-2015	0.3
Urban population growth rate (average annual %)	2010-2015	−1.2
Rural population growth rate (average annual %)	2010-2015	0.4
Urban population (%)	2014	8.6
Population aged 0-14 years (%)	2014	20.8
Population aged 60+ years (females and males, % of total)	2014	15.2/12.9
Sex ratio (males per 100 females)	2014	97.7
Life expectancy at birth (females and males, years)	2010-2015	73.6/66.3
Infant mortality rate (per 1 000 live births)	2010-2015	24.2
Fertility rate, total (live births per woman)	2010-2015	1.8
Contraceptive prevalence (ages 15-49, %)	2007-2013	42.5[j]
International migrant stock (000 and % of total population)	mid-2013	32.5/2.4
Refugees and others of concern to UNHCR	mid-2014	95
Education: Government expenditure (% of GDP)	2007-2013	3.2[k]
Education: Primary-secondary gross enrolment ratio (f/m per 100) [l]	2007-2013	94.5/93.5[m]
Education: Female third-level students (% of total)	2007-2013	55.4[m]
Intentional homicide rate (per 100,000 population)	2008-2012	28.3
Seats held by women in national parliaments (%)	2015	28.6

Environmental indicators		
Threatened species	2014	57
Forested area (% of land area)	2012	43.9
Proportion of terrestrial and marine areas protected (%)	2014	2.6
Population using improved drinking water sources (%)	2012	94.0[i]
Population using improved sanitation facilities (%)	2012	92.0
CO_2 emission estimates (000 metric tons and metric tons per capita)	2011	49 574/37.2
Energy supply per capita (Gigajoules)	2012	604.0

a Official rate. b 2011. c ISIC Rev.3 (CDE). d ISIC Rev.2. e 2008. f 2012. g ITU estimate. h Country estimate. i 2010. j 2006. k 2003. l National estimate. m 2004.

Tunisia

Region	Northern Africa	Surface area (sq km)	163 610
Population (est., 000)	11 117	Pop. density (per sq km)	68.0
Capital city	Tunis	Capital city pop. (000)	1 978[a]
Currency	Tunisian Dinar (TND)	UN membership date	12 November 1956

Economic indicators	2005	2010	2013
GDP: Gross domestic product (million current US$)	32 272	44 051	46 883
GDP: Growth rate at constant 2005 prices (annual %)	4.0	3.0	2.3
GDP per capita (current US$)	3 210.7	4 143.3	4 263.5
GNI: Gross national income per capita (current US$)	3 045.3	3 948.9	4 212.6
Gross fixed capital formation (% of GDP)	21.5	24.6	20.5
Exchange rates (national currency per US$)[b]	1.36	1.44	1.65
Balance of payments, current account (million US$)	−299	−2 104	−3 879
CPI: Consumer price index (2000=100)	114	139[c]	161
Index of industrial production (2010=100)[d]	83	100	100
Agricultural production index (2004-2006=100)	101	107	118
Food production index (2004-2006=100)	101	107	118
Unemployment (% of labour force)	14.2	13.0	13.3
Employment in industrial sector (% of employed)	32.3	32.7	33.5[e]
Employment in agricultural sector (% of employed)	18.7	17.6	16.2[e]
Labour force participation, adult female pop. (%)	24.3	24.9	25.1
Labour force participation, adult male pop. (%)	68.4	70.1	70.9
Tourist arrivals at national borders (000)[f]	6 378	6 903	6 269
Energy production, primary (Petajoules)	274	324	294[g]
Mobile-cellular subscriptions (per 100 inhabitants)	56.5	104.5	115.6
Individuals using the Internet (%)	9.7	36.8	43.8[h]

Total trade		Major trading partners			2013
	(million US$)		(% of exports)		(% of imports)
Exports	17 060.5	France	26.4	France	18.3
Imports	24 266.4	Italy	18.5	Italy	14.5
Balance	−7 205.9	Germany	9.0	Germany	7.2

Social indicators		
Population growth rate (average annual %)	2010-2015	1.1
Urban population growth rate (average annual %)	2010-2015	1.4
Rural population growth rate (average annual %)	2010-2015	0.6
Urban population (%)	2014	66.7
Population aged 0-14 years (%)	2014	23.2
Population aged 60+ years (females and males, % of total)	2014	11.9/10.6
Sex ratio (males per 100 females)	2014	98.2
Life expectancy at birth (females and males, years)	2010-2015	78.2/73.5
Infant mortality rate (per 1 000 live births)	2010-2015	15.5
Fertility rate, total (live births per woman)	2010-2015	2.0
Contraceptive prevalence (ages 15-49, %)	2007-2013	62.5
International migrant stock (000 and % of total population)[i]	mid-2013	36.5/0.3
Refugees and others of concern to UNHCR	mid-2014	1 157
Education: Government expenditure (% of GDP)	2007-2013	6.2
Education: Primary-secondary gross enrolment ratio (f/m per 100)	2007-2013	99.1/97.9
Education: Female third-level students (% of total)	2007-2013	60.4
Intentional homicide rate (per 100,000 population)	2008-2012	2.2
Seats held by women in national parliaments (%)	2015	31.3

Environmental indicators		
Threatened species	2014	82
Forested area (% of land area)	2012	6.7
Proportion of terrestrial and marine areas protected (%)	2014	3.7
Population using improved drinking water sources (%)	2012	97.0
Population using improved sanitation facilities (%)	2012	90.0
CO_2 emission estimates (000 metric tons and metric tons per capita)	2011	25 643/2.4
Energy supply per capita (Gigajoules)	2012	38.0

a Refers to Grand Tunis. b Market rate. c Series linked to former series. d ISIC Rev.4 (BCDE). e 2011. f Excluding nationals residing abroad. g 2012. h ITU estimate. i Refers to foreign citizens.

Turkey

Region	Western Asia	Surface area (sq km)	783 562
Population (est., 000)	75 837	Pop. density (per sq km)	96.8
Capital city	Ankara	Capital city pop. (000)	4 644[a]
Currency	Turkish Lira (TRY)	UN membership date	24 October 1945

Economic indicators	2005	2010	2013
GDP: Gross domestic product (million current US$)	482 986	731 144	822 149
GDP: Growth rate at constant 2005 prices (annual %)	8.4	9.2	4.1
GDP per capita (current US$)	7 129.7	10 135.4	10 971.8
GNI: Gross national income per capita (current US$)	7 118.0	10 125.3	10 935.2
Gross fixed capital formation (% of GDP)	21.0	18.9	20.3
Exchange rates (national currency per US$)[b]	1.35	1.54	2.14
Balance of payments, current account (million US$)	−21 449	−45 313	−65 034
CPI: Consumer price index (2000=100)	381[c]	578	720
Index of industrial production (2010=100)[d]	86	100	116
Agricultural production index (2004-2006=100)	101	110	125
Food production index (2004-2006=100)	101	111	127
Unemployment (% of labour force)	10.6	11.9	10.0
Employment in industrial sector (% of employed)	24.8[e]	26.2	26.0[f]
Employment in agricultural sector (% of employed)	29.5[e]	23.7	23.6[f]
Labour force participation, adult female pop. (%)	23.4	27.6	29.4
Labour force participation, adult male pop. (%)	70.3	70.7	70.8
Tourist arrivals at national borders (000)	20 273	31 364[g]	37 795[g]
Energy production, primary (Petajoules)	1 004	1 352	1 282[f]
Mobile-cellular subscriptions (per 100 inhabitants)	64.4	85.6	93.0
Individuals using the Internet (%)	15.5	39.8	46.3

Total trade		Major trading partners			2013
	(million US$)		(% of exports)		(% of imports)
Exports	151 796.5	Germany	9.0	Russian Federation	10.0
Imports	251 650.6	Iraq	7.9	China	9.8
Balance	−99 854.1	United Kingdom	5.8	Germany	9.6

Social indicators		
Population growth rate (average annual %)	2010-2015	1.2
Urban population growth rate (average annual %)	2010-2015	2.0
Rural population growth rate (average annual %)	2010-2015	−0.7
Urban population (%)	2014	72.9
Population aged 0-14 years (%)	2014	25.3
Population aged 60+ years (females and males, % of total)	2014	12.4/9.8
Sex ratio (males per 100 females)	2014	96.5
Life expectancy at birth (females and males, years)	2010-2015	78.5/71.7
Infant mortality rate (per 1 000 live births)	2010-2015	12.0
Fertility rate, total (live births per woman)	2010-2015	2.1
Contraceptive prevalence (ages 15-49, %)	2007-2013	73.0
International migrant stock (000 and % of total population)[h]	mid-2013	1 864.9/2.5
Refugees and others of concern to UNHCR	mid-2014	892 041[i]
Education: Government expenditure (% of GDP)	2007-2013	2.9[j]
Education: Primary-secondary gross enrolment ratio (f/m per 100)	2007-2013	90.2/93.5
Education: Female third-level students (% of total)	2007-2013	45.4
Intentional homicide rate (per 100,000 population)	2008-2012	2.6
Seats held by women in national parliaments (%)	2015	14.4

Environmental indicators		
Threatened species	2014	364
Forested area (% of land area)	2012	15.0
Proportion of terrestrial and marine areas protected (%)	2014	0.2
Population using improved drinking water sources (%)	2012	100.0
Population using improved sanitation facilities (%)	2012	91.0
CO_2 emission estimates (000 metric tons and metric tons per capita)	2011	320 841/4.4
Energy supply per capita (Gigajoules)	2012	66.0

a Refers to Altindag, Cankaya, Etimesgut, Golbasi, Keçioren, Mamak, Sincan and Yenimahalle. b Market rate. c Series linked to former series. d ISIC Rev.4 (BCD). e ISIC Rev.3. f 2012. g Including Turkish citizens resident abroad. h Including refugees. i Refugee population for Syrians in Turkey is a government estimate. j 2006.

Turkmenistan

Region	Central Asia	Surface area (sq km)	488 100
Population (est., 000)	5 307	Pop. density (per sq km)	10.9
Capital city	Ashgabat	Capital city pop. (000)	735
Currency	Turkmen Manat (TMT)	UN membership date	2 March 1992

Economic indicators	2005	2010	2013
GDP: Gross domestic product (million current US$)	14 189	22 148	41 851
GDP: Growth rate at constant 2005 prices (annual %)	13.0	9.2	10.2
GDP per capita (current US$)	2 988.6	4 392.7	7 986.7
GNI: Gross national income per capita (current US$)	2 781.0	4 017.1	7 369.7
Gross fixed capital formation (% of GDP)	22.9	52.9	50.7
Exchange rates (national currency per US$)[a]	...	2.85[b]	...
Agricultural production index (2004-2006=100)	104	102	103
Food production index (2004-2006=100)	102	106	109
Unemployment (% of labour force)	11.0	10.9	10.6
Labour force participation, adult female pop. (%)	47.0	46.4	46.9
Labour force participation, adult male pop. (%)	74.8	75.7	76.9
Tourist arrivals at national borders (000)	12	...	...
Energy production, primary (Petajoules)	2 584	1 982	2 853[c]
Mobile-cellular subscriptions (per 100 inhabitants)	2.2[d]	63.4	116.9[d]
Individuals using the Internet (%)[d]	1.0	3.0	9.6

Social indicators		
Population growth rate (average annual %)	2010-2015	1.3
Urban population growth rate (average annual %)	2010-2015	1.9
Rural population growth rate (average annual %)	2010-2015	0.6
Urban population (%)	2014	49.7
Population aged 0-14 years (%)	2014	28.4
Population aged 60+ years (females and males, % of total)	2014	7.6/5.7
Sex ratio (males per 100 females)	2014	96.7
Life expectancy at birth (females and males, years)	2010-2015	69.7/61.3
Infant mortality rate (per 1 000 live births)	2010-2015	46.7
Fertility rate, total (live births per woman)	2010-2015	2.3
Contraceptive prevalence (ages 15-49, %)	2007-2013	48.0[e]
International migrant stock (000 and % of total population)	mid-2013	226.3/4.3
Refugees and others of concern to UNHCR	mid-2014	7 552
Education: Government expenditure (% of GDP)	2007-2013	3.1
Education: Primary-secondary gross enrolment ratio (f/m per 100)	2007-2013	85.4/88.0
Education: Female third-level students (% of total)	2007-2013	38.5
Intentional homicide rate (per 100,000 population)	2008-2012	12.8
Seats held by women in national parliaments (%)	2015	25.8

Environmental indicators		
Threatened species	2014	49
Forested area (% of land area)	2012	8.8
Proportion of terrestrial and marine areas protected (%)	2014	3.2
Population using improved drinking water sources (%)	2012	71.0
Population using improved sanitation facilities (%)	2012	99.0
CO_2 emission estimates (000 metric tons and metric tons per capita)	2011	62 218/12.2
Energy supply per capita (Gigajoules)	2012	207.0

a UN operational exchange rate. b January 2009. c 2012. d ITU estimate. e 2006.

Turks and Caicos Islands

Region	Caribbean	Surface area (sq km)		948[a]
Population (est., 000)	34	Pop. density (per sq km)		78.5
Capital city	Cockburn Town[b]	Capital city pop. (000)		5
Currency	U.S. Dollar (USD)			

Economic indicators	2005	2010	2013
GDP: Gross domestic product (million current US$)	579	687	706
GDP: Growth rate at constant 2005 prices (annual %)	14.4	1.0	−2.1
GDP per capita (current US$)	21 877.0	22 159.5	21 337.9
GNI: Gross national income per capita (current US$)	23 937.8	24 246.9	23 347.9
Gross fixed capital formation (% of GDP)	38.7	20.5	17.1
Employment in industrial sector (% of employed)	16.8[c]	24.3[cd]	...
Employment in agricultural sector (% of employed)	1.4[c]	1.2[cd]	...
Tourist arrivals at national borders (000)	176	281	291
Energy production, primary (Petajoules)	0	0	0[e]

Total trade		Major trading partners			2013
	(million US$)[e]	(% of exports)[e]			(% of imports)[e]
Exports	11.8	United States	93.2	United States	75.4
Imports	268.5	Areas nes	6.8[f]	Bahamas	13.8
Balance	−256.7		...	Areas nes	9.1[f]

Social indicators		
Population growth rate (average annual %)	2010-2015	2.1
Urban population growth rate (average annual %)	2010-2015	2.5
Rural population growth rate (average annual %)	2010-2015	−2.4
Urban population (%)	2014	91.9
Life expectancy at birth (females and males, years)[g]	2010-2015	77.4/79.0[h]
International migrant stock (000 and % of total population)	mid-2013	11.4/34.3
Refugees and others of concern to UNHCR	mid-2014	8
Education: Female third-level students (% of total)	2007-2013	60.0
Intentional homicide rate (per 100,000 population)	2008-2012	6.6

Environmental indicators		
Threatened species	2014	48
Forested area (% of land area)	2012	36.2
Proportion of terrestrial and marine areas protected (%)	2014	3.6
CO_2 emission estimates (000 metric tons and metric tons per capita)	2011	191/6.0
Energy supply per capita (Gigajoules)	2012	86.0[i]

a Including low water level for all islands (area to shoreline). b Refers to the island of Grand Turk. c ISIC Rev.3. d 2007. e 2012. f See technical notes. g Data compiled by the United Nations Demographic Yearbook system. h 2001. i UNSD estimate.

Tuvalu

Region	Oceania-Polynesia	Surface area (sq km)	26
Population (est., 000)	10	Pop. density (per sq km)	380.5
Capital city	Funafuti	Capital city pop. (000)	6
Currency	Australian Dollar (AUD)	UN membership date	5 September 2000

Economic indicators	2005	2010	2013
GDP: Gross domestic product (million current US$)	22	32	38
GDP: Growth rate at constant 2005 prices (annual %)	–3.9	–2.7	1.3
GDP per capita (current US$)	2 258.8	3 238.5	3 882.0
GNI: Gross national income per capita (current US$)	3 868.4	5 181.7	6 388.0
Gross fixed capital formation (% of GDP)	62.6	45.6	49.7
Exchange rates (national currency per US$) [a]	1.37	0.99	1.12
Balance of payments, current account (million US$)	–4	–14	7
CPI: Consumer price index (2000=100) [b]	117	125[cd]	...
Agricultural production index (2004-2006=100)	101	111	108
Food production index (2004-2006=100)	101	111	108
Tourist arrivals at national borders (000)	1	2	...
Mobile-cellular subscriptions (per 100 inhabitants)	13.4	16.3	34.4[e]
Individuals using the Internet (%) [e]	10.0[c]	25.0	37.0

Social indicators		
Population growth rate (average annual %)	2010-2015	0.2
Urban population growth rate (average annual %)	2010-2015	1.9
Rural population growth rate (average annual %)	2010-2015	–2.1
Urban population (%)	2014	58.8
Population aged 0-14 years (%) [fg]	2014	32.8
Sex ratio (males per 100 females) [fg]	2014	103.7
Life expectancy at birth (females and males, years) [f]	2010-2015	71.9/67.4[h]
Infant mortality rate (per 1 000 live births) [f]	2010-2015	10.3[h]
Fertility rate, total (live births per woman) [f]	2010-2015	3.2[i]
Contraceptive prevalence (ages 15-49, %)	2007-2013	30.5
International migrant stock (000 and % of total population) [j]	mid-2013	0.2/1.5
Education: Primary-secondary gross enrolment ratio (f/m per 100) [k]	2007-2013	89.1/83.0
Intentional homicide rate (per 100,000 population)	2008-2012	4.2
Seats held by women in national parliaments (%)	2015	6.7

Environmental indicators		
Threatened species	2014	93
Forested area (% of land area)	2012	33.3
Proportion of terrestrial and marine areas protected (%)	2014	0.0
Population using improved drinking water sources (%)	2012	98.0
Population using improved sanitation facilities (%)	2012	83.0

a UN operational exchange rate. b Funafuti. c 2007. d Series linked to former series. e ITU estimate. f Data compiled by the Secretariat of the Pacific Community Demography Programme. g De facto estimate. h 2010. i 2009. j Refers to foreign citizens. k National estimate.

Uganda

Region	Eastern Africa	Surface area (sq km)	241 550	
Population (est., 000)	38 845	Pop. density (per sq km)	161.2	
Capital city	Kampala	Capital city pop. (000)	1 863	
Currency	Uganda Shilling (UGX)	UN membership date	25 October 1962	

Economic indicators

	2005	2010	2013
GDP: Gross domestic product (million current US$)	12 295	21 620	26 444
GDP: Growth rate at constant 2005 prices (annual %)	10.0	9.7	4.5
GDP per capita (current US$)	428.0	636.1	703.7
GNI: Gross national income per capita (current US$)	416.4	623.4	681.5
Gross fixed capital formation (% of GDP)	28.1	28.2	28.5
Exchange rates (national currency per US$)[a]	1 816.86	2 308.30	2 527.96
Balance of payments, current account (million US$)	−13	−1 696	−1 999
CPI: Consumer price index (2000=100)	124	186	266
Agricultural production index (2004-2006=100)	100	112	112
Food production index (2004-2006=100)	100	112	111
Unemployment (% of labour force)	2.0	4.2	3.8
Employment in industrial sector (% of employed)	4.5[bcde]	6.0[bcdef]	...
Employment in agricultural sector (% of employed)	71.6[bcd]	65.6[bcdf]	...
Labour force participation, adult female pop. (%)	77.2	76.1	75.8
Labour force participation, adult male pop. (%)	80.0	79.4	79.2
Tourist arrivals at national borders (000)	468	946	1 206
Energy production, primary (Petajoules)	350	379	390[g]
Mobile-cellular subscriptions (per 100 inhabitants)	4.6	37.7[h]	44.1[i]
Individuals using the Internet (%)	1.7	12.5	16.2[i]

Total trade		Major trading partners				2013
	(million US$)	(% of exports)				(% of imports)
Exports	2 407.7	Kenya	13.1	India		26.8
Imports	5 817.5	Dem. Rep. of Congo	11.1	China		10.7
Balance	−3 409.8	Sudan	9.9	Kenya		9.7

Social indicators

Population growth rate (average annual %)	2010-2015	3.3
Urban population growth rate (average annual %)	2010-2015	5.4
Rural population growth rate (average annual %)	2010-2015	3.0
Urban population (%)	2014	15.8
Population aged 0-14 years (%)	2014	48.2
Population aged 60+ years (females and males, % of total)	2014	3.9/3.5
Sex ratio (males per 100 females)	2014	100.5
Life expectancy at birth (females and males, years)	2010-2015	60.2/57.8
Infant mortality rate (per 1 000 live births)	2010-2015	57.0
Fertility rate, total (live births per woman)	2010-2015	5.9
Contraceptive prevalence (ages 15-49, %)	2007-2013	30.0
International migrant stock (000 and % of total population)[j]	mid-2013	531.4/1.4
Refugees and others of concern to UNHCR	mid-2014	440 464
Education: Government expenditure (% of GDP)	2007-2013	3.3
Education: Primary-secondary gross enrolment ratio (f/m per 100)	2007-2013	74.8/75.3
Education: Female third-level students (% of total)	2007-2013	43.7
Intentional homicide rate (per 100,000 population)	2008-2012	10.7
Seats held by women in national parliaments (%)	2015	35.0

Environmental indicators

Threatened species	2014	189
Forested area (% of land area)	2012	14.1
Proportion of terrestrial and marine areas protected (%)	2014	16.0
Population using improved drinking water sources (%)	2012	75.0
Population using improved sanitation facilities (%)	2012	34.0
CO_2 emission estimates (000 metric tons and metric tons per capita)	2011	3 799/0.1
Energy supply per capita (Gigajoules)	2012	12.0

a Principal rate. **b** ISIC Rev.3. **c** Population aged 14-64. **d** May of the current year to April of the following year. **e** Refers to manufacturing only. **f** 2009. **g** 2012. **h** December. **i** ITU estimate. **j** Including refugees.

Ukraine

Region	Eastern Europe	Surface area (sq km)	603 500
Population (est., 000)	44 941	Pop. density (per sq km)	74.4
Capital city	Kiev	Capital city pop. (000)	2 917
Currency	Hryvnia (UAH)	UN membership date	24 October 1945

Economic indicators	2005	2010	2013
GDP: Gross domestic product (million current US$)	89 239	141 209	188 350
GDP: Growth rate at constant 2005 prices (annual %)	3.1	4.1	3.2
GDP per capita (current US$)	1 893.2	3 066.4	4 163.5
GNI: Gross national income per capita (current US$)	1 871.6	3 056.1	4 142.2
Gross fixed capital formation (% of GDP)	21.9	18.1	18.1
Exchange rates (national currency per US$)[a]	5.05	7.96	7.99
Balance of payments, current account (million US$)	2 534	−3 016	−16 518
CPI: Consumer price index (2000=100)	147	287[b]	311
Index of industrial production (2010=100)[c]	...	100	103
Agricultural production index (2004-2006=100)	100	106	138
Food production index (2004-2006=100)	100	106	138
Unemployment (% of labour force)	7.2	8.1	7.9
Employment in industrial sector (% of employed)[de]	24.2	22.4[fg]	20.7[h]
Employment in agricultural sector (% of employed)[de]	19.4	15.6[fg]	17.2[h]
Labour force participation, adult female pop. (%)	52.0	52.4	53.2
Labour force participation, adult male pop. (%)	65.3	66.1	66.9
Tourist arrivals at national borders (000)	17 631	21 203	24 671
Energy production, primary (Petajoules)	3 328	3 238	3 554[h]
Mobile-cellular subscriptions (per 100 inhabitants)	63.7	117.1	138.1
Individuals using the Internet (%)	3.8[i]	23.3[j]	41.8[k]

Total trade		Major trading partners			2013
	(million US$)		(% of exports)		(% of imports)
Exports	63 320.5	Russian Federation	23.8	Russian Federation	30.2
Imports	76 986.0	Turkey	6.0	China	10.3
Balance	−13 665.5	China	4.3	Germany	8.8

Social indicators		
Population growth rate (average annual %)	2010-2015	−0.6
Urban population growth rate (average annual %)	2010-2015	−0.3
Rural population growth rate (average annual %)	2010-2015	−1.3
Urban population (%)	2014	69.5
Population aged 0-14 years (%)	2014	14.7
Population aged 60+ years (females and males, % of total)	2014	26.0/16.7
Sex ratio (males per 100 females)	2014	85.4
Life expectancy at birth (females and males, years)	2010-2015	74.3/62.8
Infant mortality rate (per 1 000 live births)	2010-2015	11.7
Fertility rate, total (live births per woman)	2010-2015	1.5
Contraceptive prevalence (ages 15-49, %)	2007-2013	65.4
International migrant stock (000 and % of total population)	mid-2013	5 151.4/11.4
Refugees and others of concern to UNHCR	mid-2014	104 007
Education: Government expenditure (% of GDP)	2007-2013	6.7
Education: Primary-secondary gross enrolment ratio (f/m per 100)	2007-2013	100.6/101.8
Education: Female third-level students (% of total)	2007-2013	53.2
Intentional homicide rate (per 100,000 population)	2008-2012	4.3
Seats held by women in national parliaments (%)	2015	11.8

Environmental indicators		
Threatened species	2014	88
Forested area (% of land area)	2012	16.8
Proportion of terrestrial and marine areas protected (%)	2014	3.9
Population using improved drinking water sources (%)	2012	98.0
Population using improved sanitation facilities (%)	2012	94.0
CO_2 emission estimates (000 metric tons and metric tons per capita)	2011	286 228/6.2
Energy supply per capita (Gigajoules)	2012	113.0

a Official rate. **b** Series linked to former series. **c** ISIC Rev.4 (BCD). **d** ISIC Rev.3. **e** Population aged 15-70. **f** 2009. **g** Break in series. **h** 2012. **i** Population aged 15 to 59 using the Internet in the last 4 weeks. **j** Population aged 5 and over. **k** ITU estimate.

United Arab Emirates

Region	Western Asia	Surface area (sq km)	83 600
Population (est., 000)	9 446	Pop. density (per sq km)	113.0
Capital city	Abu Dhabi	Capital city pop. (000)	1 114
Currency	UAE Dirham (AED)	UN membership date	9 December 1971

Economic indicators	2005	2010	2013
GDP: Gross domestic product (million current US$)	180 617	286 049	402 340
GDP: Growth rate at constant 2005 prices (annual %)	4.9	1.6	5.2
GDP per capita (current US$)	43 534.0	33 885.9	43 048.9
GNI: Gross national income per capita (current US$)	44 229.7	33 874.1	43 085.3
Gross fixed capital formation (% of GDP)	18.4	25.0	22.0
Exchange rates (national currency per US$)[a]	3.67	3.67	3.67
Agricultural production index (2004-2006=100)	105	111	73
Food production index (2004-2006=100)	105	111	73
Unemployment (% of labour force)	3.1	4.2	3.8
Employment in industrial sector (% of employed)	39.8[bcd]	23.1[cefgh]	...
Employment in agricultural sector (% of employed)	4.9[bcd]	3.8[cefgh]	...
Labour force participation, adult female pop. (%)	37.0	46.2	46.5
Labour force participation, adult male pop. (%)	91.7	89.5	92.0
Tourist arrivals at national borders (000)[i]	7 126	...	...
Energy production, primary (Petajoules)	7 293	7 286	8 128[j]
Mobile-cellular subscriptions (per 100 inhabitants)	109.3	129.4	171.9
Individuals using the Internet (%)	40.0[k]	68.0[l]	88.0[k]

Total trade		Major trading partners			2013
	(million US$)[m]	(% of exports)[mn]			(% of imports)[m]
Exports	252 556.0	Asia nes	37.8	Areas nes	23.9[n]
Imports	210 945.0	Areas nes	26.0	India	13.6
Balance	41 611.0	India	9.6	China	7.1

Social indicators		
Population growth rate (average annual %)	2010-2015	2.5
Urban population growth rate (average annual %)	2010-2015	2.9
Rural population growth rate (average annual %)	2010-2015	0.6
Urban population (%)	2014	85.3
Population aged 0-14 years (%)	2014	15.7
Population aged 60+ years (females and males, % of total)	2014	1.0/1.0
Sex ratio (males per 100 females)	2014	230.9
Life expectancy at birth (females and males, years)	2010-2015	78.1/76.1
Infant mortality rate (per 1 000 live births)	2010-2015	5.7
Fertility rate, total (live births per woman)	2010-2015	1.8
Contraceptive prevalence (ages 15-49, %)	2007-2013	27.5[o]
International migrant stock (000 and % of total population)[pq]	mid-2013	7 827.0/83.8
Refugees and others of concern to UNHCR	mid-2014	631
Education: Primary-secondary gross enrolment ratio (f/m per 100)	2007-2013	90.9/88.0[r]
Education: Female third-level students (% of total)	2007-2013	54.3
Intentional homicide rate (per 100,000 population)	2008-2012	0.7
Seats held by women in national parliaments (%)	2015	17.5

Environmental indicators		
Threatened species	2014	49
Forested area (% of land area)	2012	3.8
Proportion of terrestrial and marine areas protected (%)	2014	16.1
Population using improved drinking water sources (%)	2012	100.0
Population using improved sanitation facilities (%)	2012	98.0
CO_2 emission estimates (000 metric tons and metric tons per capita)	2011	178 484/20.0
Energy supply per capita (Gigajoules)	2012	311.0

a Official rate. b Population census. c ISIC Rev.3. d December. e 2009. f May. g Excluding labour camps. h Break in series. i Arrivals of non-resident tourists in hotels and similar establishments. j 2012. k ITU estimate. l Refers to total population. m 2011. n See technical notes. o 1995. p Refers to foreign citizens. q Including refugees. r 1999.

United Kingdom

Region	Northern Europe	Surface area (sq km)	242 495 [a]	
Population (est., 000)	63 489	Pop. density (per sq km)	261.4	
Capital city	London	Capital city pop. (000)	10 189	
Currency	Pound Sterling (GBP)	UN membership date	24 October 1945	

Economic indicators

	2005	2010	2013
GDP: Gross domestic product (million current US$)	2 412 116	2 407 934	2 678 455
GDP: Growth rate at constant 2005 prices (annual %)	2.8	1.9	1.7
GDP per capita (current US$)	40 007.6	38 796.1	42 423.4
GNI: Gross national income per capita (current US$)	40 933.2	39 223.6	42 098.2
Gross fixed capital formation (% of GDP)	18.0	16.1	16.5
Exchange rates (national currency per US$) [b]	0.58	0.64	0.61
Balance of payments, current account (million US$)	−59 406	−75 229	−114 210
CPI: Consumer price index (2000=100)	113	131	147
Index of industrial production (2010=100) [c]	110	100	96
Agricultural production index (2004-2006=100)	100	102	100
Food production index (2004-2006=100)	100	102	99
Unemployment (% of labour force)	4.8	7.9	7.5
Employment in industrial sector (% of employed)	22.2[def]	19.1	18.9[g]
Employment in agricultural sector (% of employed)	1.3[def]	1.2	1.2[g]
Labour force participation, adult female pop. (%)	55.0	55.5	55.7
Labour force participation, adult male pop. (%)	69.3	68.6	68.7
Tourist arrivals at national borders (000)	28 039	28 295	31 169
Energy production, primary (Petajoules) [h]	8 483	6 195	4 863[g]
Mobile-cellular subscriptions (per 100 inhabitants)	108.6	123.6	123.8
Individuals using the Internet (%)	70.0	85.0	89.8

Total trade / Major trading partners

Total trade	(million US$)	Major trading partners (% of exports)			2013 (% of imports)
Exports	548 041.9	Switzerland	13.0	Germany	13.5
Imports	657 222.5	United States	11.5	China	8.8
Balance	−109 180.6	Germany	8.8	United States	8.3

Social indicators

Population growth rate (average annual %)	2010-2015	0.6
Urban population growth rate (average annual %)	2010-2015	0.9
Rural population growth rate (average annual %)	2010-2015	−0.9
Urban population (%)	2014	82.3
Population aged 0-14 years (%)	2014	17.6
Population aged 60+ years (females and males, % of total)	2014	25.0/21.7
Sex ratio (males per 100 females)	2014	97.3
Life expectancy at birth (females and males, years)	2010-2015	82.4/78.5
Infant mortality rate (per 1 000 live births)	2010-2015	4.2
Fertility rate, total (live births per woman)	2010-2015	1.9
Contraceptive prevalence (ages 15-49, %) [ij]	2007-2013	84.0
International migrant stock (000 and % of total population)	mid-2013	7 824.1/12.4
Refugees and others of concern to UNHCR	mid-2014	156 831[k]
Education: Government expenditure (% of GDP) [l]	2007-2013	6.0
Education: Primary-secondary gross enrolment ratio (f/m per 100) [l]	2007-2013	101.4/101.3
Education: Female third-level students (% of total) [l]	2007-2013	56.3
Intentional homicide rate (per 100,000 population)	2008-2012	1.0
Seats held by women in national parliaments (%)	2015	22.8

Environmental indicators

Threatened species	2014	85
Forested area (% of land area)	2012	12.0
Proportion of terrestrial and marine areas protected (%)	2014	13.8
Population using improved drinking water sources (%) [l]	2012	100.0
Population using improved sanitation facilities (%) [l]	2012	100.0
CO_2 emission estimates (000 metric tons and metric tons per capita)	2011	448 236/7.2
Energy supply per capita (Gigajoules) [h]	2012	127.0

a Excluding Channel Islands (Guernsey and Jersey) and Isle of Man. b Market rate. c ISIC Rev.4 (BCDE).
d ISIC Rev.3. e Population aged 16 and over. f Second quarter. g 2012. h Including Jersey and Guernsey
for oil statistics. Excluding these islands for electricity. i Age group 16 to 49 years. j Excluding Northern
Ireland. k Refugee population refers to the end of 2013. l Including Northern Ireland.

United Republic of Tanzania

Region	Eastern Africa	Surface area (sq km) 947 303
Population (est., 000)	50 757 [a]	Pop. density (per sq km) 53.7 [a]
Capital city	Dodoma	Capital city pop. (000) 228
Currency	Tanzania Shilling (TZS)	UN membership date 14 December 1961

Economic indicators	2005	2010	2013
GDP: Gross domestic product (million current US$) [b]	18 072	30 009	44 698
GDP: Growth rate at constant 2005 prices (annual %) [b]	7.4	5.8	8.2
GDP per capita (current US$) [b]	478.7	686.5	933.5
GNI: Gross national income per capita (current US$) [b]	472.4	684.3	928.1
Gross fixed capital formation (% of GDP) [b]	26.6	29.2	29.3
Exchange rates (national currency per US$) [c]	1 165.51	1 455.15	1 578.57
Balance of payments, current account (million US$)	−1 093	−1 960	−4 703
CPI: Consumer price index (2000=100) [b]	128	192 [d]	271
Agricultural production index (2004-2006=100)	98	129	154
Food production index (2004-2006=100)	96	131	155
Unemployment (% of labour force)	2.5	3.0	3.5
Employment in industrial sector (% of employed)	4.3 [bef]	...	...
Employment in agricultural sector (% of employed)	76.5 [bef]	...	...
Labour force participation, adult female pop. (%)	88.5	88.3	88.1
Labour force participation, adult male pop. (%)	90.5	90.3	90.2
Tourist arrivals at national borders (000)	590	754	1 063
Energy production, primary (Petajoules)	665	789	843 [g]
Mobile-cellular subscriptions (per 100 inhabitants)	7.6	46.7	55.7
Individuals using the Internet (%) [h]	1.1	2.9	4.4

Total trade		Major trading partners			2013
	(million US$)	(% of exports)			(% of imports)
Exports	4 412.5	South Africa	17.3	India	18.4
Imports	12 525.4	India	17.0	Switzerland	13.0
Balance	−8 112.9	Switzerland	9.2	China	12.7

Social indicators

Population growth rate (average annual %) [a]	2010-2015	3.0
Urban population growth rate (average annual %) [a]	2010-2015	5.4
Rural population growth rate (average annual %) [a]	2010-2015	2.0
Urban population (%) [a]	2014	30.9
Population aged 0-14 years (%) [a]	2014	44.8
Population aged 60+ years (females and males, % of total) [a]	2014	5.3/4.5
Sex ratio (males per 100 females) [a]	2014	100.1
Life expectancy at birth (females and males, years) [a]	2010-2015	62.7/60.0
Infant mortality rate (per 1 000 live births) [a]	2010-2015	48.7
Fertility rate, total (live births per woman) [a]	2010-2015	5.2
Contraceptive prevalence (ages 15-49, %)	2007-2013	34.4
International migrant stock (000 and % of total population) [ai]	mid-2013	312.8/0.6
Refugees and others of concern to UNHCR	mid-2014	253 190
Education: Government expenditure (% of GDP)	2007-2013	6.2
Education: Primary-secondary gross enrolment ratio (f/m per 100)	2007-2013	67.1/66.3
Education: Female third-level students (% of total)	2007-2013	35.4
Intentional homicide rate (per 100,000 population)	2008-2012	12.7
Seats held by women in national parliaments (%)	2015	36.0

Environmental indicators

Threatened species	2014	979
Forested area (% of land area)	2012	36.8
Proportion of terrestrial and marine areas protected (%)	2014	26.1
Population using improved drinking water sources (%)	2012	53.0
Population using improved sanitation facilities (%)	2012	12.0
CO_2 emission estimates (000 metric tons and metric tons per capita)	2011	7 301/0.2
Energy supply per capita (Gigajoules)	2012	20.0

a Including Zanzibar. b Excluding Zanzibar. c Official rate. d Series linked to former series. e 2006. f ISIC Rev.2. g 2012. h ITU estimate. i Including refugees.

United States of America

Region	Northern America	Surface area (sq km)	9 833 517
Population (est., 000)	322 583	Pop. density (per sq km)	33.5
Capital city	Washington, D.C.	Capital city pop. (000)	4 896
Currency	U.S. Dollar (USD)	UN membership date	24 October 1945

Economic indicators	2005	2010	2013
GDP: Gross domestic product (million current US$)	13 093 720	14 964 380	16 768 050
GDP: Growth rate at constant 2005 prices (annual %)	3.4	2.5	2.2
GDP per capita (current US$)	43 914.2	47 924.8	52 391.9
GNI: Gross national income per capita (current US$)	44 343.8	48 426.7	53 754.9
Gross fixed capital formation (% of GDP)	22.8	18.0	18.9
Balance of payments, current account (million US$)	–745 445	–443 932	–400 253
CPI: Consumer price index (2000=100)[a]	113	127	135
Index of industrial production (2010=100)[b]	104	100	111
Agricultural production index (2004-2006=100)	100	106	108
Food production index (2004-2006=100)	100	107	110
Unemployment (% of labour force)	5.2	9.7	7.4
Employment in industrial sector (% of employed)	20.6[cd]	16.7[def]	...
Employment in agricultural sector (% of employed)	1.6[cd]	1.6[df]	...
Labour force participation, adult female pop. (%)	58.3	57.6	56.3
Labour force participation, adult male pop. (%)	72.0	69.8	68.9
Tourist arrivals at national borders (000)	49 206	60 010	69 768
Energy production, primary (Petajoules)[gh]	68 194	71 972	75 771[i]
Mobile-cellular subscriptions (per 100 inhabitants)	68.3	91.3	95.5
Individuals using the Internet (%)	68.0[j]	71.7	84.2[j]

Total trade		Major trading partners			2013
	(million US$)[g]		(% of exports)[g]		(% of imports)[g]
Exports	1 578 001.4	Canada	19.0	China	19.8
Imports	2 328 328.5	Mexico	14.3	Canada	14.5
Balance	–750 327.1	China	7.7	Mexico	12.2

Social indicators		
Population growth rate (average annual %)	2010-2015	0.8
Urban population growth rate (average annual %)	2010-2015	1.0
Rural population growth rate (average annual %)	2010-2015	–0.1
Urban population (%)	2014	81.5
Population aged 0-14 years (%)	2014	19.5
Population aged 60+ years (females and males, % of total)	2014	21.8/18.5
Sex ratio (males per 100 females)	2014	96.9
Life expectancy at birth (females and males, years)	2010-2015	81.2/76.4
Infant mortality rate (per 1 000 live births)	2010-2015	6.1
Fertility rate, total (live births per woman)	2010-2015	2.0
Contraceptive prevalence (ages 15-49, %)[k]	2007-2013	76.4
International migrant stock (000 and % of total population)	mid-2013	45 785.1/14.3
Refugees and others of concern to UNHCR	mid-2014	359 768[l]
Education: Government expenditure (% of GDP)	2007-2013	5.2
Education: Primary-secondary gross enrolment ratio (f/m per 100)	2007-2013	95.6/96.2
Education: Female third-level students (% of total)	2007-2013	57.0
Intentional homicide rate (per 100,000 population)	2008-2012	4.7
Seats held by women in national parliaments (%)	2015	19.4

Environmental indicators		
Threatened species[m]	2014	1 287
Forested area (% of land area)	2012	33.3
Proportion of terrestrial and marine areas protected (%)	2014	14.8
Population using improved drinking water sources (%)	2012	99.0
Population using improved sanitation facilities (%)	2012	100.0
CO_2 emission estimates (000 metric tons and metric tons per capita)	2011	5 305 570/16.7
Energy supply per capita (Gigajoules)[gh]	2012	280.0

a All urban consumers. b ISIC Rev.4 (BCD). c ISIC Rev.3. d Population aged 16 and over. e Excluding electricity, gas, steam and air conditioning supply and water supply. f Break in series. g Including Puerto Rico and the U.S. Virgin Islands. h Including American Samoa, Guam, Northern Mariana Islands, Johnston Atoll, Midway Islands and Wake Island. i 2012. j ITU estimate. k Age group 15 to 44 years. l Refugee population refers to the end of 2013. m Excluding United States Minor Outlying Islands.

United States Virgin Islands

Region	Caribbean	Surface area (sq km)	347
Population (est., 000)	107	Pop. density (per sq km)	307.8
Capital city	Charlotte Amalie	Capital city pop. (000)	52
Currency	U.S. Dollar (USD)		

Economic indicators	2005	2010	2013
Agricultural production index (2004-2006=100)	98	118	123
Food production index (2004-2006=100)	98	118	123
Labour force participation, adult female pop. (%)	54.9	55.2	54.0
Labour force participation, adult male pop. (%)	76.1	73.9	72.3
Tourist arrivals at national borders (000)	593	590	570
Mobile-cellular subscriptions (per 100 inhabitants)	74.5[a]	...	...
Individuals using the Internet (%)[a]	27.3	31.2	45.3

Social indicators		
Population growth rate (average annual %)	2010-2015	0.1
Urban population growth rate (average annual %)	2010-2015	0.3
Rural population growth rate (average annual %)	2010-2015	−2.9
Urban population (%)	2014	95.2
Population aged 0-14 years (%)	2014	20.8
Population aged 60+ years (females and males, % of total)	2014	24.3/22.1
Sex ratio (males per 100 females)	2014	91.2
Life expectancy at birth (females and males, years)	2010-2015	82.9/77.2
Infant mortality rate (per 1 000 live births)	2010-2015	9.4
Fertility rate, total (live births per woman)	2010-2015	2.5
Contraceptive prevalence (ages 15-49, %)[b]	2007-2013	78.4[c]
International migrant stock (000 and % of total population)	mid-2013	63.3/59.3
Education: Female third-level students (% of total)	2007-2013	76.4
Intentional homicide rate (per 100,000 population)	2008-2012	52.6

Environmental indicators		
Threatened species	2014	44
Forested area (% of land area)	2012	56.9
Proportion of terrestrial and marine areas protected (%)	2014	2.8

a ITU estimate. **b** Age group 18 to 44 years. **c** 2002.

Uruguay

Region	South America	Surface area (sq km)		176 215
Population (est., 000)	3 419	Pop. density (per sq km)		19.5
Capital city	Montevideo	Capital city pop. (000)		1 698
Currency	Uruguayan Peso (UYU)	UN membership date		18 December 1945

Economic indicators	2005	2010	2013
GDP: Gross domestic product (million current US$)	17 363	38 881	55 708
GDP: Growth rate at constant 2005 prices (annual %)	7.5	8.4	4.4
GDP per capita (current US$)	5 221.7	11 530.6	16 350.7
GNI: Gross national income per capita (current US$)	5 071.3	11 085.0	15 801.1
Gross fixed capital formation (% of GDP)	16.6	19.9	22.9
Exchange rates (national currency per US$)[a]	24.10	20.09	21.39
Balance of payments, current account (million US$)	42	−753	−3 006
CPI: Consumer price index (2000=100)[b]	162	230	293
Agricultural production index (2004-2006=100)	101	120	131
Food production index (2004-2006=100)	101	122	133
Unemployment (% of labour force)	9.0	7.2	6.6
Employment in industrial sector (% of employed)[c]	21.9[def]	21.2[g]	21.1[h]
Employment in agricultural sector (% of employed)[ci]	4.6[def]	11.8[g]	10.9[h]
Labour force participation, adult female pop. (%)	52.7	55.2	55.6
Labour force participation, adult male pop. (%)	74.1	76.7	76.8
Tourist arrivals at national borders (000)	1 808	2 353	2 683
Energy production, primary (Petajoules)	45	87	82[j]
Mobile-cellular subscriptions (per 100 inhabitants)	34.7	131.6[k]	154.6[k]
Individuals using the Internet (%)	20.1	46.4[l]	58.1[m]

Total trade		Major trading partners			2013
	(million US$)		(% of exports)		(% of imports)
Exports	9 065.8	Brazil	18.9	China	16.9
Imports	11 642.4	Free zones	16.0[n]	Brazil	15.8
Balance	−2 576.6	China	14.2	Argentina	14.2

Social indicators		
Population growth rate (average annual %)	2010-2015	0.3
Urban population growth rate (average annual %)	2010-2015	0.5
Rural population growth rate (average annual %)	2010-2015	−3.2
Urban population (%)	2014	95.2
Population aged 0-14 years (%)	2014	21.7
Population aged 60+ years (females and males, % of total)	2014	21.5/16.0
Sex ratio (males per 100 females)	2014	93.5
Life expectancy at birth (females and males, years)	2010-2015	80.5/73.6
Infant mortality rate (per 1 000 live births)	2010-2015	11.5
Fertility rate, total (live births per woman)	2010-2015	2.1
Contraceptive prevalence (ages 15-49, %)[o]	2007-2013	77.0[p]
International migrant stock (000 and % of total population)	mid-2013	73.5/2.2
Refugees and others of concern to UNHCR	mid-2014	241
Education: Government expenditure (% of GDP)	2007-2013	4.4
Education: Primary-secondary gross enrolment ratio (f/m per 100)	2007-2013	103.1/99.0
Education: Female third-level students (% of total)	2007-2013	62.5
Intentional homicide rate (per 100,000 population)	2008-2012	7.9
Seats held by women in national parliaments (%)	2015	13.1

Environmental indicators		
Threatened species	2014	103
Forested area (% of land area)	2012	10.5
Proportion of terrestrial and marine areas protected (%)	2014	1.7
Population using improved drinking water sources (%)	2012	99.0
Population using improved sanitation facilities (%)	2012	96.0
CO_2 emission estimates (000 metric tons and metric tons per capita)	2011	7 774/2.3
Energy supply per capita (Gigajoules)	2012	59.0

a Market rate. b Montevideo. c ISIC Rev.3. d Population aged 14 and over. e Urban areas. f Excluding conscripts. g Break in series. h 2011. i Including mining and quarrying. j 2012. k Including data dedicated subscriptions. l Population aged 6 and over. m ITU estimate. n See technical notes. o Age group 15 to 50 years. p 2004.

Uzbekistan

Region	Central Asia	Surface area (sq km) 447 400
Population (est., 000)	29 325	Pop. density (per sq km) 65.5
Capital city	Tashkent	Capital city pop. (000) 2 241
Currency	Uzbekistan Sum (UZS)	UN membership date 2 March 1992

Economic indicators	2005	2010	2013
GDP: Gross domestic product (million current US$)	14 396	39 526	57 210
GDP: Growth rate at constant 2005 prices (annual %)	7.0	8.5	7.0
GDP per capita (current US$)	552.8	1 423.4	1 977.3
GNI: Gross national income per capita (current US$)	551.8	1 465.3	2 064.3
Gross fixed capital formation (% of GDP)	17.9	24.7	30.8
Index of industrial production (2010=100)[a]	61	100	...
Agricultural production index (2004-2006=100)	100	127	152
Food production index (2004-2006=100)	99	135	166
Unemployment (% of labour force)	11.0	11.0	10.7
Labour force participation, adult female pop. (%)	47.5	47.6	48.1
Labour force participation, adult male pop. (%)	72.6	74.5	75.6
Tourist arrivals at national borders (000)	242	975	1 969
Energy production, primary (Petajoules)	2 365	2 303	2 376[b]
Mobile-cellular subscriptions (per 100 inhabitants)	2.8	75.5[c]	74.3[c]
Individuals using the Internet (%)	3.3	20.0[c]	38.2[c]

Social indicators		
Population growth rate (average annual %)	2010-2015	1.4
Urban population growth rate (average annual %)	2010-2015	1.5
Rural population growth rate (average annual %)	2010-2015	1.3
Urban population (%)	2014	36.3
Population aged 0-14 years (%)	2014	28.3
Population aged 60+ years (females and males, % of total)	2014	7.5/5.9
Sex ratio (males per 100 females)	2014	98.9
Life expectancy at birth (females and males, years)	2010-2015	71.6/64.9
Infant mortality rate (per 1 000 live births)	2010-2015	44.0
Fertility rate, total (live births per woman)	2010-2015	2.3
Contraceptive prevalence (ages 15-49, %)	2007-2013	64.9[d]
International migrant stock (000 and % of total population)	mid-2013	1 266.3/4.4
Refugees and others of concern to UNHCR	mid-2014	86 836[e]
Education: Primary-secondary gross enrolment ratio (f/m per 100)	2007-2013	100.0/102.4
Education: Female third-level students (% of total)	2007-2013	38.6
Intentional homicide rate (per 100,000 population)	2008-2012	3.7
Seats held by women in national parliaments (%)	2015	16.0

Environmental indicators		
Threatened species	2014	55
Forested area (% of land area)	2012	7.7
Proportion of terrestrial and marine areas protected (%)	2014	3.4
Population using improved drinking water sources (%)	2012	87.0
Population using improved sanitation facilities (%)	2012	100.0
CO_2 emission estimates (000 metric tons and metric tons per capita)	2011	114 861/4.1
Energy supply per capita (Gigajoules)	2012	71.0

a ISIC Rev.3 (CDE). **b** 2012. **c** ITU estimate. **d** 2006. **e** Stateless persons population refers to those with permanent residence reported in 2010 by the Government. Information on other categories of stateless persons population is not available.

Vanuatu

		Surface area (sq km)	12 189
Region	Oceania-Melanesia	Surface area (sq km)	12 189
Population (est., 000)	258	Pop. density (per sq km)	21.2
Capital city	Port Vila	Capital city pop. (000)	53
Currency	Vatu (VUV)	UN membership date	15 September 1981

Economic indicators	2005	2010	2013
GDP: Gross domestic product (million current US$)	395	701	800
GDP: Growth rate at constant 2005 prices (annual %)	5.3	1.6	3.2
GDP per capita (current US$)	1 886.4	2 965.8	3 165.1
GNI: Gross national income per capita (current US$)	1 762.4	2 873.8	3 010.3
Gross fixed capital formation (% of GDP)	23.4	33.9	27.7
Exchange rates (national currency per US$)[a]	112.33	93.15	97.30
Balance of payments, current account (million US$)	−34	−35	−31
CPI: Consumer price index (2000=100)	112	133	138
Agricultural production index (2004-2006=100)	100	132	138
Food production index (2004-2006=100)	100	132	138
Employment in industrial sector (% of employed)	...	7.0[bcd]	...
Employment in agricultural sector (% of employed)	...	60.5[bcd]	...
Labour force participation, adult female pop. (%)	65.3	61.5	61.5
Labour force participation, adult male pop. (%)	81.7	80.6	80.0
Tourist arrivals at national borders (000)	62	97	110
Energy production, primary (Petajoules)	1	1	1[e]
Mobile-cellular subscriptions (per 100 inhabitants)	6.1	71.9	59.3[f]
Individuals using the Internet (%)	5.1	8.0	11.3[f]

Total trade		Major trading partners			2013
	(million US$)[g]	(% of exports)[g]			(% of imports)[g]
Exports	63.5	Malaysia	20.5	Australia	29.7
Imports	280.6	Philippines	18.1	Singapore	18.2
Balance	−217.1	Australia	11.3	New Zealand	12.7

Social indicators		
Population growth rate (average annual %)	2010-2015	2.2
Urban population growth rate (average annual %)	2010-2015	3.4
Rural population growth rate (average annual %)	2010-2015	1.8
Urban population (%)	2014	25.8
Population aged 0-14 years (%)	2014	36.5
Population aged 60+ years (females and males, % of total)	2014	6.4/6.2
Sex ratio (males per 100 females)	2014	103.0
Life expectancy at birth (females and males, years)	2010-2015	73.6/69.6
Infant mortality rate (per 1 000 live births)	2010-2015	23.9
Fertility rate, total (live births per woman)	2010-2015	3.4
Contraceptive prevalence (ages 15-49, %)	2007-2013	38.4
International migrant stock (000 and % of total population)	mid-2013	3.1/1.2
Refugees and others of concern to UNHCR	mid-2014	3
Education: Government expenditure (% of GDP)	2007-2013	5.0
Education: Primary-secondary gross enrolment ratio (f/m per 100)	2007-2013	90.3/91.8
Education: Female third-level students (% of total)[h]	2007-2013	36.1[i]
Intentional homicide rate (per 100,000 population)	2008-2012	2.9
Seats held by women in national parliaments (%)	2015	0.0

Environmental indicators		
Threatened species	2014	137
Forested area (% of land area)	2012	36.1
Proportion of terrestrial and marine areas protected (%)	2014	2.3
Population using improved drinking water sources (%)	2012	91.0
Population using improved sanitation facilities (%)	2012	58.0
CO_2 emission estimates (000 metric tons and metric tons per capita)	2011	143/0.6
Energy supply per capita (Gigajoules)	2012	11.0

a Official rate. **b** 2009. **c** Population census. **d** November. **e** 2012. **f** ITU estimate. **g** 2011. **h** UNESCO estimate. **i** 2004.

Venezuela (Bolivarian Republic of)

Region	South America	Surface area (sq km)	912 050
Population (est., 000)	30 851	Pop. density (per sq km)	33.8
Capital city	Caracas	Capital city pop. (000)	2 912[a]
Currency	Bolívar (VEF)	UN membership date	15 November 1945

Economic indicators	2005	2010	2013
GDP: Gross domestic product (million current US$)	145 513	393 808	371 339
GDP: Growth rate at constant 2005 prices (annual %)	10.3	−1.5	1.3
GDP per capita (current US$)	5 444.7	13 559.3	12 213.0
GNI: Gross national income per capita (current US$)	5 362.3	13 392.1	11 826.4
Gross fixed capital formation (% of GDP)	20.3	18.7	22.2
Exchange rates (national currency per US$)[b]	2.15	2.59	6.28
Balance of payments, current account (million US$)	25 053	8 812	11 016[c]
CPI: Consumer price index (2000=100)[d]	255[e]	156[f]	335[f]
Agricultural production index (2004-2006=100)	101	109	134
Food production index (2004-2006=100)	101	109	135
Unemployment (% of labour force)	11.4	8.6	7.5
Employment in industrial sector (% of employed)[g]	20.8[h]	22.1[i]	21.2[cij]
Employment in agricultural sector (% of employed)[g]	9.7[h]	8.7[i]	7.7[cij]
Labour force participation, adult female pop. (%)	51.6	50.5	51.1
Labour force participation, adult male pop. (%)	81.5	79.3	79.2
Tourist arrivals at national borders (000)	706	526	986
Energy production, primary (Petajoules)	8 266	8 122	7 996[c]
Mobile-cellular subscriptions (per 100 inhabitants)	46.8	96.0	101.6[k]
Individuals using the Internet (%)	12.6	37.4[l]	54.9[m]

Total trade		Major trading partners			2013
	(million US$)	(% of exports)[n]			(% of imports)
Exports	87 961.2	N & C Ame nes	34.0	United States	23.3
Imports	44 951.8	Asia nes	31.9	China	17.0
Balance	43 009.4	S. America nes	15.4	Brazil	10.0

Social indicators		
Population growth rate (average annual %)	2010-2015	1.5
Urban population growth rate (average annual %)	2010-2015	1.5
Rural population growth rate (average annual %)	2010-2015	1.1
Urban population (%)	2014	88.9
Population aged 0-14 years (%)	2014	28.2
Population aged 60+ years (females and males, % of total)	2014	10.3/9.1
Sex ratio (males per 100 females)	2014	100.5
Life expectancy at birth (females and males, years)	2010-2015	77.6/71.7
Infant mortality rate (per 1 000 live births)	2010-2015	15.0
Fertility rate, total (live births per woman)	2010-2015	2.4
Contraceptive prevalence (ages 15-49, %)	2007-2013	70.3[o]
International migrant stock (000 and % of total population)	mid-2013	1 171.3/3.9
Refugees and others of concern to UNHCR	mid-2014	205 255
Education: Government expenditure (% of GDP)	2007-2013	6.9
Education: Primary-secondary gross enrolment ratio (f/m per 100)	2007-2013	99.6/96.9
Education: Female third-level students (% of total)[p]	2007-2013	62.1
Intentional homicide rate (per 100,000 population)	2008-2012	53.7
Seats held by women in national parliaments (%)	2015	17.0

Environmental indicators		
Threatened species	2014	305
Forested area (% of land area)	2012	51.8
Proportion of terrestrial and marine areas protected (%)	2014	36.7
CO_2 emission estimates (000 metric tons and metric tons per capita)	2011	188 818/6.4
Energy supply per capita (Gigajoules)	2012	111.0

a Refers to multiple municipalities and parishes (see source). **b** Official rate. **c** 2012. **d** Caracas. **e** Metropolitan areas. **f** Index base 2008=100. **g** ISIC Rev.2. **h** Second semester. **i** Break in series. **j** Average of bi-annual estimates. **k** Preliminary. **l** Country estimate. **m** ITU estimate. **n** See technical notes. **o** 1998. **p** National estimate.

Viet Nam

Region	South-Eastern Asia	
Population (est., 000)	92 548	
Capital city	Hanoi	
Currency	Dong (VND)	

Surface area (sq km)	330 972
Pop. density (per sq km)	279.0
Capital city pop. (000)	3 470[a]
UN membership date	20 September 1977

Economic indicators	2005	2010	2013
GDP: Gross domestic product (million current US$)	52 917	115 932	171 222
GDP: Growth rate at constant 2005 prices (annual %)	8.4	6.8	5.4
GDP per capita (current US$)	622.9	1 301.9	1 867.6
GNI: Gross national income per capita (current US$)	666.0	1 252.3	1 785.4
Gross fixed capital formation (% of GDP)	32.9	32.6	23.6
Exchange rates (national currency per US$)[b]	15 916.00	18 932.00	21 036.00
Balance of payments, current account (million US$)	−560	−4 276	9 471
CPI: Consumer price index (2000=100)	126[c]	208[c]	287
Index of industrial production (2010=100)[d]	...	100	119
Agricultural production index (2004-2006=100)	100	120	136
Food production index (2004-2006=100)	100	119	133
Unemployment (% of labour force)	2.1	2.6	2.0
Employment in industrial sector (% of employed)	20.2[efg]	21.3[hij]	21.1[ijk]
Employment in agricultural sector (% of employed)	51.7[efg]	48.4[hij]	47.4[ijk]
Labour force participation, adult female pop. (%)	72.6	72.3	73.0
Labour force participation, adult male pop. (%)	81.9	81.3	82.2
Tourist arrivals at national borders (000)[f]	3 477	5 050	7 572
Energy production, primary (Petajoules)	2 612	2 749	2 860[k]
Mobile-cellular subscriptions (per 100 inhabitants)	11.3	125.3	130.9[m]
Individuals using the Internet (%)	12.7	30.7	43.9[m]

Total trade		Major trading partners			2013
	(million US$)	(% of exports)			(% of imports)
Exports	132 032.9	United States	18.1	China	27.9
Imports	132 032.5	Japan	10.3	Republic of Korea	15.7
Balance	0.4	China	10.0	Japan	8.8

Social indicators		
Population growth rate (average annual %)	2010-2015	1.0
Urban population growth rate (average annual %)	2010-2015	3.0
Rural population growth rate (average annual %)	2010-2015	<
Urban population (%)	2014	33.0
Population aged 0-14 years (%)	2014	22.6
Population aged 60+ years (females and males, % of total)	2014	11.9/8.0
Sex ratio (males per 100 females)	2014	97.7
Life expectancy at birth (females and males, years)	2010-2015	80.4/71.2
Infant mortality rate (per 1 000 live births)	2010-2015	14.1
Fertility rate, total (live births per woman)	2010-2015	1.8
Contraceptive prevalence (ages 15-49, %)	2007-2013	77.8
International migrant stock (000 and % of total population)[no]	mid-2013	68.3/0.1
Refugees and others of concern to UNHCR	mid-2014	11 000
Education: Government expenditure (% of GDP)	2007-2013	6.3
Education: Female third-level students (% of total)	2007-2013	46.4
Intentional homicide rate (per 100,000 population)	2008-2012	3.3
Seats held by women in national parliaments (%)	2015	24.3

Environmental indicators		
Threatened species	2014	538
Forested area (% of land area)	2012	45.4
Proportion of terrestrial and marine areas protected (%)	2014	2.5
Population using improved drinking water sources (%)	2012	95.0
Population using improved sanitation facilities (%)	2012	75.0
CO_2 emission estimates (000 metric tons and metric tons per capita)	2011	173 211/1.9
Energy supply per capita (Gigajoules)	2012	28.0

a Refers to urban population in the city districts. b Market rate. c Series linked to former series. d ISIC Rev.4 (BCDE). e 2006. f Living standards survey. g ISIC Rev.2. h 2011. i Average of quarterly estimates. j Break in series. k 2012. l Arrivals of non-resident visitors at national borders. m ITU estimate. n Refers to foreign citizens. o Including refugees.

Wallis and Futuna Islands

Region	Oceania-Polynesia	
Population (est., 000)	13	
Capital city	Matu-Utu	
Currency	CFP Franc (XPF)	

Surface area (sq km)	142	
Pop. density (per sq km)	66.0	
Capital city pop. (000)	1	

Economic indicators	2005	2010	2013
Exchange rates (national currency per US$)[a]	100.84	90.81	86.46
Agricultural production index (2004-2006=100)	104	101	103
Food production index (2004-2006=100)	104	101	103
Individuals using the Internet (%)	6.7	8.2	9.0[bc]

Social indicators		
Population growth rate (average annual %)	2010-2015	−0.6
Rural population growth rate (average annual %)	2010-2015	−0.6
Population aged 0-14 years (%)[de]	2014	28.2
Sex ratio (males per 100 females)[de]	2014	93.7
Life expectancy at birth (females and males, years)[f]	2010-2015	75.5/73.1[g]
Infant mortality rate (per 1 000 live births)[d]	2010-2015	12.0[h]
Fertility rate, total (live births per woman)[d]	2010-2015	2.2[i]
International migrant stock (000 and % of total population)	mid-2013	2.9/21.7

Environmental indicators		
Threatened species	2014	88
Forested area (% of land area)	2012	41.9
CO_2 emission estimates (000 metric tons and metric tons per capita)	2011	26/1.8
Energy supply per capita (Gigajoules)	2012	26.0

a UN operational exchange rate. b 2012. c ITU estimate. d Data compiled by the Secretariat of the Pacific Community Demography Programme. e De facto estimate. f Data compiled by the United Nations Demographic Yearbook system. g 2003. h 2004-2012. i 2008-2012.

Western Sahara

Region	Northern Africa
Population (est., 000)	586
Capital city	El Aaiún
Currency	Morocco Dirham (MAD)

Surface area (sq km)	266 000 [a]
Pop. density (per sq km)	2.2
Capital city pop. (000)	262

Economic indicators	2005	2010	2013
Agricultural production index (2004-2006=100)	100	102	106
Food production index (2004-2006=100)	100	102	106

Social indicators		
Population growth rate (average annual %)	2010-2015	3.2
Urban population growth rate (average annual %)	2010-2015	3.3
Rural population growth rate (average annual %)	2010-2015	3.0
Urban population (%)	2014	80.9
Population aged 0-14 years (%)	2014	26.3
Population aged 60+ years (females and males, % of total)	2014	4.6/5.4
Sex ratio (males per 100 females)	2014	110.6
Life expectancy at birth (females and males, years)	2010-2015	69.8/65.9
Infant mortality rate (per 1 000 live births)	2010-2015	37.2
Fertility rate, total (live births per woman)	2010-2015	2.4
International migrant stock (000 and % of total population) [b]	mid-2013	4.9/0.9

Environmental indicators		
Threatened species	2014	40
Forested area (% of land area)	2012	2.7

a Comprising the Northern Region (former Saguia el Hamra) and Southern Region (former Rio de Oro).
b Estimate.

Yemen

Region	Western Asia	Surface area (sq km)	527 968
Population (est., 000)	24 969	Pop. density (per sq km)	47.3
Capital city	Sana'a	Capital city pop. (000)	2 833
Currency	Yemeni Rial (YER)	UN membership date	30 September 1947

Economic indicators	2005	2010	2013
GDP: Gross domestic product (million current US$)	19 041	30 907	34 714
GDP: Growth rate at constant 2005 prices (annual %)	5.1	5.7	4.8
GDP per capita (current US$)	945.5	1 357.8	1 422.3
GNI: Gross national income per capita (current US$)	868.8	1 282.5	1 360.5
Gross fixed capital formation (% of GDP)	18.3	19.8	17.6
Exchange rates (national currency per US$)[a]	195.08	213.80	214.89
Balance of payments, current account (million US$)	624	−1 054	−1 530
CPI: Consumer price index (2000=100)	174	292[b]	426
Agricultural production index (2004-2006=100)	98	136	138
Food production index (2004-2006=100)	98	137	138
Unemployment (% of labour force)	16.1	17.8	17.4
Employment in industrial sector (% of employed)	16.3[cde]	18.8[fgh]	...
Employment in agricultural sector (% of employed)	31.0[cde]	24.7[fgh]	...
Labour force participation, adult female pop. (%)	23.5	24.8	25.4
Labour force participation, adult male pop. (%)	71.0	71.2	72.2
Tourist arrivals at national borders (000)	336	1 025[i]	990[i]
Energy production, primary (Petajoules)	844	803	629[j]
Mobile-cellular subscriptions (per 100 inhabitants)	11.3	48.7	69.0[k]
Individuals using the Internet (%)	1.1[k]	12.4	20.0[k]

Total trade		Major trading partners			2013
	(million US$)		(% of exports)		(% of imports)
Exports	7 129.8	China	24.1	United Arab Emirates	16.7
Imports	13 272.9	Thailand	19.3	China	7.8
Balance	−6 143.1	Republic of Korea	12.5	Netherlands	7.7

Social indicators

Population growth rate (average annual %)	2010-2015	2.3
Urban population growth rate (average annual %)	2010-2015	4.0
Rural population growth rate (average annual %)	2010-2015	1.4
Urban population (%)	2014	34.0
Population aged 0-14 years (%)	2014	39.7
Population aged 60+ years (females and males, % of total)	2014	4.9/4.4
Sex ratio (males per 100 females)	2014	101.6
Life expectancy at birth (females and males, years)	2010-2015	64.4/61.7
Infant mortality rate (per 1 000 live births)	2010-2015	56.2
Fertility rate, total (live births per woman)	2010-2015	4.2
Contraceptive prevalence (ages 15-49, %)	2007-2013	27.7[l]
International migrant stock (000 and % of total population)[mn]	mid-2013	314.7/1.3
Refugees and others of concern to UNHCR	mid-2014	589 710
Education: Government expenditure (% of GDP)	2007-2013	4.6
Education: Primary-secondary gross enrolment ratio (f/m per 100)	2007-2013	66.9/84.7
Education: Female third-level students (% of total)	2007-2013	29.9
Intentional homicide rate (per 100,000 population)	2008-2012	4.8
Seats held by women in national parliaments (%)	2015	0.3

Environmental indicators

Threatened species	2014	285
Forested area (% of land area)	2012	1.0
Proportion of terrestrial and marine areas protected (%)	2014	0.6
Population using improved drinking water sources (%)	2012	55.0
Population using improved sanitation facilities (%)	2012	53.0
CO_2 emission estimates (000 metric tons and metric tons per capita)	2011	22 295/1.0
Energy supply per capita (Gigajoules)	2012	12.0

a Official rate. b Series linked to former series. c 2004. d Population census. e ISIC Rev.3. f Child labour survey. g Population aged 15-65. h Break in series. i Including nationals residing abroad. j 2012. k ITU estimate. l 2006. m Refers to foreign citizens. n Including refugees.

Zambia

Region	Eastern Africa	Surface area (sq km)	752 612	
Population (est., 000)	15 021	Pop. density (per sq km)	20.0	
Capital city	Lusaka	Capital city pop. (000)	2 078	
Currency	Zambia Kwacha (ZMW)	UN membership date	1 December 1964	

Economic indicators	2005	2010	2013
GDP: Gross domestic product (million current US$)	7 179	16 190	22 384
GDP: Growth rate at constant 2005 prices (annual %)	5.3	7.6	6.5
GDP per capita (current US$)	625.9	1 225.0	1 539.6
GNI: Gross national income per capita (current US$)	570.8	1 121.8	1 456.3
Gross fixed capital formation (% of GDP)	22.4	21.1	25.9
Exchange rates (national currency per US$)[a]	3.51	4.80	5.51
Balance of payments, current account (million US$)	−598	1 206	192
CPI: Consumer price index (2000=100)	251	420	508
Index of industrial production (2010=100)[b]	71	100	112
Agricultural production index (2004-2006=100)	101	162	179
Food production index (2004-2006=100)	98	170	187
Unemployment (% of labour force)	15.9	13.2	13.3
Employment in industrial sector (% of employed)	7.1[cd]	...	...
Employment in agricultural sector (% of employed)	72.2[cd]	...	...
Labour force participation, adult female pop. (%)	73.6	73.3	73.1
Labour force participation, adult male pop. (%)	86.2	85.9	85.6
Tourist arrivals at national borders (000)	669	815	915
Energy production, primary (Petajoules)	280	322	344[e]
Mobile-cellular subscriptions (per 100 inhabitants)	8.3	41.2	71.5
Individuals using the Internet (%)	2.9[f]	10.0	15.4[f]

Total trade		Major trading partners			2013
	(million US$)		(% of exports)		(% of imports)
Exports	10 594.1	Switzerland	37.0	South Africa	30.3
Imports	10 161.8	China	21.3	Dem. Rep. of Congo	18.2
Balance	432.3	Dem. Rep. of Congo	11.2	China	9.4

Social indicators		
Population growth rate (average annual %)	2010-2015	3.2
Urban population growth rate (average annual %)	2010-2015	4.3
Rural population growth rate (average annual %)	2010-2015	2.5
Urban population (%)	2014	40.5
Population aged 0-14 years (%)	2014	46.5
Population aged 60+ years (females and males, % of total)	2014	4.1/3.6
Sex ratio (males per 100 females)	2014	99.5
Life expectancy at birth (females and males, years)	2010-2015	59.5/55.9
Infant mortality rate (per 1 000 live births)	2010-2015	65.5
Fertility rate, total (live births per woman)	2010-2015	5.7
Contraceptive prevalence (ages 15-49, %)	2007-2013	40.8
International migrant stock (000 and % of total population)[g]	mid-2013	98.9/0.7
Refugees and others of concern to UNHCR	mid-2014	53 916
Education: Government expenditure (% of GDP)	2007-2013	1.4
Education: Female third-level students (% of total)[h]	2007-2013	31.6[i]
Intentional homicide rate (per 100,000 population)	2008-2012	10.7
Seats held by women in national parliaments (%)	2015	12.7

Environmental indicators		
Threatened species	2014	79
Forested area (% of land area)	2012	66.1
Proportion of terrestrial and marine areas protected (%)	2014	37.9
Population using improved drinking water sources (%)	2012	63.0
Population using improved sanitation facilities (%)	2012	43.0
CO_2 emission estimates (000 metric tons and metric tons per capita)	2011	3 047/0.2
Energy supply per capita (Gigajoules)	2012	27.0

a Official rate. **b** ISIC Rev.3 (CDE). **c** ISIC Rev.2. **d** November to December. **e** 2012. **f** ITU estimate. **g** Including refugees. **h** UNESCO estimate. **i** 2000.

Zimbabwe

Region	Eastern Africa	Surface area (sq km)	390 757	
Population (est., 000)	14 599	Pop. density (per sq km)	37.4	
Capital city	Harare	Capital city pop. (000)	1 495	
Currency	...	UN membership date	25 August 1980	

Economic indicators	2005	2010	2013
GDP: Gross domestic product (million current US$)	6 223	9 422	13 490
GDP: Growth rate at constant 2005 prices (annual %)	−4.1	11.4	4.5
GDP per capita (current US$)	489.6	720.5	953.4
GNI: Gross national income per capita (current US$)	481.7	714.0	937.5
Gross fixed capital formation (% of GDP)	2.0	21.7	13.0
Exchange rates (national currency per US$)[a]	80.77	...	...
CPI: Consumer price index (2000=100)	100[bcd]	103[e]	112[ef]
Agricultural production index (2004-2006=100)	93	101	107
Food production index (2004-2006=100)	91	96	98
Unemployment (% of labour force)	4.6	5.5	5.4
Employment in industrial sector (% of employed)	9.3[ghij]	...	...
Employment in agricultural sector (% of employed)	64.8[ghi]	...	...
Labour force participation, adult female pop. (%)	83.1	83.0	83.4
Labour force participation, adult male pop. (%)	90.1	89.5	89.8
Tourist arrivals at national borders (000)[k]	1 559	2 239	1 833
Energy production, primary (Petajoules)	379	359	381[l]
Mobile-cellular subscriptions (per 100 inhabitants)	5.1	58.9	96.4
Individuals using the Internet (%)	8.0	11.5	18.5[m]

Total trade		Major trading partners			2013
	(million US$)	(% of exports)			(% of imports)
Exports	3 507.3	South Africa	74.5	South Africa	47.5
Imports	7 704.2	Mozambique	10.5	United Kingdom	18.4
Balance	−4 196.9	United Arab Emirates	6.5	China	5.7

Social indicators		
Population growth rate (average annual %)	2010-2015	2.8
Urban population growth rate (average annual %)	2010-2015	2.3
Rural population growth rate (average annual %)	2010-2015	3.1
Urban population (%)	2014	32.5
Population aged 0-14 years (%)	2014	39.0
Population aged 60+ years (females and males, % of total)	2014	6.4/5.0
Sex ratio (males per 100 females)	2014	97.7
Life expectancy at birth (females and males, years)	2010-2015	60.8/58.8
Infant mortality rate (per 1 000 live births)	2010-2015	37.2
Fertility rate, total (live births per woman)	2010-2015	3.5
Contraceptive prevalence (ages 15-49, %)	2007-2013	58.5
International migrant stock (000 and % of total population)[n]	mid-2013	361.0/2.6
Refugees and others of concern to UNHCR	mid-2014	66 151
Education: Government expenditure (% of GDP)	2007-2013	2.0
Education: Primary-secondary gross enrolment ratio (f/m per 100)	2007-2013	80.7/82.2
Education: Female third-level students (% of total)	2007-2013	46.3
Intentional homicide rate (per 100,000 population)	2008-2012	10.6
Seats held by women in national parliaments (%)	2015	31.5

Environmental indicators		
Threatened species	2014	60
Forested area (% of land area)	2012	38.7
Proportion of terrestrial and marine areas protected (%)	2014	26.6
Population using improved drinking water sources (%)	2012	80.0
Population using improved sanitation facilities (%)	2012	40.0
CO_2 emission estimates (000 metric tons and metric tons per capita)	2011	9 861/0.7
Energy supply per capita (Gigajoules)	2012	30.0

a Official rate. b Series replacing former series. c Index base 2005=100. d Annual average is calculated as the geometric mean of monthly indices. e Index base 2009=100. f Series linked to former series. g 2004. h ISIC Rev.3. i June. j Excluding electricity, gas and water supply. k Arrivals of non-resident visitors at national borders. l 2012. m ITU estimate. n Including refugees.

Technical notes

Below are brief descriptions of the indicators presented in the country profiles. The terms are arranged in alphabetical order.

Agricultural production index: The indices are calculated by the Laspeyres formula based on the sum of price-weighted quantities of different agricultural commodities produced. The commodities covered in the computation of indices of agricultural production are all crops and livestock products originating in each country. Practically all products are covered, with the main exception of fodder crops. Production quantities of each commodity are weighted by the average international commodity prices in the base period and summed for each year. To obtain the index, the aggregate for a given year is divided by the average aggregate for the base period 2004-2006. Indices are calculated without any deductions for feed and seed and are referred to as "gross" by the Food and Agriculture Organization of the United Nations (FAO).
Source of the data: FAOSTAT database of the Food and Agriculture Organization of the United Nations, available at http://faostat3.fao.org/faostat-gateway/go/to/download/Q/QI/E (last accessed 17 March 2015).

Balance of payments is a statement summarizing the economic transactions between the residents of a country and non-residents during a specific period, usually a year. It includes transactions in goods, services, income, transfers and financial assets and liabilities. Generally, the balance of payments is divided into two major components: the current account and the capital and financial account. The data on balance of payments presented in the *World Statistics Pocketbook* correspond to the current account category. The current account is a record of all transactions in the balance of payments covering the exports and imports of goods and services, payments of income, and current transfers between residents of a country and non-residents.
Source of the data: International Monetary Fund, Balance of Payments (BOP) database (last accessed 20 January 2015).

Capital city and capital city population: The designation of any specific city as a capital city is done solely on the basis of the designation as reported by the country or area. The city can be the seat of the government as determined by the country. Some countries designate more than one city to be a capital city with a specific title function (e.g., administrative and/or legislative capital). The data refer to the year 2014.
Source of the data: The United Nations Population Division, World Urbanization Prospects: The 2014 Revision, Table 13- Urban Agglomerations, available at http://esa.un.org/unpd/wup/CD-ROM/ (last accessed 15 December 2014).

CO_2 emission estimates represent the volume of carbon dioxide (CO_2) produced during the combustion of solid, liquid, and gaseous fuels, from gas flaring and the manufacture of cement. Original data were converted to CO_2 emissions by using the

conversion formula: 1 gram Carbon = 3.667 grams CO_2, as per https://www.ipcc.ch/pdf/special-reports/srccs/srccs_annex1.pdf.
Source of the data: Global, Regional, and National Fossil-Fuel CO_2 Emissions, Carbon Dioxide Information Analysis Center, National (All countries) file, available at http://cdiac.ornl.gov/trends/emis/overview_2011.html (last accessed 14 July 2015).

Contraceptive prevalence refers to the percentage of women married or in-union aged 15 to 49 who are currently using, or whose sexual partner is using at least one method of contraception, regardless of the method used. Contraceptive methods include modern methods such as sterilization, oral hormonal pills, intra-uterine devices, condoms, injectables, implants, vaginal barrier methods and emergency contraception and traditional methods such as the rhythm, withdrawal, lactational amenorrhea method and folk methods. The data contain the most recent estimates of contraceptive prevalence between the years 2007 and 2013.
Source of the data: United Nations, Department of Economic and Social Affairs, Population Division (2014), World Contraceptive Use 2014 (POP/DB/CP/Rev2014), Survey-based Observations, available at http://www.un.org/en/development/desa/population/publications/dataset/contraception/wcu2014.shtml (last accessed 16 March 2015).

CPI: Consumer price index measures changes over time in the general level of prices of goods and services that a reference population acquires, uses or pays for consumption. A consumer price index is estimated as a series of summary measures of the period-to-period proportional change in the prices of a fixed set of consumer goods and services of constant quantity and characteristics, acquired, used or paid for by the reference population. Each summary measure is constructed as a weighted average of a large number of elementary aggregate indices. Each of the elementary aggregate indices is estimated using a sample of prices for a defined set of goods and services obtained in, or by residents of, a specific region from a given set of outlets or other sources of consumption goods and services. Unless otherwise noted, the indices here generally refer to "all items" and to the country as a whole.
Source of the data: LABORSTA Internet, International Labour Organization (ILO) database, Consumer Price Indices, Main statistics (monthly): General Indices, food indices, Table: B9, available at http://laborsta.ilo.org/data_topic_E.html (last accessed 9 April 2015).

Currency refers to those notes and coins in circulation that are commonly used to make payments. The official currency names and the ISO currency codes are those officially in use, and may be subject to change.
Source of the data: United Nations Treasury's website, available at http://treasury.un.org/operationalrates/OperationalRates.aspx (data as of 15 December 2014).

Education: Female third-level students: The number of female students at the third-level of education is expressed as a percentage of the total number of students (males and females) at the same level in a given school year. Third-level education is that which is provided at university, teachers' college, higher professional school, and which requires, as a minimum condition of admission, the successful completion of education at the second level, or evidence of the attainment of an equivalent level of knowledge. Unless otherwise indicated, the data refer to the latest available year between 2007 and 2013.
Source of the data: UNESCO Institute for Statistics website (UIS.Stat), Education statistics, Percentage of students in tertiary education who are female (%), available at http://data.uis.unesco.org/ (last accessed 24 March 2015).

Education: Government expenditure (% of GDP): Unless otherwise indicated, the data refer to the latest available year between 2007 and 2013. They show the trends in general government expenditures for educational affairs and services at pre-primary, primary, secondary and tertiary levels and subsidiary services to education, expressed as a percentage of the gross domestic product.
Source of the data: UNESCO Institute for Statistics website (UIS.Stat), Education statistics, Government expenditure on education as % of GDP (%),,available at http://data.uis.unesco.org/ (last accessed 24 March 2015).

Education: Primary and secondary gross enrolment ratio is the total enrolment in first and second levels of education, regardless of age, expressed as a percentage of the eligible official school-age population corresponding to the same level of education in a given school year. Education at the first level provides the basic elements of education (e.g. at elementary school or primary school). Education at the second level is provided at middle school, secondary school, high school, teacher-training school at this level and schools of a vocational or technical nature. Enrolment is at the beginning of the school or academic year. The gross enrolment ratio at the first and second level should include all pupils whatever their ages, whereas the population is limited to the range of official school ages. Therefore, for countries with almost universal education among the school-age population, the gross enrolment ratio will exceed 100 if the actual age distribution of pupils extends beyond the official school ages. Unless otherwise indicated, the data refer to the latest available year between 2007 and 2013.
Source of the data: UNESCO Institute for Statistics website (UIS.Stat), Education statistics, Gross enrolment ratio, primary and secondary, female (%) and Gross enrolment ratio, primary and secondary, male (%),,available at http://data.uis.unesco.org/ (last accessed 24 March 2015).

Employment in agricultural and in industrial sectors: The "employed" comprise all persons above a specified age who, during a specified brief period, either one week or one day, were in "paid employment" or in "self-employment" as defined below. "Persons in paid employment" comprise all persons in the following categories: (a) *"at work"*: persons who during the reference period performed some work for wages, salary or related payments, in cash or in kind; or (b) *"with a job but not at work"*: persons who, having already worked in their present job, were absent during the reference period and continued to have a strong attachment to their job. *"Persons in self-employment"* comprise all persons (a) *"at work"*: persons who during the reference period performed some work for profit or family gain, in cash or in kind; or (b) *"with an enterprise but not at work"*: persons with an enterprise, which may be a business enterprise, a farm or a service undertaking, who were temporarily not at work during the reference period for any specific reason. Employers, own-account workers and members of producers' co-operatives should be considered as in self-employment and should be classified as *"at work"* or *"not at work"*, as the case may be. (See ILO's Current International Recommendations on Labour Statistics). Unless otherwise indicated, the data refer to the 15 years and over age group who perform any work at all in the reference period, for pay or profit in industry (mining, manufacturing, electricity, gas and water and construction) and in agriculture. Agriculture comprises the following divisions of the International Standard Industrial Classification of All Economic Activities (ISIC), Rev. 4: crop and animal production, hunting and related service activities, forestry and lodging, and fishing and aquaculture. Data sources include the World Bank's Core Welfare Indicators Questionnaire, Eurostat's European Labour Force Survey, household income and expenditure surveys, household or labour force surveys, living standards surveys, official estimates and population censuses. The most common source of the data shown includes household or labour force surveys, Eurostat's European Labour Force Survey or official estimates. Other sources have been indicated with a footnote. Unless otherwise indicated, data refer to ISIC Rev. 4.

Source of the data: The Key Indicators of the Labour Market (KILM) database, 8th edition, International Labour Organization (ILO), Table 4A, available at http://www.ilo.org/empelm/what/WCMS_114240/lang--en/index.htm (last accessed 17 April 2015).

Energy production, primary, is the capture or extraction of fuels or energy from natural energy flows, the biosphere and natural reserves of fossil fuels within the national territory in a form suitable for use. Inert matter removed from the extracted fuels and quantities reinjected, flared or vented are not included. The resulting products are referred to as "primary" products. It excludes secondary production, that is, the manufacture of energy products through the process of transforming primary and/or other secondary fuels or energy. Data are provided in a common energy unit (Petajoule) and refer to the following primary energy sources: hard coal, brown coal, peat, oil shale, conventional crude oil, natural gas liquids (NGL), other hydrocarbons, additives and oxygenates, natural gas, fuelwood, wood residues and by-products, bagasse, animal waste, black liquor, other vegetal material and residues, biogasoline, biodiesels, bio jet kerosene, other liquid biofuels, biogases, industrial waste, municipal waste, nuclear, solar photovoltaic, solar thermal, hydro, wind, geothermal, and tide, wave and other marine sources. Peat, biomass and *wastes are included only when the production is for energy purposes. Please see International Recommendations for Energy Statistics (2011) and 2012 Energy Balances for a complete description of the methodology.*

Source of the data: The Energy Statistics Yearbook (information provided by the Industrial and Energy Statistics Section of the United Nations Statistics Division as of 23 July 2015).

Energy supply per capita *is defined as primary energy production plus imports minus exports minus international marine bunkers minus international aviation bunkers minus stock changes. For imports, exports, international bunkers and stock changes, it includes secondary energy products, in addition to primary products.*

Source of the data: The Energy Statistics Yearbook (information provided by the Industrial and Energy Statistics Section of the United Nations Statistics Division as of 23 July 2015).

Exchange rates *are shown in units of national currency per US dollar and refer to end-of-period quotations. The exchange rates are classified into broad categories, reflecting both the role of the authorities in the determination of the exchange and/or the multiplicity of exchange rates in a country. The market rate is used to describe exchange rates determined largely by market forces; the official rate is an exchange rate determined by the authorities, sometimes in a flexible manner. For countries maintaining multiple exchange arrangements, the rates are labelled principal rate, secondary rate, and tertiary rate.*

Source of the data: The International Monetary Fund, International Financial Statistics database (last accessed 15 January 2015). For those currencies for which the IMF does not publish exchange rates, non-commercial rates derived from the year-end operational rates of exchange for United Nations programmes are shown, as published by the United Nations Treasury, available at http://www.un.org/Depts/treasury/ (last accessed 15 January 2015).

Fertility rate: *The total fertility rate is a widely used summary indicator of fertility. It refers to the number of children that would be born per woman, assuming no female mortality at child bearing ages and the age-specific fertility rates of a specified country and reference period. Unless otherwise indicated, the data are the five-year average for the reference period 2010-2015.*

Source of the data: United Nations, Department of Economic and Social Affairs, Population Division (2013), World Population Prospects: The 2012 Revision, available at http://esa.un.org/wpp/Excel-Data/fertility.htm; supplemented by official national statistics published in the United Nations Demographic Yearbook 2013, Table 4, available at http://unstats.un.org/unsd/demographic/products/dyb/dyb2013.htm; and data compiled by the Secretariat of the Pacific Community (SPC) Statistics and Demography Programme, Population and demographic indicators, available at http://www.spc.int/sdp.

Technical notes (*continued*)

Food production index covers commodities that are considered edible and contain nutrients. Accordingly, coffee and tea are excluded because they have practically no nutritive value. The index numbers shown may differ from those produced by countries themselves because of differences in concepts of production, coverage, weights, time reference of data, and methods of evaluation. The data include estimates made by FAO in cases where no official or semi-official figures are available from the countries.

Source of the data: FAOSTAT database of the Food and Agriculture Organization of the United Nations, available at http://faostat3.fao.org/faostat-gateway/go/to/download/Q/QI/E (last accessed 17 March 2015).

Forested area refers to the percentage of land area occupied by forest. Forest is defined in the Food and Agriculture Organization's Global Forest Resources Assessment as land spanning more than 0.5 hectares with trees higher than 5 metres and a canopy cover of more than 10 percent, or trees able to reach these thresholds in situ. It does not include land that is predominantly under agricultural or urban land use. Data are calculated from the forest estimates divided by the land area for 2012.

Source of the data: The FAOSTAT database of the Food and Agriculture Organization of the United Nations, available at http://faostat3.fao.org/download/R/RL/E (last accessed 24 March 2015).

GDP: Gross domestic product is an aggregate measure of production equal to the sum of gross value added of all resident producer units plus that part (possibly the total) of taxes on products, less subsidies on products, that is not included in the valuation of output. It is also equal to the sum of the final uses of goods and services (all uses except intermediate consumption) measured at purchasers' prices, less the value of imports of goods and services, and equal to the sum of primary incomes distributed by resident producer units (see *System of National Accounts 2008*). The data in the *World Statistics Pocketbook* are in current United States (US) dollars and are estimates of the total production of goods and services of the countries represented in economic terms, not as a measure of the standard of living of their inhabitants. In order to have comparable coverage for as many countries as possible, these US dollar estimates are based on official GDP data in national currency, supplemented by national currency estimates prepared by the Statistics Division using additional data from national and international sources. The estimates given here are in most cases those accepted by the United Nations General Assembly's Committee on Contributions for determining United Nations members' contributions to the United Nations regular budget. The exchange rates for the conversion of GDP national currency data into US dollars are the average market rates published by the International Monetary Fund, in *International Financial Statistics*. Official exchange rates are used only when free market rates are not available. For non-members of the Fund, the conversion rates used are the average of United Nations operational rates of exchange. It should be noted that the conversion from local currency into US dollars introduces deficiencies in comparability over time and among countries which should be considered when using the data. For example, comparability over time is distorted when exchange rate fluctuations differ substantially from domestic inflation rates.

Source of the data: The National Accounts Main Aggregates Database, available at http://unstats.un.org/unsd/snaama/dnllist.asp (last accessed 10 February 2015) and the National Accounts Statistics: Analysis of Main Aggregates, compiled from national data provided to the United Nations Statistics Division.

GDP: Growth rate at constant 2005 prices *is derived on the basis of constant price series in national currency. The figures are computed as the geometric mean of annual rates of growth expressed in percentages for the years indicated.*

Source of the data: The National Accounts Main Aggregates Database, available at http://unstats.un.org/unsd/snaama/dnllist.asp (last accessed 10 February 2015) and the National Accounts Statistics: Analysis of Main Aggregates, compiled from national data provided to the United Nations Statistics Division.

GDP per capita *estimates are the value of all goods and services produced in the economy divided by the population.*

Source of the data: The National Accounts Main Aggregates Database available at http://unstats.un.org/unsd/snaama/dnllist.asp (last accessed 10 February 2015) and the National Accounts Statistics: Analysis of Main Aggregates, compiled from national data provided to the United Nations Statistics Division.

GNI: Gross national income per capita *estimates are the aggregate value of the balances of gross primary incomes for all sectors in the economy divided by the population. GNI is equal to GDP less primary incomes payable to non-resident units plus primary incomes receivable from non-resident units. In other words, GNI is equal to GDP less taxes (less subsidies) on production and imports, compensation of employees and property income payable to the rest of the world plus the corresponding items receivable from the rest of the world. Thus GNI at market prices is the sum of gross primary incomes receivable by resident institutional units/sectors. It is worth noting that GNI at market prices was called gross national product in the 1953 SNA, and it was commonly denominated GNP. In contrast to GDP, GNI is not a concept of value added, but a concept of income (see System of National Accounts 2008).*

Source of the data: The National Accounts Main Aggregates Database, available at http://unstats.un.org/unsd/snaama/dnllist.asp (last accessed 10 February 2015) and the National Accounts Statistics: Analysis of Main Aggregates, compiled from national data provided to the United Nations Statistics Division.

Gross fixed capital formation is measured by the total value of a producer's acquisitions, less disposals, of fixed assets during the accounting period plus certain specified expenditure on services that adds to the value of non-produced assets (see *System of National Accounts 2008*). The data are based on the percentage distribution of GDP in current prices.

Source of the data: The National Accounts Main Aggregates Database, available at http://unstats.un.org/unsd/snaama/dnllist.asp (last accessed 10 February 2015) and the National Accounts Statistics: Analysis of Main Aggregates, compiled from national data provided to the United Nations Statistics Division.

Index of Industrial production: The data shown here generally cover, unless otherwise noted, the International Standard Industrial Classification of All Economic Activities, Revision 4 (ISIC Rev. 4) sections B, C, D and E (i.e., mining and quarrying; manufacturing; electricity, gas, steam and air conditioning supply; and water supply, sewerage, waste management and remediation activities). The data that are footnoted as referring to ISIC Rev. 3 cover Tabulation Categories C, D and E (mining and quarrying; manufacturing; and electricity, gas and water supply).

Source of the data: United Nations Statistics Division, Environment and Energy Statistics Branch, Industrial and Energy Statistics Section, (information provided by the Industrial and Energy Statistics Section of the United Nations Statistics Division as of 20 March 2015).

Individuals using the Internet *refer to the percentage of people who used the Internet from any location and for any purpose, irrespective of the device and network used. It can be via a computer (i.e. desktop or laptop computer, tablet or similar handheld computer), mobile phone, games machine, digital TV, etc. Access can be via a fixed or mobile network. Data are obtained by countries through national household surveys and are either provided directly to the International Telecommunication Union (ITU) by national statistical offices (NSO), or ITU carries out necessary research to obtain data, for example, from NSO websites. There are certain data limits to this indicator, insofar as estimates have to be calculated for many developing countries which do not yet collect information and communications technology household statistics. Unless otherwise indicated, data refer to population aged 16 to 74.*

Source of the data: The World Telecommunication/ICT Indicators Database 2014 (18th Edition) of the International Telecommunication Union, Time series by country, available at http://www.itu.int/en/ITU-D/Statistics/Documents/statistics/2014/Individuals_Internet_2000-2013.xls (last accessed 14 January 2015).

Infant mortality rate *(per 1 000 live births) is the ratio of infant deaths (the deaths of children under one year of age) in a given year to the total number of live births in the same year. Unless otherwise noted, the rates are the five-year projected averages for the reference period 2010-2015.*

Source of the data: United Nations, Department of Economic and Social Affairs, Population Division (2013), World Population Prospects: The 2012 Revision, available at http://esa.un.org/wpp/Excel-Data/mortality.htm and supplemented by data compiled by the Secretariat of the Pacific Community (SPC) Statistics and Demography Programme, Population and demographic indicators, available at http://www.spc.int/sdp.

Intentional homicide rate: The rates are the annual number of unlawful deaths purposefully inflicted on a person by another person, reported for the year per 100 000. The data refer to the latest available year between 2008 and 2012. For most countries, country information on causes of death is not available for most causes. Estimates are therefore based on cause of death modelling and death registration data from other countries in the region. Further country-level information and data on specific causes was also used.

Source of the data: United Nations Office on Crime and Drugs, UNODC Homicide Statistics 2013, Homicide counts and rates, time series 2000-2012, available at http://www.unodc.org/gsh/en/data.html (last accessed 25 March 2015).

International migrant stock generally represents the number of persons born in a country other than that in which they live. When information on country of birth was not recorded, data on the number of persons having foreign citizenship was used instead. In the absence of any empirical data, estimates were imputed. Data refer to mid-2013. Figures for international migrant stock as a percentage of the population are the outcome of dividing the estimated international migrant stock by the estimated total population and multiplying the result by 100.

Source of the data: The United Nations Population Division, Trends in International Migrant Stock: The 2013 Revision- Migrants by age and sex, International migrant stock at mid-year by sex and by major area, region, country or area, 1990-2013,(Table 1), available at http://www.un.org/en/development/desa/population/migration/data/estimates2/e stimatestotal.shtml (last accessed 15 July 2015).

Labour force participation rate is calculated by expressing the number of persons in the labour force as a percentage of the working-age population. The labour force is the sum of the number of persons employed and the number of unemployed (see ILO's Current International Recommendations on Labour Statistics). The working-age population is the population above a certain age, prescribed for the measurement of economic characteristics. Unless otherwise noted, the data refer to the age group of 15 years and over.

Source of the data: The Key Indicators of the Labour Market (KILM) database, 8th edition, International Labour Organization (ILO), Table 1A, available at http://www.ilo.org/empelm/what/WCMS_114240/lang--en/index.htm (last accessed 12 March 2015).

Life expectancy at birth is the average number of years of life at birth (age 0) for males and females according to the expected mortality rates by age estimated for

the reference year and population. Unless otherwise indicated, the data are the five-year projected averages for the reference period 2010-2015.
Source of the data: United Nations, Department of Economic and Social Affairs, Population Division (2013), World Population Prospects: The 2012 Revision, available at http://esa.un.org/wpp/Excel-Data/mortality.htm; supplemented by official national statistics published in the United Nations Demographic Yearbook 2013, Table 21, available at http://unstats.un.org/unsd/demographic/products/dyb/dyb2013.htm; and data compiled by the Secretariat of the Pacific Community (SPC) Statistics and Demography Programme, Population and demographic indicators, available at http://www.spc.int/sdp.

Major trading partners *show the three largest trade partners (countries of last known destination and origin or consignment) in international merchandise trade transactions. In some cases a special partner is shown (i.e. Areas nes, bunkers, etc.) instead of a country and refers to one of the following special categories. Areas not elsewhere specified (Areas nes) is used (a) for low value trade, (b) if the partner designation was unknown to the country or if an error was made in the partner assignment and (c) for reasons of confidentiality. If a specific geographical location can be identified within Areas nes, then they are recorded accordingly (i.e. Other Europe nes, South America nes, North and Central America nes, Oceania nes, Other Africa nes, and Other Asia nes). Bunkers are ship stores and aircraft supplies, which consists mostly of fuels and food. Free zones belong to the geographical and economic territory of a country but not to its customs territory. For the purpose of trade statistics the transactions between the customs territory and the free zones are recorded, if the reporting country uses the Special Trade System. Free zones can be commercial free zones (duty free shops) or industrial free zones. Data are expressed as percentages of total exports and of total imports of the country, area or special partner.*
Source of the data: The United Nations Statistics Division's Commodity Trade Statistics Database (COMTRADE), available at http://comtrade.un.org and the United Nations 2014 International Trade Statistics Yearbook.

Mobile-cellular telephone subscriptions, *per 100 inhabitants refer to the number of mobile cellular telephone subscriptions in a country for each 100 inhabitants. It is calculated by dividing the number of mobile cellular telephone subscriptions by the total population and multiplied by 100.*
Source of the data: The World Telecommunication/ICT Indicators Database 2014 (18th Edition) of the International Telecommunication Union, Time series by country, available at http://www.itu.int/en/ITU-D/Statistics/Documents/statistics/2014/Mobile_cellular_2000-2013.xls (last accessed 13 January 2015).

Technical notes (*continued*)

Population aged 0-14 years refers to the population aged 0-14 years of both sexes as a percentage of total population. Unless otherwise indicated, the data refer to the year 2014.

Source of the data: United Nations, Department of Economic and Social Affairs, Population Division (2013), World Population Prospects: The 2012 Revision, available at http://esa.un.org/unpd/wpp/Excel-Data/population.htm; supplemented by data calculated from official national statistics published in the United Nations Demographic Yearbook 2013, Table 7, available at http://unstats.un.org/unsd/demographic/products/dyb/dyb2013.htm; and data compiled by the Secretariat of the Pacific Community (SPC) Statistics and Demography Programme, Population and demographic indicators, available at http://www.spc.int/sdp (last accessed 23 March 2015).

Population aged 60 years and over refers to the percentage of the female population who are 60 years and older and the percentage of the male population who are 60 years and older, respectively. Unless otherwise indicated, the data refer to the year 2014.

Source of the data: United Nations, Department of Economic and Social Affairs, Population Division (2013), World Population Prospects: The 2012 Revision, available at http://esa.un.org/wpp/Excel-Data/Interpolated.htm; supplemented by data calculated from official national statistics published in the United Nations Demographic Yearbook 2013, Table 7, available at http://unstats.un.org/unsd/demographic/products/dyb/dyb2013.htm (last accessed 23 March 2015)..

Population density refers to medium fertility estimated population per square kilometre of surface area as of 1 July 2014. Source of the data: United Nations, Department of Economic and Social Affairs, Population Division (2013), World Population Prospects: The 2012 Revision, available at http://esa.un.org/wpp/Excel-Data/population.htm (last accessed 16 December 2015).

Population estimates: Data refer to medium fertility estimated population as of 1 July 2014. The total population of a country may comprise either all usual residents of the country (de jure population) or all persons present in the country (de facto population) at the time of the census; for purposes of international comparisons, the de facto definition is recommended.

Source of the data: United Nations, Department of Economic and Social Affairs, Population Division (2013), World Population Prospects: The 2012 Revision, available at http://esa.un.org/wpp/Excel-Data/population.htm (last accessed 16 December 2015).

Population growth rate is the average annual percentage change in total population size. Unless otherwise indicated, the data refer to the period 2010-2015. Source of the data: United Nations, Department of Economic and Social Affairs, Population Division (2013), World Population Prospects: The 2012 Revision, available at http://esa.un.org/unpd/wpp/Excel-Data/population.htm (las accessed 23 March 2015)..

Population using improved drinking water sources is the percentage of the population, urban and rural, who use any of the following types of water supply for drinking: piped water, public tap, borehole or pump, protected well, protected spring or rainwater. Improved water sources do not include vendor-provided water, bottled water, tanker trucks or unprotected wells and springs. Use of an improved drinking water source is a proxy for the use of safe drinking water. Data sources for this indicator include household surveys, population census or administrative reporting systems. The data are estimated by the WHO/UNICEF Joint Monitoring Programme for Water Supply and Sanitation (JMP) based on available country sources, see www.wssinfo.org for further information.
Source of the data: World Health Organization (WHO), Global Health Observatory Data Repository, MDG Indicators, Goal 7, available at http://apps.who.int/gho/data/node.main.606?lang=en (last accessed 8 April 2015).

Population using improved sanitation facilities refers to the percentage of the population with access to facilities that hygienically separate human excreta from human, animal and insect contact. Facilities such as sewers or septic tanks, poor flush latrines and simple pit or ventilated improved pit latrines are assumed to be adequate, provided that they are not public. To be effective, facilities must be correctly constructed and properly maintained. Sanitation facilities are not considered improved when shared with other households, or open to public use. Use of an improved sanitation facility is a proxy for access to basic sanitation. Data sources for this indicator include household surveys, population census or administrative reporting systems. The data are estimated by the WHO/UNICEF Joint Monitoring Programme for Water Supply and Sanitation (JMP) based on available country sources, see www.wssinfo.org for further information.
Source of the data: World Health Organization (WHO), Global Health Observatory Data Repository, MDG Indicators, Goal 7, available at http://apps.who.int/gho/data/node.main.606?lang=en (last accessed 8 April 2015).

Proportion of terrestrial and marine protected areas to total terrestrial area refers to the sum of terrestrial protected areas as well as marine protected areas in territorial waters (up to 200 nautical miles from the coast) divided by the total area of land area (including inland waters) and territorial waters. Protected areas are recorded in the World Database on Protected Areas (WDPA), last updated in August 2014, and include the location and extent of protected areas, determined through a

GIS analysis, spanning from 1990 to present. The WDPA is a joint initiative of UNEP and IUCN, see www.unep-wcmc.org for further information.
Source of the data: United Nations Millennium Development Goals database, Goal 7, Target 7.B, available at http://mdgs.un.org/unsd/mdg/Data.aspx (last accessed 27 August 2015).

Refugees and others of concern to the Office of the United Nations High Commissioner for Refugees (UNHCR): *The 1951 United Nations Convention relating to the Status of Refugees states that a refugee is someone who, owing to a well-founded fear of being persecuted for reasons of race, religion, nationality, political opinion or membership in a particular social group, is outside the country of his or her nationality and is unable to, or owing to such fear, is unwilling to avail himself or herself of the protection of that country; or who, not having a nationality and being outside the country of his or her former habitual residence, is unable or, owing to such fear, unwilling to return to it. In this series, refugees refer to persons granted a humanitarian status and/or those granted temporary protection. Included are persons who have been granted temporary protection on a group basis. The series also includes returned refugees, asylum-seekers, stateless persons and persons displaced internally within their own country and others of concern to UNHCR.*
Source of the data: The UNHCR Mid-Year Trends 2014, Table 1: Refugees, asylum-seekers, internally displaced persons (IDPs), returnees (refugees and IDPs), stateless persons, and others of concern to UNHCR by country/territory of asylum, mid-2014 (or latest available estimates), available at http://www.unhcr.org/pages/49c3646c4d6.html (last accessed 12 March 2015). See also the website of the Internal Displacement Monitoring Centre (IDMC) for further information.

Region: *Macro geographical regions arranged according to continents and component geographical regions used for statistical purposes.*
Source of the data: The Standard Country or Area Codes and Geographical Regions for Statistical Use, Revision 4 (United Nations publication), Composition of macro geographical (continental) regions, geographical sub-regions, and selected economic and other groupings available at http://unstats.un.org/unsd/methods/m49/m49regin.htm (last accessed 12 December 2014).

Rural population growth rate *data are based on the number of persons defined as rural according to national definitions of this concept. In most cases these definitions are those used in the most recent population census.*
Source of the data: The United Nations Population Division, World Urbanization Prospects: The 2014 Revision, File 7, available at http://esa.un.org/unpd/wup/CD-ROM/Default.aspx (last accessed 15 December 2014).

Technical notes (*continued*)

Seats held by women in national parliaments refer to the number of women in the lower chamber of national parliaments expressed as a percentage of total occupied seats in the lower or single House.
Source of the data: The Inter-Parliamentary Union, Women in National Parliaments, Situation as of 1 February 2015, available at http://www.ipu.org/wmn-e/classif.htm (last accessed 24 March 2015).

Sex ratio is calculated as the ratio of the number of men to that of 100 women. Unless otherwise indicated, the data refer to the year 2014.
Source of the data: United Nations, Department of Economic and Social Affairs, Population Division (2013), World Population Prospects: The 2012 Revision, available at http://esa.un.org/unpd/wpp/Excel-Data/population.htm; supplemented by data calculated from official national statistics published in the United Nations Demographic Yearbook 2013, Table 7, available at http://unstats.un.org/unsd/demographic/products/dyb/dyb2013.htm; and data calculated from the Secretariat of the Pacific Community (SPC) Statistics and Demography Programme, Population and demographic indicators, available at http://www.spc.int/sdp (last accessed 17 April 2015)

Surface area, unless otherwise noted, refers to land area plus inland water.
Source of the data: The United Nations Demographic Yearbook 2013, Table 3, available at http://unstats.un.org/unsd/demographic/products/dyb/dyb2013.htm (last accessed 12 March 2015).

Threatened species represents the number of plants and animals that are most in need of conservation attention and are compiled by the World Conservation Union IUCN/ Species Survival Commission (SSC).
Source of the data: The IUCN Red List of Threatened Species version 2014.3: Table 5, available at http://www.iucnredlist.org/about/summary-statistics#Tables_5_6 (last accessed 12 December 2014).

Total trade: exports and imports show the movement of goods out of and into a country. Goods simply being transported through a country (goods in transit) or temporarily admitted (except for goods for inward processing) do not add to the stock of material resources of a country and are not included in the international merchandise trade statistics. In the "general trade system", the definition of the statistical territory of a country coincides with its economic territory. In the "special trade system", the definition of the statistical territory comprises only a particular part of the economic territory, mainly that part which coincides with the free circulation area for goods. "The free circulation area" is a part of the economic territory of a country within which goods "may be disposed of without Customs restrictions". In the case of exports, the transaction value is the value at which the goods were sold by the exporter, including the cost of transportation and insurance, to bring the goods onto the transporting vehicle at the frontier of the exporting *country (an FOB-type valuation). In the case of imports, the transaction value is the value at which the goods were purchased by the importer plus the cost of transportation and insurance to the frontier of the importing country (a CIF-type valuation). Both imports and exports are shown in United States dollars. Conversion from national currencies is made by means of currency conversion factors based on official exchange rates (par values or weighted averages).*

Source of the data: The United Nations Statistics Division's Commodity Trade Statistics Database (COMTRADE), available at http://comtrade.un.org. and the United Nations 2014 International Trade Statistics Yearbook.

Tourist arrivals at national borders: *An international tourist is any person who travels to a country other than that in which he or she has his or her usual residence but outside his/her usual environment for a period not exceeding 12 months and whose main purpose of visit is other than the exercise of an activity remunerated from with the country visited, and who stays at least one night in a collective or private accommodation in the country visited (see Recommendations on Tourism Statistics of the United Nations and the World Tourism Organization). Unless otherwise indicated, the data refer to arrivals of non-resident tourists at national borders.*

Source of the data: The United Nations World Tourism Organization Compendium of Yearbook Statistics (information provided by the United Nations World Tourism Organization as of 16 December 2014).

Unemployment *refers to persons above a specified age who during a specified reference period were: "without work", i.e. were not in paid employment or self-employment as defined under employment; "currently available for work", i.e. were available for paid employment or self-employment during the reference period; and "seeking work", i.e. had taken specific steps in a specified recent period to seek paid employment or self-employment. In circumstances where employment opportunities are particularly limited and where persons not working do not have easy access to formal channels for seeking employment or face social and cultural barriers when looking for a job, the "seeking work" criterion should be relaxed. National definitions of unemployment often differ from the recommended international standard definitions and thereby limit international comparability. Inter-country comparisons are also complicated by the different types of data collection systems used to obtain information on unemployed persons. Unless otherwise indicated, the data refer to the 15 years and over age group and are national employment office statistics, usually labour force surveys, compiled by the ILO. (See ILO's Current International Recommendations on Labour Statistics, 2000 Edition).*

Source of the data: The Key Indicators of the Labour Market (KILM) database, 8th edition, International Labour Organization (ILO), Table 9A, available at http://www.ilo.org/empelm/what/WCMS_114240/lang--en/index.htm (last accessed 20 March 2015).

United Nations membership dates: *The United Nations is an intergovernmental organization whose members are the countries of the world. Currently there are 192 Member States of the United Nations, some of which joined the UN by signing and ratifying the Charter of the United Nations in 1945; the other countries joined the UN later, through the adoption of a resolution admitting them to membership. The process usually follows these steps: first, the country applies for membership and makes a declaration accepting the obligations of the Charter; second, the Security Council adopts a resolution recommending that the General Assembly admit the country to membership and finally the General Assembly adopts a resolution admitting the country.*
Source of the data: The List of Member States, available at http://www.un.org/en/members/index.shtml (accessed 12 December 2014).

Urban population *is based on the number of persons defined as urban according to national definitions of this concept. In most cases these definitions are those used in the most recent population census.*
Source of the data: United Nations Population Division, World Urbanization Prospects: The 2014 Revision, CD-ROM Edition, File 1, available at http://esa.un.org/unpd/wup/CD-ROM/ (last accessed 23 March 2015)..

Urban population growth rate *is based on the number of persons defined as urban according to national definitions of this concept. In most cases these definitions are those used in the most recent population census.*
Source of the data: United Nations Population Division, World Urbanization Prospects: The 2014 Revision, CD-ROM Edition, File 6, available at http://esa.un.org/unpd/wup/CD-ROM/Default.aspx (last accessed 12 December 2014).

Statistical sources and references

Statistical sources

Carbon Dioxide Information Analysis Center, Oak Ridge, Tennessee, Global, Regional, and National Fossil-Fuel CO_2 Emissions, available at http://cdiac.ornl.gov/trends/emis/overview_2011.html.

Food and Agriculture Organization of the United Nations, Rome, FAOSTAT database, available at http://faostat3.fao.org/home/E.

International Labour Organization, Key Indicators of the Labour Market, 8th edition software, available at http://www.ilo.org/empelm/what/WCMS_114240/lang--en/index.htm.

_____, LABORSTA Internet database, available at http://laborsta.ilo.org/.

International Monetary Fund (IMF), Washington, Balance of Payments (BOP) database.

_____, International Financial Statistics (IFS) database.

Inter-Parliamentary Union, Women in National Parliaments, available at http://www.ipu.org/wmn-e/classif.htm.

International Telecommunication Union (ITU), Geneva, the World Telecommunication/ICT Indicators Database 2014 (18th Edition) database, available at http://www.itu.int/en/ITU-D/statistics/Pages/default.aspx.

International Union for Conservation of Nature (IUCN), The 2014 IUCN Red List of Threatened Species, available at http://www.iucnredlist.org/.

Secretariat of the Pacific Community (SPC) Statistics and Demography Programme, Population and demographic indicators, available at http://www.spc.int/sdp.

United Nations Educational, Scientific and Cultural Organization (UNESCO) Institute for Statistics, Montreal, UNESCO statistics database, available at http://stats.uis.unesco.org.

United Nations High Commissioner for Refugees, Geneva, UNHCR Mid-Year Trends 2014, available at http://www.unhcr.org/statistics.html.

United Nations, Department of Economic and Social Affairs, Population Division, New York, Trends in International Migrant Stock: The 2013 Revision (United Nations publication POP/DB/MIG/Stock/Rev.2013/Age), available at http://esa.un.org/unmigration/TIMSA2013/migrantstocks2013.htm?mhome.

_____, Fertility and Family Planning Section, World Contraceptive Use 2014, available at http://www.un.org/en/development/desa/population/publications/dataset/contraception/wcu2014.shtml.

_____, World Population Prospects. The 2012 Revision, available at http://esa.un.org/unpd/wpp/index.htm.

Statistical sources and references *(continued)*

_____, *World Urbanization Prospects: The 2014 Revision*, available at http://esa.un.org/unpd/wup/.

United Nations, Department of Economic and Social Affairs, Statistics Division, New York, *Commodity Trade Statistics Database (COMTRADE)*, available at http://comtrade.un.org/db/default.aspx.

_____, *Demographic Yearbook 2013* (United Nations Publication, ST/ESA/STAT/SER.R/42), available at http://unstats.un.org/unsd/demographic/products/dyb/dyb2013.htm

_____, *Energy Statistics Yearbook* (Series J, United Nations publication), available at http://unstats.un.org/unsd/energy/yearbook/default.htm.

_____, *International Trade Statistics Yearbook* (Series G, United Nations publication), available at http://comtrade.un.org/pb/.

_____, *National Accounts Statistics: Analysis of Main Aggregates* (Series X, United Nations publication), available at http://unstats.un.org/unsd/snaama/introduction.asp.

_____, *Standard Country or Area Codes for Statistical Use* (ST/ESA/STAT/SER.M/49/Rev.4) and http://unstats.un.org/unsd/methods/m49/m49.htm.

United Nations, Department of Management, Office of Programme Planning, Budget and Accounts, New York, *Treasury website*, available at http://www.un.org/Depts/treasury.

United Nations Member States website, available at http://www.un.org/en/members/.

United Nations Millennium Development Goals database available at http://mdgs.un.org/unsd/mdg/Default.aspx.

United Nations Office on Drugs and Crime, Vienna, *Homicide Statistics website*, available at http://www.unodc.org/gsh/en/data.html.

United Nations World Health Organization (WHO), Geneva, *Global Health Observatory Data Repository* available at http://www.who.int/gho/en/.

United Nations World Tourism Organization (UNWTO), Madrid, *UNWTO statistics database, Yearbook of Tourism Statistics* available at http://www.unwto.org.

Statistical sources and references (continued)

References

Food and Agriculture Organization of the United Nations (2010). *Global Forest Resources Assessment 2010* (Rome), available at http://www.fao.org/forestry/fra/fra2010/en/.

International Labour Organization (2000). *Current International Recommendations on Labour Statistics, 2000 Edition* (Geneva), available at http://www.ilo.org/public/english/bureau/stat/publ/currrec.htm.

United Nations (1951 and 1967). *Convention relating to the Status of Refugees of 1951* (United Nations, Treaty Series, vol. 189 (1954), No. 2545, p. 137), art. 1) and *Protocol relating to the Status of Refugees of 1967* (United Nations, Treaty Series, vol. 606 (1967), No. 8791, p. 267).

United Nations (1982). *Concepts and Methods in Energy Statistics, with Special Reference to Energy Accounts and Balances: A Technical Report*. Statistical Office, Series F, No. 29 and Corr. 1 (United Nations publication, Sales No. E.82.XVII.13 and corrigendum), available at http://unstats.un.org/unsd/publication/SeriesF/SeriesF_29E.pdf.

United Nations (2008). *Principles and Recommendations for Population and Housing Censuses Rev. 2*. Statistics Division, Series M, No. 67, Rev. 2 (United Nations publication, Sales No. E.07.XVII.8), available at http://unstats.un.org/unsd/publication/SeriesM/Seriesm_67rev2e.pdf.

United Nations (2008). *International Standard Industrial Classification of All Economic Activities (ISIC), Rev. 4*. Statistics Division, Series M, No. 4, Rev.4 (United Nations publication, Sales No. E.08.XVII.25), available at http://unstats.un.org/unsd/publication/SeriesM/seriesm_4rev4e.pdf.

United Nations (2004). *International Merchandise Trade Statistics: Compilers Manual*, Statistics Division, Series F, No. 87 (United Nations publication, Sales No. E.02.XVII.17), available at http://unstats.un.org/unsd/publication/SeriesF/seriesf_87e.pdf.

United Nations (2010). *International Merchandise Trade Statistics: Concepts and Definitions*, Statistics Division, Series M, No.52, Rev.3, (United Nations publication, Sales No. E.10.XVII.13), available at http://unstats.un.org/unsd/trade/EG-IMTS/IMTS%202010%20(English).pdf.

United Nations (2011). *International Recommendations for Energy Statistics (IRES)*, Statistics Division, available at http://unstats.un.org/unsd/statcom/doc11/BG-IRES.pdf.

United Nations (2015). *2012 Energy Balances*, Statistics Division, Series W, No. 21 (United Nations Publication, Sales No. E.15.XVII.13), available at http://unstats.un.org/unsd/energy/balance/2012/01.pdf.

United Nations European Commission, International Monetary Fund, Organisation for Economic Cooperation and Development and World Bank (2009). *System of*

Statistical sources and references *(continued)*

National Accounts 2008 (SNA 2008), available at http://unstats.un.org/unsd/nationalaccount/sna2008.asp.

United Nations and World Tourism Organization (2008). *International Recommendations for Tourism Statistics 2008*, Series M, No. 83/Rev.1 (United Nations publication, Sales No. E.08.XVII.28).

World Health Organization (WHO, 2007). *International Statistical Classification of Diseases and Related Health Problems*, Tenth Revision (ICD-10), (Geneva), available at http://www.who.int/classifications/icd/en/.

Related statistical products

The *World Statistics Pocketbook* can also be viewed online in PDF format at http://unstats.un.org/unsd/pocketbook/ and in UNdata at http://data.un.org/CountryProfile.aspx.

Please visit the *World Statistics Pocketbook* website for updates on UN CountryStats, an app for iPhones and iPads, available at http://unstats.un.org/unsd/pocketbook/.

Other statistical publications offering a broad cross-section of information which may be of interest to users of the *World Statistics Pocketbook* include:

The *Monthly Bulletin of Statistics* (MBS) in print and the Monthly Bulletin of Statistics Online, available at http://unstats.un.org/unsd/mbs/.

The Statistical Yearbook (SYB) in print and online in PDF format, available at http://unstats.un.org/unsd/syb/.

Both publications are available for sale in print format (see below for instructions on how to order).

For more information about other publications and online databases prepared by the United Nations Statistics Division, please visit: http://unstats.un.org/unsd/pubs/ and http://unstats.un.org/unsd/databases.htm. For additional information about the work of the United Nations Statistics Division, please visit http://unstats.un.org/unsd.

To order United Nations publications, please visit www.un.org/publications or contact:

United Nations Publications
300 East 42nd Street
New York, NY 10017
Tel: 1-888-254-4286
Fax: 1-800-338-4550
E-mail: publications@un.org

Please provide the Statistical Dissemination Section – which is responsible for producing the *World Statistics Pocketbook,* the *Monthly Bulletin of Statistics* and the *Statistical Yearbook* – your feedback and suggestions regarding these statistical products, as well as the utility of the data, by contacting statistics@un.org.